Katharine Dexter McCormick

D0169265

Katharine Dexter McCormick in 1914. At this time she had already been recognized as a formidable leader and administrator in the national suffrage movement, with a will and determination far beyond her years of experience. (Smith College Collection)

Katharine Dexter McCormick

Pioneer for Women's Rights

ARMOND FIELDS

Westport, Connecticut
London

Library of Congress Cataloging-in-Publication Data

Fields, Armond, 1930–
    Katherine Dexter McCormick : pioneer for women's rights / Armond Fields.
       p. cm.
    Includes bibliographical references and index.
    ISBN 0–275–98004–9 (alk. paper)
       1. McCormick, Katherine Dexter, 1876–1967. 2. Women social reformers—United States—Biography. 3. Suffragists—United States—Biography. 4. Feminists—United States—Biography. 5. Women—Suffrage—United States—History. 6. Birth control—United States—History. I. Title.
    HQ1413.M68F54 2003
    303.48′4′092—dc21
    [B]   2002044540

British Library Cataloguing in Publication Data is available.

Library of Congress Catalog Card Number: 2002044540
ISBN: 0–275–98004–9

First published in 2003

Praeger Publishers, 88 Post Road West, Westport, CT 06881
An imprint of Greenwood Publishing Group, Inc.
www.praeger.com

Printed in the United States of America

The paper used in this book complies with the Permanent Paper Standard issued by the National Information Standards Organization (Z39.48–1984).

10 9 8 7 6 5 4 3 2 1

"The broadest human aims and the highest human ideals are an integral part of the lives of women."

Katharine Dexter McCormick, speech at the 1911 NAWSA Convention

" . . . a woman more strange and powerful than fiction could ever invent."

Loretta McLaughlin, *The Pill, John Rock, and the Church*

"Then you came along with your fine interest and enthusiasm—with your faith and wonderful directives—and things began to happen."

Margaret Sanger

"To Katharine Dexter McCormick, we offer our thanks and admiration for her leadership and accomplishment on behalf of the women of America."

Delegates to the 1919 NAWSA "Victory" Convention

"Her unflagging concern made possible the results which today mark the difference between misery and happiness for millions of women in this world."

Tribute to Katharine Dexter McCormick by Planned Parenthood League of Massachusetts, 1965

"Her legacy is one of confidence and will to bring about further progress for women."

Prof. Margery Resnick, MIT, at Katharine Dexter McCormick's 1975 Centennial celebration

Contents

Preface   ix

The Formative Years   1

Marriage and Madness   35

Women's Suffrage   89

The League of Women Voters   135

Dr. Brill   153

The League of Women Voters (continued)   161

Birth Control   173

Dr. Kempf, the Trial, and the Aftermath   203

Birth Control (continued)   233

The Pill   259

Final Years   293

Research Sources   309

Abbreviations   313

Notes   315

Bibliography   327

Index   331

Photo essay begins after page 160

Preface

The Massachusetts Institute of Technology is unlike any of its college brethren in New England. The contrast stems not only from the courses of study MIT has traditionally offered, nor from the exotic research programs it manages on behalf of the government. Its halls of learning are mammoth structures of granite and marble recalling the Great Library in Alexandria, Egypt, or the Louvre in Paris, with hundreds of names of the great thinkers of millennia etched along its facades. On March 1, 1968, another illustrious name was being honored at a special ceremony to dedicate the newly constructed Stanley McCormick Hall, the first dormitory for women in the history of MIT.

William H. Bemis, a Cleveland-based lawyer, joined university dignitaries, Boston politicians, and cultural leaders to pay tribute to their benefactress, Katharine Dexter McCormick, the same woman many of their fathers had spent a great deal of energy denouncing in the early years of the twentieth century. She had died barely three months earlier, at the age of ninety-two. Though quite infirm at the end, she had nonetheless supervised every aspect of the dorm's construction, as might a master architect.

Bemis began the dedication. "In all the years that I knew Mrs. McCormick, I never addressed her by her first name. Today, however, she is going to be Katharine."

Many in the audience nodded in acknowledgment, as those who had known this woman clearly understood Bemis's reference. During her lifetime, few if any had ever dared address Mrs. McCormick in the familiar.

Seventy years earlier, twenty-four-year-old Katharine Dexter had en-

tered MIT as a special student to pursue a science degree in the almost
all-male institution, the first woman with such a professed goal in mind.
That she persevered, enduring the isolation and hostility of professors and
fellow students alike, to be granted a science degree in 1904 served as an
early example of a lifelong determination and resolve to attain her desired
aims.

Love intervened, momentarily. Katharine's desire to become a doctor
was emotionally sidetracked by Stanley McCormick, youngest son of Cyrus McCormick, inventor and manufacturer of the mechanized reaper.
Stanley was tall, handsome, learned, and articulate, with strong artistic
inclinations. Unknown to Katharine, he was already manifesting signs of
an incipient mental disorder.

They married after a stormy courtship. Three times Katharine agreed
to Stanley's proposals, only to break them off because of his erratic behavior. Finally, in September 1904, in the capitalistic equivalent of the
joining of royal houses, they married.

Within two years, however, Stanley's eccentric and violent behavior
forced him to be placed in a mental institution. There he was examined
by some of the world's most eminent "alienists," expert-witness psychiatrists who determined that Stanley suffered from catatonia and would
likely never recover.

As a scientist, Katharine believed there had to be some possibility of
improvement, some therapy that would lessen Stanley's distress, perhaps
even cure him. After being informed of Stanley's illness, Katharine wrote
to her mother: "Stanley needs my attention; I know he wants to live, and
I will not leave him, no matter how long it might take." Katharine kept
her promise: she protected and cared for him as long as he lived . . . more
than another forty years.

In Boston, a few years later, on a cool, windy, and rainy night, a group
of starched-collar businessmen filled a downtown meeting hall to share
and vent their outrage against women's suffrage. In a dark, damp alley
nearby, a group of socially prominent suffragists prepared themselves to
initiate a riot. Their leader was a tall, comely, dark-haired woman from
one of the city's Brahmin families. She resembled someone dressed for a
parlor lecture, not a civil disturbance. Katharine Dexter McCormick wore
her hair curled high, Gibson-style, under a hat punctuated by two ruby
pins. She was costumed in a white silk dress, accentuated by a magnificent
string of pearls and a fur boa wound tightly around her shoulders. Katharine was now a leading member of the Massachusetts Women's Alliance,
a branch of the national women's suffrage organization. Their mission: to
break up the anti-suffrage assembly and gain publicity for their cause.
Next day, the *Boston Globe* identified Katharine, the city's wealthy socialite
and "suffrage inciter," and condemned her for "unladylike behavior."

Fourteen years later, an attractive, stately, regally graying, fur-coated woman of considerable wealth and position guided her baggage through U.S. Customs at a New York dock. Katharine had returned from one of her frequent trips to the family château outside of Geneva, Switzerland. She took more than usual care to shepherd her suitcases and trunks through the intrusive process since, carefully hidden inside the trunks, sewn into her clothing, were hundreds of illegal diaphragms. Katharine was smuggling the contraband into the country for her friend and colleague, Margaret Sanger, firebrand director of a birth control clinic recently opened in New York.

Nearly thirty years later, Katharine, now seventy-seven and no less vigorous, sought and found a research doctor with the best potential formula for an easy-to-use birth control contraceptive. Thanks to her skillful leadership, persistent hectoring, and financial support, the birth control pill became a commercial reality. The *New York Times* hailed the achievement as "the most sweeping socio-medical revolution in history."

Although historians of women's suffrage, birth control, and the pill's development sometimes cite Katharine Dexter McCormick, few are familiar with the dramatic and compelling story of this remarkable woman. In more than a half century, from her first street march on behalf of the suffrage movement to her success in making birth control a safe, affordable, and respectable reality, Katharine was a driving force in nearly every crusade for women's rights—the battle for the vote, the formation of the League of Women Voters, the birth control movement, the creation of Planned Parenthood, and the development of the pill.

All this was accomplished in spite of a personal life filled with melodramatic conflicts and tragic personal losses. Katharine was a person whose public life was often deemed heroic, while her work remained largely unheralded. She preferred to practice progressive and radical politics while retaining her position in the world of America's rich. This relative anonymity occurred by personal design; she never sought nor received the public notoriety of fellow revolutionaries such as Carrie Chapman Catt, Margaret Sanger, and Eleanor Roosevelt.

The story of Katharine is not only that of an individual moving through successive epochs of social revolution. It is also a history of the clash between fundamental views and beliefs of the appropriate role of women in our society. Whether people today might label her criminal or heroine, Katharine unswervingly dedicated her entire life and most of her wealth to women's legal, social, psychological, and physical emancipation.

In her personal world, Katharine's values were clear and fixed. Distinctions between good and evil were unambiguous; "gray areas" were unknown. These characteristics mirrored both her strengths and weaknesses throughout life. Facing appalling obstacles and resentments, she triumphed over tragedies, losses, and disappointments by taking on challenges—her "duty and destiny," as she defined them. This determination reveals a brilliant, formidable, energetic, and determined woman.

Given the era in which she crusaded, there may seem, on the surface, a distance between Katharine's activities and the events affecting women today. Today, more women attend college than men. The League of Women Voters has become a bastion of social and political respectability. Planned Parenthood includes some of the most respected men and women in the world. And birth control is big business, representing wealth in excess of the gross national product of many of the world's nations.

Yet, all of these factors notwithstanding, regression and intolerance against women remain. Abortion rights, spousal abuse, sexual harassment, equal pay for equal work, and access to affordable health care continue to be highly charged issues in this country, suggesting that, unfortunately, we still do not live in a gender-equitable society.

Today, as U.S. citizens seem at once increasingly self-centered and narrow-minded, obsessed with individual freedoms, family values, crime, and the often myopic search for a piece of the American Dream, it is easy to overlook that a few brave women like Katharine Dexter McCormick dedicated their lives to achieving a far larger dream, to improve the lot of all women. One hopes that by recalling her endeavors, triumphs, and tragedies, we might rediscover the visionary spirit that made her achievements possible.

*   *   *   *   *

I have come to the conclusion that Katharine Dexter McCormick was in every sense a pioneer on behalf of women's rights. The many examples of her organizational abilities were remarkable and groundbreaking. If inclined to be single-minded and rigid, she nevertheless possessed an unflagging integrity, an overarching intelligence, and a singular gift for "getting things done." She knew all too well the price she paid to crusade for women's equality. Yet she possessed boundless courage and an unshakable belief in her goals. And she never stopped fighting.

In the end, I have articulated Katharine's life and career along two parallel pathways: first, her battle for women's rights, which took on different forms as events demanded throughout the twentieth century; second, her fight to protect her mentally disturbed husband from his own sociopathic family and the insidious experiments of the most renowned "alienists" in early twentieth-century psychiatry.

As my search lent renewed substance to Katharine's persona, her biography took on a threefold purpose: to reveal the story of an exceptional woman who made a life's commitment to assist womankind; to examine the social and personal history of the women's rights movement at its most crucial stages of development; and to provide a window through which we might better understand and respond to the forces that impact the lives of women today.

Biographies depend upon the collection of papers, archives' preserving them, and archivists making them available to researchers. I am grateful to the following sources, all of which preserved Katharine's personal and professional history and allowed me to study the material freely.

Mormon Library, Salt Lake City

New England Genealogical Library, Boston, Massachusetts

Washtenaw Historical Society, Dexter, Michigan

Massachusetts Institute of Technology Museum

Massachusetts Institute of Technology Archives/Special Collections

Massachusetts Historical Society

Chicago Historical Society

Santa Barbara Historical Society

Montecito Historical Society

McCormick Archives/State Historical Society, Madison, Wisconsin

National American Woman Suffrage Association, Library of Congress

National Woman's Party, Library of Congress

Carrie Chapman Papers, Library of Congress

League of Women Voters Papers, Library of Congress

American Birth Control League Papers, Library of Congress

Dr. Pincus Papers, Library of Congress

Schlesinger Library, Radcliffe College

Dr. Rock Papers, Houghton Library, Harvard University

Worcester Foundation for Experimental Biology

Dr. Adolph Meyer Papers, Johns Hopkins University Medical Library

Margaret Sanger Papers, Sophia Smith Collection, Smith College

Planned Parenthood Federation, McCormick Library, New York, N.Y.

Finally, loving gratitude to my wife, Sara, who has shared my obsession with Katharine and who, without jealousy of the "other woman" in my life, has continually supported me in my endeavors.

The Formative Years

One

Quickened by the first cool breezes of approaching autumn, sunshine found its way through scattered clouds to dance lightly on the packed-earth streets of Dexter, Michigan. The twenty-seventh of August, 1875, a splendid Sunday afternoon, a girl was born to Wirt and Josephine Dexter. The child was named Katharine Moore, after Wirt's grandmother and Katharine's mother.

The town of Dexter existed by the grace and effort of Samuel William Dexter, Katharine's grandfather, who had founded a village forty years earlier. Nearly all of the businesses in Dexter were owned by the Dexter family, and most of the town's population was there because of Samuel William's superb salesmanship.

Over the years, Dexter had grown to become a thriving community of over 200 residents and sixty-five houses. It boasted twice the number of churches than its single general store. The lumber mill produced much of the town's wealth. In addition, Dexter uniquely featured a train station, tangible evidence of the rail route that Wirt's father had brilliantly maneuvered through the state legislature. Unlike other nearby communities in Michigan Territory, Dexter had no saloons; Samuel William had vigorously preached temperance.

Dexter family genealogy dated back to the thirteenth century, its roots in Devonshire, England.[1] For his loyal and unswerving devotion to the King of England, Richard de Excester was appointed Governor and Lord Justice of Ireland, recently conquered and occupied by the English. The de Excester lineage prospered there until 1641, when an uprising of Irish Catholics against their Protestant overseers persuaded Richard (now)

Dexter and his family to effect a hasty escape to the British colonies in America.

In early February 1642, a group of exhausted and hungry passengers disembarked from a merchant ship just arrived from Liverpool, England. The people on the dock paid scant attention to Richard Dexter with his wife and two children, bearing their meager belongings.

Having arrived in Massachusetts Colony with some funds, however, Richard was able to purchase a forty-acre farm near the village of Malden, north of Boston. This homestead remained in the Dexter family for nearly 200 years. Successive generations of Dexters ran the farm successfully and raised large families. They also displayed a propensity for involvement in local politics and educational affairs, more often than not as voices raised in opposition to prevailing norms.

Samuel Dexter—the first of six generations of Samuels—was born in 1700 on the family farm. Eschewing farm life, Samuel was the first Dexter to graduate from Harvard, at the time a college closely affiliated with the Congregational Church. After graduation, Samuel became a minister of the First Church of Dedham and gained the reputation of being an enlightened leader of his flock. His son, Samuel II, however, rebelled against attending Harvard and, instead, became a successful Boston merchant. The business estate he accumulated ultimately became the basis for the Dexter family fortune.

Samuel II was also one of the men who repeatedly spoke out against Britain's "dangerous policies" during the years leading to the War of Independence. His agitation against the British sometimes made him a fugitive, but he always managed to escape arrest. When independence was achieved, Samuel reaped the benefits of the infant nation's new economy. In recognition of his father, he donated money to Harvard to establish the Dexter Lectureship.

His son, Samuel III, became known throughout the country as "the great lawyer." He graduated from Harvard with honors and his rapidly flourishing practice led him into politics. Samuel served in the Massachusetts Legislature's lower house for two years, was elected to the U.S. House of Representatives, and then became a U.S. Senator. President John Adams then selected him as Secretary of War. A year later, as Secretary of the Treasury, he developed the country's first national budget. President Jefferson wanted Samuel to continue in his cabinet, even offering a desirable foreign office post; however, Samuel declined, explaining that he wanted to return to his first love, practicing law among the people.

In 1824, instead of pursuing a legal career like his father, Samuel William immigrated to the Michigan Territory, where he purchased land and established the first lumber mill in the area. He married twice and lost both wives to ill health. None of the children of these marriages survived.

Samuel William, however, proved prodigious in other ways. In 1825, he plotted the town of Dexter, named after his father. The following year, he was appointed chief justice of Washtenaw County. He opened the first post office, became postmaster, and personally carried the mail to and from Ann Arbor every week.

A year after his second wife died, Samuel William married sixteen-year-old Millicent Bond. The third Mrs. Dexter, a strong, ambitious woman, became deputy postmaster and delivered the mail when her husband was in court. She also kept the records for her husband's expanding and profitable lumber business. Over a period of twenty-eight years, she bore eight children, one boy and seven girls, all of whom lived to adulthood. Millicent outlived her husband by thirty-six years, dying in 1899, at age eighty-seven.

Throughout their years together, Samuel William's business continued to expand—new mills in Elk Rapids; the founding of the town of Saginaw; establishment of the first local newspaper, the *Western Emigrant*, which gave him the opportunity to express his opinions on temperance (in favor) and Freemasonry (against). Samuel William was also one of the initial benefactors of the University of Michigan, which he served as a regent until his death in 1863.

Just east of Dexter, on a rise overlooking both a nearby stream and the town itself, Samuel William built a magnificent mansion of hand-hewn virgin white oak, with twenty-two rooms, nine fireplaces, and fifty-two windows. He named the home Gordon Hall, in memory of his mother.

A story was told that the Dexter home was a stop on the Abolitionist "underground railroad" for slaves escaping to the North before and during the Civil War. There is evidence that Millicent regularly employed black servants who were recent arrivals to Dexter. They never seemed to stay employed for very long, nor did they remain in town.

Judge Dexter was described as a tall, muscular, handsome man, physically graceful, with sparkling, penetrating eyes. He was well-spoken, an excellent orator who enjoyed engaging in debate. His contemporaries considered him a great reader and fine scholar. He was also a highly religious man. His spiritual concerns, however, were directed primarily toward aiding the poor and destitute.

Judge Samuel William Dexter died in the spring of 1863. His sizable business was turned over to Wirt, his only son; the remainder of the estate was divided among the other seven children.

The second of eight Dexter children, Wirt had been born October 25, 1832, in Dexter. A few days after his birth, the Dexter family was visited by William Wirt, the attorney general serving then President Monroe. When he inquired about the baby's name, he was told it had yet to be chosen.

"Name him Wirt," the illustrious visitor suggested. And so it was done.

Since he was the only son, much attention was paid to Wirt's upbringing. At an early age, he was reading popular history and literary books. He was taught farming and how to handle the family's business affairs. Millicent personally guided his educational development, and Wirt became an excellent student. While still a teenager, Wirt decided to practice law, emulating his father and grandfather.

Wirt began his career at the University of Michigan. He then transferred to Cazenovia Seminary, New York, where he obtained his law degree. Returning home, he quickly assumed responsibility for running his father's business. While successful in expanding the business, Wirt had little time to practice law, his first love. In 1855, he moved to Chicago to enter the law profession and, at the same time, build the family lumber business in that city.

Two events highlighted Wirt Dexter's life in 1858. Early in the year, he was admitted to the Illinois bar, and became a partner in a well-known law firm. The Michigan Central Railway, whose existence was due in part to his father's efforts, was one of the firm's primary clients.

A few months later, Wirt married a childhood friend from the Dexter area, Kate Augusta Dusenberry. After their marriage, Wirt purchased a small property on the south side of Chicago, on Prairie Avenue, where the couple built a modest home.

In February 1864, Kate and Wirt had a son, predictably named Samuel. Unfortunately, Kate became ill following childbirth and died a few months later. The baby, Samuel, died shortly thereafter.

The loss of his loved ones drove Wirt back to Gordon Hall to mourn. It was a number of months before he resumed his practice in Chicago. At thirty-two, however, he became one of the city's most eligible bachelors.

Two years later, at a dinner party given by the Henry Kings, business friends who lived nearby, Wirt was introduced to a King family relative recently arrived in Chicago. Eighteen-year-old Josephine Moore had been born in 1846 in West Springfield, Massachusetts, the only daughter of a prosperous farming family. Unlike most couples of the day, her enlightened parents believed in advanced education for their daughter. Josephine planned to be a teacher. She had chosen Knox College, in Illinois, to study for her degree. To that end, she had received permission to stay with her cousins, the Kings. For Josephine, this was the first time she had left home, indeed a pioneering adventure. Not surprisingly, Wirt was immediately attracted by her enthusiastic, independent spirit.

Wirt set out to court Josephine, and in less than six months they were married. It was a large, elegant wedding attended by most of Chicago's social elite; "a notable event," the *Chicago Tribune* reported. Less than a year later, a son, again named Samuel, was born.

During the next few years, Wirt built his law practice and his reputation. He won a number of highly publicized criminal cases, while devoting time and energy to assisting the city's poor, with both personal contributions and charitable activities. The years 1871 to 1874 would demonstrate Wirt's capacity for leadership and sense of values.

As the nation's, if not the world's, lumber capital, Chicago was a city built almost entirely of wood—houses, churches, stores, grain elevators, factories, streets, and sidewalks. The year 1871 was unusually dry in Chicago. By autumn, the city was desiccated kindling waiting for a spark to ignite it.

On the evening of October 8, a fire started in a barn on the southwest side of the city.[2] Within minutes, fanned by strong winds, the flames raced north and east through the city. Fire brigades were quickly overwhelmed. All they could do was warn people living ahead of the fire to evacuate as fast as possible. The resulting exodus created impassable traffic jams, as families in wagons piled high with household goods attempted an increasingly desperate escape. Tragically, many never got past their own neighborhoods. Hopes that a body of water would stop the fire were shattered when flames leapt across the Chicago River, devouring north side structures and driving panic-stricken families toward Lincoln Park. Thousands found refuge only by wading neck-deep into Lake Michigan.

Wirt witnessed the fire in its initial stages from his home on Prairie Avenue. He quickly moved Josephine and Sam south, away from the fire's prevailing direction. The conflagration raged for over twenty-four hours, leveling the downtown and most north side homes and businesses. The Great Fire, as it was later called, killed more than 300 people, left 90,000 homeless, and destroyed more than $200 million worth of property.

The homeless masses now awaited the first shipment of provisions—food, water, and clothing. Army troops attempted to restore gas and water supplies. Nearly all business and government records housed in downtown offices were destroyed. Reliable news was impossible to obtain because newspaper offices had been burnt out as well. Yet, a few days after the fire, Chicago's leading business and civic leaders publicly and boldly proclaimed that they would "speedily rebuild the city" and that the "cessation of industry would be short."

Three years before the fire, a group of leading businessmen had formed the Relief and Aid Society, a private charitable agency that supported the city's poor. With a budget of $25,000 a year, the society helped more than 3,000 people each year. Its executive board was headed by Wirt Dexter. Among its members were Marshall Field, George Pullman, and Henry King, all men who knew how to design, coordinate, and implement complex ventures.

Five days after the fire, in what was considered a controversial decision by detractors of local government, the mayor of Chicago appointed the Relief and Aid Society to take charge of public relief. The society assumed total responsibility for rebuilding the city, a charge that included the receipt and distribution of all supplies. With this new mandate, the society became the city's social welfare agency as well.[3]

With Josephine serving as her husband's assistant and secretary, the Dexter home was turned into the society's headquarters. For the next two years, the Dexter home became a meeting place for city planners, builders, merchants, civic administrators, and newspeople. A portion of the home was set aside for ordering goods and materials and distributing these throughout the city.

At the same time that the society devoted itself to Chicago's reconstruction, Prairie Avenue began to attract the city's elite as a most desirable place to build their new mansions.

Prior to the Great Fire, Prairie Avenue had been a quiet residential area of modest homes, built after the Civil War. It was convenient to downtown and only a few blocks from the lake. Behind it lay the railroad tracks, but these served as buffers between the residential and industrial parts of Chicago. After the fire, however, Prairie Avenue became Chicago's first "gold coast."[4]

Within a few years, Prairie Avenue contained the most magnificent— indeed, pretentious—homes in the city, built by the new industrial elite: Armour, Otis, Pullman, Field, Kimball, Studebaker, and Kellogg. An 1880 guidebook called Prairie Avenue "the choicest property in Chicago" and went on to note, "These residences are characterized by a much higher degree of taste and appreciation of the true principles of residential architecture than has been characteristic of the west of the Western continent."

In the winter of 1874, when Wirt Dexter returned to his law practice, he was not only a neighbor to the city's richest entrepreneurs, he had become their lawyer as well. The Dexter household had again settled into some degree of normalcy. Sam, now seven, had begun school. Wirt and Josephine decided it was time to have another child.

Two months before the baby was due, Josephine took the train to Dexter and Gordon Hall. Under Millicent's care, she awaited the birth.

The local celebration to honor newborn Katharine Moore Dexter continued an entire week. It was attended by relatives, townspeople, and guests who came from as far afield as Saginaw, though not by Wirt or Sam, both of whom remained in Chicago. Wirt was involved in defending a poor woman accused of shooting a constable. Sam had just begun his elementary education at the Haven School for Boys. It would be several more months, just as snows began to curtail rail travel in Michigan, before Wirt got his first look at the infant daughter who would soon become his great pride.

Two

In late 1875, Prairie Avenue was surfaced with high-grade cobblestone. Gas streetlights had recently been installed. The avenue was lined with stately shade trees, well-swept wooden sidewalks, and carefully pruned shrubbery. Majestic oaks, tall wrought-iron fences, and ivy vines largely concealed the facades of mansions, except for their ornate entranceways. Peering through a front gate, one could view garden fountains; elegantly carved doors with large, ornamented brass door knockers; ornamental grillwork; polished wood paneling; and imported stained-glass windows.

Visitors to the neighborhood were awed by the châteaulike structures, lofty brick chimneys, decorated balconies, and sloping grill-lined roofs. They anticipated seeing members of these "aristocratic" families boarding luxurious carriages or sitting high and handsome on sleek horses prancing down the street. Situated in the center of this opulence was number 1620, the Dexter "cottage," a comparatively modest two-story home with an open, friendly, wide front porch.[1]

Katharine's nursery was on the second floor, facing Prairie Avenue. Elaborately decorated by Josephine with paintings and wall hangings, the nursery boasted the best of Victorian children's furniture, including a traditional Dexter family wooden rocking crib now adorned with ruffles. Adjacent to the nursery was a playroom, already filled with toys, some saved from Sam's early childhood. A hobbyhorse, an heirloom given to Sam by his grandmother, was now Katharine's to use, and it quickly became her favorite toy.

Excerpts from written accounts of the family suggest that Josephine was an attentive mother, though not overly warm or affectionate toward Katharine. The task of nurture was assigned to Cathrine Johnson, the Dexters' oldest maid, who had been with the family in Michigan before Wirt and Josephine were married. The Dexters also employed four other household servants—a maid to attend Sam, a cook, a butler, and a coachman. Johnson's sole responsibility was to care for Katharine.[2]

More important to Josephine was her self-imposed responsibility to perpetuate the Dexter family heritage and legacy. She was said to be so proud of being a Dexter—if only by marriage—and so imbued with the Dexter ancestry that little was ever revealed of her own family and background. Thanks to Josephine, the Dexter mythos became a vital part of her children's learning.

With single-minded zeal, Josephine carried out the daily etiquette that governed Victorian social behavior. It was as if each of her daily activities was a means by which she could affirm the nobility and elegance of her own station. Later references from Katharine's letters suggest that her mother's behavior often became so overbearing that she and Sam politely removed themselves from such situations whenever they were able.

At the same time, however, Josephine expressed a strong commitment to her children's education, not only through formal schooling in the best private institutions available, but also though travel and exposure to literature, music, and art. This was especially true for Katharine, as Josephine stressed the importance of her daughter's becoming "a well-bred woman with learning." It was hardly surprising that, as Katharine grew into girlhood and was urged to expand her own horizons, a close relationship between mother and daughter never really materialized.

At age six, Katharine was enrolled at Mrs. Stella Loring's School for Girls, at Prairie Avenue and Twenty-eighth Street. The school had been started by Prairie Avenue families who wished to have a nearby institution to educate their daughters, particularly to prepare them for Chicago society. Along with her "finishing school" curriculum, Mrs. Loring also emphasized academics. Katharine was deemed an excellent student. According to school reports, however, she admitted to not showing interest for her classes in "manners."

By the middle of elementary school, Katharine's personality had become quite defined, at least in the eyes of school personnel. She was described as a serious child, mature for her age, focused, a high achiever, but rarely outgoing with her peers. Photographs of Katharine from this period tend to support these observations: an attractive girl, with dark hair and dark eyes, serious beyond her years, her steady gaze and erect posture suggesting a determination and sincere self-assurance uncommon for a young girl raised in a sheltered and affluent home.

While her girlfriends talked of parties and dresses, Katharine was more concerned with searching for artifacts of the Fort Dearborn Massacre, a site just down the block from the Dexter home. Nor did she easily make friends at school. Given the choice between attending a Prairie Avenue birthday party or accompanying her father on a horseback ride, she chose the latter. In fact, Katharine preferred to participate in activities initiated by her father or brother.

Early in her childhood, Katharine learned that her mother was a supporter of the suffrage movement, as defined then in the speeches and writings of Susan B. Anthony and Elizabeth Cady Stanton.[3] Josephine Dexter was not, however, a publicly participating member, since such behavior would not have been considered socially acceptable among her peers. Like other upper-class women, Josephine gave time and money for benevolent and charitable efforts. At the time, women of her class did not challenge the legal, political, and economic privileges enjoyed by men, nor would they entertain the more militant actions of suffrage leaders, who insisted that such privileges should be rights enjoyed by both sexes. When questioned, Josephine maintained that, by her charitable activities on behalf of needy women, she was filling a special need.

Josephine's actual views were likely kept under firm self-control so as to protect her social position. Like many of her wealthy female contemporaries, she believed that women could achieve equality or even "rise above men" by actions more oblique and sentiments more refined. Often, as an example of her views, she talked of her business experiences with men, many of them Wirt's peers, during their involvement in Chicago's rebuilding period.

Nonetheless, Josephine admitted to advocating "prudent sex," a euphemism employed by wealthy suffrage proponents to describe the practice of contraception for deliberate birth limitation. She obviously practiced it—only two pregnancies during twenty-four years of marriage, with a seven-year separation between the births of Samuel and Katharine.

There is no question that Katharine was influenced by her mother's involvement with the suffrage movement. Early conversations had to have been confusing to young Katharine; and while she appeared to embrace her mother's value system regarding suffrage, she had not yet determined whether these beliefs would become her own. In any case, they were not readily expressed until a personal tragedy later struck the family.

Interestingly, Wirt never questioned his wife's views. In fact, when women's rights became a topic of public conversation, Wirt strongly supported the right of women to gain access to the prerogatives men enjoyed. Of course, within the milieu of Chicago's wealthy families, men like Wirt could be more outspoken about such perspectives than could their wives. As Katharine became more aware of the subtle differences in viewpoint between her father and mother, she tended to agree more with Wirt than with Josephine.

The relationship between Sam and Katharine further illuminated the Dexter family dynamics. "Young Sam," as he was fondly called by relatives and friends, was seven years older than Katharine, endowed with the special prerogatives of a firstborn son. Sam was a bright, handsome, eager child; his introduction into the Dexter universe consisted of a unique participation in his parents' civic responsibilities that had so dramatically engulfed the Dexter home as the Relief and Aid Society worked toward Chicago's rehabilitation. Assigned the job of messenger, carrying notes between groups of businessmen working on various projects, Sam grew up familiar to all parties. He was early recognized for his devotion to duty, as well as for the mutual respect that developed between him and the city's most renowned leaders. Sam's parents were indeed proud of their son, and he in turn more than fulfilled their expectations.

Four-year-old Sam had viewed all of this frenetic activity as mysterious, but as all parties seemed to appreciate his company, he found the situation full of fun. It proved a major disappointment for him when the Dexter home returned to normal and Sam had to begin school, a regimen not nearly as exciting or interesting. When Katharine arrived home, however, Sam quickly became attached to her and proclaimed himself her protector.

From the moment she first became aware of Sam, Katharine adored her brother. Sam seemed to anticipate her every need, seemed to know what she was thinking and how she felt. When Katharine suffered a childhood hurt, a kiss by Sam healed the injury. When her maid, Cathrine Johnson, was unable or unwilling to fulfill a request, Sam came to her rescue. At home, they were inseparable. When they walked on the street together, Sam held her hand, walked at her pace, and carefully helped her across the unpaved streets so her clothes would not become soiled. Sam often read to Katharine, stories they both enjoyed, like the popular Wild West dime magazines and Anna Seawall's new novel, *Black Beauty*.[4]

Sam excelled at the Haven School, a private boys' academy on the south side of Chicago. He was a happy child, a fine student, athletic, and a true companion to his peers. When a group activity was assigned, it was Samuel who assumed the leadership, and his classmates were happy to follow. No one was surprised when he graduated at the top of his class. When Sam went off to preparatory school, Katharine keenly missed her brother's companionship.

Even before graduating from preparatory school, Sam declared his intention "to become a lawyer." During his prep-school years, Sam worked part-time at his father's law firm, "to get a view on the business," according to Wirt. After graduation, before continuing his education at Harvard, Sam was rewarded with a summer trip to London. There, he promptly obtained a job driving a carriage at a well-known hotel to supplement his allowance.

Although Wirt was involved in many public activities, he desired above all to be a family man, spending as much time as possible at home. Each day, he dedicated hours to Samuel and Katharine. Wirt taught Katharine to ride, and they were often seen together astride Wirt's horse as they rode around the neighborhood. Wirt and Josephine enjoyed music and theater and often included young Katharine and Samuel. In later years, Katharine's memories of such times with her father were invariably associated with enjoyable adventures.[5]

After Katharine's arrival, one of the first visitors to the Dexter household was the famed British actress Ellen Terry. She and the Dexters had already become friends. A few years before, when Terry had visited Chicago to perform, the city had not yet reopened its hotels, which had been closed by the fire. The Dexters offered to shelter Terry. From that time on, Terry stayed with the Dexters whenever appearing in Chicago theaters. Terry grew very fond of Katharine; in her letters to the Dexters, she always wanted to know how "Dottie," her nickname for Katharine, was doing. Baby Katharine was enthralled with Terry and, at age three, announced her intention to become an actress, "just like Aunt Ellen."[6]

Wirt took pride in his home as a center of intellectual life. He loved books and spent much of his time reading not only law, but also history and literature. His friends included many of the country's leading literary figures, among them James Russell Lowell, Charles Dudley Warner, and Ralph Waldo Emerson. All were entertained at the Dexter home.

When social issues were debated, Wirt was considered a "liberal thinker." During one election, Wirt told the local Law and Order Party he could not support its demand for Sunday business closings since he believed in the rightfulness of "free sabbaths." Still, he backed the party's reform candidates because they were more concerned than most with the shape of Chicago city government. Wirt fought strongly against corrupt and dishonest local politicians, whom he labeled "bummers," asserting that they thought nothing for the "greater good of the city." The *Tribune* described him as a man who would always attract attention. "Handsome, courtly, of almost military bearing," the *Tribune* declared, "he is, in physical presence as well as other attributes, a perfect example of a well-bred American gentleman, and his bearing and manner were such as could not but command respect."[7]

Sam and Katharine were no doubt somewhat wonder-struck by the larger-than-life public figure who was their father. At home, however, Wirt was quiet, relaxed, and affectionate toward his children; he strove to maintain a separation between his personal and business lives. He rarely lectured Sam or Katharine about values and morals; one only had to listen to his words and observe his deeds to understand his philosophy.

Besides the arts, Wirt's hobbies included riding, hunting, and fishing, all favorite sports of his when he was a young man in Michigan. Each summer, one of his favorite outings was a hunting trip in Missouri with the governor, a personal friend of long acquaintance.

Wirt respected religion but belonged to none of the recognized churches.

He attended meetings at Professor Swing's Central Music Hall, a group loosely affiliated with the Congregational Church. Professor Swing had officiated at Wirt and Josephine's wedding and had become a close friend.

The Dexters loved to tour and often took vacations in Europe. While still in their teens, both Samuel and Katharine had visited England, France, and Switzerland. Katharine enjoyed these excursions with her parents and the opportunity to learn about other cultures and languages. When she was allowed some freedom to explore on her own, she decided it was to her advantage to learn French and German.

Besides the rigors of school and the excitement of adventures with her family, Katharine's early-teen life included parties and dancing, usually staged by Prairie Avenue neighbors. Almost every mansion on the street had a ballroom, so that dances for young people were frequent. Rarely did anyone patronize downtown hotels to seek entertainment.

Johnny Hand and his Orchestra played at most of these private occasions. Hand had built a reputation for performing exclusively for the city's social elite. A joke circulated that if St. Peter himself were to invite Hand to conduct a heavenly orchestra, he would first inquire if the people attending the concert would be first-class.

The most famous of these events was hosted by the Marshall Fields for their two children, Marshall, seventeen, and Ethel, thirteen, a classmate of Katharine. It was the custom of Mrs. Field to give a Christmas party for her children, to which all of the young people from the neighborhood were invited. Now that her children were older, the holiday festivity had been expanded to a formal ball, which included all parents as well.

Gilbert and Sullivan's *Mikado* had recently played in Chicago, and Mrs. Field decided to sponsor a *Mikado* costume ball. Decorators transformed the Field mansion into a miniature Japanese town. The great front hall was decorated with a copy of the stage set from the second act of *Mikado*. A miniature pagoda, under which Johnny Hand's Orchestra was seated, was erected on one side of the ballroom. In appropriate costume, Mrs. Field led the cotillion, the feature of the event.

On the night of the ball, December 15, 1889, Prairie Avenue was illuminated by calcium lights from Sixteenth Street to Twenty-second Street. More than five hundred guests attended the event. Party favors of linen, silver, and foodstuffs from Paris were distributed among the guests. Newspapers reported that the ball cost almost $75,000.[8]

Katharine and her friends had learned to dance at Bournique's Dancing Academy on Twenty-third Street, near Prairie Avenue. It was there that the children of the elite learned the steps of the waltz, schottische, and polka. And it was there that thirteen-year-old Katharine first became acquainted with fourteen-year-old Stanley McCormick. Stanley was the youngest son of Cyrus McCormick, inventor, manufacturer, distributor, and multimillionaire, thanks to his patent on the mechanized reaper. Ironically, Wirt's Relief and Aid Society had persuaded McCormick to keep his factory in Chicago after the Great Fire.[9]

While the McCormicks did not live on Prairie Avenue—they had chosen to build an ornate, châteaulike mansion on Rush Street, on Chicago's north side, the better to distinguish themselves from the city's other wealthy families—their standing gave them entree to the entertainments of the Prairie Avenue plutocrats. For her part, Katharine remembered Stanley as being good-looking, tall, an excellent dancer, but very shy. Years later, she discovered that Stanley had been attracted to her and had begged his mother, Nettie, to arrange for him to meet Katharine again. Nettie, however, had refused his request and admonished her son for his interest in girls.

In the spring of 1890, in anticipation of a visit to matriarch Millicent and Wirt's sisters, the family prepared for a trip to Dexter, Michigan. Wirt had been hard at work as counselor to and board member of the Burlington Railroad. Josephine was involved with a group of women friends conferring at the moment with Jane Addams and Ellen Starr about an innovative (some called it sacrilegious) idea to establish and operate a settlement house for the destitute on Chicago's south side. Addams needed funds, and the matrons from Prairie Avenue were interested in the project.

After four highly successful years at Harvard, replete with scholastic and athletic honors, Sam was about to graduate with a law degree. He was planning to spend the summer apprenticing at his father's firm. Katharine, a pretty, self-assured fourteen-year-old, was attempting to convince her mother to let her take a European tour on her own.

May 19, 1890, was a cloudy, humid day in Chicago, heavy with the portent of rain. Wirt had come to the office prepared with an umbrella, since he planned to walk home after work, no matter the weather, as was his habit. It was another in a series of long days attending to railroad business, and Wirt decided to remain in his office to complete the work, although the other employees had already left for the day. Dinner would have to wait.

On his hands and knees while rummaging through some boxes, Wirt was seized with a sudden, severe shooting pain in his chest. It took his breath away for a moment, then quickly subsided. Wirt was shaken enough to call a doctor to examine him. The doctor arrived in minutes and told Wirt that he was very ill. A carriage was called, and Wirt was driven home as rapidly as possible. He arrived home earlier than expected; Josephine and Katharine greeted him at the door with some surprise.

Supported by the coachman, Wirt staggered up the porch stairs, where Josephine joined in assisting him to his bedroom. Dr. Johnson, Wirt's personal physician and friend, arrived shortly, examined him, and immediately gave him hot applications and stimulants to reduce the chest pain. Dr. Johnson told Wirt he had suffered a severe heart attack and would likely require hospital care. Johnson went downstairs to call the hospital for an ambulance. The pain subsiding momentarily, Wirt asked to be moved to his easy chair.

About a half-hour later, with Dr. Johnson, Josephine, and Katharine attending him, Wirt suddenly gasped, clutched his chest against the increasing pain, and slumped back in his chair. Wirt Dexter had died.

Josephine slumped to the floor and began sobbing, Wirt's hand still in her own. Katharine had also fallen to the floor, dazed, speechless, afraid to breathe; but no tears came to her eyes. Both she and Josephine were assisted to their bedrooms and given a sedative. Not until Wirt Dexter's funeral services did Katharine cry, as if in final affirmation of her father's unexpected, indeed shocking, death.

During the hours that immediately followed his passing, Dr. Johnson made the arrangements for Wirt's funeral and prepared the legal papers. Mrs. Pullman was called in to assist Josephine. Her cousins, the Kings, were asked to take over burial arrangements. Samuel was sent a wire informing him, in simple, unaffected telegraphic language, about the death of his father.

Samuel arrived in Chicago two days later, and the funeral took place at the Dexter home that afternoon. According to Wirt's wishes, the funeral was simple and brief. Dr. Swing read a few familiar psalms from Samuel William Dexter's Bible and paid his final respects to an old friend. Wirt's body lay in a plain black casket, graced by a wreath of laurel. Surrounding the casket were Wirt's neighbors and virtually every lawyer and businessman he had known. Speaking of Wirt's life, the Reverend Robert Collyer, head of the local Westminster Church, told of his great gifts and liberality of thought. "His power over injustice was great, as his convictions were strong," Collyer proclaimed. "He always advocated that which he himself sincerely believed, and his intense earnestness was the subtle power of the substance of truth itself."

The casket was closed and carried out of the house. Two carriages carried Josephine, Katharine, and close relatives to Graceland Cemetery, where, during the darkening moments of the day, Wirt Dexter was laid to rest. The *Chicago Tribune* devoted its entire front page to Wirt's passing, listing at length his contributions to the city and describing in detail his death and funeral services. The city mourned a dear friend and benefactor.

After the funeral, some neighbors lingered late, not wishing to leave Josephine alone. Katharine, still under Dr. Johnson's care, had retired.

Later in the evening, the sounds of footsteps descending the porch stairs were echoed by the massive oaks in front of No. 1620. Quiet words of condolence and encouragement were exchanged between Josephine and her neighbors, but she, better than anyone, understood the manners of the rich. Soon, she would be in social limbo, bereft of the human contact and activity upon which she had thrived, relegated to the constrained position defined for spinsters and bereaved widows. A powerful extension of Wirt Dexter while he lived, now, at age forty-two, with his death, she had lost most of the benefits her social acumen had accumulated. Nor would Katharine fare much better at school and with apparent friends.

In the Dexter study, Josephine had turned down the lamps and pulled a chair up to the fire that had been lit to provide her sufficient warmth. Three times she read the eulogy offered by Reverend Collyer. With tears in her eyes, she stared for a long while at the dying embers. Finally, she put aside the paper and forced herself to think about prospects for the future.

Taking paper and pen from the desk, she set about writing a letter to a family friend in Boston. Her days in Chicago were numbered, she wrote. "I now have to decide what to do about mine and my daughter's future."

Three

Unable to concentrate on her studies, Katharine had withdrawn from school the last weeks of the school year. Nor could she involve herself in any other activities, since each one seemed to remind her of her father. All she cared to do was count the days until she and Josephine would leave Chicago.

For Katharine, the long, slow train to Boston carried with it a heavy burden of grief. Never, even in her most girlish moods, would she have been described as a typical teenager. Now, she was at her most serious, more like a grieving woman than a child.

The train from Buffalo to Albany ran a winding, tortuous route through the Appalachian Mountains. Its slow passage, rattling over trestle bridges and chugging noisily through tiny farm communities, should have delighted a young girl. Yet unlike her mother, who visualized the possibilities of a life rebuilt in Boston, Katharine seemed to view the prospect as an imposed exile.

Josephine had friends and relatives in Boston. She had asked them for help to get settled in the city. Money was no problem, since she had been the sole beneficiary of Wirt's considerable estate. Along with the Prairie Avenue home, Wirt had owned seven pieces of commercial property on South Wabash Avenue in Chicago, all of them occupied by business concerns. His will included his share of the law firm, one-third ownership in Gordon Hall, and various lumber and iron works scattered throughout Michigan. In addition, Wirt owned more than $100,000 in railroad stocks and bonds. The Wabash properties alone would bring Josephine more than $51,000 a year in rents.[1]

In July, when Josephine and Katharine reached Boston, they rented a home on Beacon Street. It was to serve as temporary quarters until Josephine could find a more suitable home. In the meantime, the majority of their furnishings remained at Prairie Avenue.

In the fall, Katharine was ready to enter secondary school. Josephine wanted her to major in music and literature and prepare for her introduction into Boston society. Instead, Katharine announced her desire to take courses in the sciences because she wanted to become a scientist. Not surprisingly, Katharine's declaration was met with some concern. Josephine was convinced that the Dexter heritage would be best served by her daughter's development into a young woman of social refinement and grace. In conjunction with her obvious intellect, these would make her a fine prize for some young Boston Brahmin.

To Josephine's dismay, Katharine strongly disagreed, firm in her determination "to become a scientist, not a debutante." After some lengthy debates, mother and daughter compromised. Katharine was enrolled in Miss Hershey's School for Girls, a Back Bay finishing school, but one also noted for its academic excellence.

Little is known about Katharine's years at Miss Hershey's except that she excelled in academic courses and was reported to be indifferent to those teaching social etiquette. School authorities reported to Josephine that Katharine associated little with classmates, evidently considering them rather frivolous. An English class essay revealed Katharine's disdain for Boston society as a whole. She wrote: "The Boston citizen is provincial, intolerant, and narrow-minded; suspicious, conservative, doesn't want to change, since any moral and material change will be for the worse."[2] Josephine expressed great concern regarding her daughter's views of the very society she was destined to enter.

Even family social activities among literary and artistic people (such as Henry James) offered little to stimulate Katharine. She dutifully obeyed her mother's requests, but concentrated primarily on her studies. She now talked about becoming a surgeon.

Katharine debuted into Back Bay society in the fall of 1893. She was a tall, dark-haired, beautiful young woman whose poise and maturity made her seem older than her eighteen years. To judge from a portrait and photographs taken near the time of her debut, she was a serious, confident, and determined person. Yet her luminous eyes also revealed sorrow and loneliness.

As if to understate her social position and femininity, in none of these pictures did she wear any jewelry, the typical adornment of young society women. Atypical of the day's styles, her long hair was parted in the center and pulled to a bun in the back. Katharine had few real female friends. Unlike her fellow debutantes, she showed little interest in men, with the exception of her adored brother.

Twenty-five-year-old Sam was an intelligent, handsome young man, destined to follow in his illustrious father's footsteps. His Harvard undergraduate days had been replete with academic excellence and personal popularity. He had the honor of being chosen president of his class at Harvard each year. Nicknamed "Big Sam" due to his athletic prowess and leadership qualities, he was continually singled out by his peers, owing to his "qualities of heart and stature." In his senior year, Sam was elected marshall on Class Day, a prestigious honor at Harvard.

He had entered law school in Cambridge, obtained a degree—only a month after his father's sudden death—and decided, against his mother's wishes, to apprentice with his late father's firm. Josephine wanted him to remain in Boston.

During the summer of 1893, while the Dexters were vacationing at Newport, Rhode Island, Sam met Elsie Clews, a pretty Barnard College sophomore, whose family owned an oceanfront cottage on Narragansett Bay.[3] A brilliant student, fluent in both French and German, Elsie was described by her teachers as "an earnest young woman planning her future." Sam was immediately attracted to Elsie because she was unlike other women he knew. Likewise, Elsie found Sam an attractive companion.

Elsie and Sam spent the summer sharing interests, from swimming and riding to reading classical literature. After Sam returned to Chicago to begin his law practice, they maintained an active correspondence. Sam visited Elsie during the Christmas holidays, and it appeared their relationship was moving toward marriage.

Initially, Katharine did not have much direct contact with Elsie; but what she knew of her, including long written descriptions from Sam, engendered regard and admiration. Here was a woman whom she could respect, Katharine thought, the kind of person she would like to emulate. Josephine too was quite pleased with Elsie and hoped that a marriage would soon take place. In an April 1894 letter from Elsie to Sam, she discussed the possibility of having a family with him.

Sam was admitted to the Chicago bar in May 1894. To celebrate his admission, he returned to Boston to visit his mother and sister. It was to be a defining moment of triumph, as one of his life goals was to "fill the place made vacant by my father."

After arriving in Boston, he complained of a slight cold but paid little attention to the discomfort. While resting at home, Sam was suddenly stricken with severe headaches, nausea, and a high fever. Dr. Putnam, the family doctor, was called; Sam was taken to St. Margaret's Hospital for observation. "Am at the hospital with a slight fever," he wrote Elsie. "Don't know when I shall be out."[4]

Sam's original symptoms soon developed into neck and back spasms, alarming Dr. Putnam. Within three days, his illness finally diagnosed as spinal meningitis, Sam would be dead.

Knowing Sam had only a few hours to live, Dr. Putnam called Josephine and Katharine to the hospital. It was clear to Putnam that Sam was suffering from a fatal disease and there was little the medical profession could do about it. Putnam's primary responsibility, he believed, was to attend to Sam's family.

When Josephine and Katharine arrived at the hospital, Putnam took them aside to report on Sam's condition. Embracing Josephine, he said, "My dear Mrs. Dexter." He paused a frightening moment. "It is my sorrowful task to tell you that Sam will not recover from his illness. He has but a few hours alive." Putnam held her tightly while she sobbed on his shoulder.

Josephine was inconsolable. The most cruel and fearful event a mother could ever be asked to endure, the death of a child, was about to befall her. Through all of this, Katharine, stunned by the news, sat motionless and speechless, recalling her father's last moments.

During the last hour of his life, Sam became comatose. Taking both his hands in hers, Josephine could feel his presence fading. When Putnam announced Sam's passing, Josephine fell upon his body, weeping uncontrollably. Katharine covered her already tear-stained face and noted to no one in particular, "Now my dear brother is gone, too."

Josephine wished to conduct Sam's funeral at their Prairie Avenue home and to bury him next to Wirt in Graceland Cemetery. Old friends in Chicago assisted in making the arrangements. Reaching Chicago, Katharine displayed a courageous, solemn calm to those observing her, but inside, her heart and mind were racked by the loss of her adored brother.

Professor David Swing presided at Sam's funeral services. In attendance were many of the same people who had been present at Wirt's funeral four years earlier. Josephine and Katharine, attired in black, stood to one side, the casket flanked by neighbors and friends who had known and delighted in young Sam. In his brief sermon, Professor Swing referred to the recent Dexter family tragedies but also proffered hope for the living.

What sunny hours have passed over this roof and through these halls. Hither many of us came to find friendship, sympathy, and high happiness. Today we must place the beloved son by the side of the beloved father. He was anxious to fill the place made vacant by his noble father, and he was learning to be just, learning to be kind to everyone. His was a simple heart, strong and natural. To Josephine and Katharine, strength will enable you to live in communion and realize the presence of that world by which we are surrounded.[5]

For Katharine, however, grief was tempered by anger. "Why were my loved ones taken from me?" she wrote grandmother Millicent. "What kind of God would make us so unhappy?" And to the equally grieving Elsie, she asked: "What of our lives now?"

After some weeks in seclusion, analyzing her current situation, considering all that she had come to know of life, Katharine wrote to Elsie: "I have concluded that justice seemed better served to those who took control of their own lives. One cannot depend on faith for sustenance." Katharine reasoned, "Sentiment must be met with intellect to survive."[6]

Four

To escape the sad memories and seek personal renewal, Josephine planned an extensive trip to Europe for herself and Katharine. Although Katharine had planned to begin work toward a science degree, she felt she had to be a companion for her bereaved mother. The trip would extend for almost eighteen months, until Josephine believed she was ready to resume a normal life in Boston. For Katharine, it would prove a frustrating postponement of her scientific career.

A unique friendship had developed among Elsie Crews, Josephine, and Katharine. While in Europe, both wrote to Elsie frequently, their letters filled with recitations of the days' events, places visited, and people seen. Katharine, particularly, enjoyed corresponding with Elsie, as it gave her an opportunity to share her experiences and feelings. She wrote of literature and riding; she recalled earlier, happier times. The letters between them displayed a mutual respect, and there was no question that Katharine embraced aspects of Elsie's life philosophy into her own.[1]

Josephine took it upon herself to be Elsie's surrogate mother, in an attempt to lift her spirits and, at the same time, share their mutual loss. While Josephine often reiterated her respect for Elsie's atypical goals in life, her recommendations about the proper role of women resembled the views that she urged upon Katharine.

The long European trip did offer numerous benefits for Katharine. She improved her fluency in French and German, and three months in Italy helped her learn Italian. Almost daily tours of museums and historical monuments broadened her knowledge of each country's culture. Besides swimming and riding, Katharine took up fencing, which also happened to be one of Elsie's favorite sports. Most evenings were spent at social events or the theater. It seemed to Katharine that Josephine would never tolerate a moment's pause, for fear of lapsing into melancholy.

Throughout the entire trip, a ritualized truce existed between Katharine and her mother. Josephine continually reminded Katharine of the necessity to marry. After all, she was the proper age—many of her friends in Boston were already wed—and, most important to Josephine, the Dexter family heritage now depended on Katharine's producing an heir.

Katharine, however, rejected her mother's advice. She was formulating her own plans; once back in Boston, she wanted to pursue a scientific education, with the same enthusiasm and commitment demonstrated by her friend, Elsie.

While mother and daughter were traveling through Switzerland, near the end of their tour, Josephine discovered the perfect home in which to reside during her frequent trips to the continent. In the small town of Nyons, just outside Geneva, stood the Château de Prangins, and, indeed, the estate embodied its impressive name. Not twenty years earlier, the château had been owned by Joseph Napoleon, who had used it as his summer residence.[2]

Standing on the front veranda of this imposing structure, Katharine had an unrestricted view across Lake Geneva, as far as the mountains on the French side of the border. Below the broad stone porch was a wide gravel roadway, running in a semicircle around the edge of the property toward large, ornate iron gates that opened onto the road to Geneva. Beyond this roadway stretched a wide expanse of manicured lawn, strategically shaded by trees and bushes, extending to the lake's edge. On one side of the château was a garden crisscrossed by walkways etched by low stone borders, each distinct plot replete with flowers, potted trees, and occasional benches. Above the flowers rose pedestals upon which perched stone-sculpted figures of nymphs. Viewing the garden for the first time, Katharine was enthralled by its beauty and serenity.

Inside the château, Katharine strolled through long, dark hallways with high, rounded ceilings and chandeliers comprising countless gas-filled lamps clustered in fleur-de-lis designs. Gilt-framed portraits of anonymous royalty hung from the walls. There were no rugs on the inlaid parquet floors, so Katharine's footsteps echoed loudly throughout the hall, lending human substance to the otherwise inanimate surroundings.

As she passed from room to room, Katharine encountered sculpted mantelpieces topped with candelabra, vases, and clocks mounted on miniature Ionic columns. Walls were covered with tapestries of pastoral scenes, gaslight fixtures, busts and cameos. Bookcases, filled with leather-bound multivolume sets, reached to the ceiling. The floors in these rooms were accented with small, fringed Oriental rugs, upon which stood voluptuously upholstered chairs, counterbalanced by severe, straight-backed armchairs of cloth and highly polished wood. On the small tables were fringed lamps, surrounded with miniature prints in gilt-edged frames.

With the château's heady mixture of art and kitsch, this first visit seemed fanciful to Katharine. It was the garden, however, that proved her greatest enjoyment, with its alluring atmosphere of sights, sounds, and fragrances.

To Josephine, the château seemed the perfect venue in which to spend a summer, hosting dinners and parties, inviting friends for vacations. Owning and running the château made her feel like a member of royalty.

In November 1895, Josephine and Katharine returned to Boston. Josephine's first effort was to find a permanent residence, in the proper neighborhood, of course. Katharine immediately entered a local college to begin her fervently desired education. Within a few weeks, however, she expressed frustration because the school's science curriculum was weak and the classes offered little challenge. She stopped attending classes but remained determined to find another school that would meet her requirements.

Josephine found a four-story stone and brick structure, already furnished, at 393 Commonwealth Avenue, and she purchased it from the last descendant of an old Boston family, who badly needed the money. This section of Boston, called Back Bay, was almost European in style. The majestic homes on this street were built so close to one another that they seemed to share common walls. They were solidly constructed of New England granite; it was as if the owners had intended these edifices to last forever. For Josephine, this part of Boston epitomized the city's steadfast and tasteful tradition.

An austere mix of Gothic and Yankee design, these buildings projected imposing facades. Number 393 was protected by large, ornate iron gates facing the tree-lined street. Tall, rectangular windows displayed elegantly tasseled flowered silk drapes. Rooms with magisterial ceilings exhibited various pieces of sumptuous Victorian furniture and wall tapestries. And no Boston manse was complete without a finely appointed, dark mahogany, thickly carpeted circular staircase. Josephine had the Prairie Avenue home sold with most of its furnishings. Only Wirt's desk, rocking chair, and library (absent legal tomes) were kept.

Katharine's room was tastefully decorated but simple in its furnishings—a bed, a dressing table, a lounge, and an armoire. The design of this furniture was unmistakable, and an astute observer could quickly notice the identity of the French manufacturer. The wainscoted, vertically striped wallpapered walls featured English and French prints. On the oval dressing table were simply framed photographs of her father and brother.

Katharine now began to explore other schools that she hoped would meet her requirements. She visited Harvard and talked to the director of

Radcliffe College, the new women's division. When Katharine expressed her desire to study biology and asked to see the school's chemistry laboratory, she was told, "We do our chemistry in the bathroom."

Katharine then decided to talk to administrators at the Massachusetts Institute of Technology. The Walker Building housed both the architecture and biology departments, though hardly with equal emphasis. A friend joked, "Architecture is at the top of the building and biology underneath, but you have to look for it."

Katharine sought out Charles-Edward Winslow, professor of biology, to discuss the courses she would need for a degree. As he guided her through the building, he pointed to a number of large, equipment-filled rooms. "You'd have an opportunity to use these laboratories," he assured her, "if you decided to study biology." Katharine looked around the rooms with anticipation; they convinced her that MIT was the school to meet her needs.

The Massachusetts Institute of Technology, at the time often referred to as "Boston Tech," had been founded in 1861. The campus was later moved to Cambridge and extended along the Charles River almost directly opposite the Dexter residence on Commonwealth Avenue. The school quickly established itself as one of the premier science-focused universities in the United States and became known for combining a rigorous undergraduate education with thorough scientific research in all of its programs.

It was also a school primarily for men, not only because few women at the time aspired to science degrees, but also because educational and social barriers had been established at the school to discourage women from attending. Only forty-four women were enrolled at MIT in 1896, and only one woman had ever graduated from the institute.

No matter the barriers, Katharine was convinced that MIT was the only school where she could pursue her interest in biology. In the fall of 1896, she applied for admission and was permitted to take the required entrance examinations. Although she passed the tests, examiners offered to admit her only as a special student. She was informed that a number of preparatory classes had to be taken before she could become a full-fledged degree student. "Music and French do not replace pre-science courses," the admissions director told her.

Katharine quickly discovered that the prerequisite work that had been outlined for her would take three years to complete. Besides these stringent curriculum demands, she was warned that the school would make it difficult for a woman to pursue a degree, particularly one in science, a male-dominated field. Nevertheless, Katharine was undeterred.

Upon beginning her preparatory classes, Katharine found that men and women seldom spoke to one another, even in classroom discussions. Nor were any extracurricular activities available for women. Her first confrontation occurred when she accidentally challenged MIT's strict dress code. "I was sharply commented upon, about the shorter length of my dress. 'Well,' I responded, 'I don't want it to touch the unclean floors.'"

For the next three years, Katharine's life was almost entirely filled with long hours of study, library research, reports, and exams. Often, she found herself the only woman in class. She was shunned by male classmates and, sometimes, by teachers.

The ever-insistent Josephine suggested that there must be opportunities to meet potential suitors at school social events, but Katharine treated these get-togethers with disdain. As she frequently stated to her mother, she did not want to compromise her goal of becoming an official degree student at MIT.

In September 1899, at age twenty-four, Katharine prepared to take the entrance exams that, if passed, would allow her to enroll as a degree student. Preparation was difficult, and Katharine knew that she would have to prove her abilities with a superior performance, because of the school's prejudicial attitudes toward women. Katharine passed the exams easily, and the MIT governing board granted her entrance, albeit reluctantly. Katharine, euphoric over her victory, was now ready to launch her studies toward a degree in biology. Her ultimate goal: to become a surgeon.

While Josephine was pleased by her daughter's academic accomplishments—she did not hesitate in telling people of her daughter's affiliation with MIT—she harbored strong doubts that Katharine would ever marry. She hoped and prayed, however, that her daughter might meet a prospective mate at school, even if he were not the prince of industry or law that she herself would have preferred.

In her first year at MIT, Katharine's coursework consisted of general subjects—English composition, algebra, American history, and world science. English composition, however, was the only course that gave her an opportunity for personal expression. For her first assignment, Katharine was asked to write about her preparations for MIT, the instructor seeking information from the students regarding their earlier training and scientific inclinations. Instead, Katharine chose to write, somewhat sarcastically, about the barriers she had had to overcome to enter MIT and the challenges that the school had presented.

The Massachusetts Institute of Technology! How much I have heard about it! How admirable it was said to be, and how thorough and practical the training it afforded. I heard how scientific it was in all ways, even to proclaiming the doctrine of Evolution by permitting the survival of only the fittest of students. Above all I had heard of its almost insurmountable difficulties. It was described to me how they confronted the pale student on entering and how they pursued him as he grew paler and yet more pale through the death march of four years. All of this I shuddered to hear. Why, I ask myself, does not some one enter this Institute of Technology so fully prepared that his work becomes a mere pastime to him, that he can enjoy to the full the social and athletic advantages; so that he issue from the ordeal stronger in body and more cheerful in mind than ever before? Why, I again ask myself, should I not be the one to accomplish this; to demonstrate how irresistible is the combination of health and an institute education? 'Ah,' I was answered sadly, 'that will make no difference; the difficulties will remain as great.' Still, I resolved to try.[3]

Her instructor commented positively on her correct form, careful punctuation, and good margins. However, he was displeased with her remarks about the school and its students; and he declared, "You quite misunderstood the subject." Still, Katharine received a C for her efforts.

Katharine's next essay assignment dealt with her personal impressions of fellow students. For the first time, her perceptions and opinions about men were revealed. No wonder she showed a lack of interest in her fellow students.

I saw a few men here, a few men there. Two or three girls in passing. And from these many instantaneous glimpses finally formed the 'moving picture' of my impression. This, I find, I can separate into two classes of impressions which I might call the physical and the physiognomical. As to the former, I was forcibly impressed by the lack of physical development. The men were undersized; there was a head forward-flat chest look about them. Very few stood or walked well. They gave one the idea that throughout their life they had ignored their physical condition. They did not appear firm (solid?) or fit muscularly. They lacked that vigor of health so necessary to the appearance of every one, and which particularly belongs to the young man, who, however, can acquire it only by the correct use and training of his body.[4]

While the instructor indicated he did not agree with Katharine's assessment of male students, he acknowledged that her observations were "mature in thought" and "full of careful observation." Having met the requirements of the assignment, Katharine received an A.

Successive themes revealed her improved command of subject matter and style of expression; by the end of the year, Katharine was consistently getting As, although her instructor continued to disagree with her perceptions of men and their apparent state of health. In another essay, Katharine took issue with what she perceived to be an overemphasis on academics, to the detriment of personal health at MIT, a topic that seemed to be of increasing importance to her. Even scientists should have "all round physical development," she believed.[5]

Yet Katharine also expressed occasional uncertainties about her direction and abilities, not surprising in such a pervasively antifemale environment. In her last class essay, a creative writing assignment open to any subject, these self-doubts were exposed. Katharine imagined herself blind and questioned her ability to deal with the consequences. Nevertheless, after personal introspection, she went on to challenge the imagined obstacles.

It occurred to me to call someone, and then I reflected how painful the first interview would be with all its pity and sympathy, and I felt I could not bear it until I had recovered myself. There was so much to do. My life must be reorganized and rearranged. I tried to think if I could ever walk in the country. I knew I could never ride or drive myself again. I was puzzled to think how it would be with my friends. Should I be the same with them? The thought was full of pain. How could I be the same when I could share in so few of the pleasures that bring friends together. Would my life shrink and shrink into itself?

Slowly I seemed to think out my way. I would not lead an invalid life of stagnation; I would try to learn and grow. I could still work and study; I could take physical exercise; I could have music. I did not want to be found hopelessly staring upwards. I preferred to have them know that I did not fear the dark. Look! I am going to act the part of one who is blind. It is said to be difficult; watch and see if I can do it well![6]

This essay disclosed significant features of Katharine's emerging philosophy. It suggested an ability to deal rationally with emotionally charged issues and to carefully think out alternative options to resolve them. It indicated a refusal to engage in self-pity or to depend on others for assistance. Most importantly, Katharine demonstrated a resoluteness to overcome any barriers that she perceived to stand in her way.

During the next few years, Katharine worked with the same zeal. By the end of each term, she demonstrated a strong command for the material. Her note taking and research were systematic, detailed, and comprehensive. Excellent exam results showed diligent preparation and clear understanding of the information. By her third year, Katharine was recognized, although hesitantly, as an excellent science student. Her self-assurance in academic matters also influenced her social interests, and these now spread beyond the boundaries of MIT.

Down the road from Katharine's campus, another young woman was speaking out on behalf of women's rights. While a senior at Radcliffe College, Maud Wood Park had voiced her support for Susan B. Anthony and expressed the belief that women should be given the opportunity to govern themselves. In addition, she appealed to other women to become more actively involved in the growing suffrage movement.[7]

After graduation, Park contacted recent college graduates in the Boston area for the purpose of forming a suffrage group. In March 1900, a meeting of college women was to take place before the National Suffrage Convention, in Washington, D.C. The college women in Boston agreed it would be beneficial to organize and send a delegate to the national meeting; Maud Wood Park was appointed to represent them.

Upon Park's return, the group prepared a charter, elected officers, and named themselves the College Equal Suffrage League. The organization's twenty-five charter members came from Radcliffe, Wellesley, and Boston University. CESL's objective was to promote suffrage sentiment among college women, both before and after graduation, and to stimulate an interest in the movement for equal rights. They became the first organization to promote the suffrage movement at the college level.

To attract new members, the group sponsored "dramatic entertainments" at Association Hall in Boston. Skits were presented to the assembled.[8] For example, one skit told the story of an Irish girl who became a suffragist in defiance of the Church. Another skit, entitled "The Judgement of Minerva," presented two opposing groups—one prosuffrage, the other antisuffrage—which came before the Greek goddess to plead their cases about women's rights. To no one's surprise, Minerva gave her blessing to the prosuffragists. These performances were reported in the women's column of the *Boston Globe* because the participants, as well as the audience, represented many socially elite families in the city. Katharine was invited to one of these presentations, which she attended.

Because the group seemed to synthesize her feelings about women's status in college, Katharine was immediately attracted to the CESL. She joined at once and became the first member to represent women at MIT. Joining the League was also the beginning of a long working friendship with Maud Wood Park, who became a colleague in the National American Woman Suffrage Alliance (NAWSA) and was later elected the first president of the League of Women Voters. When MIT authorities refused Katharine's request for the organization to meet on campus, 393 Commonwealth became the CESL's assembly place.

Two other almost simultaneous events very likely influenced Katharine's involvement in the league. Emma Goldman, a young anarchist and gifted orator, had recently been released from a New York City prison, to which she had been sentenced for inciting a riot at a hunger demonstration. Nelly Bly, a journalist for the *New York World*, featured Goldman in her articles and quickly turned Goldman into a celebrity. Within a short time, Goldman was touring the country on the lecture circuit, preaching the tenets of the suffrage movement. While in Boston, Goldman spoke before the CESL and met with its members, including Katharine. Goldman's thesis was very attractive to these young, upper-class women, in large part because she strongly advocated the use of birth control and freedom of sexual expression.

Prior to Katharine's joining the league, a book by Kate Chopin, *The Awakening,* had been published. Chopin's themes dealt with personal autonomy and sexual freedom and were considered a major breakthrough for women's freedom of expression at the time. Although the book was vilified and condemned by the Church and press, it was read by many "enlightened" women, among whom were members of the CESL. In a number of her letters, Katharine referred to these episodes as influential in her decision to join the CESL.

Katharine began her own lobbying campaign in chemistry class. School policy dictated that women who attended classes must always wear hats. At the turn of the century, fashionable women's hats were rather large, with wide brims and feathers. Katharine believed that they not only interfered with chemistry experiments but were potentially dangerous as well.

She discussed the situation with her professor and, when nothing was done, went to the school administration with her recommendation, namely, that women in laboratory classes need not wear hats. When they disregarded her request, Katharine ostentatiously refused to wear her hat in class. This breach of classroom etiquette and school rules immediately gained her the attention of the department. At first, her professors appealed to her to follow school rules. She refused and countered by suggesting that all women at MIT need not wear hats to any class. Shortly after, the chemistry department announced that, for reasons of safety, women would no longer have to wear hats in their lab classes.

Katharine had now completed three years of study, passing all of her courses with excellent grades and the respectful, if grudging, approval of her professors. Biology remained her declared major, and her expressed desire was to study medicine after graduation. For her last year at MIT, along with doing advanced work in biology, she was required to write an honors thesis, which had to be an original experiment in her major area. There was no question that her last year at MIT would be the hardest and most demanding yet. Before the beginning of her senior year, Katharine and Josephine decided to take a brief vacation at Beverly Farms, an exclusive resort near Boston.

On the afternoon of September 1, 1903, thirty-year-old bachelor Stanley McCormick was racing his automobile through the Massachusetts countryside on his way to Boston. As it was late in the day, Stanley decided to stop at Beverly Farms to spend the night. At dinner, elegantly served in the plush Art Nouveau–style restaurant, Stanley recognized Katharine seated at a nearby table. It had been sixteen years since they last met, at a Prairie Avenue dancing class, but he had not forgotten the positive impression she had made, or the frustration of not being allowed by his mother to see her again. When he introduced himself, Katharine, likewise, was newly impressed by this tall, lean, and handsome man.

Katharine agreed to a walk with Stanley in the garden after dinner, anticipating the usual, time-honored ritual of light social discourse. Instead, an animated Stanley talked intensely about his views of life and launched into a lively monologue on the benefits of socialism. Surprised, and somewhat put off, Katharine suggested that they discuss a "happier" topic, as the subject matter distressed her.

In lieu of a lighter topic, however, Stanley began to relate the story of his personal life.[9] He revealed himself to be artistic in ability and taste, but admitted that his mother was placing pressure on him to enter the family business.

"What do you think I should do?" he asked Katharine. "Please help me decide."

Katharine was quite taken aback by Stanley's behavior. They had just become reacquainted after many years, and she was not about to offer him advice. Still, there was no denying his sincerity and passion. He was educated, athletic, and good-looking; and Josephine would be pleased to know he was the youngest son of the celebrated Cyrus McCormick. Certainly Katharine knew that being raised in a family with a formidable legacy and considerable wealth often generated extraordinary pressure. Stanley's behavior, perhaps somewhat eccentric and impassioned, could therefore be viewed as understandable. It would be pleasant to see him again.

Marriage and Madness

Five

Cyrus McCormick was a tyrannical father whose vindictive, petty feuds with power barons and Pullman baggage handlers alike bordered on monomania. His wife, Nettie, treated his frequent rages with saccharine bromides. In turn, she harassed her children with religious zealotry and obsessions, from every detail of their dress to bizarre health fads and remedies. Two of the couple's children died shortly after birth. Three were closet sociopaths. The remaining two proved to be psychotic and required long-term hospitalization.[1]

Cyrus McCormick was born in 1809 on a farm in Walnut Grove, Virginia. His father was a hardworking farmer but a failure in his attempts to invent various kinds of farm machinery, one of which was a primitive reaping device. Raised as an old-fashioned "bluestocking" Presbyterian, McCormick acquired from his father the belief that life was a constant battle. In consequence, Cyrus developed into a young man with a rugged disposition, accompanied by a forceful, persevering assault against all perceived obstacles. Cyrus refused to be beaten, although he had difficulty discriminating between small and large issues, confronting both with the same amount of relentless energy.

What the father had envisioned, the son delivered. The rich prairie wheat lands were available, if a practical method could be found to harvest bountiful crops. There was a lack of sufficient farm labor to do the harvesting, and the flat farmlands made a mechanical reaper a product with spectacular potential.

At twenty-two, Cyrus demonstrated a prototype; three years later, he patented an improved model. With sixty dollars in his pocket, the model in his wagon, Cyrus rode to Chicago to set up a factory. Within a few years, the McCormick reaper was being used throughout the country. The reaper had transformed Chicago into America's grain capital and McCormick into one of its youngest millionaires.

Cyrus committed his entire life to business. He was serious to the point of absolute humorlessness, resisted anything resembling a social life, and had no time for either family or friends. Whether they were employees, customers, or the increasing phalanx of outsiders seeking financial assistance or political favors, his interaction with others was strictly business.

Ironically, this myopic focus on business made Cyrus a tempting target for promoters and charlatans. Easily flattered and gullible, he believed everyone to be honest, particularly if they carried credentials to prove their merit. Not surprisingly, he was tricked many times. If, however, he discovered the fraud, regardless of its extent, he became implacably vindictive and never failed to "get even" with any "enemy."

Cyrus demonstrated his extraordinary will when the Great Fire of 1871 totally destroyed his factory. With a lifetime of accomplishment in smoking ruin, Cyrus planned to rebuild elsewhere, having taken this setback as a personal affront. As the rehabilitation of Chicago began, the Relief and Aid Society, headed by Wirt Dexter, persuaded Cyrus to remain in the city. In a typical example of his ability to attack adversity, he rebuilt his factory into a state-of-the-art manufacturing facility, incorporating the most advanced technology of the day. This further increased his fortune, so that he became one of America's richest men.

Cyrus was fifty years old when he decided to marry. He needed an equally obsessive mate, and finding a woman to meet his requirements would be difficult. She arrived in the person of twenty-three-year-old Nettie Fowler.

Nettie Fowler was Cyrus's spiritual soul mate. Born in 1835, she spent her girlhood near Clayton, New York, on the St. Lawrence River, where she learned the hard life of commercial river entrepreneurs. In 1857, Nettie came to Chicago to visit friends and was introduced to Cyrus McCormick. That he professed love for her almost immediately suggests a remarkable union. This was, after all, a man who had never developed an emotional attachment to anyone. In 1858, they were married in a quiet ceremony; and Nettie became her husband's partner in all aspects of his life.

Along with ruling the household and raising the children, Nettie involved herself in the administration of her husband's business. She became co-operator of the company and, when Cyrus's health began to fail, took over supervision of the entire enterprise.

Nettie brought several talents to this unique collaboration. She possessed an accurate memory for details. The energy she devoted to organization and planning often drove business associates to distraction. Intractable once a decision was made, she remained unswervingly committed to her own perception of duty. Whatever the goal, nothing could sidetrack her in the drive toward her desired ends. Moreover, like her husband, she too had difficulty discriminating between the essential and the irrelevant.

Her personal life was no less a challenge. Nettie was obsessed with the latest medical literature and health crazes. Often, she would "catch" ailments to inspire sympathy or distract an antagonist. She became a master of the indirect maneuver, although there is little evidence that she was consciously aware of her behavior. She was committed to personal health and hygiene for her children. When they went out to play, she layered them with shirts, sweaters, overcoats, and hats, regardless of the weather or season. If Nettie "sensed" a child catching cold, the child went to bed and stayed there for days. Her letters were full of advice: avoid drafts, eat properly, wear boots; "always full of health and business," a daughter complained. Ever on the alert for incipient illness, Nettie had a sizable stock of remedies and prescriptions ready to be instantly administered— flannel around the throat, bran for stomach pain, camphorated oil for a cold.

Nettie was equally obsessed about God's evaluation of her. She remained convinced throughout her life that all misfortune was a direct punishment from God for her lack of physical vigor or religious discipline. When two infant children died of illness, Nettie believed she had been solely responsible. "God is punishing me for my sins, my procrastination, my slothfulness," she repeated for months after the infants died.

Nettie practiced daily prayer. She offered Thanksgiving every morning in the library, and Sundays were devoted entirely to the Lord, starting in the morning with church and Sunday school, Bible readings in the afternoon, and a return to church in the evening. Nettie turned the McCormick home into a sanctuary for traveling seminarians, gospel ministers, and evangelical missionaries.

During the sum total of their waking moments, the children remained under Nettie's imperious eyes. She believed it was her duty to inquire into the smallest detail of each child's life. When they were especially good, she rewarded them with sweets; when they misbehaved, she shut them in a dark closet.

The older children pictured Nettie as someone "carrying heavy weights" who "embraced her burdens as an aspirant to sainthood." As her daughter Anita once wrote: "Laughter embarrassed her, irony escaped her, and time-wasting angered her."

Nettie made sure that sex in any form was repressed. The carnal was profane and unmentionable. Nettie preached the goodness of "virginal innocence" and the challenge to "keep the pure pages of youth unsullied." She taught the children to avoid sexual thoughts and to conceal their naked bodies, even from siblings or playmates of the same sex.

In contrast, Cyrus's interactions with his children were rare encounters, and those were mostly unsatisfactory. He raged indiscriminately and disproportionately against them, prompting Nettie to intercede and soothe him with encouragement: "It will be all right, father." Cyrus wielded parental authority from a distance yet demanded an unyielding level of perfection, in speech and in manner. If one of the children mispronounced a word when they were reading the Bible, he would cuff and rebuke them. Harold and Stanley, the two youngest, regarded this chastising old man with fear.

The oldest child, Cyrus Jr., had the dubious advantage of having known his father when the man was still in his prime. He was considered the most stable of the children, having developed a defense of "Yes, father (mother), you are right. What can I do to please you?" His younger brothers and sisters were never this passive and, consequently, suffered greater anxiety and distress.

Several of the children, notably Mary Virginia and Stanley, showed artistic talent. Mary Virginia, the older, was affectionate and sweet. In her early teens, she became an accomplished pianist, but she soon developed bouts of weeping, shortness of breath, insomnia, neurasthenia, and frequent episodes of frenzied prayer. Nettie's typical response was a combination of recrimination and medicinal remedies. Shortly after Cyrus died, Mary Virginia broke down. She was diagnosed as suffering from dementia praecox and was placed in a sanitarium. She remained under nursing care, a scattered, impulsive, and bizarre patient until her death.

The next in line, Anita, was highly intelligent and displayed an uncanny knack for thinking out and solving complex problems. However, she suffered from an inability to make decisions. In reaction to her parents, Anita agonized over every situation, delaying the moment for decision or, in many situations, making no decision at all. She was the only child to declare her independence from Nettie, but even this hard-won freedom was nominal until Nettie died.

If Nettie spoiled anyone, it was Harold. He was two years older than Stanley but was treated as equal to his younger brother. Described as bighearted, lively, and easygoing, he revealed the least visible effects of his mother's attentions, although he showed little individuality or motivation. He did not care to have his mother delving into every detail of his life, yet he appeared to accept it in a relaxed manner.

Stanley McCormick was born in Chicago, November 2, 1874.[2] The construction of the fabled McCormick mansion was begun at his birth. It took five years to complete, but once built, it ushered in an era of opulence on North Rush Street. Three stories tall, designed in the French Empire style, it defined Victorian taste and aristocratic bravura. No home in Chicago was its rival. The mansion was filled with imported tapestries, hand-carved mahogany paneling, parquet floors, giant chandeliers of bronze

and glass, doors and windows framed with ebony wood inlaid with ornamental tin. The dining room ceiling incorporated the embossed names
of the McCormick children, surrounded by sheaves of flowing grain. Stanley, however, was the only child to be raised in this mansion. Watching
over him were his mother and thirteen servants.

As a young child, Stanley was fair, gentle, bright, dutiful, and unusually
shy. In every aspect of his life, Nettie had a profound influence; and, not
surprisingly, he sought his mother's constant approval. She selected his
playmates, often telling him, "Now that boy I think (or I don't think) you
should get acquainted with." When he misbehaved, he was forced to con-
fess under sharp questioning and was then taken upstairs for a spanking
or shut away in a closet. When, as a teenager, he began to go out, she
demanded that he get to bed early and directed a maid to telephone him
to come home at the appointed time.

Nettie was dissatisfied with the quality of Stanley's education, which
necessitated a nomadic journey through different schools and tutors. Stanley attended five schools and had three tutors before entering Princeton.
In spite of the discontinuity, Stanley approached his studies with intelligence and sensitivity. He was anxious to do well and maintained a high
standing in his classes.

Since he and Harold were raised as virtual twins, both of them were in
the same freshman class at Princeton. By virtue of his intellect, Stanley
became a leader in class; Harold, on the other hand, just managed to
scrape through. According to family letters, Stanley graduated in 1895,
cum laude, "carrying Harold through on his hip."

Harold did not care for the comparisons with his brother. Relations
between them were strained. Harold represented the college rascal—social, popular, studiously frivolous, and frequently in the company of beautiful women. Stanley was the assiduous student and worked hard to
develop his athletic abilities, gaining some recognition by playing on the
Princeton varsity tennis team. But where Harold embodied the college
bon vivant, Stanley retreated, hesitant and slow to make friends. He was
quiet and introspective, his approach to others painfully tentative. Stanley
was always on the alert to avoid hurting anyone, and he was apprehensive
about sharing his personal burdens.

In their last year at Princeton, the brothers became estranged when
Harold became interested in a particular woman. He lost whatever interest he had in school, preferring to court his girlfriend, Edith Rockefeller
(daughter of John D. Rockefeller).[3] Stanley had never before contended
with a permanent rival, one who would replace him as Harold's helper.
When Harold married Edith in 1895, a hurt and angry Stanley stayed on
campus rather than attend the wedding.

During his first year at Princeton, Stanley discovered art. He enjoyed
its freedom and found he could create with less effort than was necessary

for his regular studies. During the summer, against Nettie's wishes, he attended the Art Students' League in New York, where teachers praised his aptitude and strong line. Stanley seriously considered becoming an artist, but Nettie reminded him of his responsibility toward the family business. In Nettie's opinion, art's association with the disreputable world of Bohemia made it an unacceptable career choice. She thought Stanley would be safe in business, but art, "goodness knows what might happen to him."

Immediately after his graduation from Princeton, as a reward for his fine school record, Nettie took Stanley on an extended trip to Europe, Africa, and the Middle East.[4] Their journey continued for more than a year. The tour ended in Paris, where they planned to stay for several months. While in Paris, Stanley persuaded Nettie to allow him to take art lessons. Again, his teachers believed he had talent and encouraged him to continue his fine work. Faced with a choice between his own inclinations and his mother's preferences, Stanley coincidentally had his first sexual experience with a woman he met at art school. The liaison left him distraught, suffering from the belief that he had committed a sin. People could tell what he had done just by looking at him, he suspected. He became so ashamed that he avoided classes that the woman attended.[5]

Nettie was not about to forfeit her child to the frivolous world of art. She used an acquired nervous condition to force their return to Chicago. At the same time, Stanley developed a torpor, with vague symptoms that suggested ill health. In London, he was taken to a doctor who diagnosed his "illness" as possibly the early signs of tuberculosis. He had no choice but to return to Chicago to recuperate.

Now back in Chicago, Stanley reluctantly entered the family business. While his brothers treated him as an equal, the processes and vocabulary of commerce confused him, and he lacked the knowledge to make any kind of particular contribution to the business.[6] To make up for these deficiencies, Cyrus Jr., suggested that Stanley study law, subject matter that might appeal to his analytical mind.

Thus, Stanley spent a year at Northwestern University Law School studying finance, patents, and policy, earning high grades and commendations from his professors. In 1897, Cyrus Jr. gave Stanley responsibility to handle certain aspects of company finances. Since the family was not yet sure what role he should play in the business, Stanley was identified as a consultant rather than an employee. Uneasy about the job demands, he could, at least, decide his own hours. At the same time, however, he continued to suffer undiagnosed health problems that periodically kept him away from the business.

In 1898, with the intention of buying them out, the McCormick Harvesting Machine Company entered into negotiations with a manufacturing rival, the Deering Company. Stanley was assigned the position of financial expert in the negotiations, providing the diligence necessary for such arcane matters. The deal hinged on McCormick's ability to raise enough capital to finalize a purchase. Harold was given the job of persuading his father-in-law, John D. Rockefeller, to loan the necessary money. Rockefeller, however, refused, which caused a bitter breakdown between the potential partners. Instead, a competitive battle ensued.

Deeply disappointed by the breakdown in negotiations, Stanley exhibited signs of physical frailty and withdrew from the company. The McCormick family doctor said that he "appeared to be a little weak in the chest" and recommended that Stanley go to Arizona to recuperate. With a Princeton friend, John Garrett, Stanley purchased a 45,000-acre cattle ranch. For the next two years, Stanley remained aloof from the family business.

In 1900, the family persuaded Stanley to represent the company at the International Exposition in Paris, a suggestion he willingly embraced. He took complete charge of company exhibits and managed all of the company's business affairs there. Thanks to Stanley, the company gained considerable international exposure and won two gold medals for innovative technology. After six months of frenetic activity, however, Stanley's health again declined, and he returned to the Arizona ranch.

When Deering and McCormick finally agreed to a merger—the new company would be named International Harvester—Cyrus Jr. appointed Stanley comptroller, over Nettie's objections. Unfortunately, overwork and nervousness in his new job forced Stanley again to go back to the ranch. Recovery took longer this time. He wrote Cyrus Jr. that "the condition of last fall and this winter has been the consequence of an accumulated taxation on my nervous energy, and recuperation has been slower than I hoped."

The following year, when Stanley returned to Chicago, the family noticed his increasingly nervous self-consciousness and indecision. He had considerable trouble completing daily tasks. The situation became so critical that Cyrus Jr. called a family meeting to decide what to do about Stanley. After hours of debate and argument, Nettie's suggestion that Stanley be made superintendent of factories prevailed. It was a position designed to remove him from the family's daily business deliberations. Yet the new assignment actually worsened his nervous condition. In one reported episode, during a routine business meeting, an agitated Stanley argued with the plant manager about a number of procedures. Stanley suddenly went pale, threw his papers aside, stood up, and walked out of the room, to the shock of the group. This outburst necessitated another trip to the ranch.

To the family, there was no doubt that Stanley was ill, and his affliction appeared to be more mental than physical. There certainly existed several obvious irritants: work-related stress; family relationships; and Stanley's own personal insecurities. In addition, Stanley had recently consulted a doctor about his sexual adequacy.

He reported a number of reasons to the doctor for the consultation. Nettie's prohibitions on anything sexual had apparently affected him. In college, when he started to masturbate, he believed it would make him unfit for marriage. To guard against these urges, he built himself a harness to wear at night. The brief relationship with the art student in Paris made him believe he had sinned and caused self-doubt about his potency. After examining Stanley, the doctor found him physically fit and healthy, yet Stanley remained unconvinced. Now, any kind of emotional interchange, even with family members, made him nervous and withdrawn.

Of course, the family grew concerned about Stanley's emotional behavior. Mary Virginia had been hospitalized for years. They hardly needed new troubles or additional public whispers. When Stanley suggested that he would like to do some traveling, family members were relieved. Stanley enjoyed the privacy of the road, away from family and business pressures. In turn, the family felt relieved of the burden for any emotional complications that might occur. Even Nettie, attached as she was to her youngest, permitted his "vacations" as a necessary diversion.

Stanley's doctor recommended a change of scenery as therapeutic, and he liked to journey to different locales. In September 1903, thirty-year-old Stanley McCormick chose an automobile tour of New England.

The autumn countryside soothed him. Its craggy, rolling hills, replete with forests of changing colors, was a visual delight. He enjoyed the dirt roads of Massachusetts, exhilarated by the wind in his face and the long, brown cloud of dust trailing behind his open automobile. He motored without regard to speed, delighted simply in driving without supervision, without rules, and without familial judgment.

Stanley was familiar with this part of the state, remembering there was a restaurant nearby. Unfettered by schedule, he decided to stop, clean up, and have a leisurely meal. Parking his roadster, he discarded driving coat, gloves, and goggles and entered the restaurant.

In the restroom, Stanley approached the mirror and gazed into the glass. He lurched back in surprise. For some reason, he was unable to see his image in the mirror. Taken aback, suddenly frightened, he stared again, searching for his reflection. Still nothing. This was not possible, he said to himself. Incredulous, he grabbed the sides of the porcelain sink tightly. Sweating profusely, he felt his arms and legs quaking as he willed himself to become visible. Despite his most vigorous efforts, nothing materialized.

In panic now, he fled the restaurant, screaming uncontrollably, "My God, I'm blind to my own face!" His body shaking in grief, Stanley buried his head in his arms against the steering wheel and sobbed.

The next day, ostensibly recovered as he always seemed to be after an emotional episode, Stanley stopped at Beverly Farms to spend the night.

At dinner, Stanley recognized Katharine Dexter seated at a nearby table with an older woman. Sixteen years had elapsed since they had practiced waltzing at the dancing school on Prairie Avenue. And now, there she sat, wearing a soft white linen suit and a beautiful feathered hat. Her classically beautiful features were framed by long, flowing dark hair. Yet, he remembered, she still had the same serious eyes. To Stanley, Katharine had become a very attractive young woman.

Six

Stanley approached the Dexter table to introduce himself. Recognizing him as the son of Cyrus McCormick, Josephine was delighted. Katharine observed Stanley's friendly expression and saw features that appealed to her, perhaps his strong, lean face or the affable curve of his lips as he smiled.[1]

"Would you care to take a walk after dinner?" he inquired.

Pleased by his offer, Katharine readily agreed. She anticipated a pleasant stroll through the Beverly Farms garden, still filled with late-summer blooms.

As they made their way around the extensive garden, Stanley began talking ardently about his views of life. Then he launched into an animated monologue on socialism. This was not the kind of after-dinner conversation Katharine had anticipated. She considered herself well informed about the various social and political systems of the time, and she was already an avowed suffragist. Stanley's grasp of the subject matter seemed to her insightful, but she thought his timing was clumsy. Katharine requested they discuss a "happier" subject.

Stanley flushed; perhaps he had been too aggressive. Taking a calming breath, he lowered his voice and, more slowly, began to talk about his life again. He confided to Katharine that he was at a "monumental juncture," a possible turning point "of great import" in his life. He believed himself to be an artist. But, he explained, his outlook and emotional makeup were in direct conflict with his family's views. "They want me to enter the business. What do you think I should do?" In an almost pleading voice, he entreated, "Please help me decide."

Quite taken aback, Katharine was not sure how to answer. What an odd conversation this was, she thought. We've just become reacquainted after sixteen years, and Stanley is talking to me as if we were old friends. Yet there was no denying his sincerity and passion. Indeed, the genuine concern expressed in his eyes touched her.

Still, Stanley's demeanor perplexed her. As they circled back toward the resort's main sitting room, he took her hand in his and held it tightly. "Tell me your honest opinion," he begged her. "Please."

Gently but firmly, Katharine pulled her hand from his grasp and replied, "I don't know what might be right for you, Mr. McCormick. But I believe in being unerringly true to one's own nature." With a subtle gesture of good night, Katharine left Stanley to his indecision.

The next day, so she could begin preparations for her final year at MIT, Katharine and her mother returned to Boston. Stanley refused to accept her departure. He followed her back home to "continue our conversations," he explained apologetically. Katharine admittedly felt flattered by his attention.

For the next two weeks, Stanley courted Katharine with flowers and dinners. His enthusiastic attention and romantic qualities were disarming, she thought. Yet he remained preoccupied with morose topics of conversation. From day to day, his behavior was unpredictable, a mixture of self-deprecation and ardent wooing. Surely, Stanley was better than the picture he painted of himself, Katharine assumed. How could a person with his obvious intelligence and sensitivity condemn himself so thoroughly? The conundrum both troubled and intrigued her.

At the end of the month, Stanley proposed marriage. Instead of asking her directly, however, he posed a hypothetical question, presenting the hypothetical mate as a man with many shortcomings. Katharine refused the proposal outright.

"You talk about all the world's problems as if they affect you personally," she replied. "You talk about yourself in a negative manner. Why? And why are you so anxious about getting my point of view? People of character do not indulge themselves with such melancholy attitudes."

Absorbing her every word, Stanley remained silent.

"I cannot have these problems intrude into my life," Katharine continued, "or interfere with my last year of school. Life, Stanley, should be lived in harmony with one's honest self. Strength of purpose gives you meaning."

"That's how I would like it to be," he answered.

"But you make it difficult for yourself," she pointed out.

"Will it ever be possible?" he asked.

Katharine admired his tenacity. She had to admit she was moved by his expressions of affection, even if they were often interspersed with recurrent personal distress.

"Stanley, please," she entreated. "I need to devote all my attention to school. This is just not the time."

"Will the time ever come?"

Katharine was unable to give Stanley an answer since she was not sure herself what demands would have to be faced in the coming year. His time in Boston coming to an end, Stanley had to meet his mother, vacationing at an Adirondacks resort. He was disappointed about being separated from Katharine but promised to write her often. While she was glad to have time to devote to school, the turbulent emotional currents between them did unsettle her.

Stanley wrote letters to Katharine every day. They were so gloomy and self-questioning, however, that she left them unread for a week, then read them all together to minimize their depressive content. In contrast, Katharine attempted to keep her letters to him light, describing classroom activities and CESL meetings. As soon as the holiday with his mother could be concluded, Stanley returned to Boston in November to continue courting Katharine.

Upon his return, Stanley relished the little time she had for him because of her studies, but he mentioned nothing about his original proposal to her. Besides the normal coursework, Katharine began research on her senior honors thesis, required of all science majors. It necessitated a good deal of time in the laboratory.

Still, he courted her. His professions of love, with flowers and gifts, excited her. Stanley seemed willing to give her freedom to pursue a scientific career, to many people neither a feminine nor a socially appropriate occupation for an upper-class woman. Moreover, Katharine was aware of her own limitations. She was an educated twenty-nine-year-old who had definite beliefs and goals, and whose relationships with people were perceived to be distant. Nonetheless, here was a man who claimed he adored her and desired marriage. Some kind of emotional chemistry had to be responsible for this attraction, she believed.

At Stanley's invitation, Katharine agreed to visit Chicago during the Christmas holidays. She had not returned since her brother's funeral and would be able to visit old family friends. It would also give her an opportunity to meet the McCormick family. While Stanley mentioned his discomfort at the prospect, it represented the natural next step in any courtship. He arranged a dinner in her honor, to be given at Harold's home, with Stanley; Harold; his wife, Edith; Anita; and Nettie acting as hosts. Stanley had asked Harold for support in his pursuit of Katharine, and his brother was delighted to oblige.

Katharine, accustomed to the protocol for such family gatherings, was lovely and self-possessed. Harold and Edith charmed her and were themselves charmed, quite taken with Katharine's intelligence and impressed with her upcoming graduation from MIT. Anita and Nettie felt otherwise.

Anita doubted Katharine's sincerity about Stanley and felt her brother's affection to be far too one-way. Katharine perceived Anita's coolness toward her as snobbery, thinking Anita was more preoccupied with social status than personal feelings. For Nettie, Katharine simply did not meet her stringent standards for Stanley. Nettie ignored Katharine throughout the entire evening, pretending that Stanley was alone.

Nettie's behavior put Stanley in a state of tension. He had predicted his mother's reaction but hoped everyone else would be friendly and accepting. Through it all, Katharine appeared to take Nettie's coolness lightly, with almost clinical detachment, sensing that "his mother might be defensive about the possibility of losing her youngest son."

Seeking to keep his beloved protected, Stanley became more agitated with each passing moment. For her part, Katharine actually enjoyed the contest. She might appear serious and reserved, but she loved a challenge. She would not be intimidated by Nettie's disdain.

On the way back from Harold and Edith's dinner, Nettie asked to be dropped off first, before Stanley accompanied Katharine to her hotel. When they stopped at the gate of the Rush Street mansion, Stanley escorted his mother to the door. As she embraced him good night, Nettie attempted to restrain him from returning to the carriage.

"It's late, and you should go to bed," she insisted, while holding tight to Stanley.

Embarrassed, he did not want to appear to be struggling with his mother; so he tried to appease her with a promise to return home as soon as he could. Still, she would not release him. Shaken, Stanley finally managed to extricate himself. Katharine observed this interaction with some concern and discomfort. In light of his obvious agitation about the episode, as they continued to the hotel, she said nothing to him, depending on the silence of the ride to give him time to relax.

During the two weeks they spent together, Stanley confided to Katharine his difficulties with Nettie. His words seemed to carry the weight of confession, and his discomfiture was obvious. He revealed that his mother did not care for Katharine, which was no surprise to her. Even his sister, Anita, suggested that his interest in Katharine was not "the big love" he would have someday "with the right girl." Stanley concluded by conceding that any person who needed this sort of management must be someone "who had never done anything worthwhile." Responding to Stanley's remarks, Katharine admonished him for saying such things about himself. She believed his self-assessment unjust, and she suggested that he consult a doctor to discuss these issues.

The next day, Stanley went to see the family physician, Dr. Favill. In a moment of self-revelation, Stanley shared his fears that perhaps he suffered from the same illness that had affected Mary Virginia. "Nonsense," Favill assured him. "You have only a light nervous prostration," he declared. Certainly there was nothing in his condition to prohibit a marriage. Dr. Favill further prescribed that Stanley take a vacation. "Go abroad and take a walking trip," he advised.

Her relationship with Stanley continued to trouble Katharine. She admired his intelligence, sensitivity, and artistic inclinations; but she was exasperated with his frequent retreats into self-denigration. Having met Nettie and observed her behavior toward Stanley, Katharine believed that Stanley's only salvation lay in a permanent separation from his mother. Moreover, Katharine now came to believe she could stabilize his sometimes idiosyncratic behavior through loving attention and sensible care.

At the same time, Katharine was evaluating her own needs with respect to the relationship. Stanley came from a respected family and was physically fit. He was the type of person of whom her father might well have been proud. Such a union could produce an heir to perpetuate the Dexter family legacy, an event that would undoubtedly please her mother. Perhaps she was not consumed with the same passion toward him as he felt toward her, but then, she had never felt an intense connection to any man, except her father and brother. Katharine could easily see herself as Stanley's "guide," assisting him in finding life more enjoyable and giving him the support he sought. The prospect of their marriage offered a fascinating challenge for her.

In February 1904, Stanley sent a telegram to Harold, announcing his engagement to Katharine. That day, in his diary, Harold wrote: "Stanley told me today the secret of his heart. We hope and pray his hopes may be fulfilled."[2]

Hearing the news, Nettie flew into a rage, declaring that she strongly opposed the engagement and questioning Stanley's fitness to marry. In contrast, Josephine could not have been more delighted with the announcement. Finally, her daughter was to be married; and to a handsome son of the illustrious McCormick family.

The engagement commitment, however, did not improve Stanley's feelings about himself. Thanks to Nettie, his nervous reactions and self-diagnosed health problems monopolized letters to Katharine. If anything, it seemed that the engagement had actually heightened Stanley's symptoms. Not surprisingly, Katharine expressed displeasure with this behavior and told Stanley the distractions were having a detrimental effect on her studies. After another month of Stanley's moody letters, Katharine decided what she believed best at this point in her life. She wrote him: "I'm dispirited about having you as a companion for a woman who preferred light to shadows." With that, she informed him that she was breaking the engagement.

The force of her statement appeared to snap Stanley out of his self-absorption. He acknowledged his behavior was scuttling their relationship, but at the same time, he refused to accept her change of heart. He took the next train to Boston to persuade her of his love, and he promised to be "happy-minded." Katharine accepted his apology and promise, but she requested some time to evaluate his actions. For the next few months, Stanley's letters were "normal," his behavior and opinions reasonable.

In June 1904, Stanley returned to Boston, with the intent to once again persuade Katharine to an engagement. Katharine's graduation from MIT was only days away. She was the only woman in the senior class, only the second woman to receive a degree from the school since its inception, and, most importantly, the first woman to receive a science degree.

Graduation ceremonies were held in the MIT chapel, hot and stuffy due to the press of participants and observers, all dressed in society's finest. Attending the event were Josephine, Stanley, some family and friends, and Katharine's colleagues from the College Equal Suffrage League. For league members, this was an especially gratifying event. Much to the chagrin and embarrassment of university dignitaries, they cheered loudly when Katharine received her diploma from the MIT president. They knew too well the barriers Katharine had surmounted for seven years and applauded her for bravery, fortitude, and commitment. That evening, at 393 Commonwealth, the graduation celebration culminated with the announcement of Katharine and Stanley's engagement.

The engagement was no sooner announced, however, than Stanley reverted to his previous erratic behavior. In a heated discussion between them, Stanley confessed to Katharine that he had been a masturbator and feared it might make him unfit for marriage. "Stanley," she responded, "I think that is ridiculous."

Nettie wrote a cold, unfriendly letter to Katharine, expressing qualified approval for the engagement but none for the prospective bride. When Stanley told her of receiving a letter from his mother, filled with unsolicited advice, she could easily imagine what Nettie had written her son. The situation had become so charged, Katharine decided to leave at once for the Dexter château in Switzerland, to relax and "clear her head" from the complications created by Stanley and his family. Stanley begged to accompany her, but she refused.

On the day she was to leave Boston, Stanley did not come to the train station to say good-bye. Katharine was heartbroken. Crying as she rode to New York and convinced that she had finally been bested, Katharine wrote to Nettie, ending the engagement. She felt she now understood who ruled Stanley's life and could well imagine Nettie's delight when the letter was delivered. At this moment, a commitment to "save" Stanley did not seem worth the emotional cost. She must now mentally prepare herself to continue her career in science, separate from this ardent yet ambivalent suitor. As a haven from the emotional turmoil, the gardens of the Château de Prangins seemed inviting.

To her great surprise, the next day, at the dock of the liner *Mauritania*,

Stanley reappeared. Before he could speak, Katharine told him bluntly and with feeling that their relationship had little chance to survive, due to his mood swings and his interfering mother. She also told him about the letter to Nettie, declaring the end of the engagement.

Stanley seemed so emotionally charged that he ignored her words, waving them away with a sweep of his arms. "I have something really important to share with you," he said excitedly.

He had just visited an eminent specialist who had examined his genitals. "They are normal!" he exclaimed.

Because of Stanley's continuing obsession about his sexual fitness, Katharine knew this information was of no small import to him. While she sympathized with his joy, she attempted to explain her decision once again. Yet nothing seemed to divert his maniacal attention. He continued to prattle on about his physical condition, even as she boarded the ship.

As she looked back and saw how agitated Stanley was, the sight touched her deeply. Desperately, he seemed to need her. She heard his excited voice calling after her, talking nonstop about the miracle, as the gangplank was raised.

Did Stanley actually not understand what she had told him? She had broken their engagement, and she needed time to be alone.

Seven

The summer of 1904 began cool and clear. At the château, abundant spring snow and rain had nourished the flowers, and the trees appeared even greener and more full-bodied than usual. Katharine enjoyed early-morning walks along the paths bordering Lake Geneva and found sitting in the garden, her personal garden, restorative.

The distance between her and life back in Boston was sufficient to allow her to relax and contemplate the distracting and puzzling events of the past year. She wrote letters to friends and relatives. She read. She practiced French and German.

Still, Stanley continued to occupy her thoughts. Katharine wondered why Stanley had not written since they parted; it was not like him. Was he ill? Upset? Speeding around the countryside?

Her thoughts reviewed every aspect of their turbulent courtship. Had she been wrong to break off the engagement? Stanley seemed both dashing and helpless. Despite her reserve, she enjoyed his direct expressions of love. And his erratic behavior could possibly be excused as reflecting the eccentricities characteristic of the very rich. Yet he seemed not to understand that she had actually ended their engagement.

Yet Katharine felt guilty about leaving Stanley vulnerable to his unbalanced mother. He had never been given the opportunity to flourish, disengaged from Nettie's control, Katharine reasoned. Here, in the quiet of the Swiss garden, she had to admit she still cared for him and believed that he needed her. But why had he not written?

In fact, Stanley was already on his way to join her. Nettie had attempted to use Katharine's letter as an argument against their relationship. "Can't you see, Stanley? She broke the engagement because she doesn't love you." Anita, too, tried to persuade him: "Katharine is not your true love." In spite of these family exhortations, Stanley booked passage to Le Havre. He wanted to see Katharine as soon as he was able. He had to prove his love for her and his desire for them to be married.

Less than a month after their separation at the dock in New York, Stanley was standing on Katharine's doorstep in Nyons. He arrived with gifts—jewelry, books, flowers—to convince her that his love was sincere. No sooner had he crossed the threshold than he entreated her, "Please marry me. I love you dearly."

Surprised by and taken with his ardor, she remained cautious. Stanley looked ill or maybe just exhausted from his journey. She had to be more certain about his mental health before committing to anything. "Relax and rest for a few weeks. We'll talk about plans then," she assured him.

The kindness of her reception encouraged Stanley. In a matter of days, his color returned, and his nervousness abated. Each morning, he came to the château to pick her up in his rented touring car, and they drove off together, to return for dinner at a fine restaurant in Geneva. Separated from his family by an ocean, Stanley seemed to flourish. Katharine was delighted by his attentions and his seriousness of purpose. They thoroughly enjoyed the time together.

Their freedom and his passion rekindled the relationship so that, in early August, they again discussed marriage. Katharine had almost forgotten, or at least put aside, her concern about Stanley's erratic behavior. Stanley, in turn, exuded confidence as he proved an increasingly successful suitor.

On August 14, Katharine told her mother she was going to marry Stanley. The next day, Harold received a cable from Stanley: "Great news. September 15. Happy event occurs Geneva." When Harold informed Nettie of Stanley's announcement, she immediately fell ill. "I am distracted with anxiety," she cried, and she remained bedridden for days, mourning the "loss" of her son.

To Harold and Anita, Stanley's impending marriage proved vexing. Stanley had asked Harold to be his best man. No one, he believed, knew him better nor had been more sympathetic to his pursuit of Katharine. He expected Harold to offer greater support than other family members. To Stanley's surprise, however, Harold turned him down, insisting that he had to attend to "business affairs," a decision that annoyed and disappointed Stanley. Anita claimed she was unable to change her schedule and apologized to her brother for not being able to attend "his happiest day." Only Cyrus Jr., his wife, and Nettie planned to attend the wedding. Nettie saw to it that publicity of the marriage was minimized in Chicago. Only a brief article in the society section of the *Chicago Tribune* announced the betrothal. "Re: Stanley McCormick and Katharine Dexter. The engagement was announced only recently. In fact, the word came from abroad where both young people have spent the greater part of the summer. The wedding will be quietly celebrated. Mrs. McCormick, Mr. and Mrs. Cyrus McCormick, and their son plan to attend. The couple plan to live in Chicago, where both are well known."[1]

Up to the day the McCormicks were to arrive from Chicago, Stanley appeared cheerful and calm, and Katharine herself had grown more confident of their relationship. She had been relying on a regimen of steady, rational support to keep Stanley in balance, and he obviously enjoyed her attention. She was now telling herself, "It will probably turn out right, after all."

Three days before the wedding, they drove to the train station to meet the McCormicks. Stanley seemed a little nervous, but Katharine expected it. Josephine, demonstrating her unerring instinct for perfect social planning, had arranged a full day of activities for the group, starting with a formal lunch at the château. The McCormicks would get an opportunity to see the Dexter estate, and, as the perfect hostess, Josephine would begin the process of uniting these two "royal" families. The lunch was followed by an elegant ceremony at the home of Geneva's mayor, who presented the McCormicks the key to the city. Finally, the entourage engaged in the ritual of eating Swiss chocolate—for good luck—on the city's landmark Suspension Bridge. The first day went successfully, remarkable for its harmony and splendid in its pomp.

The following day, the group drove to a nearby village to enjoy a prenuptial breakfast. On the way back to the château, however, Stanley was stopped by a policeman and briefly arrested for speeding. His calm demeanor suddenly collapsed. Rigid and unforgiving, Nettie refused to acknowledge his apology, remaining stonily silent. Katharine hoped that he would get them safely home, where she might calm him.

Once back at the château, as the couple ascended the stairs to the drawing room, Stanley suddenly went pale and tremulous. He begged Katharine to forgive him for breaking the law, which, she reminded him, she already had.

"Sit, Stanley. Please calm down. It is not a matter of great importance."

Forgiving him, however, did nothing to lessen the tension; instead, it triggered the now familiar rambling monologue about his condition. Katharine attempted to stem the flow of words by gently placing her hand over his mouth, but Stanley seemed incapable of stopping. Finally, in frustration, Katharine cried, "Stanley, this is an overreaction. It has to stop!"

"Overreaction?" he shouted. "I am bedeviled. Don't you remember, I masturbated? What better evidence of my lack of strength. Don't you realize the pain? How could I be a good husband?"

Sick of his self-denigrating monologue and disturbed by his obsession with sex, Katharine angrily scolded him. "Stanley, you are so placed in life, you can do anything you like. Pay some attention to me and the marriage now, and your strength will return." And she added, "See a physician again if you feel the need."

Yet, Katharine herself felt constrained. It was now too late to postpone the wedding, nor was she about to turn and run. She resolved to remain strong. It was obvious that Stanley needed her, and she was determined to help him. Their honeymoon would cure him, she tried to convince herself.

"Stanley, you are going to visit a doctor. This is nonsense, and it has to be put to rest."

The next morning, Stanley consulted a local physician, who, like so many before him, pronounced Stanley fit. His composure returned with the positive professional report.

On September 15, at 11:30 A.M., at the Hotel de Ville, Katharine Dexter, in an elegant embroidered wedding gown, and Stanley McCormick, in a tailed tuxedo with silk lapels, appeared before the mayor of Nyons, who performed a brief civil ceremony.[2] The town required considerable paperwork to make the marriage official, and the mayor proudly guided the newlyweds through the administrative maze, which included the usual signatures for the civil servants in attendance. Next, the group moved on to the Church of the Macabees for the religious ceremony, conducted by the Reverend Mr. Frothingham, a Dexter family friend who had been brought from Boston. Cyrus Jr. spent the entire time attending his mother, who appeared dazed by the events.

In a solemn ceremony, Katharine and Stanley exchanged vows under the tall shadow of Reverend Frothingham, who in his comments alluded to the joyous joining of two distinguished families. Shortly after, the participants drove to the Hotel Beau Rivage for the reception. In her bridal gown, Katharine radiated beauty and cool confidence, while Stanley seemed hesitant, somewhat unsure of himself, as if he were struggling with an inner turmoil. As they posed for wedding pictures, he appeared to be "hanging on" to Katharine.

Based on information supplied by the McCormicks, the *Chicago Tribune* society page reported on the wedding: "The bride wore an exquisitely embroidered gown of white French muslin, with a magnificent set of pearls, given by the groom. Mrs. Dexter's costume was of mauve musseline and Mrs. McCormick's a gray brocade. After the religious ceremony, an afternoon reception was served at the Hotel Beau Rivage. They left in the afternoon for a touring trip in an automobile. Their plans for the winter are not known."[3]

The reality, however, was very different from what was described in the news release. Because Nettie had decided to remain in Geneva for a month, Katharine and Stanley were forced to stay at the hotel. Reluctantly,

Nettie agreed to embark from Liverpool with Josephine, but only after the newlyweds promised to take them there.

Her decision to remain in Nyons entailed several requests, primarily to have Stanley visit her at least twice a week. Because these visits might initiate erratic behavior from Stanley, Katharine decided that luncheons, including herself and Josephine, would minimize the pressure on Stanley. Since this arrangement thwarted Nettie's attempt to be alone with Stanley, she was quite displeased. Not surprisingly, her loathing for Katharine increased. In a letter to Harold and Anita, her hostility toward Katharine was obvious. "If Katharine were obliged to choose between her husband and her mother, it would not be her husband that she would choose."[4]

For the newlyweds, the situation caused increasing discomfort. They would both have loved to be free of their mothers. As often as she could, Nettie sought to reattach her psychological umbilical to Stanley. For her part, Josephine spent the time luxuriating in the social implications of her daughter's marriage.

Finding the continuous pretense of social obligation tiresome, Katharine grew increasingly irritated. She could see Stanley's bouts of panic increasing in frequency. He fretted about his potency. He was having problems talking both to Nettie and to Josephine. He was hesitant to go out in public. Each time, Katharine tried to reassure him that it would soon be all right. "We did not get married just to entertain our mothers," she reminded him.

Still, the situation remained distressful to Stanley, particularly his sexual performance. Troubled and afraid to come to bed, he spent hours late into the night writing letters. Often, Katharine would not see him until dawn. The pattern repeated itself for several days. It would then abruptly cease, only to return a few days later. During the day, however, Stanley seemed thoroughly relaxed. The two would then escape by motoring or hiking in the mountains. During these moments, Katharine remembered why they had married. Only with the onset of evening did another side of her husband emerge. Katharine was convinced the mothers' departure could not come fast enough.

During the slow trek to Liverpool, by way of Paris and London, the tension grew: four people confined in a motorcar, the trip made days longer because Stanley was forced to drive at slower speeds to accommodate his mother's demands. As decorum and politeness were invoked to keep the experience civil, Katharine focused her entire efforts on providing support for Stanley, primarily to protect him from Nettie's attempts to "possess" her son.

Nettie hated to leave Stanley. In her diary, on the day she sailed, she wrote these prophetic words:

Our parting was the saddest we ever had. It seemed as sad for him as for me. He looked very careworn. His countenance looked very drawn, and showed an ashen cast that alarmed me. I am deeply distressed. As soon as the steamer was in the stream, I felt I had done wrong to leave Europe. I feel a foreboding of something, I know not what. I thought of tuberculosis among other reasons for his decline.[5]

In contrast, the couple felt palpable relief at Nettie and Josephine's departure. Katharine had always believed that Stanley's emotional health was directly tied to his mother's proximity, and her analysis had been borne out by the events of the past month. This was not a moment of transition from one phase of their honeymoon to another, she believed, but rather an actual release from familial bondage.

They returned to the mainland, determined to enjoy every simple pleasure. They stopped frequently to wander around the countryside, then sped away to the next unplanned destination. Stanley's financial records were a diary of their activities: theaters, ice-skating, fine dinners, an auto touring club. Upon arriving in Paris, they went shopping specifically for art, looking for works among a group of French artists recently labeled by the country's art establishment, the "Impressionists." They purchased six oil paintings for slightly over $10,000—works by such artists as Monet, Sisley, and Morisot—and had them shipped back to Boston.

Their return to Paris, with its numerous art gallery visits, reminded Stanley of his thwarted art career. Again, he talked about giving up the family business to study art. Rather than agreeing with him, however, Katharine suggested that Stanley simply decide for himself what he wanted. "I have no preconceived expectations," she explained. "It's up to you to decide."

Nevertheless, Stanley insisted that she advocate a position, an opinion to which he could respond. Indeed, he was looking for an anchor. In his mind, Katharine's reluctance to support one life direction over another made him feel even more out of control. In frustration, he admitted to her, "I feel unequal to the demands for adjustment to satisfy you."[6]

Katharine noticed additional signs of emotional trouble. Stanley fussed over unimportant details of daily life, rediscovered an overwhelming concern for world problems, and became increasingly melancholy over the dichotomy between his mother's vision for him and the prospects of independence offered by his wife. In a moment of frustration, he cried, "My life has become so inharmonious, I don't know what to do." Finally, they agreed it might be time to discuss these problems with a doctor.

Back in Geneva, they visited Dr. Diemal, whom the Dexters had consulted in the past. According to the doctor, Stanley was in good health; he could find nothing physically wrong that might be contributing to his turmoil. Perhaps, the doctor suggested, Stanley was suffering from mental exhaustion due to his bouts of anxiety. To minimize Stanley's stress, he recommended that they settle in one place for a few months. In addition, the doctor recommended that they avoid any sexual intimacy during this time. The couple decided to stay in St. Moritz to relax and enjoy the winter sports.

The next two months saw only marginal improvement. Some days, Stanley seemed relaxed, enjoying his surroundings. Other days, he stayed in bed reading newspapers and refused to talk to anyone, including Katharine. There were other times, mostly at night, when Katharine could not get him to bed.

During the spring, they traveled to Italy, a trip that was marked by further erratic episodes. In Milan, Stanley returned one evening after a walk, threw himself on the bed, and sobbed inconsolably. Yet he refused to tell Katharine the cause of his distress. Katharine felt bewildered by this new emotional outburst. Insisting that he tell her what he felt, Katharine elicited from Stanley his admission to a "queer experience of unconsciousness" in which he "felt terribly alone." Stanley then rambled on until dawn, under Katharine's watchful attention.

With the honeymoon coming to a close, the question of where they would live was again discussed. To Katharine's surprise, Stanley changed his mind, declaring that he wanted to continue in the family business, which, of course, meant living in Chicago. Katharine argued against it, feeling they would have less stress in Boston. But Stanley insisted that the family needed him to deal with business expansion plans. When Katharine pointed out the problem of Nettie's proximity, Stanley promised to manage his mother, although Katharine strongly doubted his ability to do so.

In what seemed to Katharine a campaign to "entrap" Stanley, Nettie continued to send telegrams to her son, advising him what to eat, what to wear, and which sites to visit. When Stanley mentioned they were going to visit Monte Carlo, Nettie sent a series of night letters persuading him not to go there because it was "a den of evil."

At the same time, the McCormick family convened to decide about Stanley's future in the business, since his unstable condition made responsible employment problematic. Their deliberations centered on considering a slate of officers "which may come when Stanley retires," an event they all clearly hoped would come soon.[7]

As the couple prepared to return to the United States, Stanley's nervousness increased. He developed a new fixation, this one regarding his underwear—its weight, texture, and material. Each morning, he made extensive observations of the temperature and studied the weather forecast before selecting his underwear of the day. This process reached its climax when they were packing to take the train to Le Havre. Katharine found Stanley with his clothes strewn around the room and nothing yet packed.

"Please hurry," she urged him. He reacted indignantly. "I have postponed the trip," he declared.

On June 6, 1905, the morning was partly cloudy with spotty banks of fog beginning to burn off, as the great black and red liner *Kaiser Wilhelm II* entered New York Harbor. The harbor was uncrowded except for a few tugs pulling barges downstream. The barges were laden with coal to fuel the large furnaces that kept temperatures in New York buildings comfortable. As the liner passed, tugs sounded their horns; seamen waved jovially, as they did to all the great passenger liners. In spite of the early-morning arrival, crowds were already gathered at the dock, waiting anxiously to greet the disembarking passengers. Most of the passengers themselves were already on deck, leaning against the railings, watching as the ship gracefully maneuvered into its slip. Some cheered as it approached; others shouted and waved to friends and relatives they identified on the dock. Near the passenger gangway, Harold and Edith waited to meet Katharine and Stanley. It had been almost nine months since their marriage, a year since both of them had departed from New York for the Dexter château.

As the boat dropped anchor, Katharine's thoughts glided over the year's events. A year ago, she had been a college graduate and single; now she was married "for better or for worse." She had pictured her life as a series of considered, intentional decisions, whether intellectual, emotional, or physical. Now, uncomfortably, she found herself in the vortex of a turbulence barely under her control, maybe not under her control at all. A good scientist should not have been so careless, she admonished herself. Yet, love was never logical.

Katharine and Stanley were glad to be back in the States. As they descended the gangplank, Harold and Edith immediately noticed how tired they both looked, the lines in their faces, their slower pace. Stanley, in particular, had a look of apprehension as he approached. The look, however, quickly disappeared when they smiled and reached out to embrace him. They were genuinely pleased to see him, knowing some of the ordeals he had endured in the past months. Stanley still confided in Harold and had written about his problems, including those related to sex. Harold admitted to having difficulty understanding the reasons that these problems had occurred with Katharine, since he and Edith perceived her as a brilliant, attractive, and popular young woman, one who wanted only to support Stanley. Of course, some of her ideas were different than Stanley's, but, Harold reasoned, petty squabbles never upset people to the point of making them ill.

Katharine was surprised to see Harold and Edith waiting to meet them and reacted somewhat defensively. It was, indeed, a nice gesture, but why were they there? To "rescue" Stanley? Had Nettie sent them to reestablish her control over him? And yet, she acknowledged to herself, Nettie would likely accomplish that goal anyway, once they returned to Chicago and Stanley went back into the family business.

Harold and Edith accompanied the couple to Boston, to visit with Josephine before traveling to Chicago. Josephine, too, noticed the fatigue in their faces, although they seemed happy to be together. She had no idea what had occurred on the long honeymoon trip because Katharine had written nothing about the problems. Moreover, since this visit was so short, Josephine did not have the opportunity to question her daughter.

The train trip to Chicago heightened Katharine's apprehension, as well as Stanley's. How many times had she taken this journey? Each time, it seemed to her, the trip had been taken to fulfill some sad obligation. She was filled with melancholy and foreboding. There was so much to attend to—finding a place to live; improving relations with the McCormick family; and, above all, Stanley's health.

They arrived to a grand dinner at the McCormick mansion on Rush Street. Nettie, resplendent in her most elegant gown, stood tense and strained at the front door, waiting for the carriage to pull up. Rushing down the stairs to embrace Stanley, she held him affectionately, crying over and over, "Thank God you are home." She clutched his arm and led him into the house. Katharine, Harold, and Edith followed.[8]

The McCormick dining room was brilliantly lit with newly installed electric fixtures, embedded in the neo-Greek-style chandeliers. On the Chippendale dining table was a brocaded, silver-tasseled cloth, highlighted by china from Limoges, silverware from Milan, and glassware from Venice. Within this luxurious setting, Stanley was to be feted, upon the occasion of his long-awaited return to McCormickland. It was an impressive reunion for everyone except Katharine.

Anita offered her apartment to the couple while Katharine found a place to live. The next day, Harold and Cyrus Jr. took Stanley to the office to discuss his new duties. Edith and Katharine went shopping for household needs and had an opportunity to talk about the family. It seemed that Edith was having some doubts about her marriage to Harold.

Within a few weeks, however, Katharine realized that she was too uncomfortable staying in Chicago. Again, the debate surfaced between Stanley and Katharine about where to live. "The company needs me," he argued. "But it will be more restful for both of us in Boston," she replied. To no avail.

In early September, Katharine returned to Boston and quickly purchased a home in Brookline, at 87 Gardner Road. It was a suburban neighborhood of stately two-story homes on curving, tree-lined streets. Much of the furniture was moved from 393 Commonwealth Avenue. Adorning the walls were the paintings and tapestries purchased in France. Placed on the mantel, on tables, and in glass cases were artifacts brought back from the honeymoon trip.

Stanley remained in Chicago and decided to move back to Rush Street. ("It could not have been his own idea," Katharine believed.) Almost immediately, bouts of restlessness again began to interfere with both his work and sleep. He seemed perpetually unhappy. He handled paperwork and meetings unsuccessfully, frequently distracted by the smallest diversion. Even having been assigned an assistant to help him, he struggled.

Finally, both Cyrus Jr. and Harold agreed that Stanley should return to Katharine.[9] Nettie objected, however, claiming that "Stanley will only feel worse leaving Chicago." Nonetheless, his behavior became increasingly worrisome, and the McCormicks did not want to incur gossip that might harm their reputation or their business.

Embarrassed by his inability to deal with business affairs and persuaded by his brothers to leave Chicago, Stanley returned to Brookline. Katharine, now quite sensitive to his mood swings, tried to avoid situations that might unsettle him. She was not always successful.

One night, in the midst of a dance at a ball they were attending, Stanley stopped abruptly and stood rigidly on the floor, staring and perspiring profusely. With some difficulty, Katharine got him home. For several days after, he was silent, unable to talk except with hesitation. He had momentary blackouts. He had difficulty making decisions, even on what clothes to wear each day. And he continued to be troubled by fears about his potency. Katharine realized that their relationship had become tenuous, yet Stanley did not seem to be aware of her concerns.

In early January, citing the family's need for him, Stanley persuaded Katharine to allow him to travel to Chicago. Immediately upon his arrival, Harold noticed the change in his brother's behavior, remarking to Anita that Stanley was "going downhill." To avoid any potential problems, Harold suggested that he go back to Brookline "to rest." Unofficially, Stanley was giving up his position as comptroller in the company, but he did not seem to care. He never visited Chicago again.[10]

Indeed, Stanley's health was declining. He was now being seen by the Dexter family physician, who attempted to monitor his erratic episodes and counsel both Stanley and Katharine how they might best be handled. Stanley remained detached from the impact of his behavior. Weary and dejected, Katharine withdrew from him. She moved into a separate bedroom. Depending on his behavior, she would lock her bedroom door at night.

Since everyone was aware that he could no longer function in business, in June 1906, Stanley officially resigned his position at International Harvester. As a way to ease Stanley's mind about the resignation, Katharine decided it would be helpful for them to go to a cabin in the Maine woods, where, she hoped, he could regain his health. On the day they planned to leave, however, Nettie arrived unexpectedly, along with her maid, secretary, nurse, and grandchild. She just happened to be on her way to a resort in New Hampshire. Nettie's visit ravaged the household for five days.

It took three days after Nettie's departure for Katharine to calm Stanley sufficiently to leave for Maine. Their time in the woods seemed to lessen Stanley's nervousness, and he ate and slept well. During the entire time, however, he remained silent, took hikes by himself, and ignored Katharine. One day, he found her crying but paid no attention. On another occasion, he abruptly left her in the woods, returning to the cabin alone.

"I'm not sure how much more I can endure," Katharine wrote her mother. "I'm alarmed by his moods and fixations and angry with his thoughtlessness." Yet she continued to grieve for him, knowing she was facing difficult choices. She admitted to Josephine that she "no longer loved him when he acted like a child." Prior to the marriage, Katharine had wished to pursue her own interests, but now all of her time and energy were devoted to keeping Stanley stable. It appeared to her that Stanley needed a caretaker more than a wife, and she bridled at the implications.

In September, they went to the docks to meet Josephine, who was returning from Switzerland. They arrived late and, unaware that a permit was required for entrance, ignored the gateman and attempted to reach the ship. The gateman seized Stanley, and a fight ensued. It ended with Katharine skewering the gateman with her umbrella. While they waited for Josephine to disembark, Stanley sat on the ground, quiet, dazed, and ashen.[11]

A few days later, when Stanley seemed calm and relaxed, Katharine raised an issue that had been troubling her for many months, particularly of late, as her own strength was increasingly challenged. "There is no reason why you should not discharge your physical obligations," she informed him. "Please, Stanley, I want an heir."[12]

Stanley tried, and failed. His failure shook him uncontrollably, and he retired to his bedroom in deep despair. The next four days became a personal horror for both Stanley and Katharine.

The following day necessitated a visit with Josephine. On their arrival at 393, Stanley abruptly left Katharine, proclaiming excitedly, "I have to look up a German teacher." (The family doctor had suggested that Stanley study German to help reduce his nervousness.) Before he departed, he promised to meet her at a specific restaurant for lunch. Katharine waited an hour before giving up. Instead, a few hours later, Stanley appeared at 393, looking for Katharine. "Where is she?" he asked Josephine. "I was supposed to meet her for lunch."

When Katharine returned to her mother's house, Stanley seized her by the arm. Pushing and dragging her up the staircase into the study, he locked the door. Falling to the floor, he cried, "I beg you not to leave me! I'm afraid you don't love me any more! You can't have affection for someone who forgets!"

With great effort, Katharine was able to persuade him to return home, where they could discuss their problems privately. During the entire trip to Brookline, Stanley was silent, brooding in the corner of the carriage. Dismayed by this newest episode, Katharine was herself close to breaking down.

That evening, after a bath, Stanley seemed more relaxed. When they began to talk of the day's events, however, he became quite agitated. At bedtime, he declared, "I don't want to go to bed," a familiar refrain to Katharine. Finally, he agreed to rest in his room.

The next morning, Stanley visited a dentist to have a tooth repaired. While there, he got into a fight with the dentist, during which he sustained a black eye, skinned nose, and cut lip. When he arrived at home, Katharine was shocked to see her disheveled husband and attempted to soothe his injuries. The more he related the episode, however, the more agitated he became. Jumping up, he ran out the door, shouting, "I'm going back to beat him up." In fact, Stanley did have a second encounter, this time with the elevator operator, who ordered him out of the dentist's office building.

When Stanley returned home a few hours later, he was accompanied by a reluctant and fearful German teacher, who apologized to Katharine for allowing himself to be forced by Stanley to come along. Disturbed by this succession of bizarre events, Katharine at last called Dr. Putnam, a physician affiliated with the McLean Hospital, a mental institution, to seek guidance on how to deal with Stanley. Putnam promised to visit her the next day. That evening, Stanley retired to his room and remained there throughout the night, to Katharine's great relief. She herself could not sleep. Stanley was rapidly slipping from reality, she concluded, and she felt powerless to do anything about it.[13]

At lunch the following day, when a friend came to visit, Stanley grabbed her handbag and pushed her up the front steps. When she tried to leave, Stanley took her arm and said, "I'm going with you."

At that moment, Dr. Putnam arrived. Assisted by a male nurse, he took Stanley up to his room. He assured Stanley that they would remain with him and be available if he needed them. Stanley was quite polite to the doctor and accepted their help.

A few hours later, however, Stanley wished to leave the house, explaining to Katharine that he wanted to see a man about his motorcar. When Stanley agreed to join her for "some fresh air," an attempt by Katharine to divert his attention, their walk lasted only a few minutes before he ran off, leaving Katharine dazed and alone.

Dr. Putnam was immediately informed and prepared to go out to find him, worried that Stanley might injure himself. Yet no sooner had the doctor and his assistant walked out the front door than Stanley reappeared. He was taken to his room and put to bed, with the nurse assigned to watch over him during the night.

When the nurse entered the bedroom, however, Stanley, half-dressed, attacked him, ran down the stairs, and bolted out of the house. Putnam, the nurse, and some helpful neighbors were finally able to subdue him and return him to bed. This time, as a precautionary measure, Putnam applied restraints to make sure that Stanley would not escape again. Throughout the night, Stanley struggled against the restraints, alternately shouting obscenities and begging to be released.

Downstairs, in the drawing room, Katharine slumped in her chair, exhausted and dispirited, hands covering her tear-filled eyes. "Is there any hope for Stanley?" she asked Putnam.

"We'll have to see how he behaves in the morning, Mrs. McCormick. Right now, he does not appear to be stable enough to be left alone."

Sitting beside her and taking her hand, he continued," I'm concerned about you, too, Mrs. McCormick. This situation has obviously been going on for months, and I can see it has affected you, as well." Yes, she thought to herself, even before we were married.

The next morning, Katharine and Putnam reviewed Stanley's condition. His continued shouting and moaning could be heard clearly from upstairs.

"With your permission, we are going to take your husband to the hospital," Putnam declared, "so we can observe his behavior more diligently." Resigned to the inevitable, Katharine nodded her approval.

Eight

From her bedroom window, Katharine watched the dawn gradually break over the mansion roofs of Back Bay. Upon returning from McLean Hospital, rather than go back to her silent and empty home, she had chosen to stay with her mother.

Now, Katharine stood in her former bedroom, exhausted, leaning against the high double French doors that opened onto Commonwealth Avenue. She heard the clip-clop of horses' hooves, signaling the early-morning arrival of ice and milk delivery wagons. After some reflective moments, she drew the heavy damask curtains across the windows and walked to her writing desk.

Slowly removing the pins that kept her hair in its usual tasteful coiffure, she let it fall carelessly over her shoulders. With a deep but determined sigh, she thought of Stanley's hospitalization and the McCormicks' impending arrival. "How am I going to deal with these issues?" she wondered as she mulled over the possible alternatives available to her.

The previous morning, when Stanley had been admitted to McLean Hospital, he was alternately pugnacious and delusional, one moment struggling with nurses, the next moment calling out for Jack London. On the admission form, doctors had tentatively diagnosed Stanley to be manic-depressive. Under "heredity," based on Katharine's information, the doctors noted: "all the McCormick family of nervous temperament; mother eccentric; older sister insane." Everyone's hope was that a period of complete rest would "restore Stanley's spirits."[1]

The ordeal had been unsettling. As Katharine put pen to paper, a momentary fear seized her imagination. "My marriage to Stanley," she gasped. "What have I done?" A brief sensation of panic overwhelmed her, visions of three tumultuous years flashing through her mind.

Shaking her head, as if to rid herself of the negative sentiments, and grasping the pen tightly, she submerged the feeling quickly. There were important issues that had to be dealt with immediately.

That afternoon, Katharine visited Dr. Putnam at McLean. While she was anxious to discover how Stanley had spent the night, she was more interested in discussing with Putnam how to manage the upcoming meetings with the McCormicks. At this very moment, Nettie, Harold, and Anita were on their way to Boston.

"The McCormicks will be arriving tomorrow," she informed Putnam. "Without a doubt, I'll be subjected to a cross-examination about the events of the previous days."

"Do you think you're strong enough to talk about it, Mrs. McCormick?" inquired Putnam.

Katharine paused a moment to reflect. "I believe I can handle it. But Nettie will demand all the painful details and will likely disapprove of my decision to put Stanley here. There's got to be a point where her oppressive hysteria is restrained. Maybe Harold or Anita can help."

With little alternative in the pressing moment, Katharine unburdened herself to Dr. Putnam. "Why can't we talk about what might have contributed to his illness?" She went on: "They weren't fair with me. Why didn't they tell me about Stanley's earlier symptoms? And Nettie, who didn't want me to marry her 'dear child,' why did she agree to it?"

Putnam leaned forward in his chair and took her hand. "You know, Mrs. McCormick, they will never discuss these issues. You must remember that the McCormicks have already had to deal with Mary Virginia's mental problems. To Nettie, her decline must have been traumatic. Can you imagine the embarrassment and shame the family will feel when they have to acknowledge another child's mental illness?"

Katharine, however, refused to concede the point. "Nettie will claim I knew about his problems before we were married. She will likely suggest I'm the cause of his current condition. You're suggesting that their concern for appearances motivated them to ignore Stanley's behavior?"

"I'm suggesting that social prominence brings with it an enormous weight of public expectations, and especially so for Nettie," Putnam pointed out.

Still uncomfortable with his assessment, Katharine concluded the discussion. "Nothing Nettie does is unpremeditated. Whatever she accuses me of, I won't let the McCormick definition of morality affect what has to be done for Stanley." Having delivered her opinion, Katharine shook Putnam's hand and exited the hospital.

To Harold, this trip was first of all a business matter. He had alerted the McCormick lawyer, Cyrus Bentley, to be prepared to negotiate any "family business." The company's accountant had been instructed to pay all of Stanley's bills and debts. A list of his securities and income had to be consolidated.[2]

Nettie had her own agenda. She was not about to leave Stanley in the hands of "that conspiring woman." She had already launched a vigorous letter-writing campaign, dispatching missives to Stanley's doctors at McLean, as well as to family and friends who might provide additional leverage and support for her position. To the doctors, she recommended specific treatments; to everyone else, she bemoaned her "little boy's condition." Woven into every letter was the recurring theme of Katharine's marital neglect and spousal failures.

In a letter to Dr. Billings, superintendent of McLean Hospital, Nettie offered her own explanation for Stanley's breakdown: "He misinterpreted the intentions of those around him, which led to intense resentment, then resistance." Billings chose not to respond until she had visited the hospital, which angered Nettie.[3]

The meeting between the McCormicks and Katharine was surprisingly brief. They exchanged documents, which would be studied by their respective lawyers. Conversation was civil but dripping with hostility. In detail, Katharine described Stanley's situation at McLean, but all Nettie wanted to do was see "her darling boy" as quickly as possible.

Nettie refused to talk to Katharine directly, instead communicating through Anita. As the parties were leaving, however, this did not prevent her from declaring out loud that Katharine had never cared for Stanley. Jabbing a trembling finger at her, Nettie accused Katharine of "withholding love from him, instead of providing comfort for my child."

After the meeting, Katharine wrote to Bentley, outlining her plan regarding Stanley's care. She proposed that official guardianship be delayed until "we see what Stanley's condition is likely to be." In the meantime, Katharine suggested that she and Anita "equally share the responsibility."[4]

When Anita reported this proposal to Nettie, Nettie became so disturbed, it compelled her to return to the sanitarium for rest and prayer. She wailed, "She wants to take over Stanley's affairs! How can Anita share responsibility when she lives in Chicago?"

Bentley relayed to Katharine a counterproposal stipulating that he, Bentley, be made a party to any further negotiations and that Harold and Anita exclusively handle Stanley's business affairs.

To no one's surprise, Katharine considered the McCormick family's demands totally unacceptable. In response, she suggested forming a "board of trustees," with her personal right to veto any decisions.

Anita marveled at Katharine's audacity. "Who is this woman?" she wrote Nettie. "She behaves like a lawyer."

While at the sanitarium, Nettie continued her letter-writing campaign. Cyrus and Harold met with Bentley to discuss further strategy.

In the meantime, Stanley's behavior ranged from total withdrawal to moments of complete lucidity. Doctors' notes reported a period of steady improvement—he was sleeping well, gaining weight—and discussed his symptoms frankly. He wrote daily letters to Katharine, most of them quite clear and natural. On those occasions when he had a "violent episode" (undefined by the doctors), he was placed in cold baths to calm him.

During his calm periods, Katharine was allowed to visit him, along with occasional visits by Anita and Josephine. Yet the doctors noticed a specific pattern of behavior: after Katharine visited Stanley, he became upset and unruly. This behavior soon became generalized to all females. Since it appeared that women were too provocative for Stanley, all female nurses and aides were removed from his care. How they planned to deal with Katharine's visits was another matter.

Two male nurses, McKillop and Tompkins, were assigned to Stanley to provide twenty-four-hour care and supervision. For some years before coming to McLean, McKillop had been an experienced mental hospital attendant. He had a reputation for patience and calm and the ability to gain the confidence of his wards. Tompkins had little experience and was apprenticed to McKillop. Their supervision of Stanley initiated a unique friendship between patient and attendants, one that continued almost forty years, until Stanley's death.

Stanley's rigid rehabilitation program resembled that used for any mentally disturbed patient at McLean. In the morning, after breakfast, he walked or played billiards, followed by a period of rest. Before lunch, he was given a massage. After lunch, he received visitors or played cards with his attendants. Later, he went to the gymnasium to exercise. After dinner, he would walk or read before retiring.

The pattern never changed, except when he became disturbed or refused to follow orders, at which point he was placed in a frigid bath. Once a week, a doctor attempted to explore his state of mind. The doctors believed they had achieved a major breakthrough when Stanley admitted that he had been impotent in his marriage. No wonder, they deduced, he became upset when Katharine came to visit.

After two months of monitoring Stanley's condition, however, Katharine expressed dissatisfaction with the situation, believing little was being accomplished to help her husband. She was particularly distressed by the use of cold baths whenever Stanley refused to cooperate. Nor did she care for the doctors' attempts to reduce the frequency of her visits.

About the same time that Katharine was speaking to the doctors about Stanley's condition, Stanley suffered "a relapse." Even though he admitted he could feed himself, Stanley chose to be fed through a tube to his stomach. He attacked a doctor and made a feeble attempt at suicide by trying to hang himself with the drawstrings of his pajamas, even though McKillop was in the room with him. When informed of the episodes, Katharine became exasperated with the regimen of care and demanded a change. She and Anita decided to consult Dr. Adolf Meyer, an expert in the emerging field of psychotherapy and reputed to be the most influential figure in American psychiatry. At the time, Dr. Meyer was practicing in New York City. Katharine hoped that he might lend some "science" to Stanley's rehabilitation.

Adolf Meyer was a Swiss neurologist who had emigrated to the United States in 1892. He quickly gained a reputation by modernizing the medical school teaching of psychiatry. His primary focus was psychobiology, a term he created to describe an approach that emphasized a person's mental state as being influenced by a combination of biological and environmental factors. Meyer claimed to examine a person's life history and relate it to the disease itself in order to identify experiences that might have contributed to the patient's mental illness. Some practitioners viewed his ideas as radical, but the majority believed them to be sound and innovative. Meyer had found that his theories were attractive to members of the city's social elite, thus assuring him of a prestigious following.[5]

Katharine had been aware of Meyer's reputation and was in general agreement with his methods. Persuading herself that Dr. Meyer would reveal new possibilities for Stanley's recovery, she asked him to examine Stanley, which he agreed to do.

Meyer's diagnosis proved disturbing to everyone. After a thorough examination of the patient and interviews with Katharine; Cyrus; Harold; Anita; and Dr. Favill, the McCormick's family doctor—Nettie refused to participate—Meyer submitted a report with the declaration that Stanley suffered from catatonia, a form of dementia praecox. His report also suggested that Stanley's chances for recovery "were extremely dim."[6]

Due to Meyer's diagnosis, Katharine became even more determined to gain sole control over Stanley's care, and she immediately wrote to Bentley stating her demands. Harold and Anita had received the report with a mixture of distress and resignation, remembering the ordeal of their older sister, Mary Virginia. They were not sure what to do. Still at the sanitarium, Nettie refused to acknowledge Meyer's report and continued to pray fervently for Stanley's recovery.

Realizing the need to take a different approach, so as to either harness or divert Katharine's intention to "take over" Stanley's care, Bentley and Dr. Favill devised a strategy to persuade her to divorce Stanley, or at least agree to an annulment. A sizable financial offering, they believed, could win her over to their point of view. They convinced Meyer that Stanley's best hope for recovery was to be rid of Katharine's influence. Meyer agreed and accepted a consultancy from the McCormicks to convince

Katharine that a divorce would help Stanley. He completely miscalculated Katharine's resolve.

Upon Meyer's recommendation—and agreement from Katharine and the McCormicks—Dr. Gilbert Van Tassel Hamilton, a young resident at McLean Hospital, was assigned as Stanley's full-time physician. Born in Frazeyberg, Ohio, in January 1877, Dr. Hamilton had obtained a medical degree from Jefferson Medical College in 1901 and had interned at the Jewish Hospital in Philadelphia. His excellent work gained him a position as assistant superintendent at the State Hospital for the Insane in Warren, Pennsylvania. In 1905, he was offered the job of resident psychiatrist at McLean. Hamilton was considered an "advanced" figure in the new field of mental health. His recent studies on the sexual behavior of apes, as a link to human sexuality, were highly regarded by Dr. Meyer, who believed that, with this background, Hamilton would be the perfect doctor for Stanley.

Initial meetings between Hamilton and Stanley went well, and a bond of trust seems to have been developed. Katharine was satisfied with the appointment and even more pleased when Hamilton began sending daily reports of Stanley's activities to both her and Anita. Nonetheless, when Hamilton suggested that, at least for the time being, no family members visit Stanley, Katharine became personally offended and sought out Dr. Meyer's opinion. "How can I monitor Stanley's care if I'm unable to visit him?" she pointed out to Meyer. Katharine was quite taken aback when Meyer supported Hamilton, but she accepted the recommendation, albeit reluctantly. The decision resulted in a temporary cessation of debate between the parties, and it might have quieted the rhetoric for some time, except for Nettie's sharp reaction.

Nettie immediately appealed to Bentley and Favill to intervene. As an alternative to "the poor treatment" Stanley was receiving at McLean, she suggested he be moved to another hospital, preferably one in Chicago. Dr. Favill calmly put her off by pointing out that "no change of location should be presently considered, in order to maintain Stanley's recovery." Nettie, however, remained unconvinced, and she renewed her letter-writing campaign to all the doctors involved in the case. She expressed a fear that, by their questioning Stanley about his behavior, he would come to believe he was "unsound." At the same time, Nettie remained critical of Katharine, assailing her selfishness for refusing to relinquish Stanley's care to his family.[7]

Nettie, Cyrus, Harold, Anita, Cyrus Bentley, and Dr. Favill, representing McCormick interests, met with Katharine, representing herself. Taking the initiative, Katharine stated firmly that she intended to assume full responsibility for Stanley. The McCormicks were shocked and claimed her demand was a personal affront to their "rights" as family members and, although the assumption remained unspoken, a threat to their control of

Stanley's estate. Two hours of heated debate, with oblique accusations cast across the table, ended in an impasse, the only agreement among them being to persuade Dr. Hamilton to permit the resumption of visits by Katharine and the family.

Under pressure, Hamilton agreed to the visitations, which unfortunately quickly reignited Stanley's previously strong reactions against Katharine and Anita. During Katharine's first visit, Stanley hid in another room to avoid meeting his wife. At the next visit, he was reported to have attacked her, although it appears more likely the episode was exaggerated by Hamilton to curtail all visits until "Stanley had become more stabilized."

His decision had implications well beyond what anyone could have imagined at the time. The ban—prohibiting visits between Stanley and Katharine (and any other woman)—continued for almost twenty years. Their contact would be limited to letters, telegrams, gift giving, and Katharine's occasional glimpses of Stanley from hidden locations.

A meeting between Katharine and Dr. Meyer became an opportunity for Meyer to convince her that both she and Stanley would be "better off"—Katharine winced at Meyer's use of the phrase—if she divorced him. Katharine bluntly told Meyer that "I will never divorce Stanley nor retreat from my desire to assist in his recovery. Nor am I interested in your opinion of this matter."

Meyer reported the discussion to Bentley and Favill, telling them that he was convinced Katharine would never remove herself from the situation, nor would she ever "give in" to the McCormicks. "She views it as her personal duty," he wrote, "and she will never deviate from that position."

With opposing sides delineated but the issue clearly unresolved, the argument regarding Stanley's care and guardianship temporarily subsided. The combatants now anxiously awaited Hamilton's reports, hoping for any signs of improvement. While Katharine had expended considerable time and labor over the "McCormick affair"—so dubbed by the press—she managed to devote some of her energies and attention to the College Equal Suffrage League, now an active, growing organization.

Under the direction of the energetic and charismatic Maud Wood Park, the College Equal Suffrage League had attracted membership from colleges beyond its Boston origins. In 1904, Park began organizing chapters in Massachusetts and Connecticut. In 1906, the CESL was represented at the annual National American Woman Suffrage Alliance (NAWSA) convention and had petitioned to become an affiliated auxiliary. To their disappointment, NAWSA rejected the petition due to the group's limited representation.

When Katharine first volunteered, Park had immediately enlisted her aid to gain affiliation with the national organization by attending the 1907 convention as the league's representative from Massachusetts. The convention afforded Katharine an opportunity to meet leaders of the national organization, some of whom would become close working colleagues when, a decade later, NAWSA was fighting for the women's vote.

Reverend Anna Howard Shaw, a protégé of Susan B. Anthony, was president of NAWSA, having assumed the leadership in 1904 when Carrie Chapman Catt became ill. Her ordination in 1880 as the first female Methodist minister capped an extraordinary journey that began with her emigration from England before her twelfth birthday, through years of pioneer homesteading, then to a teaching position. In 1886, while studying at Boston University, she joined the suffrage movement, having been greatly influenced by Julia Ward Howe, Lucy Stone, and Mary Eastman. Mrs. Shaw helped found the Women's Christian Temperance Union (WCTU) and became one of the organization's premier promoters. An eloquent and evangelistic speaker, she gained the reputation for having spoken "in every state of the union."[8]

By 1908, four states had passed suffrage laws: Wyoming, Colorado, Idaho, and Utah. Reverend Shaw's fiery rhetoric helped drive membership rolls from 17,000 to more than 100,000. A national headquarters office was about to open in New York City, on Fifth Avenue. A major fundraising campaign, under the direction of M. Cary Thomas, president of Bryn Mawr College, raised $60,000, mostly from well-to-do matrons. Katharine had donated $500 to NAWSA.

These suffrage movement successes ignited equally vociferous opposition, particularly in New England. Composed of businessmen, members of the church, and ladies who insisted that the majority of women did not wish to vote, groups of antisuffragists held passionate meetings to denounce women seeking equal rights as people in search of "free love." They distributed brochures and pamphlets that featured pornographic material to intimidate voters and harassed them at the polls. Suffragist appeals to the police were summarily ignored.

While Reverend Shaw earned her reputation for eloquence, she was unable to manage NAWSA's operations particularly well. Amid mounting hostility toward the organization, she demonstrated little ability to keep NAWSA cohesive. She possessed a strong will, but she could not effectively mediate disputes over doctrinal issues, which often escalated into personality clashes. Thus, state organizations worked to build their own groups, while NAWSA foundered. Shaw found herself leading an organization in disarray, with countless board resignations and support for women's rights losing momentum at the polls.

At their initial meeting, Shaw was impressed with Katharine's intelligence and MIT science degree and immediately attempted to recruit her for a national committee. While intrigued by the opportunity, Katharine refused, citing her responsibilities at home. She did, however, indicate an interest in NAWSA's Massachusetts chapter. Shaw introduced her to Mary Ware Dennett, secretary and recruiter for the state chapter, and Katharine agreed to discuss possible involvement at some future date.

Katharine also met Carrie Chapman Catt, the former NAWSA president and current leader of the recently formed International Woman Suffrage Alliance (IWSA). Catt recognized the value of Katharine's European travel experiences and her fluency in both German and French and urged her to join IWSA. Again, Katharine refused the flattering offer.

Nonetheless, Katharine was buoyed by her experiences at the convention, which implied there was a place for her talents and interests. "And what better purpose," Catt submitted, "than for women's rights?"

Nine

To everyone's surprise, Stanley remained coherent and stable during the next few months. He wrote letters to Katharine and his mother, reported on his golf games with McKillop and Tompkins, and talked of the summer home in Marion, Massachusetts, recently built for him and his wife. On Mother's Day, he wished Nettie "an ocean of love for you, dear Mother." Stanley also expressed anticipation to visit his new summer home in July, since Dr. Hamilton's assessment of his condition was "encouraging."

Unfortunately, the prospect of actually leaving the protection of the hospital triggered a severe reversal in his behavior. In his subsequent report to Katharine and Anita on Stanley's condition, Hamilton wrote: "Stanley talks incoherently and seems to be under the power of disturbing ideas and dominating influences. He is tormented with feelings he wants to express."[1]

"What does all this mean?" Katharine wanted to know. According to Hamilton, the only effective method to suppress these anxieties was cold bath treatments. Katharine trembled with anger when she read Hamilton's report. There had to be more humane ways to treat Stanley's condition.

Katharine called for another conclave to discuss Stanley's latest episode. The meeting was attended by Bentley, Dr. Favill, and Anita. They all agreed that some "other line" should be tried, but disagreed as to what form it should take. Katharine questioned Hamilton's handling of the situation but agreed to let him remain in full control for the next three months.

To discuss Katharine's ongoing "interference" in Stanley's care, Anita secretly met with Dr. Meyer. In the McCormicks' opinion, whatever the origin of Stanley's problems, Katharine was the catalyst. Anita asked Meyer to convince Katharine to divorce Stanley. While he agreed with her view, Meyer reminded Anita of his recent failure in attempting to sell Katharine on the benefits of divorce. Still, Anita implored him to pursue the effort and offered Meyer an additional fee to discuss again with Katharine the subject of divorce. Sent after the meeting, a note from Anita to Katharine promised that "if you agree to a divorce, the McCormicks would make it worthwhile."

Shortly after, at Meyer's instigation, he and Katharine met to discuss the divorce issue. Meyer pleaded that, in Stanley's best interests, the couple should separate. While Katharine admitted she was prepared to "do anything necessary to ensure Stanley's recovery," even if a dissolution of their marriage took place, "I am unwilling to give up a guardianship role."

"But a full separation is necessary," Meyer argued, "being best for all involved."

"For the McCormicks especially?" Katharine queried sarcastically.

The exchange heightened Katharine's suspicion that Meyer, regardless of his skill as a doctor, was siding with her adversaries. She warned herself to be more careful in dealing with him. Nonetheless, the discussion ended with Katharine's reaffirming her intent to continue supervising Stanley's care.

Katharine felt herself further isolated when her mother seemed to side with Dr. Meyer and the McCormicks. Josephine had expressed unhappiness with the outcome of the marriage and was very concerned that the Dexter line was in jeopardy. "Now might be the best time to separate from Stanley," she counseled her daughter. Katharine fervently disagreed.

As Katharine explained to her mother, "Nettie is behind it all; the person who damaged Stanley initially." Katharine was convinced that just the thought of her relinquishing his care was to Nettie, by itself, sufficient to "save" him. "Whatever anyone says, Mother, I'll care for him as long as it is necessary."

Miraculously, to this point, everyone accepted the fact that Dr. Hamilton was doing an excellent job with Stanley, skillfully and successfully ministering to his needs, except for the cold baths. Hamilton was conscientious, tactful, sympathetic, and gentle, and Stanley responded well to the empathic treatment. The patient/doctor relationship had grown to the point where Stanley even assisted Hamilton with his ape experiments. Katharine continued to monitor activities and exchanged letters with Stanley but, following Hamilton's orders, viewed him only from a distance. Reflecting on the physical separation from her husband, Katharine wrote her mother about "the difficult decision that grieved me nightly."

The McCormicks' efforts to remove Katharine's guardianship continued. Dr. Favill proposed a number of new strategies against her, "but they should be gone about with circumspection, particularly fortified by the absolute advice of medical men." Favill had tried to persuade Dr. Hamilton to talk to Katharine about divorce, but he refused.

When Nettie heard of Dr. Favill's failure to influence Hamilton, she wrote Dr. Hamilton's wife and sent along a blanket for Stanley, "to keep the precious child warm." Another letter, this one to Dr. Hamilton directly, bewailed Stanley's condition and suggested an "oxygen cure for him."[2]

To Nettie's intrusive letters, Hamilton responded tactfully yet firmly:

I have promised all that I will not communicate with any members of the family. The complexity of the situation seems to demand such a policy, and, of course, I wish to be faithful to a promise which I know to be part of carefully thought out plans. Please do not think me insensitive to your anxiety and to the most sacred of all claims upon my sympathies, but I should be unworthy of the duties allotted me were I to evade my promise in any way.[3]

Recognizing that she would obtain nothing from Dr. Hamilton, Nettie again wrote to Mrs. Hamilton, to thank her husband "for all that Doctor has been to my dear, dear, suffering child, a boy so noble, so good, as son, husband, brother, and friend." Mrs. Hamilton passed the letter on to her husband with a smile and a shake of the head.

Katharine was told of the content of Nettie's letters, which, combined with the constant pressures applied to her by Bentley, Favill, and Meyer, caused her to write a forceful letter to Anita, reiterating her commitment to Stanley.[4]

"It is primarily my right and responsibility to take care of Stanley," she informed Anita. "I am responsible to Stanley for the conduct of his business affairs during his illness, and it is my desire to be as business-like in their execution as Stanley would wish and as he would be himself."

Exasperated and angry, Anita reported Katharine's latest statement to the family. In an emotional outburst of frustration, she recommended that, somehow, Katharine be "removed." Silence from all parties for the next several weeks underscored the impasse.

A note from Dr. Hamilton, however, temporarily deflected the guardians' attention to the doctor himself. He revealed that he had received a job offer from another institution. Hamilton proposed that, if he decided to take the job, Dr. Favill should take over, at least temporarily. Not surprisingly, Katharine emphatically rejected the plan. "This would seem like handing Stanley back to the family," she wrote her mother.

Instead, Katharine proposed an alternative: Dr. Hamilton in charge, with total control, including permission to consult other doctors if he so desired; a separate venue for Stanley, with three nurses in attendance; and an increase in Hamilton's salary, paid for by her.

Convinced that Hamilton wanted to eliminate "the effect of Katharine's impulses," Anita believed Katharine's proposal to be opportune. Conversely, Katharine believed that Hamilton was sympathetic to her position and was influenced by her scientific approach. Much to Katharine's surprise, Anita persuaded the family to agree to the proposal.

A week later, Stanley was removed from McLean Hospital to a private home, under the direction of Dr. Hamilton and the nurses McKillop and Tompkins. During the next several months, while Stanley vacillated between periods of calmness, engaged lucidity, and rigid silence, the ongoing controversy simmered just beneath a surface of strictly observed civility.

The veneer again shattered when Dr. Favill, at the direction of Cyrus Bentley and Harold, raised the issue of Stanley's expenses; they were running more than $1,500 a month, he reported. Favill suggested that Hamilton and Meyer look for ways to reduce costs. Katharine's response was immediate and clear-cut.

"The direct initiation of all expenses concerning Stanley has rested with me, and I have assumed entire responsibility for them." Repeated pleas by Cyrus Bentley to discuss Stanley's expenses did nothing to alter Katharine's position. Again, the confrontation recessed.

In May 1908, the McCormicks and Katharine met to review Stanley's condition and progress. At the meeting, Dr. Hamilton reported on the radical swings in Stanley's moods and behavior during the past months. Under Katharine's astute questioning, he admitted that Stanley's recovery would be a very long process, "years rather than months." For those still hoping for a quick recovery, this was a disturbing prognosis.

It was Katharine who suggested that Stanley be removed from the private home to a venue where he could receive more personal care, in a more pleasant environment. "Why not Riven Rock?" Anita proposed; Riven Rock was the McCormick estate in Montecito, California. Ironically, the estate had been purchased twelve years earlier as a personal sanitarium for Mary Virginia, Stanley's psychotic older sister.

In a *San Francisco Chronicle* article featuring Santa Barbara landmarks, Riven Rock had been featured as early as 1883. "Among the curiosities to be seen in the Montecito Valley is a granite boulder at least thirty feet in diameter, through which a tender young live-oak sapling has forced its way, splitting the solid stone in two, and as it grew in strength and size, actually dividing the rock several feet apart."[5]

A former newspaper editor from the Midwest, O. A. Stafford, had bought Riven Rock in 1876. He cleared the land of trees and undergrowth. Stones removed from the fields were made into massive rock walls that bordered the farm. Stafford had planted 100 lemon and 400 orange trees. He cultivated the land until 1896, when he sold the property to Nettie and Harold McCormick to house Mary Virginia.

In early 1897, Nettie, Harold, and Stanley had spent the summer preparing plans for the property. A stone mansion was designed and excavations of the terrain were conducted. An old farmhouse was moved, to serve later as a lodge and gardener's cottage. Groundbreaking for the mansion had taken place in August 1897, under Stanley's supervision.

The mansion itself was 101 by 78 feet in size (nearly 8,000 square feet), two stories high, with a bell tower at one end. Its architecture was of the Mission style, with rounded arches. Ludovici tiles, moss green in color, covered the roof. A broad stone porch with low brick walls extended across the entire front of the mansion.

In 1898, the property was enlarged when Stanley purchased another fifty-three acres, making the total estate eighty-seven acres. The mansion was completed the following year, along with a barn. In addition, a private golf course of nine holes was laid out in front of the mansion. Mary Virginia lived at Riven Rock until 1904, when she was moved to a sanitarium in Huntsville, Alabama. The estate had remained vacant, except for a crew of more than fifty maintenance people and gardeners.

Initially, Katharine was ambivalent about the move to Riven Rock. It would necessitate long and tiring train trips during the year and require special attention because of the need to supervise a large estate and its employees. Most important, however, would be the continental distance between her, Stanley, and Dr. Hamilton. She wondered if she could supervise the estate from so far away. And could she endure the long separations from Stanley? Yet it was an undeniably beautiful location, providing an almost paradisiacal calm and mild climate. Stanley might well benefit from such a peaceful environment, she speculated.

The McCormicks, too, were uncertain. They had long wished for Stanley to be moved to another location, preferably away from Katharine's proximity. But Riven Rock? The estate was a long way from Chicago, the family, and their legal and medical support system. Yet they, too, felt a familiar place might contribute to Stanley's recovery.

In June 1908, accompanied by Dr. Hamilton, McKillop, and Tompkins, Stanley was transported to the Riven Rock estate in a private train. Katharine had successfully persuaded Hamilton to remain in charge of Stanley's care by agreeing to let him continue his animal research experiments, with a promise to build a fully equipped primate laboratory, the first of its kind in the world. Hamilton would also be provided with a number of apes, so as to continue his experiments concerning their sexual behavior. Both Hamilton and Katharine expressed the hope that the results of these experiments would in some way contribute to Stanley's recovery.

Katharine also convinced McKillop and Tompkins to move with Stanley. She reasoned correctly that their affection for Stanley, and his pleasure in their friendship, would lend continuity and security to his care. They and Dr. Hamilton had already worked well together for almost two years.

Stanley's first glimpse of Riven Rock recalled his earlier involvement with the estate. The majestic oaks, the vines of ivy, and the strong scent of rose and orange blossoms beckoned him. Spread out before his eyes were winding paths—he had designed them—and a lazy creek that cut directly through the property, bordered by rhododendrons and azaleas. Stepping out onto the raised stone terrace, Stanley could scan the surrounding countryside—the ocean and Channel Islands to the west, the Santa Barbara Mountains to the north and east, a vast embrace of beautiful natural barriers. Nevertheless, taken together, they formed a veritable, permanent prison for Stanley. Within weeks of his arrival, locals labeled Riven Rock Stanley's "gilded cage."

In conjunction with their agreement to move Stanley to Riven Rock, the McCormicks prevailed upon Katharine to consider hiring another doctor to examine him. In discussions with the McCormicks, Dr. Meyer had recommended an outside psychiatrist who might reaffirm the diagnosis and, they hoped, reemphasize the need to remove Katharine from supervising Stanley's care. The McCormicks seized on this recommendation and immediately contacted Meyer's selection, Dr. Emil Kraepelin, of Munich, Germany, to examine Stanley. Katharine reluctantly consented to the examination but reiterated that Dr. Hamilton remained in full charge and retained full power to accept or reject any outside diagnoses or recommendations.

Nettie and Anita just happened to be in Germany when the decision was agreed upon, and they quickly traveled to Munich to see Dr. Kraepelin. After Kraepelin accepted the job, agreeing to evaluate Stanley for a substantial fee, Nettie told him her story.

From the late nineteenth through the early twentieth centuries, Dr. Emil Kraepelin was one of the most important figures in European psychiatry.[6] He had been a professor at Dorpot (1886–1891) and Heidelberg (1891–1902) and was now head of psychiatry at the university in Munich. He had already achieved a reputation for his contributions to the classification of psychotic disorders, coining the terms and describing the symptoms for two major functional psychoses, dementia praecox and manic-depressive disorders. Dr. Kraepelin was accompanied to California by Dr. August Hoch, a friend of Meyer and a Kraepelin protégé who was then practicing at the Psychiatric Hospital in New York.

Stanley's examination by Kraepelin took place over a five-day period in the middle of August. Besides data obtained from interviews with the patient, medical records were examined and interviews were conducted with Dr. Hamilton, Anita, and Katharine. A twenty-six-page report followed.[7] Kraepelin and Hoch outlined their analyses in four categories: diagnosis, prognosis, treatment, and legal issues. Unfortunately, they left the estate before any substantive questions could be asked regarding their findings and interpretations.

Their report concluded that Stanley was suffering from a form of dementia praecox called catatonia. The doctors believed that the illness had been brought about by years of internal family conflicts—art versus business, independence versus dependence—a lack of good health, indecision, depression and irritability, leading to violent acts and sexual episodes, hallucinations, apathy and rigidity, unmotivated exhilaration, irregular food intake, and a lack of awareness of his surroundings.

The prognosis was guarded but far from encouraging. The doctors discussed the nature of this "acute illness" and admitted they were unable to predict its duration. "A very grave disorder," they called it.

Current treatment was determined to be excellent. A continuation of cold baths and sedation were recommended to deal with violent and excitable episodes. Any special mental treatment, such as personal discussions with the patient, was considered not yet practicable because he remained "inaccessible."

Introduction of new medical personnel could possibly cause relapses. That issue would have to be addressed since it was believed that the current nursing staff could not be counted on for future years.

Regarding legal issues, Kraepelin and Hoch recommended that a single conservator be appointed to eliminate debate and argument and "to instigate and adopt all measures necessary for the care and treatment of the patient." But who would it be? And how would the person be selected? Each side came away with a different interpretation of the report.

Katharine was quite satisfied with the report and believed it was a mandate for her to remain Stanley's guardian. The McCormicks, however, saw the report as an argument to replace Katharine. Moreover, Nettie was greatly disturbed by the doctors' conclusions, since they suggested that she might have contributed to her son's illness. It further increased her own hypochondria, religious fervor, and hatred for Katharine. For the time being, the Kraepelin report muted the McCormicks' ambition to do battle with Katharine, just as it convinced Katharine that her role as Stanley's wife was to be his lifelong caretaker.

The McCormicks now focused their attention on Stanley's fortune. He was worth more than ten million dollars at the time and they wished to prevent Katharine from obtaining any part of it. Cyrus Bentley was instructed to see what legal grounds he might be able to manufacture to block Katharine's rights as Stanley's wife, since existing law provided very few opportunities for women to own property. After exploring the possibilities, however, Bentley determined that the only way to accomplish the desired end was "to persuade Katharine to divorce Stanley, an approach which we had already tried and failed."

Based on the move to Riven Rock and her own evaluation of Dr. Kraepelin's report, Katharine was given another opportunity to weigh her extraordinary relationship with Stanley. Was it best to remove herself from Stanley and his abrasive family? Or was it her responsibility and duty to assist her husband to the best of her ability? Her conclusions showed a

strong inclination to continue assisting Stanley. In the process of her evaluation, Katharine became conscious of other factors that very likely influenced her to remain Stanley's defender. Indeed, she now saw herself as
his caretaker and protector.

The premature deaths of her father and brother undoubtedly played an
important role. Due to circumstances beyond her control, she had been
unable to care in any way for Wirt or Samuel. In contrast, she now had
the opportunity to oversee her husband's care and seek his cure.

Admitting to herself that she had no desire ever again to be dependent
on men, she reasoned that remaining with Stanley would serve to protect
her against further heartbreak. The three men who had been the loves of
her life had, unfortunately, brought only sadness.

Staying married to Stanley offered other advantages. The mantle of the
McCormick name gave Katharine a broader orbit, greater influence, and
more flexibility to engage in activities otherwise deemed inappropriate
for women. She also believed it was a legitimate way to avoid any future
intimate relationships with men and, therefore, any emotional situations
that could leave her vulnerable to their vagaries. "No more male-induced
personal disasters," she wrote her mother, who received the disturbing
news with sadness. Josephine had desperately hoped that she would
someday become a grandmother.

The train trip from Boston to Santa Barbara took five days. The solitary
hours gave Katharine the opportunity to make plans for her stay at Riven
Rock. Upon arrival, she had to arrange for Stanley's first Christmas at the
estate, as well as organize routines and work responsibilities for the maintenance crews. Now that the Kraepelin report had been digested, she had
to discuss treatment plans with Dr. Hamilton. And she knew that Hamilton would want to discuss construction of the promised primate lab.

At the beginning of the new year, Katharine planned to go to court to
have Stanley declared legally insane. She would then have the power to
make a legitimate custody claim against the McCormicks. The hearing
would take place in a Santa Barbara court instead of Chicago, where the
McCormicks would have had more legal leverage.

Katharine was also thinking about her previous conversations with
Maud Wood Park, Reverend Shaw, and Carrie Chapman Catt. They were
obviously interested in her participation in the suffrage movement and
believed that she could make a contribution to their causes. To allocate
time and energy to their organizations would be easier now, Katharine
guessed. She promised herself to talk to them when she returned to
Boston.

When the train arrived in Pasadena, McKillop was waiting in Stanley's
roadster to drive Katharine to Riven Rock, a three-hour ramble over dirt
roads and through endless groves of oranges. Katharine eagerly questioned McKillop about Stanley's condition. "He's doing as well as can be

expected, Mrs. McCormick," the noncommittal words sounding as if he had repeated them hundreds of times before. She would have to press Dr. Hamilton to obtain the factual information she sought.

Katharine stayed in a cottage in nearby Montecito, only a few minutes from Riven Rock. McKillop picked her up and drove her back each day. After the inclement weather in Boston, southern California was like an oasis. What a pleasant place to live . . . someday, she thought.

Each day, when Stanley retired to his room, Dr. Hamilton summoned Katharine to discuss the business of the estate. A large Christmas tree had been erected in the stone mansion, but without ornaments, since, according to Hamilton, these might excite Stanley. Katharine made sure that everyone working at Riven Rock received holiday gifts.

Discussions with Hamilton ranged from the planting of flowers to the purchase of a new car for Stanley's daily drives. A summary of Stanley's condition was prepared and sent to the McCormicks, since they were not planning to visit Stanley until spring. Dr. Hamilton indicated that routines had been established and would be continued until Stanley was more verbally accessible. Civility prevailing, Katharine wrote Anita, telling her that she would be stopping in Chicago and would be happy to update her about Stanley. "You will, I am sure, be so kind as to tell me frankly if this is not convenient," she added.

Christmas Day at Riven Rock was unlike any holiday Katharine had ever experienced. The weather was warm and the sun bright; the surrounding landscape was covered with lush greenery. Except for a few decorated trees and door wreaths she had seen in Montecito, one could not tell it was really the holiday season. Life at Riven Rock was unchanging. Only variations in Stanley's behavior modified the routine.

It was the unaccustomed, almost unnatural quiet that most affected Katharine. There were times she forced herself to escape to the seashore or the town of Santa Barbara to see people, to feel the vital, vibrant pulse of activity. If for no other reason than to maintain her own equilibrium, she acknowledged, it would be necessary to leave soon. Katharine found herself more depressed than she had imagined possible. Aware of her increasing anxiety, Dr. Hamilton wisely recommended that Katharine leave after New Year's Day. She considered it a welcome and well-timed suggestion.

After a final glimpse of Stanley, rigid in his rocking chair on the mansion's stone terrace, Katharine departed in the roadster, making her way back to Pasadena, the train, and a long, mournful journey home.

Women's Suffrage

Ten

Strategically located a short distance from Back Bay's elegant residences, where most of its members lived, the offices of the Massachusetts Woman Suffrage Alliance (MWSA) were located on Boylston Street. The organization was led by Mrs. Susan Fitzgerald, a member of one of Boston's illustrious families who had recently supplied considerable financial support to Irish politicians to help them retake the city's leadership.

Mrs. Fitzgerald, however, was anathema to most politicians and to the hierarchy of the Catholic church, both of whom strongly opposed the suffrage movement. Due to her social position and the influential composition of the association's membership, the opposition was forced to coexist with her. Meanwhile, Mrs. Fitzgerald took full advantage of the leverage afforded by her situation. She confidently sent out members to give speeches and recruit followers, unbothered by recurring, not always subtle "suggestions" to curtail the group's activities. Not surprisingly, the MWSA was one of the most energetic and adventurous groups within NAWSA at the time.

Mary Ware Dennett was Mrs. Fitzgerald's skillful field general. Born in Worcester, Massachusetts, thirty-seven years old, a former interior designer now divorced with three children, Dennett had been elected field secretary of the organization the previous year. During that time, with remarkable zeal and determination, she organized and participated in dozens of field trips throughout the state, speaking on behalf of suffrage, distributing pamphlets, and recruiting hundreds of women to the cause. Dennett was later to become NAWSA's national corresponding secretary, at the same time that Mrs. Fitzgerald was elected to the national board, an attempt to bring energy and vitality into the faltering organization.

Having met Dennett at an earlier NAWSA convention, Katharine was familiar with her activities and infectious enthusiasm. As a learning experience for Katharine, Mrs. Fitzgerald suggested that she travel with Dennett on one of the field trips. "It won't be an easy jaunt," she cautioned, "but the experience will be invaluable to you." Katharine accepted the assignment with keen anticipation.

For the next two months, Katharine, Dennett, and other association members toured many of the towns and villages in eastern and central Massachusetts.[1] They described their crusade as "preaching for the cause."

"We visited three towns a day, with meetings in each," Katharine wrote Stanley.[2] "It was one long scramble from beginning to end, sleeping, eating, traveling, speaking, with hardly a moment anywhere for so much as a fresh washing or a shampoo."

"But it was interesting," she continued, "wonderfully so, and instructive. Certainly to us, and we fondly hope it was to the various batches of the populace who were the recipients of our message. We averaged reaching about 700 people a day," Katharine enthused, "and had the benefit of a very large amount of newspaper notice, most of which was not of the yellow sort."

To her mother, Katharine reported, "Certainly, there has been no other form of suffrage work in the state that has begun to promise so well for results." Reading Katharine's letters, Josephine noticed an ardor in her attitude that had been missing for years.

Katharine described a typical day in the field. Upon arriving in a town, they instructed the conductor, "Leave us in the busiest part of town." They found the nearest drugstore and asked the druggist if they could leave their suitcases there. Ready for work, the group unfurled a banner, unpacked leaflets, and began distributing literature to passersby and patrons of surrounding shops. One member went to the police station to announce their intentions and then visited the local newspaper to get reporters to follow their progress through town.

"Where is the best place for a meeting?" they asked townspeople.

Invariably, it was the park. Suffrage meetings were held in the evening, when people would be free of work. By that time, everyone in town had been alerted that "the suffragists had arrived." As one member reported the experience, "The crowds always came, as a crowd always comes to a fire."

Katharine also discovered that women in these communities responded well to their message of "justice." They did not need to be "jollied or scolded" to see that suffrage was a necessary part of their lives. Most of the meetings were favorably received, and many women joined the association.

In two towns, the traveling group sponsored garden parties; in another, the suffragists joined a circus parade. In Fall River, they persuaded two storeowners to wrap a colored flyer in each parcel. In Lawrence, they made a balloon ascension and showered down literature on the crowd. Frequently, they spoke from vaudeville stages, as well as on the streets. During Katharine's first expedition, the group held ninety-seven meetings and talked to more than 25,000 people.

When Katharine returned home, she was both exhausted and exhilarated. Like a religious convert, Katharine believed that she had found her calling. And, after two months of daily speeches and debates, she had developed a great deal of confidence when facing crowds.

With only a brief rest, Katharine, Dennett, Fitzgerald, and other members scheduled a series of evening meetings at Boston Common. At first, attendance was small. To better advertise their meetings, suffrage buttons and pamphlets were distributed, posters mounted, and large kites flown. The crowds grew, and it was soon discovered that these kinds of meetings were the best to reach city audiences.

By this time, the campaigners had become resourceful. At Nantasket, a large beach at the southern end of Boston Harbor, police prevented speakers from congregating on the beach. In response, Katharine and her sisters strode knee-deep into the water, carrying aloft their banners, and spoke from the sea to audiences gathered on the shore. For the first time, Katharine was mentioned in the newspaper, for having defied police orders to proclaim her suffragist creed.

Katharine had now become one of the leading speakers for the association. Her fearless attitude toward hecklers was particularly noted.

Eleven

Katharine glanced nervously at the clock. It showed three minutes to nine. She, Cyrus Bentley, and Dr. Hamilton were waiting to be ushered into Judge Crow's office.[1]

In March 1909, Katharine had petitioned the Santa Barbara Superior Court to declare Stanley insane. She had also requested the creation of a collaborative guardianship, consisting of herself, Dr. Henry Favill, and Cyrus Bentley. The hearing was delayed a month, however, because Bentley claimed he was unable to make the trip to California "for business reasons." Actually, he was spending this time attempting to get the hearing moved to Chicago.

They were no sooner seated than Judge Crow began questioning Dr. Hamilton. Do you know Mr. Stanley McCormick? For how long? Describe his condition. Any progress toward recovery? Dr. Hamilton answered all of the judge's questions succinctly and directly, identifying Stanley's current mental condition.

Thus, based on the testimony presented, Judge Crow declared Stanley McCormick insane, by reason of catatonia, and declared there was no doubt in his mind that Stanley required continuous care.

Katharine then testified on behalf of the proposed guardianship, requesting that she, Cyrus Bentley, and Dr. Favill be Stanley's guardians.

"What particular reasons have you for desiring that they be appointed guardians with you?" inquired the judge.

"I made the request," Katharine responded, "because Mr. Bentley and Dr. Favill are and have been for a great many years the personal friends of myself and Mr. McCormick, as well as professional advisors."

With no further questioning, Judge Crow formally designated Katharine, Bentley, and Dr. Favill to be Stanley's legal guardians. As part of the agreement, they would meet quarterly to discuss Stanley's business affairs and finances regarding the operation of Riven Rock. Katharine was then elected personally to supervise the estate, since neither Bentley nor Favill had the time to get away from their regular duties in Chicago.[2]

When Bentley related the results of the meeting to the McCormicks, they expressed great concern about possible newspaper articles reporting another insanity in the family. They requested that court proceedings not be made public. Nettie, specifically, appealed to Judge Crow: "I would respectfully ask if you will not kindly exercise your powers as Judge of the Superior Court, to the end of keeping the further records of this case within your private file as 'proceedings in chambers.'"

Judge Crow, however, noted that the information was in the public domain and indicated that he could not prevent newspapers from reporting the case. Bentley quickly sent Nettie a telegram warning her about the possibility of negative newspaper coverage. "Impossible to secure private hearing or prevent publication, but everything possible has been done to avoid unpleasant notices."[3]

Newspapers across the country headlined:

"Stanley McCormick Insane; A Prisoner."[4]

"Millionaire Is Guarded."[5]

"Son of 'King' Incompetent."[6]

"Nurses Guard Millionaire."[7]

The McCormicks, particularly Nettie, were greatly distressed by the publicity. Indeed, the embarrassment so obsessed Nettie that she avoided social affairs for more than six months.

Visiting Riven Rock to prepare for the holiday season, Katharine found Stanley unchanged. According to Hamilton, the only activity that seemed to focus Stanley on his surroundings were daily motorcar rides.

The daily rides, however, had met with resistance from neighbors, who expressed concern about "the mad McCormick" driving on local roads. Katharine quickly defused the situation by assuring the "town fathers" that Stanley was always accompanied by "two strong male nurses and was always in restraints."

Construction had been started on the primate lab, along with a sprinkler system whose pipes ran to trees surrounding the mansion. Hamilton believed that water spray, like cold baths, would relax Stanley. If Stanley became agitated, the sprinkler system would be turned on and a fine

spray, falling from the trees, would cover the area. Whether this therapeutic method succeeded or not was never discussed or recorded.

Following Christmas activities, Katharine returned to Boston to meet
with Bentley and Favill, examine the estate's 1909 expenses, and establish
a budget for 1910. Graciously, the men agreed to meet her in Boston. Katharine had no idea that they were in fact intending to initiate a new campaign to pressure her into divorcing Stanley.

The disposition of Stanley's ranch in Arizona was the meeting's first
order of business. The ranch now consisted of 7,000 acres and thirty-five
employees and had been badly neglected in recent years. Using the insanity declaration as evidence, the guardians had assumed control of the
ranch, but they decided now not to sell the property immediately because
"the results would not have been favorable."

Riven Rock's budget was then addressed. For its first year, total expenses for Stanley's care amounted to more than $52,000, of which salaries
accounted for $29,000. In addition, Favill and Bentley each received
$12,000 for serving as guardians. The remaining expenses were attribut-
able to utilities, auto repair, equipment, household and laundry supplies,
and travel expenses. Only Katharine's travel to and from Riven Rock was
paid by the estate; all other expenses she incurred were her own responsibility, as she had insisted.

After agreeing that the year's expenses were justified, the guardians
prepared a 1910 budget of $55,000, which the court later accepted. The
information was somehow leaked to the Santa Barbara newspaper, which
promptly published an article about Stanley's "gilded cage." The article
pointed out that Stanley's annual expenses at Riven Rock were more than
the president of the United States earned in a year.

After completion of the business affairs, Bentley presented Katharine
with a proposal to dissolve her marriage with Stanley. Quite taken aback
by the proposal—the divorce would grant her a good deal of money to
be paid over many years—she asked for time to consider the offer.

For the next month, several letters and telegrams passed between Bentley and the McCormicks. They discussed the plan, surmising that, if they
were to refine it, the proposal might prove even more attractive. "Money
will surely change her mind," Anita believed.[8] Dr. Meyer, however, attempted to warn them otherwise.

"I have only to say that I find nothing in her words, conduct, or demeanor sufficient to justify such a judgement," Meyer wrote to Anita.

Indeed, Meyer was correct. Bentley made a final proposal to Katharine,
and her response was a clear refusal.

"I do not desire a dissolution of the marriage," she wrote Bentley, "nor
am I convinced its annulment or divorce will better the conditions of
Stanley's life."[9]

Katharine had been offered one-third of the net income of Stanley's properties purported to be more than $500,000 a year, paid to her in whatever installments she desired. As Bentley reported to the McCormicks, "She has definitely and finally agreed to nothing!" Although asked to intercede on behalf of the McCormicks, Dr. Meyer refused, concluding that "further involvement would do nothing to alter Katharine's position."

Katharine's refusal initiated a period of relative calm and diminished further confrontations for a number of years. However, hostility from the McCormicks remained. Nevertheless, Katharine's recent experiences in the suffrage movement appeared to have inspired her and strengthened her resolve.

Twelve

In early 1910, the Massachusetts Woman Suffrage Alliance initiated a lobbying campaign that urged state legislators to pass a constitutional amendment allowing women to vote. Hearings were attended by mothers, mission and church workers, teachers, social workers, saleswomen, clerks, and college women, many of them transported to the state capitol building by Boston's suffragists. A large group marched to the State House and presented themselves before legislators, demonstrating and demanding the vote. Katharine participated in this campaign by organizing transportation and housing the visitors. The measure, however, was soundly defeated on March 31, by a vote of 148 to 47. Nonetheless, suffragists left the State House encouraged by their efforts and pleased with the number and variety of women who had participated in the demonstration.

During the summer, a number of Massachusetts Alliance members traveled to New York City to take part in NAWSA's first sponsored suffrage parade. Newspapers called the parade "a successful occurrence," although some were amazed that such an event had actually taken place. The suffragists paraded briskly down Fifth Avenue, accompanied by a number of women's marching bands, dressed in the latest finery. They marched four abreast in a line blocks long, waving to thousands of spectators. Some wore bright-colored sashes that revealed their NAWSA affiliation. Others carried large signs and banners demanding the vote for women. Placards mentioned the shirtwaist factory fire (March 25, 1911, in New York City; the worst factory fire in the history of the city) as an example of suppression of women. Other participants passed out pamphlets to crowds who were watching and cheering the procession, in some places eight deep on the sidewalks. Surprisingly, hecklers were few, and those who hurled epithets or shouted obscenities at the women were quickly silenced by those surrounding them. It was Katharine's first suffrage parade; she was duly impressed by the participation of women representing all social classes. She was also impressed by the seriousness of their demeanor.

The summer also included another tour of Massachusetts towns, speaking and signing up members. Katharine did not participate in all of the trips, however, because she had just been elected the organization's auditor, with responsibility to manage all finances. Her decision to accept this position was likely influenced by recent negative publicity.

Local newspapers had reported her involvement in recruiting members and her "unseemly" speech making. Representatives of Boston's social elite were so discomfited that they passed on "suggestions" to Josephine about how embarrassing it had become to them. In addition, powerful Catholic church spokesmen publicly condemned the suffrage movement and its adherents as irreligious. As a result of these pressures, Josephine found herself defending Katharine and the Dexter name from assault by the Boston establishment. "Please be less conspicuous," she appealed to her daughter. After careful thought, Katharine agreed. In fact, she considered, she could possibly accomplish more if she remained "behind the scenes."

The 1910 NAWSA convention was held in Washington, D.C. Katharine attended as a representative of the Massachusetts chapter. A review of the year's activities illustrated the suffragists' significant progress.[1] Ida Husted Harper, chair of the National Press Committee, reported that more than 3,000 newspaper articles on women's suffrage had been published during the year, including 2,311 editorials, of which half favored the movement. This was a decided increase in favorable coverage from previous years. More than a hundred magazine articles had been published, and two movies portraying suffrage favorably were released to theaters around the country. Harper concluded her report by declaring, "It is doubtful if there was such a record in all the preceding ten years combined."

Harriet Stanton Blatch chaired a symposium on open-air meetings, at which Katharine was one of the speakers. She described the results achieved in Massachusetts, adding her own observations of the enthusiasm with which women recognized and embraced the suffrage crusade. Reports on enrollment, education, political organization, trade unions, and parents' clubs all indicated increased membership and participation.

One major negative, however, was publicly revealed to convention members. NAWSA had lost money, due primarily to its sizable increase in membership, which required the accumulation of sizable debts. Membership fees were unable to cover the added expense of new members, so fees would have to be raised to sustain the continued growth of the organization. Carefully omitted from the discussions was the increasing decay of NAWSA leadership under Reverend Shaw, a situation that very likely contributed to the resignation of some key board members. Some members openly called for Carrie Chapman Catt to return.

At the time, Catt's time and energy were committed to other women's organizations. She was president of the International Woman Suffrage Alliance, a group she had organized in 1902. She was also the primary force behind the formation of the New York Suffrage Party. New York was the state she believed the most influential because it was the largest, richest, and most dominant in national politics.[2] She expressed a willingness to attend NAWSA's conventions, but it was clear that she could contribute little more for the present.

Given Catt's unavailability, Reverend Shaw was reelected president, along with a slate of holdovers and one new member, Mary Ware Dennett. It was thought that Dennett's election would likely contribute to the improvement of field activities but, admittedly, would do little to improve internal operations. The convention ended with a call for further efforts to pass suffrage laws in California, Arizona, and Oregon during the coming year. Yet how much could the group really accomplish with limited funds and weak operational leadership?

For the first time, the Democratic Party had placed a resolution on the agenda favoring the submission of women's suffrage to a vote in the next election. The Republican Party fought its inclusion, claiming that most women in the state did not want the vote. Suffragists vigorously lobbied Republicans to accept the resolution, at least to allow the issue to appear on the ballot. Among those giving speeches at the legislative hearings was Katharine, who was identified by the local press as making "a persuasive plea" to politicians. Nonetheless, the resolution was defeated.

Katharine spent the next several months working to improve the financial viability of the Massachusetts branch. She quickly found that many current members were behind on dues, and others who had made pledges had not yet honored them. Devoting long hours and employing tenacious follow-through and hard bargaining, Katharine obtained funds for the organization to operate in the black for the coming year. Shaw became aware of the Massachusetts branch's solvency. She would not forget Katharine's financial virtuosity.

In addition to her efforts on behalf of the Massachusetts branch, Katharine was elected membership chair of the College Equal Suffrage League. She believed that the group could serve as a feeder of new members to the national organization. She initiated an aggressive campaign to enlist college women in Boston. She held frequent afternoon teas at 393 Commonwealth, where she led discussions on the latest issues facing educated women. The first meeting attracted eight women. By the fifth meeting, more than fifty attended, and many were persuaded to participate in up-coming recruitment tours of the state.

As Katharine explained it, foremost on their agenda was "the emancipation of women, both as a human being and as a sex being," since this issue was particularly applicable to the new generation of college-educated women. Much was said of the opportunities created by the nineteenth-century suffragists, and they were challenged to continue "this progressive movement." Katharine spoke of her classroom experiences at MIT and how the professorial staff had treated her. Citing her recent battles with the McCormicks as examples, she emphasized the need to protect women's rights.

The 1911 NAWSA convention, held in Louisville, Kentucky, cheered the passage of suffrage in California. It had been a very close win, with the margin in favor amounting to one vote per precinct. In 1912, votes for suffrage were to take place in Arizona, Oregon, and Kansas, and NAWSA anticipated a positive outcome, as the legislatures in these states were already in favor. A climate of confidence at the convention saved Reverend Shaw's presidency for another year, but her staff was shuffled by the national board to reflect the need for improved operations. Jane Addams, of Hull House fame, was elected first vice president; Mary Ware Dennett was reelected; Susan Fitzgerald, the former Massachusetts branch president, was elected recording secretary; Mrs. Robert La Follette became first auditor; and Katharine Dexter McCormick was appointed an at-large member of the NAWSA board.[3] The new board held heated discussions addressing operational changes, particularly the creation of a new, more proactive constitution.

In her acceptance speech, Katharine emphasized the positive influence of the movement on women who committed to the suffrage cause. It could easily have been taken as an autobiographical statement.

So much attention has been given to the growth and development of the movement for woman suffrage that the effect on women themselves has been lost sight of or has been little considered, but today it is becoming clear that the cause of suffrage is more valuable to the individual woman than she is to the cause. The woman suffrage movement offers the broadest field for contact with life. To come into contact with this movement means to some individuals to enter a larger world of thought than they had known before; to others it means approaching the same world in a more real and effective way. To all it gives a wider horizon in the recognition of one fact—that the broadest human aims and the highest human ideals are an integral part of the lives of women.[4]

Katharine's speech was heartily cheered and later reproduced in pamphlets to be distributed to NAWSA branches across the country. Newspapers covering the convention also published portions of the speech, pointing out the national board's new "enthusiasm." In spite of her desire for minimal exposure, Katharine quickly found herself identified as a visible and active board member.

Carrie Chapman Catt had been attending the convention, heard Katharine's speech, and quickly recognized her potential for Catt's International Woman Suffrage Alliance. She hastened to recruit Katharine, not only as a member of the organization but also as an IWSA board member.

When Catt had first become president of IWSA in 1902, she was also president of NAWSA. In 1904, she resigned her position in NAWSA, declaring that she was "just worn out." Records suggest, however, that the declining health of both her husband and her mother strongly influenced the decision. In 1905, Catt's husband suffered a fatal heart attack. Catt became deeply depressed by the loss and withdrew from domestic suffrage activities for a number of years.

The main purpose of ISWA was to promote and undertake campaigns to promote universal suffrage. When the group first began, it found that only five countries had woman suffrage organizations—Great Britain, the United States, Norway, Sweden, and Holland. Representatives from Canada and Australia also attended the first conference in Washington, D.C., because they had expressed interest in forming a women's group. By 1911, representatives from twenty-six countries attended a meeting in Genoa, Italy, to formulate programs for the next two years. Now healthy, Catt directed the organization with vigor.

Catt was a persuasive recruiter, and Katharine was inspired by her emotional appeal to join and serve ISWA. Catt had recognized Katharine's abilities—her fiscal, oratorical, and writing skills; knowledge of French and German; and her familiarity with European cultures—and suggested that she take over as the organization's corresponding secretary. Katharine agreed to be nominated and, a few months later, was easily elected to the position.[5]

Catt was an eloquent, charismatic speaker and an outstanding organizer, but she was a mediocre writer. After Katharine took over, ISWA became visible in the international press. This marked the beginning of a challenging but successful business relationship spanning more than fifteen years.

Now, Katharine's personal challenge focused on her ability to balance the responsibilities of various tasks and offices and accomplish them all successfully.

Thirteen

In early 1912, "monkey business" at Riven Rock forced Katharine to pay a quick visit to the estate. According to Dr. Hamilton, Stanley's condition had improved, essentially due to his daily motorcar rides accompanied by a new resident of the estate, an orangutan named Julius. The local press saw the situation differently.

Julius had recently been purchased by Dr. Hamilton in San Francisco from an old sea captain. Julius was considered an intelligent and friendly ape, one who would fit well into Hamilton's continuing experiments, although "naughty" on occasion. The ape sat next to Stanley on his daily rides, much to the patient's delight. Often, they were seen to be arm in arm. Unfortunately, during these excursions Julius enjoyed jumping on the seat to show off his genitals as they drove past roadside observers.

Local newspapers gleefully reported the incidents in detail and rebuked Dr. Hamilton for allowing such "unsavory displays" to continue. Hamilton, however, was reluctant to alter the routine because of its positive effect on Stanley. When Katharine was apprised of the delicate situation, she found it amusing, although she took care not to share the humor of the episodes with Hamilton. After all, she thought, they had serious implications.

The McCormicks, in contrast, were quite disturbed by the reports and demanded that Hamilton keep Julius caged. The situation was finally resolved a few months later when Julius attacked an estate gardener and had to be permanently confined. In a moment of sympathetic lucidity, Stanley expressed unhappiness that "my former companion had to be imprisoned."

Meanwhile, because Mrs. La Follette had abruptly resigned her position as NAWSA's auditor, Katharine was recalled to Washington, D.C., by Reverend Shaw. Shaw had recommended that Katharine fill the position, remembering her management of the Massachusetts Alliance's finances. Although a few older board members felt Katharine "had only recently come in close touch with the national association," Shaw believed Katharine had the ability to run the office, and her decision prevailed.[1]

Getting to understand NAWSA's byzantine bookkeeping methods was Katharine's first task. She found the records in reasonably good shape but the publication *The Woman's Journal* deeply in debt. When Katharine revealed the problem to the national board, it debated whether the publication should continue, and if the answer was yes, where the money would come from. Three days of discussion generated no resolution of the issue. Finally, Katharine recommended the *Journal* be continued because of its publicity value, and she offered $500 to help pay off its debts. Other board members followed her lead, and donations more than covered the need. In addition, Katharine recommended that copies of the *Journal* be sent to all members of the U.S. Congress.[2]

For the first time in eight years, Katharine decided to take a brief vacation at the family château in Nyons, although with mixed emotions. With lingering clarity, she remembered the marriage ceremonies and the tensions with Stanley and Nettie. Still, the château gardens had often served as an escape from the stresses in her life; and she could use some rest.

Yet two weeks later, Katharine took the opportunity to visit various members of ISWA who were in the process of planning the organization's next conference in Budapest, Austria-Hungary. Since she knew her new position as an officeholder and as Mrs. Catt's speechwriter would place her in the vortex of convention activities, she wished to become part of the planning team. When her mother chided Katharine about her definition of "a rest," Katharine replied, "Even a rest becomes business. I just can't seem to sit quietly for very long. I have to control my time in the best way I can." Josephine shook her head in exasperation.

What Katharine did not share with her mother was her need to stay busy, to keep her mind occupied with "meaningful" projects. Two months earlier, a meeting with Dr. Putnam had touched on the subject. Once he found out about Katharine's current responsibilities, he inquired whether she believed this constant activity was healthy, mentally and physically. Her reply to the question, she recalled, came too fast and was too obvious.

"You are being too defensive, Mrs. McCormick, about the very things in which you choose to participate," Putnam responded. "You ought to be thinking carefully about the motivations of your actions. And what about Riven Rock and Stanley?"

Actually, Katharine had been reviewing plans for the coming year at

Riven Rock, hoping that the situation would remain stable so that she could concentrate more fully on suffrage affairs.

No sooner had she returned to Boston, however, than she received a letter from John Chapman, the McCormicks' auditor, demanding a new review of Stanley's business affairs. Riven Rock's expenses and the new year's budget also had to be reviewed with Bentley and Dr. Favill. Katharine found that the yearly budget had now risen to more than $60,000, with Bentley and Favill together receiving $13,500 of that amount for consultation. She believed the money going to her fellow guardians would be better spent on Stanley's care, but the legal agreement prevented her from effecting any change. Wages for Dr. Hamilton and other personnel amounted to $22,000. At their meeting, the guardians agreed to increase expenses for Riven Rock to nearly $62,000.

The guardian meeting also uncovered a new attempt by Nettie to enlist another prestigious analyst to examine Stanley, "another challenge to my supervision of Stanley's care," Katharine guessed. This time, Nettie had contacted Dr. Carl Gustave Jung, the eminent Viennese psychoanalyst, to visit Riven Rock and evaluate Stanley. In spite of a lucrative offer, Jung expressed little interest in traveling to California, and the matter was dropped.[3]

Philadelphia was the site selected for NAWSA's 1912 convention. The number of women attending the convention was more than double that of any previous year. Actions both inside and outside the convention center signaled an increasing exuberance for the movement, and newspapers reported convention activities in detail. They speculated that the cause had gained renewed interest because of the successful passage of suffrage in Arizona, Kansas, and Oregon. Nine states had granted the vote to women.

A highlight of the first session was a report on *The Woman's Journal*. While the board generally agreed the *Journal* had become a formidable communications tool for NAWSA, the magazine had again fallen into debt. "The expenses had increased and funds had not been supplied to meet them," reported Alice Stone Blackwell, the magazine's editor. Nor was a report from the national treasurer encouraging. She indicated that NAWSA had a small balance at the end of the year, but the additional debt incurred by the *Journal* had created a $5,000 deficit. Reverend Shaw turned to the board and asked, "Where could the money be raised to pay off the debt and continue next year's publication of the *Journal?*" No one immediately offered any ideas.

Hesitatingly, Katharine raised her hand, was recognized, and slowly rose to speak. Beginning quietly but seemingly gaining assurance as she spoke, Katharine reviewed the situation with the *Journal* and the difficulty obtaining funds to continue its publication. "Remember what we had to go through last year," she said. Then, Katharine fumbled with her purse, extracted an envelope, and handed it to Shaw.

"Here is a check for $6,000 to eliminate the deficit and fund the magazine for the coming year," she said. "And, I beg you, please keep my donation anonymous."[4]

Katharine sat down. The board appeared stunned to silence for a moment. Then, in an emotional release of gratitude and relief, the members rose from their chairs and erupted in cheers and applause. Nothing resembling this kind of action had ever occurred in NAWSA's existence, and the board had been overwhelmed by Katharine's gesture.

Another highlight of the convention was the discussion and development of policy declarations about the need for women police officers, judges, and jurors. Speakers described the poor conditions facing women in large cities: "From the time of the arrest of a woman to the final disposition of her case, she is handicapped by being in the charge of and surrounded by men."

"What does this have to do with suffrage?" a number of delegates asked.

"This has to do with women's rights," answered Katharine, "and women's rights have to do with suffrage."

Delegates were assigned to investigate and to work for improved conditions in their own localities, since the national organization could devote neither money nor people to the issue. For the 1913 year, Reverend Shaw and the board were easily reelected. Nonetheless, the seeds of upheaval within the organization took root when Alice Paul and Lucy Burns, without the approval of the national board, transformed a previously inactive committee into a militant faction.

Alice Paul's first efforts for votes for women took place in England, where she worked with British militants and spent time in prison for her militancy.[5] She was highly educated, temperamental, driven, and charismatic. Paul had graduated from Swarthmore College in 1905 and spent the next several years working in charitable and settlement houses, but she found them a frustrating experience. In 1908, she traveled to England and enrolled in the London School of Economics. Once there, she was recruited to join the English suffrage movement, which had become a strong, outspoken, militant organization.

A year later, Paul returned to the United States and entered the doctoral program at the University of Pennsylvania. In Philadelphia, she joined the suffrage movement and chose to concentrate her energies on recruiting clerical and factory workers. She resumed a friendship with Lucy Burns from their London days. Burns was a similarly young, stubborn, and outspoken campaigner, schooled by the Pankhurst Women's Social and Political Union in Scotland.

After the 1912 NAWSA convention, Paul and Burns took over leadership of the dormant Congressional Committee of NAWSA and recruited three women, Dora Lewis, Crystal Eastman, and Mary Ritter Beard, all of whom had strong labor-movement experience. Paul openly expressed her dissatisfaction with NAWSA's "educational approach" to obtain passage of the woman's vote. Instead, she believed that a more direct confrontation to "punish the party in power," a strategy patterned after British suffragists' experiences, was the best way to get results.

At the 1912 convention, Paul and the NAWSA board argued strategy and tactics but came to no agreement. Instead, the debate ended in a standoff.[6] Completely on her own, Paul turned to planning the first of many marches, this one scheduled for the day before Woodrow Wilson's inauguration as president. The march was to take place in front of the White House.

News of the proposed march split the national board. Should they embrace a political strategy or an educational one? Katharine voiced her support for NAWSA's educational approach, believing it to be the more productive. Her strongly worded argument all but alienated her from Paul and precipitated a debate with the young firebrand about adherence to NAWSA's policies.

During the convention, Katharine's personal life took an unexpected turn. At one of the evening dinners, she met Mrs. Frank (Julia) Roessing, who had recently joined NAWSA and was serving as a Pennsylvania delegate. A resident of Pittsburgh and a member of the city's social elite, she had received a sizable estate from her husband as the result of a divorce. Not surprisingly, the two women found much in common. Subsequently, they were seen together at convention meetings and social affairs. Within a short time, Julia Roessing was being referred to as Katharine's "constant companion." Their open relationship reflected an intimate friendship that was to continue for almost twenty years. Some years later, when Katharine was questioned about her alliance with Julia, she described it as "the most honest form of female behavior."

Near the closing of the convention, NAWSA's treasurer, Jessie Ashley, submitted her resignation, citing fatigue and family matters. Ashley had been a close associate of Reverend Shaw for some years, and rumors suggested that she had been pressured by certain board members to resign. Fitzgerald and Dennett proposed that Katharine be elected treasurer to replace Ashley, and they immediately began a lobbying campaign to promote her nomination for the position. At the next board meeting, Katharine was nominated and easily won the job as NAWSA's treasurer.

Although some members complained about the abrupt change, Reverend Shaw sensed no collusion. When she announced Katharine's elevation in office, Shaw declared to the board, "To me, personally, the entrance of Mrs. Stanley McCormick into our work has been a source of the deepest gratification and comfort."[7] Shaw also noted Katharine's organizational and administrative experience, the first time those skills were publicly recognized. Both Fitzgerald and Dennett viewed Katharine's appointment as an opportunity for NAWSA to improve its operations and, strategically, as an important step toward Shaw's removal as president.

Katharine's initial recommendation to the board as treasurer was an increase in dues and assessments (from NAWSA's branches nationwide) to supplement the association's funding base. The board unanimously approved her proposal and voted to have her initiate a program as quickly as possible to collect the needed funds.

Meanwhile, as she had promised, on the day before Wilson's inauguration, Alice Paul, members of her Congressional Committee, and almost 8,000 suffragists boldly marched down Pennsylvania Avenue, upstaging most of the preinaugural festivities. A newspaper reported that, when Wilson arrived at the site of the festivities, he asked where the crowds were. "Everyone's at the suffrage parade," he was told.

All along Pennsylvania Avenue, suffrage banners, held high over the marchers' heads, proclaimed their cause: "We demand an amendment to the Constitution of the United States enfranchising the women of the country." Marchers sang songs and repeated suffrage slogans, and ridiculed Wilson and Congress as well. Newspaper reporters and photographers followed the entire suffrage parade, guaranteeing that the street actions would receive national coverage.

There was no question that Paul's single-minded, focused plan and skillful execution made this event an amazing and dramatic episode in the increasingly heated battle for the women's vote. Historians believe that Paul's orchestrated demonstration likely contributed to the launching of a new era for the suffrage movement.

Newspapers headlined and photographed attacks made on the marchers by hecklers and police. The marchers received no police protection. When hecklers began harassing the women by hurling objects and obscenities, one parade observer, Secretary of War Stimson, called out the army cavalry to separate the battling groups. Still, some police arrested a number of women and carted them off to jail. Women across the country were outraged, and the incoming Wilson administration was embarrassed by the incident.

NAWSA board members were dismayed and visibly shaken by Paul's march and subsequent street confrontation, believing the action had decidedly hampered their efforts to win favor with the new president and Congress. Historians suggest that Wilson's delayed acceptance of suffrage was due primarily to this episode.

In an attempt to separate NAWSA's goals from those of Paul's street action, Katharine, as spokesperson for NAWSA, wrote a letter to the *New York Times*. The resulting article was headlined: "On Militant Women: Treasurer of National Suffrage Body Says It Is Dumb."

Some of our members approve the course pursued, and many are opposed to it. In regard to our recent appeal for contributions to the funds of the National association, I would say that their appeal is solely for educational and legislative work of our association. Whatever may be the opinions held by our members, the fact remains that the National association is not a militant suffrage association, that there is no militant association among our many branches.[8]

Most NAWSA members rallied behind Katharine; however, some elements still decried NAWSA's "soft" approach and, while they denounced militancy, urged the national organization to become more confrontational. The article identified Katharine as being against militancy and, thus, against Alice Paul, who was emerging as a popular suffrage street fighter. Unfortunately, Katharine's position got lost in the wake of Paul's mushrooming media coverage, the newspapers reporting her every move and every action that precipitated a street skirmish. Although many of these events were NAWSA-inspired and definitely nonmilitant, the press nevertheless attributed them to Paul and her followers. By the end of 1913, Paul's actions so diverged from NAWSA policies that her group voted to become an independent and rival suffrage organization, as well as to begin the publication of its own newspaper, *The Suffragist.*

Regrettably for Katharine, her public debate with Paul brought unwanted publicity. Newspaper reporters now wanted to know more about this mysterious, elegant woman who spoke for NAWSA.

The *New York Times* was the first to reveal her background. It published an article titled "Love Is Loyal, Hope Is Gone," with the subtitles "Society Favorite Clings to Demented Husband" and "Wife Comes to Visit but Cannot See Him."[9] It was an evocative tale that described her marriage to Stanley. The story told of her socialite upbringing, courtship, and marriage to "poor" Stanley McCormick. It portrayed her as an upper-class woman who had extensive social connections and was a "society favorite" in New York, Boston, and Chicago. It described Katharine as a "grieving" woman, "sacrificing her life" and "suffering in silence" at the demise of her marriage. But not a word of her suffrage activities was mentioned.

Katharine was irate about the way she had been portrayed and the omission of significant facts that she believed were most important to the suffrage movement. The description of Stanley's plight was particularly irritating, because it demeaned him at a time when she was trying hard to protect his name. Overall, the article clearly revealed the barriers facing women like herself who were attempting to gain respectable recognition. It also jeopardized her desired anonymity and provided ammunition to the McCormicks to question the legitimacy of her guardianship role. The experience also caused Katharine to reflect about continuing her suffrage efforts. Sensing her doubts, Mrs. Catt gave Katharine the inspiration to continue.

The ISWA was about to open its international convention in Budapest; and Catt called on Katharine to assist her in the preparation of an agenda and speeches, although these assignments went beyond Katharine's role as a U.S. delegate and corresponding secretary. Knowing that her involvement with NAWSA would soon increase, Mrs. Catt made the gesture of resigning as IWSA's president, although she did not want to relinquish the post. To no one's surprise, the convention delegates prevailed upon Mrs. Catt to remain as their leader. To assist her, a slate was drawn up for a new board, with those receiving the highest number of votes to constitute its membership. Five members were elected, among them Mrs. Katharine Dexter McCormick of the United States.[10] During the convention, Katharine and Mrs. Catt began discussing how they believed NAWSA should be run.

After the Budapest convention, at Katharine's insistence, IWSA's governing board traveled to Geneva to continue its policy-making deliberations. Being so familiar with the site, she assumed responsibility for arranging accommodations and venues. Ironically, the meetings were held in the same hotel where Katharine and Stanley had had their wedding reception. The British diplomatic delegation, in full ambassadorial regalia, gave a reception for the women; they were later reprimanded by the Home Office for openly supporting the suffrage movement. Lady Astor sponsored a dinner party for the group, and Katharine and Josephine hosted a garden party at the château, which Josephine later described to a friend in Boston as "my elegant social gathering."

On her return to Boston in September, Katharine conferred with Susan Fitzgerald and Mary Ware Dennett about upcoming NAWSA strategy. They agreed to continue their efforts to revitalize the national organization and "get Mrs. Catt back as president."

"Look what we have accomplished in the last four years," Dennett declared. "Think how much more can be accomplished in the next four years."

A few weeks later, in Newport, Rhode Island, an exclusive seaside resort, Katharine forcefully reiterated her suffrage commitment. T. Talcot Williams, head of the Columbia School of Journalism and an ardent spokesperson against suffrage, was making a well-advertised speech at a crowded and already "worked up" antisuffrage rally. As he was about to begin his speech, a group of "society" suffragists, led by Katharine, climbed onto the stage and pushed Williams away from the podium. Others in the group shouted suffrage slogans at the audience. The crowd, incensed by the intrusion and the woman-handling of their speaker, surged forward to accost the suffragists. Luckily for Katharine and company, police reacted quickly and stepped in to prevent a riot, guiding suffragists off the stand and away from the angry crowd. The suffragist objective, however, had been fulfilled; the meeting had been broken up.

Williams threatened to sue Katharine and her colleagues, but nothing ever came of his threats. Local newspapers wanted to know why NAWSA had suddenly become so militant, seemingly in violation of its own policies.

Newspapers headlined: "Newport Society Suffragists Rout Anti's In Rally." A picture of Katharine—actually one taken from an oil painting made several years earlier—was included in the story, along with reports of her "unladylike behavior."[11] When Katharine was interviewed to obtain her side of the episode, she was quoted as saying, "This is another instance of the truth that our work has been chiefly effective. We urge all women to join our ranks for the cause." With that declaration of defiance, Katharine went home to prepare for NAWSA's next national convention, strategically located in Washington, D.C., bringing together members from across the country to storm legislative offices and face the disturbing issue of Alice Paul's independent militant activities.

Unfortunately, events leading up to NAWSA's 1913 convention caused additional turmoil within the organization itself and threatened to derail efforts to lobby President Wilson and Congress. In his State of the Union message, Woodrow Wilson had failed to mention anything about women's suffrage. In response, Alice Paul headed a delegation to the White House to lobby Wilson to support a women's vote amendment. While the former president of Princeton University greeted the delegation in his usual gentlemanly fashion, his message was anything but positive. He bluntly told the assembled women that their petitions, although signed by thousands of women, would not alter his position on suffrage. He also told them that he would not unduly pressure Congress on the issue. Amid shouts of protest, Wilson departed the meeting, surrounded by his advisors and security personnel. Wilson's dismissive response convinced Paul that her only alternative was militant action.

Shortly afterward, apparently in competition with Paul, Reverend Shaw led a delegation of fifty high-profile women, among them Katharine, to meet Wilson and ask pointedly why he had not mentioned suffrage in his speech. He smoothly deflected their pleas but could not ignore their influence. To push its agenda, NAWSA had enlisted the aid of Louis Brandeis, an eminent lawyer, soon to be elevated to the U.S. Supreme Court, and Helen Gardener, a Washington, D.C., socialite with many influential friends, to get Wilson's ear about the influence women wielded in states already committed to suffrage. When Wilson's wife sided with the suffragists, he began to listen. Still, the situation with Paul's group troubled him and made him reluctant to appear conciliatory toward them, particularly as it was reported that Paul and NAWSA were in heated conflict.

In fact, NAWSA's attempts to limit Paul's operations were failing, and she continued to build a separate organization from within NAWSA itself. Katharine found herself unable to collect dues from these renegade members, and when she threatened to drop them from NAWSA's membership rolls, they countered with a threat to support Paul's emerging group. By the time of the 1913 convention, Paul claimed to have more than a thousand members, most of them former NAWSA adherents.

At the convention, NAWSA demanded that Paul stop her independent operation and make her group accountable to the board. Paul categorically refused; in consequence, the board removed her from the chair of the Congressional Committee. After the separation, Paul's Congressional Union immediately embarked on a militant campaign, much to NAWSA's dismay.

Since Katharine was already deeply involved in the debate between the two groups, she was selected NAWSA's spokesperson for its nonmilitant, educational lobbying position. Whereas Paul preached confrontation and pressure politics, Katharine argued for calm persuasion and tact. It became a debate as much about social class as it was about suffrage. Cast in that light, Katharine had difficulty spreading NAWSA's philosophy, particularly as it was reported in newspapers.

Paul did not hesitate to embarrass Wilson and Congress. Katharine, now strongly supported by Mrs. Catt, who was quickly assuming greater visibility in NAWSA, stressed that discretion, quiet social reform, and proof of women's leadership abilities would ultimately win over Wilson and Congress. At the same time, Katharine had to convince NAWSA's nervous members that their relatively genteel methods were more effective than Paul's confrontational tactics. To them, she argued that "the Congressional Union is harmful to the cause. Yes, without reservation, as to our policy. Yes, without reservation, as to method," she declared.[12]

In addition, she stated, "There is no aspect or application of their policy which NAWSA does not view not only with disapprobation, but with grave misgivings for the future success of the Cause." Katharine's speech appeared to have held members; nevertheless, there was movement from within its ranks for NAWSA itself to become more proactive.

In a letter to Alice Paul, later published in many newspapers, Katharine warned her to stop the Congressional Union's misrepresentation of NAWSA's support of the woman's vote amendment.

On account of the importance of the big suffrage campaign now under way in the East, the officers of the National Association have made every effort to avoid inter-suffrage disputes, with their resulting harmful publicity. But owing to the recent persistent misrepresentation by the Congressional Union in regard to our attitude on the Susan B. Anthony Amendment, we wish you to desist from such activities. Those who regard it are forgetting that, in the game of politics, an intellectual grasp of a given situation, combined with the necessary acumen, is often of more value than emotional fervor, however exalted.[13]

Although they actually knew little about each other, the ill will between Alice Paul and Katharine Dexter McCormick grew increasingly personal. Paul perceived and spoke of Katharine as the privileged woman who practiced suffrage as a "time-filler." Katharine, in turn, pointedly questioned Paul's personal motives and her apparent need for self-aggrandizement. It was an argument from which neither benefited, but it did clearly identify the existence of two decidedly different suffrage groups coexisting, however uncomfortably, to procure the vote for women. It was an odd alliance, but one that later proved to be successful.

Katharine was also devoting considerable time to reorganizing the treasurer's role in NAWSA. She found that accounts had not been well documented and financial reporting had been erratic; it was nothing illegal or shady, just the work of inexperienced people. The plan to revise NAWSA's constitution also meant revising the role of treasurer, and Katharine prepared a job description that represented her view of the responsibilities of and skills required for the position. Dues, assessments, and allocation of funds took on a new importance, and Katharine managed them with an iron hand.[14]

Following the NAWSA convention, Katharine made a quick trip to Riven Rock to oversee the now annual Christmas festivities. While Dr. Hamilton reported minimal change in Stanley's condition, he waxed eloquent about the results of his experiments with the primate lab's apes. Katharine only wanted to know, "Have the findings of your work helped in dealing with Stanley's illness?" Hamilton had to admit he did not know.

Dr. Hamilton was about to publish a professional article explaining the primate lab and its work, "A Study of Sexual Tendencies in Monkeys and Baboons."[15] The article would present the findings of the first in a series of investigative studies conducted by Hamilton. Almost two decades later, his work would be summarized in a landmark book, *A Research in Marriage* (1929), the first of its kind published in the United States dealing with human sexuality. One of his associates in these studies was a young and eager doctor by the name of Albert Kinsey.

Hamilton's investigations dealt with abnormal sexual behavior in apes, through which he sought information on its biological significance, particularly with regard to how such knowledge might be transferred to better understand "human perversion" (Hamilton's words). It was Katharine's hope, and Hamilton's stated objective, that findings from the research would provide insight into Stanley's problems and how they might be successfully modified. Both Dr. Favill and Dr. Meyer, however, believed Hamilton's efforts on behalf of Stanley to be a waste of time, although Meyer lauded his primate research. Though most of the costs for building and maintaining the primate lab had been included in Riven Rock's yearly expenses, Katharine spent an additional $50,000 on the project as part of her promise to seek a cure for her husband.

At the same time, Alice Paul's activities were upsetting and threatening NAWSA's very existence. Paul's Congressional Union was attracting women who were dissatisfied with NAWSA's gradual strategy. Talented social and trade union organizers were joining the union, believing it to be more compatible with their own methods of operation. Much to NAWSA's concern, the union also attracted some upper-class women. One of these was Alva Belmont, who had already publicly and financially supported striking garment workers a few years earlier. Her financial donations allowed the union to carry out street activities that garnered a great deal of public notoriety.

Throughout the spring and summer of 1914, Paul's organization also threatened to overshadow NAWSA's lobbying efforts. Though attractive to the outsider, the Congressional Union was not a democratically run operation. Paul was forceful and uncompromising, and she demanded strong allegiance, devotion, and commitment to her cause. When asked about their group, members unhesitatingly proclaimed, "Paul is the Party!" yet, nevertheless, they loyally continued to follow her lead.

The Congressional Union displayed other attractions as well. It was clearly a one-issue group. It was not afraid to challenge authority, from President Wilson to local police. In comparison to NAWSA, it was made up of younger members and favorably compared its vocal, vibrant leader with the less-than-dynamic Reverend Shaw, who was sixty-seven years old. Moreover, it appealed to a broader spectrum of women, from factory and clerical workers to society matrons.

NAWSA was clearly aware of these threats to its organization, but, unfortunately, at the moment, its own leadership was in disarray. Shaw's abilities were now being questioned publicly, and she became a target of derision from members of her own board. State campaigns to sponsor passage of the vote for women were disorganized and split regarding their loyalty to Shaw. The introduction in Congress of a new amendment to diminish the chances for suffrage laws to be passed in several states caused further consternation among members. Emerging as a spokesperson for NAWSA, Mrs. Catt called the amendment "a bomb thrown into the national suffrage camp." In contrast, Alice Paul was unfazed by the proposed legislation, commenting that it would not interfere with the Congressional Union's purposes.

Katharine stepped in to condemn the amendment, in an attempt to quell internal dissension and return NAWSA to the primary operational issues it faced. "We have already drafted a resolution that will give aid to states," she reminded members, "and our goal is to bring into the suffrage column at least fifteen more states. Do not forget that we want suffrage to soon be an accomplished fact."

To some members, Katharine's statement of policy seemed clear and realistic. To others, it did little to answer their questions about the proposed antisuffrage amendment's effect on NAWSA policies, particularly its financial allocations. Would it help or hurt NAWSA's cause, they wanted to know. The debate continued into NAWSA's next convention.

Because of her increasing responsibilities in the treasurer's job and as a policy debater, Katharine decided she had to move to New York City, where she rented an apartment a few blocks away from NAWSA's Fifth Avenue offices. The apartment was spare, having almost more people than pieces of furniture. Attending Katharine's needs were a private secretary, a housekeeper, and a cook. To make her environment a bit "homier," she brought pictures of Stanley and their honeymoon travels. She also brought along her files on all the issues dealing with Stanley and the McCormicks, so that any problems could be quickly addressed when the occasion arose.

In addition to her treasurer's responsibilities, the board asked Katharine to head a committee to establish a speaker's bureau and assist in raising additional funds for key state campaigns. The board had already attempted to raise funds but had been largely unsuccessful, and Katharine quickly found the task to be equally frustrating. She had estimated the committee needed $50,000 to conduct active campaigns, but they had less than $13,000. Her report to Shaw would have been humorous had it not been so painfully true: "We collected and distributed in cash a less amount than would be used on the campaign of a city alderman in an off year."[16] Shaw did not immediately respond to Katharine's assessment, but the board wanted to know, "What can you do to increase funds?"

Within days, Katharine returned to the board with a number of plans. She recommended a "self sacrifice" day, where members would sacrifice "something personal" and donate that amount to NAWSA. Amazingly, nearly $10,000 was collected. Another effort, which Katharine labeled "the melting pot," in which high-profile women were each asked to solicit six other people to match their own contributions, proved to be a much less successful enterprise, netting only $3,000. The additional $13,000 collected went to campaigns in New York, New Jersey, and Pennsylvania.

There is evidence to suggest that Katharine freely donated to the committee she headed, but exact amounts are unknown. Some board members spread the jest that Katharine was not only NAWSA's treasurer, but its treasury as well.

Held in Nashville, Tennessee, the 1914 NAWSA convention opened with a long, fractious debate on the pending antisuffrage legislative amendment, with no resolution reached. The debate dramatically heightened board members' distress regarding the resolve of NAWSA leadership and its future strategy. The resulting vote for the following year's officers clearly revealed the delegates' concern.

Three hundred fifteen delegates were entitled to vote. Running for president again, Reverend Shaw received 192 votes, only 62 percent of the total, much less than she had ever before received. Demonstrating their unhappiness with Shaw, one hundred twenty-three delegates chose to abstain. In addition, Jane Addams declined to serve another term as first vice president. Although Mrs. Desha Breckinbridge had been reelected second vice president, she abruptly resigned.

Quickly, a new set of candidates had to be assembled and voted upon. Susan Fitzgerald approached Katharine and asked her to run for office, but Katharine was reluctant to assume any more responsibility. A private meeting was hastily called, which Mrs. Catt, now actively planning to take over NAWSA again, attended. She persuaded Katharine to run for first vice president. If she won the office, Mrs. Catt pointed out, Katharine would be in a position to forward Catt's takeover and serve as Catt's personal lieutenant in future operations. With rapid efficiency, meeting attendees fanned out in all directions, telling delegates that a vote for Katharine was a vote for the reinvigoration of NAWSA, and if they hesitated, NAWSA would likely lose its suffrage reputation to Alice Paul's militants.

Katharine received 55 percent of the vote—many delegates remained uneasy with her—and she was elected first vice president of NAWSA.[17] Some delegates balked at the "backroom" nature of the nomination. Others voted for Katharine believing that this was the first step toward Mrs. Catt's return to NAWSA's presidency. The new board, still headed by Reverend Shaw, included only two previous board members, Katharine and Susan Fitzgerald.

When Katharine gave her final report as treasurer to the assembled delegates, she noted that receipts for the year had exceeded $67,000, although the original budget had been $42,000. Most of the money had been allocated, with the additional funds raised going to campaigning states.

Susan Fitzgerald rose and commended Katharine on her efforts as treasurer, and other delegates applauded as well. Maud Wood Park rose and cited Katharine's reorganization of the office and her successful efforts through various fund-raising activities. Katharine replied with gratitude: "You have all, dear presidents and members of the sixty-three affiliated associations, been most kind to your treasurer; and she has deeply appreciated your forbearance." In the front row, enthusiastically leading the applause for Katharine, sat Mrs. Catt.

Clearly, Katharine was aware of the new job's challenges. Support for Shaw was rapidly eroding, and Katharine judged that Mrs. Catt would likely take over leadership of NAWSA within months, if not weeks. In the meantime, to effect a steady transition, she and the board would have to set and maintain an unswerving course for NAWSA until the new leadership arrived. A Chicago office had recently opened; it would have to be staffed and plans made for its operation. Fieldwork in various states, speeches booked, groups visited and solicited, new suffrage clubs begun—all this had to be organized and implemented. Above all, the lobbying campaign in Congress had to be improved and coordinated. And with the threatened increase in hostilities from Paul's Congressional Union, both against legislators and against NAWSA policies, NAWSA leaders had to be prepared to deal with them.

Katharine had no doubts about the goals nor any illusions concerning the hazards. She knew what would be expected of her and what she had to accomplish. Nevertheless, she was now convinced that a leading role in NAWSA was her rightful place. Katharine had found her voice and her cause.

Fourteen

The suffrage movement appeared to be in confusion. The public was puzzled by newspaper reports of conflict within its leadership. Alice Paul and her Congressional Union had recently separated from NAWSA and pursued a strategy of civil disobedience to embarrass President Wilson and Congress. NAWSA leadership had been in transition, with members attempting to remove Reverend Shaw quickly and replace her with Mrs. Catt. At the same time, NAWSA's financial support was eroding because of its internal disorder; with a national convention about to begin, members doubted that anything meaningful could be accomplished.

Reverend Shaw's surprise reelection as NAWSA president in 1914 only delayed clarification of the organization's leadership and direction. She retained office by a bare majority, many delegates again abstaining to show their displeasure with her leadership. A faction of delegates lobbied for Mrs. Catt to run for president, but she refused their request, at least for the immediate future. No one seemed to know why she had turned down the offer when it was obvious that she wanted the job.

Intense debate concerning NAWSA's direction ended in an impasse. Its only outcome was to further divide NAWSA delegates between pro-Shaw and pro-Catt partisans.

As she assumed her new duties as NAWSA's first vice president, Katharine found herself in a difficult position. She would not have run for the job but for Mrs. Catt's insistence, yet Catt, for reasons unknown, remained on the sidelines. The two had discussed strategy to revitalize the organization, but for the moment, Katharine had to carry the load on her own. While Mrs. Catt expressed confidence in Katharine's understanding of the problems and goals of NAWSA, it would have been helpful had she received more guidance from the person who aspired to be president.

Reverend Shaw's decision to relinquish primary responsibility for NAWSA's daily operations placed increased demands on Katharine. After her reelection as president, Shaw quietly removed herself from the everyday workings of the organization and privately admitted that this would be her last year as president. Katharine now had to assume many of Shaw's responsibilities, as well as her own; and board members depended on her to maintain NAWSA's operations during this period of change. It seemed that everyone waited for Mrs. Catt to take over.

At the same time Katharine sought stability for NAWSA, Alice Paul's strategy of "street militancy" generated a great deal of press coverage. Borrowing its methods from British suffragists, Paul's organization announced its intent to direct all efforts against the political party in power, namely, President Wilson and the Democrats. The goal was to "punish" the entire Democratic Party, even those who might have been sympathetic to the cause. It began its campaign by picketing in front of the White House, to embarrass Wilson and obtain as much public (and police) attention as possible.

Once Paul broke with NAWSA, she moved quickly to seize the initiative and capture the public's imagination as the recognized leader of the national suffrage movement. Her strategy was based on using the media for publicity and the streets to bring her message directly to the people. There was no question that her tactics had infused women's suffrage with renewed interest and excitement at the same time that NAWSA appeared to lack direction.

Yet, even with noisy pickets at the White House gates, Wilson seemed uninterested in, indeed, indifferent to suffrage activities. Persistent heckling during his speeches, however, gained attention for the issue. Wilson's wife and members of his cabinet sent him daily reports of Paul's actions. Wilson concluded that the issue could no longer be avoided and that continued inaction on the suffrage question would not be politically condoned. But which direction would Wilson choose to take?

Meanwhile, Katharine devoted long hours to improving NAWSA's management and operations, if for no other reason than to prepare for Mrs. Catt's assumption of leadership. Away from the national board, she had persuaded Mrs. Catt and Maud Wood Park to meet and discuss business issues and operational decisions.

Katharine's typical day began at 6:00 A.M. By 7:00 she was walking to NAWSA headquarters to open the offices. Arriving at work an hour before anyone else enabled her to attend to logistical problems. Once the staff got to work, most of the day was spent on operational tasks. Katharine usually had her lunch brought in, although at least once a week, a meeting with state officers or legislative personnel required a restaurant setting.

She worked until 8:00 P.M. each evening to communicate with Midwestern and Western offices. By the time she arrived home, the cook had dinner ready—hot if she was on time, cold if she arrived late. Evenings were usually spent examining newspapers and attending to correspondence, particularly those letters dealing with Riven Rock activities.

Some evenings she dined with Julia Roessing, and the two were often seen together strolling Fifth Avenue, stopping in front of store windows to assess the latest fashions. It was reported that Katharine made infrequent visits to the opera and legitimate theater, both of which she enjoyed but for which she had little time. These activities seem to have been her only forms of recreation.

On the basis of discussions with Catt and Park, Katharine moved to reinstitute direct communications between national headquarters and state branches, paying particular attention to those that had pending elections on the women's vote. For these crucial states, she allocated additional funds for publicity and assigned cadres of canvassers to get out the vote. To better coordinate publicity efforts, Katharine took over management of the Press Committee. Brochures, pamphlets, and news releases were prepared and distributed on a timely basis. She introduced a letter-writing campaign designed to deluge newspapers around the country with correspondence promoting NAWSA's accomplishments and goals.

Of particular concern for Katharine was the need for a concerted effort to separate NAWSA from Alice Paul's street tactics. Since her first confrontations with Paul, this had become a serious issue for Katharine. In fact, she was determined to clarify NAWSA's position so well that there would be no question as to which suffrage group was more "true to the cause."

For weeks, Katharine worked with the national treasurer and state auditors to initiate fund-raising campaigns. Not only did increasing expenses have to be covered, but plans to lobby Congress also required a sizable amount of additional money.

With Mrs. Catt and Maud Wood Park, Katharine formed a working team to develop plans for an aggressive lobbying campaign aimed at Congress. The plan was to be put into operation once Mrs. Catt was elected president.

In spite of her closeness with Mrs. Catt during this period, Katharine experienced mixed feelings about her. She viewed this senior suffrage warrior as a mentor and supporter but sometimes speculated that she herself was being used for some "grand purpose." She had observed that Mrs. Catt often switched from reasoned planning to evangelistic preaching, and Katharine found it difficult to separate Catt's zeal from the development of meaningful strategy. Yet Mrs. Catt accepted Katharine's speech writing with minimal changes and leaned on her for the detailed planning necessary to put specific programs into operation. When they worked together, the collaboration was invigorating. When Katharine worked alone on these plans, she often wondered about Mrs. Catt's real intention. Still, events were proceeding so quickly that Katharine found little time to address these questions and doubts.

At this very moment, Mrs. Catt was touring New York to "sell" passage of a women's vote referendum. Catt had agreed to lead the Empire State Campaign Committee and founded the New York State Woman Suffrage Party, an umbrella group to coordinate suffrage organizations, whose efforts to that time had not been united.

Even though the referendum was defeated, Mrs. Catt's efforts created a formidable suffrage organization in New York and substantially increased her following in the one state she believed was most important to winning the eventual vote in Congress. The next national convention was only a few months away, and Mrs. Catt now prepared to make her move to gain NAWSA's presidency.

Along with her usual daily responsibilities, Katharine found herself having to deal with a delicate internal problem involving an old friend and sometime mentor, Mary Ware Dennett. Relations between the national board and Dennett had become strained, not because of any policy disagreement, but rather due to Dennett's increasing involvement in the emerging birth control movement.

A year before, birth control firebrand Margaret Sanger had formed the National Birth Control League, a vehicle to educate women in the use of birth control methods. As a result, Sanger was forced to flee to Europe to avoid prosecution for violating the Comstock laws against distribution of "obscene" literature. While Sanger was out of the country, Dennett and a number of prominent women reorganized the NBCL. Dennett wanted the organization to be more law-abiding. When Sanger returned from her European exile, she was angered by Dennett's takeover and proceeded to wrest control back "from my usurper." Sanger's supreme pleasure at the time was to see newspaper articles freely quoting the term she had coined: "birth control."[1]

Dennett and Sanger were unable to effect a compromise (since they refused to meet to discuss the problem), and each continued with her separate strategy for a number of years, albeit in support of the same cause. In the process, one thing that Dennett taught Sanger was the advantage of soliciting support from society women.

As was common practice among NAWSA board members, Dennett had pledged money to the organization as a portion of her 1915 dues. When she was late in honoring the pledge, Katharine wrote to remind her of the obligation, pointing out NAWSA's critical needs. In response, Dennett not only refused to honor the pledge, but also refused to pay her yearly membership dues. The situation proved difficult for Katharine.

Initially, Katharine approached Dennett in a businesslike but friendly manner, requesting payment. Dennett cited her involvement with the NBCL as the reason she currently had no available funds. They met twice to discuss the situation but came to no agreement. During these meetings, however, Katharine acquired her first information on birth control issues and learned about Margaret Sanger and her challenging activities. Still, Dennett refused to pay dues, leaving Katharine no choice but to recommend her removal from NAWSA's board and membership in the organization. When informed of the possible consequences, Dennett offered no protest, saying her interests were now solely focused on the NBCL.

With no other choice available, Katharine sent a formal letter to Dennett, informing her of her dismissal from NAWSA.[2] Displeased with "the tone" of the letter, Dennett accused Katharine of forcing her out of NAWSA, supposedly because she had refused to support Mrs. Catt. While no evidence suggested this was a conscious plot, rumors insinuated that there had been an effort to purge all anti-Catt members from the national board. Dennett never spoke to Katharine again.

Shortly before the 1915 NAWSA convention opened, Reverend Shaw publicly announced her resignation as president. Immediately, a group of delegates initiated action to draft Mrs. Catt as Shaw's replacement, and the speed with which they acted suggested preconvention planning. Delegates were taken aback, however, when Mrs. Catt hesitated to accept the draft "due to my continuing work with the New York suffrage organization." In reality, Catt's reluctance was feigned. While she publicly stated, "I am a hesitant spectator," Catt privately demanded that, if she accepted the position, she be permitted to select the national board.

Additional support for Mrs. Catt came in the form of a $900,000 bequest from Mrs. Frank Leslie, the wife of a prominent publisher, who had died in 1914. The money given to Mrs. Catt, Leslie's old friend, was to assist in the enfranchisement of women. By this single event, Mrs. Catt gained substantial power in NAWSA, and the organization gained financing when it was most needed.

With almost total unanimity, Carrie Chapman Catt was elected NAWSA president.[3] Prior to the actual balloting, in a gesture of goodwill, Reverend Shaw asked the delegates for the privilege of casting the first vote for Mrs. Catt, "the woman who from the beginning has been my choice, the one who more than any other I long to see occupy the position of your president."[4] Mrs. Catt's handpicked board was also elected, with no opposition. Katharine continued as NAWSA's first vice president and Mrs. Catt's chief aide.

The "secret plan" that Catt, Park, and Katharine had planned was immediately put into operation, its sole purpose to persuade Congress to pass the women's vote amendment. Called "the Winning Plan" by suffrage leaders and "the Front Door Lobby" by the press, it had the initial objective of consolidating and streamlining NAWSA forces for a large-scale offensive aimed at both federal and state levels, since a constitutional amendment required passage by two-thirds of the states. To assume the operational responsibilities of this plan, Katharine had to temporarily relinquish her first vice presidential duties. To replace her, Katharine recommended Julia Roessing, "my friend and companion." Through this arrangement, Katharine could assist Julia whenever it proved necessary.

Katharine's first assignment was to develop plans for states where suffrage had not yet passed but appeared to be near at hand. NAWSA forces in these states were provided funds to wage a vigorous fight during the next election. In states where suffrage was proving difficult to pass, Katharine recommended local efforts. Where suffrage was already law, lobbying pressure was to be applied to the state's congressional representatives in Washington, D.C.

By the middle of 1916, the structure of NAWSA's lobbying committee had been formed and its operation begun. Working with Katharine was Maud Wood Park, the committee's chair; Helen Gardener, the Washington, D.C., insider with links to Wilson's cabinet; and Jeanette Rankin, from Montana, who planned to run for a House of Representatives seat in the fall election. This was a formidable array of women familiar with high-stakes politics.

According to the planning committee, members were to research designated legislators to discover the best arguments by which to obtain their support. In addition, NAWSA individual members led groups from various sections of the country that descended on Washington, D.C., in "relays" to assist the national office and, while there, lobby their state representatives. Other members appeared at Congressional social functions to buttonhole key legislators and "educate" them about the amendment. Legislators complained that they could not turn around without meeting a suffrage representative—exactly what NAWSA had hoped to achieve.

Mrs. Catt's goal was to make legislators believe it was advantageous, if not essential to their own political futures, to support suffrage. The almost daily contacts with members of Congress quickly taught Katharine and her colleagues the intricacies of politics, and their vigorous, relentless lobbying impressed upon Congress NAWSA's steely determination. Newspapers noted that NAWSA appeared to be "on the move" again.

Yet President Wilson hesitated to support suffrage, even though 1916 was an election year. He was put off by the negative publicity generated by Alice Paul's newly named National Woman's Party, particularly their constant attacks on him. Rather than suffrage, most important to him was getting reelected and preparing the country for war. Characteristically, Wilson planned to run on a platform proclaiming "he kept us out of war." At the same time, however, he secretly ordered military training in preparation for the country's entry into the largely European conflict.

Both NAWSA and NWP were frustrated by President Wilson's inattention, as well as continuing Congressional evasion. Still, the passage of the voting rights amendment was in sight. NWP decided to increase its street agitation tactics. NAWSA decided to increase lobbying pressure on members of Congress.

Asked to chair yet another committee to publicize NAWSA's lobbying activities, Katharine was called upon to intensify the organization's efforts in this vital area. Her knowledge of the lobbying campaign and her past experience developing publicity programs made Katharine the obvious choice to run the new committee. Immediately, she hired a number of press professionals and obtained money from the Leslie bequest to begin operations. She made a special effort to report events and "successes" in a nonthreatening manner, in contrast to NWP's aggressive, confrontational publicity; and her strategy appeared to be working.

Katharine recruited Julia Roessing to assist her on this committee. Julia marveled at the hours and days Katharine spent on these assignments. "How do you do it?" she asked. "Don't you often get tired?"

"Of course," Katharine admitted. "But I've accepted these duties; and they must be fulfilled, to the best of my ability."

Katharine's colleagues worried about her health, but no one dared to raise the subject with her, not even Julia. Actually, Julia was beginning to have doubts about her relationship with Katharine, since work conspired to limit their time together.

Mrs. Catt strategically scheduled the NAWSA convention for September, in Atlantic City, just prior to the 1916 national elections. She planned to present "the "Winning Plan" to the delegates to get them energized. Simultaneously, she wanted to use the convention to pressure President Wilson to support suffrage, as well as clearly to distinguish NAWSA from NWP's "stupendous stupidity," as Mrs. Catt often described it. Her timing proved to be excellent.

With women in twelve states now having obtained the vote, with both presidential nominating conventions witness to suffragist parades, and with both parties tentatively endorsing woman suffrage, Mrs. Catt felt it was time to approach President Wilson and, at the same time, give him the political opportunity to express a positive attitude on the issue. She invited both Wilson and the Republican Party candidate, Charles Evans Hughes, to speak at the NAWSA convention. Hughes, campaigning in the West, declined the invitation. Wilson, along with his wife and several Cabinet members, chose to attend.

In front of a large crowd of expectant delegates, Wilson gave a rousing speech recognizing women's "increasingly significant role" and acknowledged suffrage as "something which has not only come to stay but has come with conquering power." Finally, Wilson had endorsed women's suffrage. The delegates cheered loudly, chanting in unison, "Wilson for president."

Later in the convention, Mrs. Catt explained "the Winning Plan" to the delegates and the national press. "Now, all NAWSA efforts will be directed toward passage of the federal suffrage amendment," she declared. When Katharine spoke, she announced that "each state will coordinate its campaigns with the national board to maximize our impact." In addition, she stated, "Money would be available for each state participating in the effort."

Mrs. Catt then concluded the speech making with "a call to arms" and "a victory for NAWSA!" With evangelical zeal, Catt literally shouted at the delegates, her fingers jabbing emphatically, her arms upraised:

If you are to seize the victory, that change must take place in this hall, here and now. The crisis is here, but if the call goes unheeded, if our women think it means the vote without a struggle, if they think other women can and will pay the price of their emancipation, the hour may pass and our political liberty may not be won. The character of a man is measured by his will. The same is true of a movement. Then will to be free![5]

The delegates rose to their feet and cheered and applauded for more than ten minutes. When they departed the convention hall, one could feel their energy and determination.

In a series of workshops, Katharine trained delegates in how to use publicity effectively and how to "sell" the federal amendment. She led seminars to familiarize delegates with details of "the Winning Plan." As explained to the delegates, in implementing the new plan, Mrs. Catt and Maud Wood Park were to be the "outside force." Katharine was assigned to manage NAWSA's internal operations.

In the 1916 national election, Wilson was reelected president, winning all the states that had already granted suffrage to women. Three women had run for seats in the House of Representatives. Jeanette Rankin, a key member of NAWSA's board, won the seat from Montana, the first woman in U.S. history to be elected to Congress. It had been a great victory for the suffrage movement. Ironically, on the day that Rankin was sworn in, Wilson asked Congress to declare war against Germany. NAWSA and the suffrage movement now faced another crucial test—establishing women's credibility and loyalty to the nation.

Prior to Wilson's second inauguration, Alice Paul met with the president, but she reported to the press that the interview had been unsatisfactory. NWP members returned to picketing the White House, somewhat more loudly and aggressively than before. On the day of the inaugural, a thousand protesting NWP members marched around the White House shouting, "Mr. President, how long must women wait for liberty?"

To newspaper reporters, Katharine labeled these activities "scandalous" and "detrimental to the suffrage movement." Immediately following the inaugural festivities, NASWA offered its services to the government if war should be declared. At the time, no one could have imagined how important that offer was to become.

In one of his initial wartime decisions, Wilson selected Newton D. Baker to be Secretary of War. Baker had graduated from Johns Hopkins University in 1892, having been a student in Wilson's classes, where the two became close friends. After receiving a law degree, Baker was appointed secretary to the Postmaster General during Grover Cleveland's administration. As a lawyer practicing in Cleveland, Ohio, Baker was elected city solicitor in 1909 and mayor in 1912, serving two terms. Declining to run for mayor in 1916, Baker had returned to private practice. Shortly after, Wilson asked him to join the Cabinet and head the War Department.

Baker was an outspoken supporter of suffrage. Some historians suggest that Baker was particularly influential in persuading Wilson to support the suffrage movement. In his new position, Baker quickly got women involved in the war effort. He attached a contingent of nurses to the army and sent 11,000 of them to support U.S. troops in France. Announcing this action, Baker declared, "The success of the United States in the making of this war is just as much in the hands of the women of America as in the hands of soldiers in the army."[6]

Baker also created the Council of Defense, an organization to unite and coordinate war efforts at home. To assist in planning council activities, he appointed a committee of nationally prominent women to consider and advise "how the assistance of the women of America may be made available in the prosecution of the war." Three NAWSA board members— Katharine, Mrs. Catt, and Reverend Shaw—were asked to serve on the committee. Their meeting represented the beginning of a public policy partnership between Katharine and Newton Baker that lasted more than thirty years.

The committee's deliberations resulted in the formation of the Woman's Committee of the National Council of Defense, and Katharine was unanimously appointed its chair. As determined by the council, the committee's responsibilities included food conservation, collection of Red Cross supplies, child welfare, and the protection of women in industry. Although the committee had no precedent to guide it and little time to work out procedures, NAWSA's operational structure enabled it quickly to initiate programs throughout the country. This increased visibility and stature, along with significant contributions of time and energy, gained NAWSA substantial recognition and respect.

For Katharine, it meant a new challenge for her skills and a tremendous amount of work. She wrote to Stanley about the new assignment: "I've been made chair of a committee to help the war effort. I know it will mean a great deal of effort on my part, but I'll have plenty of help from my NAWSA colleagues. I'm so enthused about the job, I can't wait to begin."

When the McCormicks heard of Katharine's appointment, they hoped the job would prevent her from visiting Riven Rock and "disturbing" Stanley. In fact, however, a new disturbance was about to upset Stanley's guardianship and demand Katharine's immediate intervention.

Fifteen

Dr. Favill had unexpectedly died. Cyrus Bentley sent Katharine a telegram advising her of Favill's passing and requested an immediate meeting to select a new guardian. On their own, the McCormicks decided that Anita should replace Dr. Favill. With support coming from Bentley and Dr. Meyer, they hoped Katharine could be convinced to accept Anita. They were wrong.

Upon receipt of Bentley's telegram, Katharine wrote him, "I want to recommend Dr. Smith Ely Jelliffe." Dr. Jelliffe was a prominent psychoanalyst and one of a new school believing that chemical reactions in the body were responsible for mental illness. Neither accepting nor rejecting her recommendation, Bentley proposed that, if Katharine was so interested in seeking a doctor, why not Dr. Meyer?

Her reaction to Bentley's suggestion was anything but complimentary to Meyer. "My opinion in regard to Dr. Meyer is that he may be an interesting and perhaps valuable consultant; but that his point of view is too much concerned with his own theories, and that these theories are vague."[1]

She went on with her appraisal of Meyer. "I believe that Dr. Meyer is not the type of mind, nor the kind of person, to grasp in a practical way all sides of a situation; and no one to turn to for sound judgment and advice."

When Bentley shared this information with the McCormicks, Nettie bewailed that "this uncompromising woman has now rejected Anita and Dr. Meyer, and there is no containing her disregard for Stanley." In spite of Nettie's outburst, the ever-diplomatic Bentley asked Katharine why she recommended Dr. Jelliffe.

"He might be very helpful to us," she responded. "We need someone who can be a check on Dr. Hamilton, one on whose judgment we can count." For the first time, Katharine openly expressed concern about Hamilton since reports of his "restlessness" had been periodically sent to her.

Rather than doing the job himself, Hamilton had asked Katharine to dismiss a gardener. In response to the request, she questioned his "executive ability." Instead of replying to Katharine, Hamilton wrote to Bentley, claiming he was "in disfavor with Mrs. McCormick." When Bentley reported this to Katharine, she replied that it was only the result of her efforts "to get him to be more business-like." Why had he contacted Bentley instead of her? she asked.

Under her relentless questioning, Bentley admitted that, in a recent letter, Hamilton had referred to Katharine's latest intrusive visit to Riven Rock, bringing with her "her personal friend" (Julia Roessing). Katharine became incensed at the implication. She defended her visitor as "a companion during my cross-country trips," suggesting to Bentley that Hamilton seemed to be losing interest in Stanley "and we should be prepared to deal with this issue in the near future."

As instructed, Bentley contacted Dr. Jelliffe, who agreed to examine Stanley as a possible first step toward assuming Dr. Favill's position as guardian. This immediately precipitated a discussion among the McCormicks about accepting Dr. Jelliffe, since he was Katharine's choice.

Dr. Jelliffe's report on Stanley's condition reiterated what had already been known. Jelliffe went on to describe Santa Barbara as having "great advantage" over Eastern localities (including Chicago) and argued against moving Stanley at this time. He supported the relationship Dr. Hamilton had established with the patient but questioned Hamilton's skill as a psychoanalyst, suggesting that he was not adequately trained. As regarded McKillop and the corps of personal caretakers, Jelliffe stated, "They deserve the highest recognition for the capable handling of the patient." The McCormicks were not at all pleased with his report and thus did not accept Katharine's choice of him as the new guardian.

Discussion between Katharine and the McCormicks about a replacement for Dr. Favill continued for weeks, but nothing was resolved, other than for Stanley to remain at Riven Rock.

Shortly thereafter, Dr. Hamilton precipitated another crisis when he unexpectedly submitted his resignation, claiming he was "burned out."[2] Nor did Katharine attempt to get him to reconsider the decision. The McCormicks blamed Katharine for Hamilton's abrupt resignation, and they were frightened. Would Hamilton's replacement favor Katharine? How would the change affect "our dear Stanley?" Dr. Favill had not yet been replaced, and Katharine undoubtedly would be difficult to deal with, Anita concluded. The family turned to Cyrus Bentley and Dr. Meyer for assistance.

Katharine believed that a competent doctor had to be found quickly, and it was likely that agreement with the McCormicks would prove elusive. The lack of a replacement for Dr. Favill was a good example of the McCormicks' inability to make a decision, though many candidates had been examined. Dealing with the McCormicks was no easier today than it had been ten years ago, Katharine thought.

Much to everyone's surprise, the search for a physician to replace Dr. Hamilton turned out to be easier than anticipated. Dr. Meyer had recommended Dr. Hoch, who had recently retired from practice in New York and was available. Dr. Hoch had accompanied Dr. Kraepelin at Stanley's 1908 examination and coauthored their report. At the moment, Hoch was preparing a book dealing with the various forms of schizophrenia. "What better person to take over for Dr. Hamilton?" Dr. Meyer advised. What Meyer and Hoch did not share with Katharine and the McCormicks was Hoch's worsening heart condition.

Since Dr. Hoch was not able to take over Stanley's care immediately, Meyer persuaded the guardians to hire Dr. Nathanial Brush on temporary assignment. Dr. Brush had been working at Johns Hopkins Clinic, under Meyer's supervision. He was quickly dispatched to meet Hamilton and learn the Riven Rock routines. Stanley greeted Brush with indifference. Hamilton, however, offered Brush a good deal of guidance, including a warning about "outside interferences" that had often disrupted his work.[3]

A few days later, Dr. Hamilton departed Riven Rock quietly. When he informed the patient of his impending departure, Stanley seemed unable to comprehend what Hamilton was saying. As long as McKillop and Tompkins were there every day to be with Stanley, that seemed to satisfy him. The primate lab was closed, and the apes were sold to various zoos. It would be some years before the laboratory and cages were torn down, totally erasing their previous existence. Today, no one seems able to pinpoint where the lab and cages were once located.

With little debate, Dr. Hoch was hired and, accompanied by his wife, arrived at Riven Rock early in April 1918. A cottage on the estate had been prepared to serve as the couple's home. When Dr. Hoch began his supervision of Stanley, Stanley expressed almost total indifference to him.

From the beginning, it became apparent that Dr. Hoch cared equally little about Stanley and assigned most of the work to McKillop and Tompkins. Hoch spent most of his time working on his book and ministering to his own heart condition. (It was later discovered that Hoch had included a good deal of information about Stanley's condition in his manuscript, citing specific examples of behavior and therapy, much of the material collected before Hoch had arrived at Riven Rock.)

McKillop quickly informed Katharine of Hoch's inattention to Stanley.

Regrettably, she was unable to request his removal so soon after hiring him; her complaints to the McCormicks would have been viewed as another attempt to seize control of Stanley's care. She could, however, recommend alternative tests that might offer new approaches toward his rehabilitation. She immediately wrote to Dr. Hoch and Cyrus Bentley asking for new tests to evaluate Stanley's current condition. Actually, she had once before asked Hamilton and Meyer for these tests, but they had refused her.

"About two years ago I took up very earnestly the general question of having Stanley examined for internal glandular deficiency," she began. In the letter, she described the kinds of tests she would like to have administered and the doctors she would like to hire to conduct the tests. In conclusion, she all but demanded that the tests be conducted: "I believe it to be an important part of the investigation; and until it is done, I shall not feel we have even touched on a very vital side of the general situation."[4]

Armed with Dr. Meyer's support, Hoch declined Katharine's request, saying that he believed "it would disturb Stanley too much." Letters to Meyer and Anita indicated his irritation at Katharine's "interference."

A few months later, Katharine again wrote to Hoch and Bentley, asking for an examination of Stanley from "the physiological standpoint." Having recently become acquainted with the latest advances dealing with the relationship of the body's chemical processes and mental disturbance, Katharine thought that such an examination might uncover new evidence about Stanley's condition. Her actions revealed an interest in the new field of endocrinology and its possible connection to schizophrenia, a route Katharine was to pursue aggressively in coming years.

Again, Dr. Hoch, backed by Meyer, refused Katharine's request. His decision only intensified her concern about Hoch's lack of interest in Stanley, and with McKillop's letters as evidence, she requested that Bentley dismiss Hoch immediately.

After speaking with the McCormicks, Bentley declined Katharine's request, saying that "Dr. Hoch will remain Stanley's physician until further notice." The impasse persisted.

The League of Women Voters

Sixteen

Before Katharine had an opportunity to begin work on the new assignment, Mrs. Catt handed her an article from the National Anti-Suffrage Association that had recently appeared in a New York newspaper. "Answer it as you wish," Catt told Katharine, "but let them know we're no pushovers."

In the article, the National Anti-Suffrage Association accused NAWSA of being pro-German and unpatriotic, and having supposedly solicited funds for their personal use—deliberately inflammatory comments in a big-city newspaper. The president of this organization was Mrs. James W. Wadsworth Jr., wife of the Republican U.S. Senator from New York, a longtime, outspoken opponent of suffrage and a leader in defeating the suffrage resolution in the state the previous year.

To begin with, Katharine called on a number of sympathetic New York legislators to give speeches in Albany defending NAWSA and labeling Wadsworth a "hate-monger." To answer Mrs. Wadsworth, Katharine wrote a letter to the newspaper suggesting that the naive Mrs. Wadsworth had been "misled" and that she would be pleased to receive the woman in NAWSA's offices to share the organization's financial records. While Mrs. Wadsworth never responded to Katharine's offer, letters that followed in the newspaper were all in support of suffrage.

In October, a street parade staged by the NWP in front of the White House turned into a violent confrontation between picketers and hecklers, the latter reported to have been an organized group of men determined to "rough up" and intimidate the marchers. When the women attempted to defend themselves, they were arrested by police and summarily jailed.

While in jail, they received harsh treatment, which the press reported in detail. Judges exacerbated the episode. What had begun as simple misdemeanor jailings turned into sixty-day sentences. In response, the NWP demanded that its members be recognized as political prisoners subjected to "administrative terrorism." Shortly afterward, Alice Paul was arrested and given a seven-month sentence for picketing. Paul was placed in a psychiatric ward and force-fed when she went on a hunger strike. Each day, the press reported on her incarceration with excruciating detail.

On November 14, a "night of terror" was precipitated when thirty-three NWP picketers were arrested for protesting Alice Paul's treatment. Soldiers and police attacked them, destroyed and burned their banners and signs, and dragged them off to jail. In an apparent antisuffrage frenzy, many picketers were beaten, injured, and handcuffed to cell doors. The jailed women began a hunger strike; jailers force-fed them as they were bound and restrained. Photos of this aggressive violence against the jailed women appeared in newspapers across the country. Public opinion against these police actions became so strong that Wilson ordered the police to release the women immediately.

Still, Wilson labeled the NWP "unreasonable radicals." In addition, he attempted to block publicity for the NWP by asking newspapers to downplay the organization's activities. The press, however, called his request "censorship." Wilson also ordered the Secret Service, recently formed to monitor anti-American activity, to watch NWP leaders closely and report on their contacts and actions.

In spite of his comments about the NWP, Wilson wanted to demonstrate his continued support for suffrage. He wrote to Mrs. Catt, telling her that he was aware that NAWSA was not a part of the "street militancy," but he defended the police response to the volatile situation. He could not have made a more egregious tactical error.

Acting as NAWSA's spokesperson, Katharine attacked Wilson's statement, pointing out that, although NWP action was irresponsible, "all women are being unduly prosecuted by law agencies." For its part, the NWP accused the president of supporting police brutality.

On one hand, NAWSA was pleased that Wilson viewed it as a "respectful" organization. Nonetheless, Mrs. Catt and the national board were quite disturbed by the NWP/police confrontations because of their negative influence on key legislators in Congress, and they rushed to reduce the possible damage to their efforts.

Now an open supporter of NAWSA, Secretary of War Newton Baker attempted to convince Wilson that the episodes of jailing and physical abuse of women had caused doubts about his domestic war efforts. How could a president claim to be fighting for democracy in Europe, Baker argued, while at the same time he denied women the vote in the United States?

In December 1917, Mrs. Catt opened NAWSA's convention in Washington, D.C., by reading letters from the Governor of Texas and the mayors of Houston and Dallas, asking NAWSA to consider their cities for the following year's convention. These letters represented the first major recognition of the political attraction of suffrage coming from non–suffrage state leaders. To the assembled delegates, Katharine reported the success of NAWSA's vigorous campaigning, resulting in the passage of the women's vote in five states, including Arkansas, the first southern state to grant suffrage. She also affirmed that New York's second attempt at a resolution permitting the women's vote had proven victorious, thus adding five million women to the electorate. She indicated that the victory in New York sent a clear message to Congress regarding NAWSA's growing influence and the increasing power women would wield in future elections.[1]

Mrs. Catt was unanimously reelected, as was the entire national board; Katharine was again selected first vice president. The featured speaker at the convention was Secretary of War Newton Baker. His speech outlined women's contributions to the war effort and NAWSA's skillful organization in bringing these efforts to fruition. Again, he took the opportunity to reaffirm his belief that men and women should share equally in America's democracy: "Men and women are essentially partners and . . . the democracy which we are trying to establish, is one which recognizes the rights of all the persons in that society."[2]

When Secretary Baker announced the formation of a new committee on women's defense work, he named Katharine chairperson of its War Services Department. When Katharine rose to speak about the new assignment, she described the group's objectives and structure for the coming year. She and Baker had already worked out the functioning of the organization weeks ahead of the announcement.

Mrs. Catt's convention-ending speech served notice to Congress of NAWSA's determination. Pointing in the direction of the Capitol Building, she declared, "Woman suffrage is inevitable—you know it!" Delegates' cheers rocked the auditorium.

Later in December, when Congress convened, it readily acknowledged the impact of the New York State suffrage victory—women now had the opportunity to affect choices for nearly 45 percent of the Electoral College. As a result, the House of Representatives established a Woman's Suffrage Committee (even though Jeanette Rankin, the only woman in the House, was omitted from the panel) and set January 10, 1918, as the date to vote on the suffrage amendment. The day before the vote, Wilson appeared before the House and pled for passage. The House vote barely met the necessary two-thirds majority. The battle for Senate passage now began.

For Katharine, the amendment's initial victory meant the culmination of four years of a total personal commitment to suffrage. How many times had she visited legislators? Two hundred? Three hundred? More? How many meetings had she attended to plot strategy, discuss assignments, argue budgets, and inspire colleagues? Whether she was walking the long marble corridors and sweeping staircases of the Capitol or working in the cramped, dimly lit, uncomfortable NAWSA offices, Katharine's circumscribed world seemed an abstract universe, pompous and preposterous at the same time. It had been a unique battlefield upon which Katharine and her associates had fought a vigorous, bruising war, men against women, with men having held the distinct advantage. But now, victory was in sight.

However, it also appeared that Katharine's ongoing commitments had affected her relationship with Julia Roessing. Unexpectedly, Julia resigned her position in NAWSA and returned to her home in Pittsburgh, claiming fatigue and family problems. Her abrupt departure likely had more to do with the increasingly strained nature of her intimacy with Katharine.

During the summer of 1918, the NWP's activities fueled further antisuffrage protests. When the Senate failed to pass the suffrage amendment—it was defeated by only two votes—the NWP again picketed the White House, which engendered further confrontations with police. In contrast, NAWSA focused its attention on a group of key senators and, prior to the general election, lobbied them to support suffrage. They offered a not-so-veiled threat—that if the reluctant senators did not vote for suffrage, NAWSA would endorse their opponents. The position was as militant an action as NAWSA had ever undertaken.

When Congress shifted its attention back to domestic issues after the war ended, suffrage became its top priority. Thus, the NWP increased White House picketing; NAWSA increased its visits with senators. Before leaving for the Paris peace conference, Wilson prodded Congress to pass the amendment quickly, because the Democrats had lost their majority in the Senate and would relinquish power in March. Nonetheless, a coalition of conservative Southern Democrats and Republicans initiated a number of delaying tactics and prevented a vote.

Through her association with Secretary Baker, Katharine had urged Wilson to include women in the American delegation at the peace conference in Versailles. She argued that "peace is a concern for both men and women." No women, however, were present at the Versailles conference; Wilson had ignored the request.

Due to the war and its conclusion, no NAWSA convention had been scheduled for 1918. Instead, the meeting was delayed until March 1919. NAWSA selected St. Louis, Missouri, because of its central location. The venue was designed to attract as many national representatives as possible. In addition to NAWSA members, observers from other American and Canadian women's organizations were invited to attend. The national board agreed to call this 1919 meeting the Jubilee Convention, not only to celebrate the approaching passage of the amendment, but also to celebrate the fiftieth anniversary of the national suffrage movement.

At the same time that preparations for the convention were being made, Mrs. Catt and Katharine were deep in discussion about the future of NAWSA after the women's vote had been attained. Both agreed the organization should continue, but in what form? And what goals should such an organization promote in order to represent all women?

For weeks they struggled to develop the outline of a structure to succeed NAWSA. The challenge was intimidating. How could they hold together a suffrage army of two million women and focus them on a new agenda? How could they reorient attitudes in light of historical experience, based on the feelings, habits, and expectations of all classes of women? The more Mrs. Catt and Katharine deliberated such questions, the more overwhelming the task seemed to be.

Yet they succeeded in putting together an outline for the proposed organization, seeking input from board members but primarily hoping for their agreement to the plan. After considerable debate, the board agreed that, temporarily, the new organization would be an auxiliary of NAWSA, led by the NAWSA board, until further clarification of the issues and structure was achieved.

However, the national board encountered difficulties when it sought to transform the common goal of suffrage, for which all had diligently worked, into a commitment for more limited, specific goals. Each individual, it seemed, had her own list of objectives. This forced the group to develop a set of procedures to reconcile disputes, although that effort took a sizable emotional toll. Some members walked out, because they had no interests beyond suffrage; some boycotted the meetings; still others accused Mrs. Catt of imposing her personal views on everyone else. Mrs. Catt and Katharine quickly realized that no new organization, however formulated, would capture the imagination, win the loyalty, and reflect the interests of a majority of suffragists. Only the most active, ambitious, and politicized of women would entertain new collaborative goals, but getting them to participate would require a heroic effort.

Still, since initial reactions to the new organization were positive, the board voted to continue planning for NAWSA's eventual transition. In fact, two goals were generally agreed upon: to promote the political education of newly enfranchised women, and to establish procedures that would give women an opportunity to take part in the governing process. Other goals were put off to a later date. After some debate, the board chose a tentative name for the new body: the National League of Women Voters. Their stated purpose: a country in which all voters speak English, read their own ballots, and honor the American flag.

In a rousing, pulpit-pounding speech to the convention, Mrs. Catt asked the rhetorical question: "Why should there be a League of Women Voters?" She challenged the assembled suffragists to "stay on the battlefield as an army of women citizens." She urged them to "finish the fight" to "reconstruct the nation." In closing, she implored the delegates to "improve and extend civic education to create an informed electorate."[3] Applause and cheers from the delegates were noticeably light.

While the delegates overwhelmingly adopted the recommendation that NAWSA be dissolved when its work was finished and that a new organization be launched, many departed the conference believing their work had been done and they could now go home, exhausted but successful. Mrs. Catt's speech had succeeded in galvanizing those who fully embraced the new body, but it also drove away many who were no longer motivated to continue the battle. The issue would become even more fractious at future meetings.

During one of the sessions, Katharine, as chairperson, reported on NAWSA's war service programs.[4] She had organized the group into four sections: Thrift, Food Production, Industrial Protection for Women, and Americanization. Branches of each section had been formed by NAWSA's state groups, with specific people selected to liaise with national headquarters. The success of these sections persuaded the War Department to add two more sections—selling liberty bonds and creating an overseas hospital service.

As an example of women's contributions to the war effort, Katharine reported on the success of training women for agricultural work. "Early in the spring of 1917, a number of organizations undertook to register and place women who could and would be agricultural labor. A Woman's Land Army was created in thirty states, and more than 15,000 were placed on the land."

Katharine also shared an interesting anecdote dealing with her attempt to get women appointed to a work committee headed by Samuel Gompers, president of the American Federation of Labor.

"I'm pleased to see that you've supported laws regulating the conditions and hours of work for women," Katharine had told Mr. Gompers.

"Thanks for the compliment, Mrs. McCormick," responded Gompers. "We're doing what we can for women."

"Then why don't you have a woman representative on your committee?" Katharine asked.

"I'm sorry," he replied, "but our policies bar women from committees."

"Then your policies ought to be changed to reflect the new roles of women in the labor movement," Katharine suggested. Gompers said he would look into it.

Katharine also reviewed the successes of the Overseas Hospital Service. "In conjunction with the dispatch of Army nurses to Europe by Secretary of War Newton Baker," she related, "a women's auxiliary was sent to assist nurses, administer hospitals, and supervise purchase of

supplies. Twelve thousand women were recruited and trained to participate in this program."

In response to Katharine's report, delegates called from the floor for a
resolution to commend Katharine for her War Service Department accomplishments. The resolution read: "From May, 1917, to the middle of March,
1919, the committee labored unceasingly to perform its great task. There
can be no doubt that the splendid war work of the suffragists has been a
principal factor in the rededication of the Federal Amendment. To Katharine Dexter McCormick, we offer our thanks and admiration for her leadership and accomplishment on behalf of the women of America."[5]

The delegates rose to their feet, applauded, and sang "For She's A Jolly
Good Fellow." Katharine, somewhat embarrassed and taken aback by the
ovation, nodded her thanks and retreated from the podium.

The following day, with Katharine again serving as chair, delegates debated long and hard before voting to accept a draft constitution for the
league.[6] Under Katharine's guidance, fourteen resolutions, all but one,
were passed by the delegates. The resolution defeated (number 5) was for
approval of a national memorial to the soldiers of '17 (1917) and '76 (1776).
It was rejected outright, because women serving in those wars had received no recognition.

At the convention's final session, a name for the new organization was
agreed upon. According to press accounts, however, the matter was not
resolved by the delegates themselves but rather by representatives of six
major metropolitan newspapers, who voted unanimously for the "National League of Women Voters." The name was then officially adopted
by the delegates. Some believed it was no coincidence that, in a number
of earlier speeches, Mrs. Catt had alluded to the new organization by that
name.

In the convention's final moments, a committee was selected to develop
plans and procedures for the 1920 convention. Katharine, along with Mrs.
Jenkins (Wyoming) and Mrs. Stuart (Illinois), were appointed to lead the
committee. Katharine wired Julia, asking if she would be interested in
assisting the committee; Julia replied in the affirmative.

At the conclusion of the convention, Katharine returned to Boston to
visit briefly with her mother but primarily to rest. Exhausted from months
of campaigning and the intense atmosphere at the convention, Katharine
believed she needed some time to reflect on her activities and their implications for her own future. While she had been exhilarated by the formation
of the league that she and Mrs. Catt had single-handedly produced, she
harbored doubts that its purposes would ever be fulfilled.

Mrs. Catt and a number of her enthusiastic followers wished to promote
the league as a politically oriented organization. Katharine preferred to
see more emphasis on social services. She and Mrs. Catt would have to
iron out their differences of opinion and of direction. In the meantime,

Katharine spent a refreshing week in activities having nothing to do with either suffrage or Riven Rock.

Yet no sooner had the convention closed than controversy surfaced about the league and its avowed political orientation. Some politicians and members of the press openly expressed their reservations about the league, believing it would compete with existing political parties. Unfortunately, Mrs. Catt's response to those accusations only made the accusers more suspicious when she declared, "The League is political but not partisan."

Arguments about the league became even more rancorous when, in April 1919, the Women's Republican Club of New York passed a resolution denouncing the League of Women Voters as "encouraging dissension between men and women voters whose interests are identical." Further, the resolution declared that a "non-partisan" party would use its power "regardless of party principles of government" and would be a "menace to our national life."[7] The text of the resolution was sent to all suffrage leaders in the enfranchised states and all major newspapers.

While the actions of the NAWSA convention appeared to threaten political party members in general, it was a group of women who sought actively to block the league. They were led by Ruth Hanna McCormick of Illinois. Ruth Hanna, daughter of the famous Mark Hanna, New York Republican political boss, had married a cousin of Cyrus McCormick.[8] A few years previously, she had served on NAWSA's board. Now she was vehemently fighting its successor. Because the Republican Party had supported suffrage earlier than the Democrats and believed it had much to gain by passage of the amendment, Ruth Hanna McCormick believed existence of the league would significantly dilute that Republican advantage. Enter Katharine into the fray. The press thrilled to the combat: McCormick versus McCormick. Contentious challengers from the same celebrated family!

Katharine declared Ruth McCormick's beliefs "misplaced" and suggested that her party affiliation "clouded her views of the League." Ruth countered by claiming the "interests of the nation were inseparable from the interests of her party."

Katharine responded, "The League happens to be everything you think it is not, and none of the things you think it is. What interests me is your willingness to announce that you are at war with those who won you the vote."[9]

Unfortunately, Ruth McCormick's personal animosity toward the league led to a further lack of understanding and increased hostility that was not to be allayed for many years. Even some women from the Democratic Party found fault with the new organization. Mrs. Catt railed at these women's opinions.

"We are not radicals," she declared. "We women are going to be the pudding sticks inside each party, pushing it forward to do the right thing."

Some were offended by her comments. Others brushed them off as typical "Catt-calls." In any case, Mrs. Catt was not doing a very good job of selling the league.

Katharine viewed these internal conflicts as examples of old habits and loyalties being forced to fit into more constricted civic responsibilities, and she foresaw a long battle to legitimize the league. And what of her own goals, to see the league more involved in community service and public health? Katharine had her doubts. The challenge appeared daunting, and Mrs. Catt was not helping with her portentous declarations.

When the league's initial committee meeting convened, debate immediately centered on how authority would be organized and allocated. A decision had to be made. But who should have the power to make it? No one could agree. They turned to Mrs. Catt for direction.

First, without debate, Mrs. Catt designated a committee to draft a constitution for the league, a unilateral action that was met with incredulity. "But what about the constitution that was adopted by the delegates in St. Louis three months ago?" asked a puzzled Katharine. Mrs. Catt responded that "the constitution created at the last convention was only for the enfranchised states." Katharine, among others, disagreed. "I and others believed it was passed with all states in mind," she insisted.

Mrs. Catt disputed Katharine's remarks. She believed the constitution still remained to be "worked on." She further complicated the discussion by raising questions about NAWSA's continuing existence, the league's relationship with the IWSA (of which Catt was president), and NAWSA's current financial responsibilities. Again, Katharine expressed surprise at Mrs. Catt's questions, since she believed these issues had been resolved at the convention. Nonetheless, Mrs. Catt's ruling prevailed. For the first time, Katharine entertained serious doubts about Mrs. Catt's agenda and her own commitment to the league.

Her loyalty was shaken even more when, as a member of the league Committee on Social Hygiene, she made a recommendation to sponsor a session on "social morality." Without hesitation, Mrs. Catt expressed her disapproval of such a session because it "might raise" controversial issues like birth control and contraception. Katharine pushed to have the session included in the convention agenda, but Mrs. Catt countered that delegates from the last convention had not authorized it, precisely the reverse of her argument in support of a new constitution.

Katharine was not at all pleased with Mrs. Catt's disagreement. It seemed obvious to her that Catt did not want to deal with such fundamental issues, opting instead to promote her own program. Again, Katharine found herself disturbed with her mentor's antagonistic posture.

Little regarding the constitution was decided at this meeting. The group did acknowledge, however, that once the goal of suffrage was achieved, interest in the league would likely decline and potentially weaken the new organization's influence. Due to this possibility, the members voted to keep the league a nonpartisan body and promote political education. How that goal was to be accomplished was not discussed.

Frustrated by the inability of the committee to resolve league issues, Katharine returned to planning the 1920 convention, with the assistance of Julia Roessing. It was to be designated the Victory Convention, ostensibly the last for NAWSA, and the first for the League of Women Voters. While Katharine shared her belief in the new organization with Julia, her enthusiasm to assist Mrs. Catt had greatly diminished.

Her thoughts were abruptly rechanneled when she received a telegram from Riven Rock. Dr. Hoch had suffered a severe heart attack and was near death.

Who would replace Hoch, she wondered. The process of selection would surely become a challenge, as it had many times before. Quickly boarding a train for Pasadena, Katharine now had five days to formulate plans before meeting with Cyrus Bentley and Anita.

Seventeen

Heavy rain was falling when Katharine arrived in Pasadena. Umbrella in hand, the ever-reliable McKillop awaited her as she stepped down from the train.

"Dr. Hoch died yesterday," he reported solemnly.

During the long car trip to Riven Rock, McKillop told Katharine about Hoch's last days. After his heart attack, Hoch had drifted into a coma and never awoke from it, his wife and a local doctor at his side during the final hours. No one else had been in attendance, nor was anyone else informed of the event. To make sure that Stanley would not see the ambulance that carried away Hoch's body, the removal took place late at night. Later, McKillop informed Stanley of Dr. Hoch's fatal heart attack. Stanley merely shrugged his shoulders, apparently unaffected by the news.

McKillop also told Katharine a bizarre story about a new system of written communication that Bentley and Anita were hastily composing. They had become very concerned that outsiders—"snoopy newspaper reporters," McKillop suggested—might uncover recent events at Riven Rock. The previous week, he reported, inquisitive reporters had been rebuffed at the gate following a rumor that "someone" on the estate was near death.

To guard against what Bentley and Anita believed to be "insidious intruders" (Bentley's words) and the possible revelation of "sensational events" (Anita's words) at Riven Rock, they decided to formulate a code for use when sending letters and cables between family members, lawyers, and doctors. As McKillop related the story, Katharine thought the entire exercise was ridiculous.

McKillop had been correct. When Katharine arrived at her Santa Barbara hotel, a breathless Bentley was first to greet her. "We need to convene immediately, Mrs. McCormick. Anita and I have an urgent issue to discuss with you." Even before she was able to retire to her room, Bentley dragooned her into the lounge where Anita was waiting, papers spread across the table before her.

During the meeting, Katharine was surprised to discover the two plotters more interested in setting up their code system and obtaining her agreement to use it than in finding a replacement for Dr. Hoch. She tried to bring up the critical situation facing them, but she was unable to deflect attention away from Bentley and Anita's "urgent" task. In Katharine's view, they had concocted an elaborate diversion to avoid dealing with the "Hoch problem."

Having already worked many hours on their project, Bentley and Anita produced a long list of words used in usual correspondence and carefully selected alternative meanings for them. For example, "ancestor" stood for Stanley, "mitigate" meant Riven Rock, and "arbitrator" identified Katharine. Code words had also been created for all members of the McCormick family; all doctors; cities; and even specific emotions, like "sadness" and "excitement." Katharine was taken aback by their intense preoccupation and earnestness. Unwilling to share in the exercise, she politely excused herself and retired to her room.

Later, when Bentley attempted to compose a letter to Dr. Meyer explaining the current crisis, it took him nearly the entire day to prepare it. As the hours passed, Katharine again reminded Bentley of the need to discuss the selection of a new doctor for Stanley, but she was unable to distract him.

The following morning, Katharine dispatched two messages: one to Bentley, saying, "I will not agree to the use of your newly fashioned code system," which effectively killed it; and the other to Dr. Meyer, requesting a recommendation for a doctor to replace Hoch.[1] Raising a sensitive issue with Meyer, Katharine asked about her visiting Stanley, reminding him that Dr. Hoch had delayed her request six months previously because it might "introduce unnecessary complications." Meyer quickly cabled her that "no decision on this issue should be made until a new doctor is installed."

When Dr. Nathanial Brush, the physician who had temporarily stepped in during the transition from Hamilton to Hoch, heard that Dr. Hoch had died, he wrote Dr. Meyer, asking to be returned to Riven Rock to become Stanley's care manager. Meyer, eager to settle the resident doctor situation with as little fuss as possible, forwarded the letter to the guardians along with an affirmative recommendation.[2] In a matter of days, Brush met with

Katharine, Bentley, and Anita. All agreed that Brush would make a reasonably good replacement, although Katharine pointed out his lack of
psychiatric knowledge and experience. No matter to the McCormicks; it
was an easy solution to an otherwise difficult appointment.

Early in 1920, Dr. Brush was officially hired to take over as Riven Rock's
physician-in-charge. In what appeared to be a generous offer, Dr. Meyer
volunteered to counsel Brush "if and when he requested it." Katharine,
however, had no inkling that Anita had hired Meyer as a consultant (apart
from his consultant role regarding Stanley) to "oversee" Brush's activities.
Nor were any of the guardians aware that Meyer directed Brush to send
him monthly reports, not only those dealing with Stanley's condition, but
also others regarding all activities at Riven Rock, including copies of letters received and sent by family members.[3]

Dr. Brush's reacquaintance with Stanley seemed to begin well. Brush
found Stanley more conversational, coherent, and responsive to people.
He was writing letters, listening to music, and watching movies. What
had previously been Dr. Hamilton's offices had been converted into a
theater, its walls entirely lined with cork, with a raised projection booth
installed at one end of the building. These were activities that Dr. Hoch
had casually instituted to "fill Stanley's time."

Brush wrote Meyer confidently: "The meeting far exceeded anything
that I had thought possible; it was just as natural in every respect as one
could hope for. The two years of my absence have been marked with an
abeyance of all the old traits so prominent in 1917." Meyer warned him
not to be taken in by these gestures of friendliness, "as they may be of a
temporary nature only."

Meyer was correct in his prediction. Within two weeks of Brush's arrival, Stanley attempted a series of escapes from Riven Rock. While most
were thwarted before they could be carried out, one of them generated a
good deal of public interest.

When a grocery delivery truck leaving Riven Rock drove through the
gate, Stanley had jumped onto its rear bumper. After the truck had moved
beyond the gate, he jumped off and ran into the woods. Immediately, an
alarm went off, alerting Brush and the other employees. McKillop ran to
follow Stanley. Tompkins reported what had occurred, and various
groups, each armed with restraints, fanned out in different directions from
the gate in pursuit of Stanley. It took several hours to find him. A neighbor
notified local newspapers of the escape. When Stanley was found hiding
behind a rock not far from the gate, he willingly returned to the estate,
laughing all the way at his "keepers" for having outsmarted them. The
newspapers reported Stanley's escape—"Madman on the Loose" was
their headline—and demanded he be guarded more carefully to avoid
any "unpleasant episodes" with neighbors since, of course, he was an
"unstable person."

Dr. Brush was alarmed by the adventure, having been taken completely by surprise. He cabled Meyer for advice. He also wrote the guardians regarding Stanley's exploits. Their reactions were typical. Katharine expressed a good deal of concern—"Stanley could have been injured," she wrote—and suggested that Dr. Brush had clearly demonstrated his inability to deal with Stanley. The McCormicks did everything in their power to suppress newspaper coverage of the episode, particularly to prevent the story from becoming news beyond Santa Barbara. Cyrus Bentley was immediately dispatched to get "a close look" at the situation.

Bentley's visit appeared to stabilize the situation, as did the precaution of locking Stanley in his room whenever deliveries were made to Riven Rock. When Brush wrote to Meyer, he seemed relieved. "His visit has been most helpful in many ways, and I feel confident that from now on we will be all working together for the one cause."

A particularly sensitive issue Brush brought up in his letter gained immediate attention from Meyer, that of Katharine's letters to Stanley possibly having a "negative effect" on the patient. Brush suggested that "careful attention had to be paid to their content, for fear it might upset Stanley for some unknown reason."[4] Meyer agreed and told Brush he would discuss this issue with the guardians.

When Katharine heard of this accusation, she at once labeled it "censorship" and questioned Brush as to why he had made the recommendation. She quickly discovered from Brush that a form of censorship was already occurring. When Stanley dictated letters to her, she had been receiving edited versions, since many of his incoherences had been excised. Letters Stanley had been receiving from Katharine had been read to him by Dr. Brush and then filed away. Certain passages, those Brush considered to be potentially disruptive, were never shared with Stanley.

Katharine was incensed and demanded that the procedure cease immediately. "If I find that Dr. Brush has in any way manipulated these letters one more time, he shall be removed!" She produced two letters recently received from Stanley and demanded to know what had been omitted from them, as well as from those that she had written him.

None of the letters were ever produced; however, Bentley apologized for "the inconvenience" and assured Katharine that no censorship would ever occur again.[5] Although Katharine remained suspicious that some kind of censorship continued, she refrained from raising the issue, at least for the time being.

Brush now sent Meyer weekly reports recounting Stanley's disruptive behavior. In letters to the guardians, however, he did not report these violent outbursts, food throwing, exhibitionist masturbation, and long periods of self-imposed silence. It had quickly become obvious to Meyer that Dr. Brush was not equipped to deal with these episodes and that Brush's efforts to care for Stanley would be, at best, for maintenance only.

None of Brush's numerous reports suggested that therapeutic measures were being taken. Since Meyer was primarily responsible for recommending Brush to the position, he had to do something to defuse the potentially explosive situation, and to deflect criticism of his own less than effective oversight.

The guardians were totally unaware of the situation at Riven Rock until they and Dr. Meyer met in Chicago to review the new yearly budget. Meyer brought up Dr. Brush's limited psychiatric training, but he mentioned none of the recent events in detail. No one suggested getting rid of Brush—that would have precipitated another crisis in the apparently perennial saga of finding doctors for Stanley—but Katharine took the opportunity to recommend that endocrine testing and psychoanalysis be considered for Stanley. To her surprise, the group generally agreed that it might be worthwhile to pursue such efforts. As usual, however, the guardians were undecided as to how or with whom to initiate them. Dr. Meyer offered his expertise regarding the best tests to use and the doctors best qualified to conduct them. Due to her ongoing suspicions about the doctor's motives, however, Katharine refused to acknowledge Meyer's suggestions.

Debate regarding the use and benefits of psychoanalysis were even more inconclusive, with Meyer challenging each of the alternatives discussed. In apparent desperation, Katharine declared that she would investigate the various psychoanalytic schools herself and, on the basis of her research, make a recommendation to the group. Everyone seemed satisfied with her proposal, if for no other reason than that it delayed the necessity to make a decision.

In reality, Katharine had other important reasons for making this recommendation. Recent conversations with Julia and her mother, as well as her own perplexity with regard to causes and commitments, had persuaded her to consider undergoing therapy herself.

A number of obvious issues appear to have been weighing on Katharine's mind heavily enough that she believed a professional perspective might assist her in clarifying her feelings and motivations. The tumultuous events of the past few years—the suffrage movement, the NAWSA/NWP conflict, her recent suspicions about Mrs. Catt's agenda and the direction of the league—had all appeared to "pile up" in her mind. An ongoing concern was Stanley and the continual disputes with the McCormicks; Katharine nervously waited for the next crisis to occur. Finally, Katharine's relationship with Julia weighed on her heart and mind. She had not really decided whether their friendship was offering emotional support or not.

Katharine had become a ravenous reader of medical journals and felt comfortable in managing diagnosis-related matters. She had convinced herself that this was a pivotal point in her life. She was forty-five years old, had successfully carved a career for herself in causes on behalf of women, and had sworn a duty to Stanley, but Katharine believed she was entering a time of transitions. What would they bring? What direction would they take? To her mother she confided, "Analysis could very possibly offer clearer direction and purpose."

During the next several months, Katharine visited four psychiatrists to interrogate them about their methods. She finally settled on the theory and techniques of Dr. Abraham A. Brill, at the time one of the country's eminent Freudian practitioners and spokesmen. She told Julia she had chosen Dr. Brill because he was "brisk and business-like."

Dr. Brill

Eighteen

"Normality is my goal for patients," Dr. Brill declared to Katharine. "The normal, average life. That is quite an achievement, you know."[1]

"Could my life ever be considered normal?" Katharine queried.

"Do not call it subnormal until you can understand it," Brill answered.

In 1889, at the age of fifteen, Abraham A. Brill had immigrated to the United States, arriving from Austria-Hungary with three dollars in his pocket. As quickly as he could manage, he had fled from his parents, an uneducated and authoritarian father who often beat him, and a mother who fervently wanted him to become a rabbi. Brill had rejected his religious faith and sworn never to succumb to what he described as a domestic dictatorship. Poor but driven to better himself, Brill took a variety of menial jobs to work his way through New York University. Seeking to take entrance exams at Columbia University's Medical School, he worked for a year at two jobs to obtain the necessary funds and passed the exams in exemplary fashion.

In 1905, Brill graduated from Columbia with a degree in medicine. Interning in hospitals and clinics for two years, he saved enough money to attend Vienna's Burgholzi University for a year, studying psychiatry. There he discovered Sigmund Freud and, under the direction of the already eminent professor, encountered the school of psychiatry he sought. Brill decided to become both a practitioner of and a spokesperson for Freud's work; he translated his mentor's writings into English, making them available in the United States for the first time. In 1911, Brill founded the New York Psychoanalytic Society, based on the belief that only trained physicians were equipped to practice psychoanalysis. By 1920, Brill had developed an outstanding reputation, both as Freud's champion in the United States and as a renowned therapist whose techniques overturned many of the traditional practices in the profession.[2]

After evaluating a number of psychiatrists, Katharine selected Dr. Brill as "a vehicle to better understanding" for herself and, through her, for Stanley. Thus committed, she visited Brill regularly several times a week for more than six months. Only Julia knew of her decision.

Within a matter of a few sessions, Brill had identified three issues he believed Katharine needed to explore: her relationship with Stanley and the McCormicks; her motivation to crusade for women's rights; and her personal relationships with other women.

"Of course, they are intertwined," he indicated, "but we shall attempt to give each one meaning and understanding." Katharine's therapeutic experience was about to begin.

"Was your marriage to Stanley ever sexually consummated?" Brill asked bluntly.

"Do you mean did we ever engage in sexual intercourse?" Katharine replied, somewhat defensively. "Because, early in our honeymoon, we did often."

"No, Mrs. McCormick," he pursued. "I mean did Stanley achieve orgasm at any time?"

"As far as I know, he did not," she answered.

"Do you have any idea why he was unable to perform?" Brill asked.

Katharine recited all she knew about the McCormick family, how Stanley had been raised, his failure as an artist and as a businessman, and the courtship, honeymoon, and final days of their companionship prior to his hospitalization.

"Stanley was born into a family that rivaled the dynasties of the Rockefellers, Vanderbilts, and Carnegies at the turn of the century," Katharine began. "The family had already had its share of nervous problems." Mary Virginia had gone insane at age nineteen; a cousin, Medill, was unsuccessfully treated by Carl Gustav Jung and later committed suicide; Harold, Stanley's older brother, had undergone years of periodic analysis, with unknown results.

"Stanley had been a lifelong introvert with an artistic flair," Katharine explained, "which was one of the reasons I became attracted to him." She pointed out, however, that she had not known of his earlier "illnesses" and "nervous conditions" until after they were married. "I believe I was never told of Stanley's problems because the McCormicks wanted Stanley married to get out of caring for him and to remove him from the business."

Katharine knew of Stanley's sexual problems because he had revealed them to her on frequent occasions, but she believed them to be a form of guilt and self-doubt brought on by his mother's overbearing presence. "I believed if I could remove him from his mother's influence, he could live a normal life, like a normal man. Obviously, I was wrong; and persuading Stanley to perform his sexual duties strained our relationship all the more."

"And how do you judge your marriage today?" Brill asked.

"I view it as an unfortunate venture," Katharine acknowledged with resignation.

As Brill further explored Katharine's feelings regarding the decision to marry Stanley, there were several occasions when she wept so deeply that conversation was interrupted. The forbearing analyst allowed Katharine all the time she needed to vent her frustrations and sadness.

As Brill meticulously explained, Katharine's marriage situation had become a raging battleground between two mothers, Nettie and Katharine, to gain control over Stanley. Katharine readily admitted her wish to protect Stanley from his irrational family.

"But was it also a way to avoid sexual intimacy," Brill prodded, "while maintaining the marriage?"

Katharine found Brill's question difficult to answer. She resisted Brill's implication, referring often to her mother's desire for her to produce a Dexter heir.

"Then, you were defying your mother as well," Brill interjected.

Once her motivations were clearly delineated by Brill, Katharine could trace her initial, almost naive behavior toward Stanley during their turbulent courtship. "You wanted to battle the McCormicks for possession of Stanley," Brill declared, "and once you won, you took over his mother's role. Stanley was sufficiently confused at the time, and his reasoning could not cope with the perception he would be having sexual relations with his 'mother.'"

Unsettled, Katharine alluded to her many efforts to offer Stanley approval. "But he also feared your disapproval, Mrs. McCormick. You were just too strong-willed and self-confident," Brill pointed out. "In that way, Stanley had perceived you and Nettie to be alike."

"So the more we fought over him," Katharine added in recognition, "the more Stanley became confused."

"And that is why he wanted to leave both of you behind, why he escaped into illness. It was his protection against the demands being made of him."

For weeks, they worked on Katharine's motivations, not only to remain married to Stanley, but also to seek a cure for his illness. While Brill suggested that Katharine wished to assume the role of "mother" rather than "lover," he also assured her that she was not entirely to blame for Stanley's condition, as the McCormicks continuously maintained. Recent research, he indicated, revealed that schizophrenia often began during adolescence and that Stanley had exhibited the first outward signs of the disease in college, well before his marriage. Obviously, Stanley's long-enduring relations with Nettie and his siblings only aggravated the illness. "Your behavior toward him seemed to be the catalyst," Brill explained, "that precipitated the breakdown. I doubt that Stanley will ever recover as long as he remains at Riven Rock," he opined.

Brill also examined Katharine's increasingly "mothering" compensatory behavior over the years. Not surprisingly, it had begun after the deaths of Wirt and Samuel, primarily due to her guilt at their deaths and, later, her increasing desperation to "save" Stanley from a similar fate. "But," Brill continued, "instead of using personal sensitivity and loving care, you used your scientific training to manage conflicts and problem solving."

Katharine admitted she had attempted to overwhelm the McCormicks and Stanley's doctors with her scientific knowledge, and she still did, using science to "prove" her opinions. "It was my only protection against male authority," Katharine explained. "It was also," Brill added pointedly, "the means to block the deep emotional feelings you had for the loss of all three of 'your men.'"

As interpreted by Brill, Katharine had perceived the McCormicks as representing "everything irrational in life." Her exclusion from seeing Stanley back in 1907 had only strengthened her resolve and determination to remain involved in his care, and to control his environment and the decisions made by his doctors. "That you made demands of men, professionals in their own fields, and gained success, gave you confidence to 'push limits' even further," Brill explained, "even though they might extirpate the situation."

Still, Katharine sought to defend her feelings to Brill about the failures of men, particularly as they attempted to "keep women down." The doctor countered by accusing her of "liking" crises, so she could display her talents and abilities by solving them. "The fact that you function so well as a leader in the suffrage movement has been due to the crises you resolved and the admiration you received from both colleagues and enemies," Brill explained.

Nonetheless, Brill explained, admiration was not love. Under intense questioning, Katharine admitted having experienced three "love affairs" in her life—with her father, her brother, and Stanley—"and they all met with tragedy. Love had been stolen from me," she cried.

Katharine went on to reveal that she had, for years, harbored anger and frustration toward the men who "robbed" her of love. Due to these experiences, she had decided that men could not be trusted; they could not be supportive, nor were they as strong as they boasted.

"So, then," Brill concluded, "the fact that you could 'be like a man,' excel in a man's school, become a scientist, organize and administer with masculine efficiency, and handle great sums of money expediently, proved you needed no man for support."

"Nor do I need them now," Katharine quickly responded. "Maybe even less than before."

"Nevertheless," Brill cautioned, "you have to deal with men and respect their interests, just as you want them to honor yours." Whereupon Brill demonstrated to Katharine that the more success she attained, the more she sought opportunities to excel. "The process has become as important as the end result," he pointed out.

"Is it not true that, throughout the months of therapy, you have displayed little emotion publicly, that you have attended to your responsibilities with vigor?" Brill proposed. "That you have kept your personal feelings separate from the demands of suffrage shows both your strength and your weakness."

Under Brill's relentless interrogation, Katharine often chafed at his diagnosis. Still, she admitted that their conversations had definitely clarified her commitment to the needs of women as a means for personal fulfillment and identification. Characteristically, Brill did not let her self-congratulatory comment pass.

"And the more evident your motivations," Brill commented, "the more determined you are to carry them out. Correct, Mrs. McCormick?" She reluctantly nodded in agreement.

"Not surprising, then, that you perceived the suffrage movement and the league as a gratifying choice." Accolades from people like Mrs. Catt, Reverend Shaw, and Newton Baker were important, "but a different kind of love came from Mrs. Roessing," Brill interjected. "Am I not accurate in my assessment?"

"Yes," Katharine replied. "And it makes me uncomfortable."

For the next several weeks, Katharine and Dr. Brill explored her feelings about Mrs. Roessing and the strains in their relationship that had recently escalated. Katharine admitted feeling positive about the friendship but revealed that she was hesitant to continue for fear of being hurt. As Brill analyzed the situation, he explained that Katharine's years of sexual repression, thanks to Josephine and her desire for a Dexter heir, as well as the unfulfilled intimacy with Stanley, had been responsible for blocking total acceptance of her relationship with Julia. Brill was direct in his recommendation: "If you're comfortable with the friendship, don't be afraid of it. It's your way to obtain love."

During their final sessions, Brill pointed out how much more relaxed Katharine seemed to be. "My colleagues have mentioned it as well," Katharine acknowledged, "and without any deterioration of my work habits."

"You now know that you don't have to be a 'mother' to everyone, Mrs. McCormick, as you are observing," said Brill. "Discussion is a vital force. Talking about issues enlightens, defuses, and offers alternatives," he declared. "Find someone to talk to."

Brill also cautioned Katharine that any new resolve on her part had to be tempered with greater sensitivity. "Otherwise," he concluded, "your talents, abilities, and, don't forget, your money, will be wasted."

At the conclusion of the therapy with Dr. Brill, Katharine excused herself from suffrage duties temporarily to go to the château. She told Brill it would give her some time to think. He agreed it was a good idea after months of intensive examination. "We can talk whenever you feel the need," he offered.

Katharine discovered herself quite deflated by the end of their discussions. Yet, she felt exhilarated by what she believed had been accomplished.

Katharine was born at Gordon Hall, Dexter, Michigan. The mansion has a long and distinguished history, from having served as a stop on the Underground Railroad during the Civil War to housing University of Michigan students in the 1980s. (Courtesy MIT Museum)

Josephine Dexter, Katharine's mother, became imbued with the Dexter heritage and passed its virtues
on to her children. Yet all of her efforts failed to perpetuate the Dexter lineage, a fact that would prove
to be a continuing disappointment to her throughout her life. (Courtesy MIT Museum)

Eight-year-old Katharine was a serious, motivated student. From the start, she was a loner who eschewed the social activities of her peers. (Courtesy MIT Museum)

Wirt Dexter, one of Chicago's most outstanding lawyers, represented the poor, spoke out on behalf of
human rights, and contributed to charities that
championed the destitute.

At age fourteen, Katharine and her mother moved to Boston after the untimely death of Wirt in 1890. She began "finishing school" there, but it was many months before she recovered from the loss of her father. (Courtesy MIT Museum)

Katharine's older brother, Samuel, whom she adored, was handsome, intelligent, and personable. After graduating from Harvard and preparing to enter his father's former law firm, Samuel was struck down by meningitis in 1894. His death was a profound loss to Josephine, but was especially devastating to Katharine. (Courtesy MIT Museum)

In 1903, as a third-year student at MIT, Katharine had overcome the isolation and hostility she encountered from male students and
faculty to fashion an outstanding academic
record. She had decided to become a doctor.
(Courtesy MIT Museum)

Chemistry was one of Katharine's favorite classes. This photograph was taken prior to her campaign to allow women to remove their hats in class because they inhibited the ability of women to perform experiments. She won her battle; department administrators finally changed the rules for reasons of safety. (Courtesy MIT Museum)

Nettie McCormick and Stanley, her youngest child, after his graduation from Princeton. Following an eighteen-month European grand tour, she expected him to assume a position in the company. The first signs of his schizophrenia were already apparent and exacerbated his indecision. (Courtesy Wisconsin Historical Society)

Katharine and Stanley seemed to be the ideal couple—attractive, sensitive, intelligent, artistically
inclined, and from equally affluent backgrounds.
Still, Katharine broke off their engagement three
times due to Stanley's erratic behavior. (Courtesy
MIT Museum)

The marriage of Katharine Dexter and Stanley McCormick at the Château Prangins in September 1904 resembled the union of two royal houses. Within two years, Stanley would have to be placed in a mental institution; he remained under psychiatric care and supervision for the rest of his life. (Courtesy MIT Museum)

Shortly after their honeymoon, a doctor recommended the couple remain in St. Moritz for several months in order to "calm" Stanley. They should "refrain from any sexual activity during that time," the doctor advised, "to speed Stanley's healing." (Courtesy Wisconsin Historical Society)

Dr. Adolf Meyer, an eminent psychiatrist from Johns Hopkins University, became a McCormick consultant after Stanley was transferred to Riven Rock. He and Katharine feuded for more than twenty years regarding Stanley's care.

Reverend Anna Howard Shaw was president of the National American Woman Suffrage Association for more than ten years. An eloquent, evangelistic, and charismatic speaker, Shaw helped the suffrage organization to grow, but her organizational abilities were limited.

The McCormick estate, Riven Rock, near Montecito, California, became Stanley's "gilded cage," as neighbors labeled it, where the young, insane millionaire spent his days under twenty-four-hour care and supervision. (Courtesy Santa Barbara Historical Society)

Suffragists "on the road." One of Katharine's first assignments for the Massachusetts suffrage organization was to travel to towns and villages in the state to recruit women "for the cause." The group: (1) Florence Luscomb, (2) Susan W. Fitzgerald, (3) Teresa Crowley, (4) Margaret Foley, (5) Mrs. Stanley McCormick. (Courtesy of The Schlesinger Library, Radcliffe Institute, Harvard University)

Suffrage's charismatic leader and moral arbiter, Carrie Chapman Catt, president of NAWSA, as well as president of the International Woman Suffrage Alliance (IWSA), and cofounder with Katharine of the League of Women Voters. (Courtesy of The Schlesinger Library, Radcliffe Institute, Harvard University)

A group portrait of the IWSA board members at their 1913 meeting in Budapest, Austria-Hungary. Katharine is seated, second from the left. Next to her on the right are Anna Shaw and Jane Addams of Hull House, Chicago. (Courtesy MIT Museum)

One of the many demonstrations NAWSA undertook to promote suffrage. Apart from her administrative duties, Katherine (left) often appeared in street parades. (Courtesy MIT Museum)

Secretary of War Newton
Baker formed the Women's
Council of National De-
fense at the beginning of
World War I and chose
Katharine to head the or-
ganization. A strong ad-
vocate for women's rights,
Baker later became Katha-
rine's personal attorney
and advisor.

Women's Council of National Defense members included, seated, third from left, Ida Tarbell; standing to the right of Tarbell, Katharine; and seated to the right of Tarbell, Anna Shaw and Mrs. Catt. (Courtesy MIT Museum)

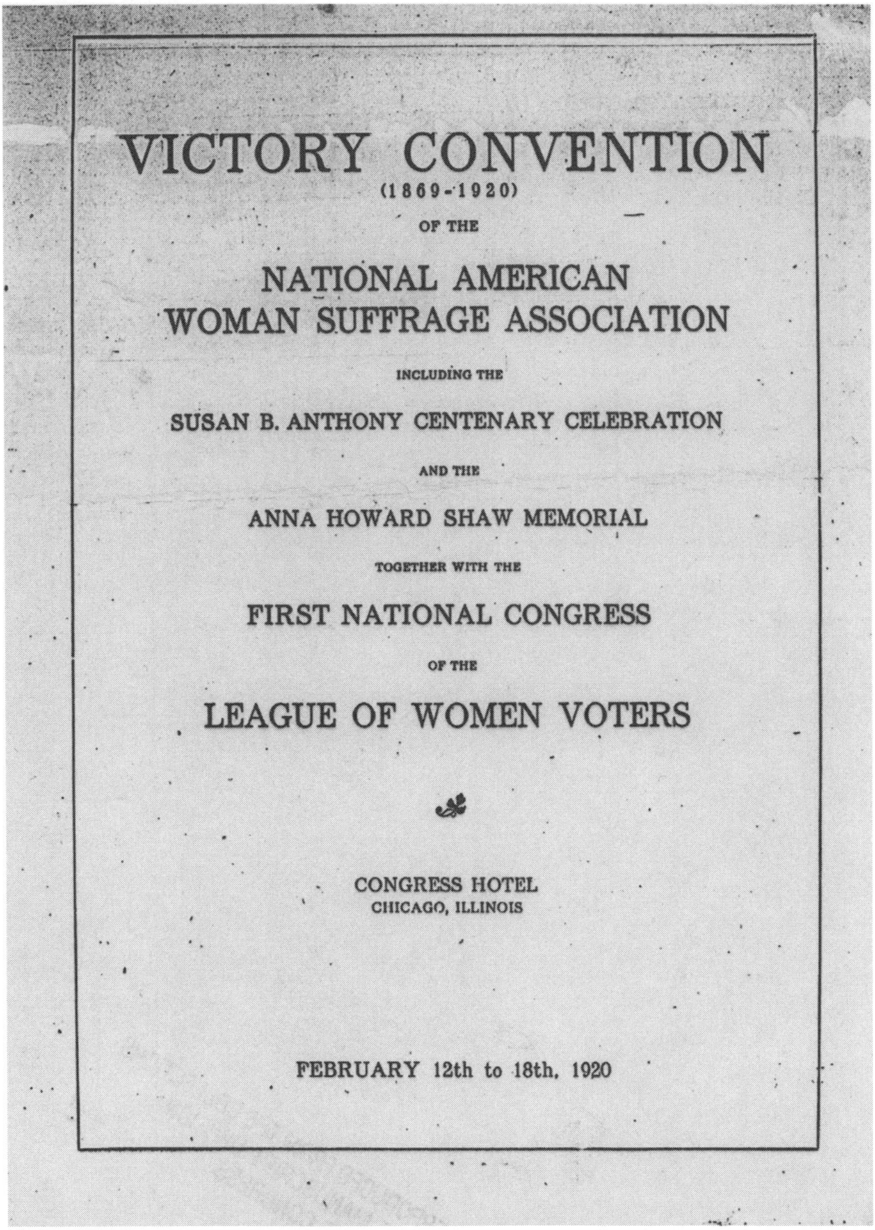

VICTORY CONVENTION
(1869-1920)

OF THE

NATIONAL AMERICAN WOMAN SUFFRAGE ASSOCIATION

INCLUDING THE

SUSAN B. ANTHONY CENTENARY CELEBRATION

AND THE

ANNA HOWARD SHAW MEMORIAL

TOGETHER WITH THE

FIRST NATIONAL CONGRESS

OF THE

LEAGUE OF WOMEN VOTERS

CONGRESS HOTEL
CHICAGO, ILLINOIS

FEBRUARY 12th to 18th, 1920

Program cover from the Victory Convention, 1920, honoring the passage of the Nineteenth Amendment to the U.S. Constitution, granting women the right to vote. It was NAWSA's last official meeting and the first for the League of Women Voters.

A rare photograph of Margaret Sanger, outspoken crusader for birth control, circa 1920. For more than forty years, Katharine supported Sanger with contributions ranging from direct financial aid to smuggling diaphragms into the United States for use in Sanger's clinics.

In 1927, Dr. Edward Kempf, a Freudian psychiatrist, was hired by Stanley's guardians at the unprecedented annual salary of $120,000. Within months of Kempf's appointment, a rift developed between him and Katharine regarding Stanley's care.

Headline from the *New York Evening Graphic Magazine* for a feature article on the contentious court battle. Articles similar to this appeared in newspapers across the country during the trial: McCormick versus McCormick, with Freud in the middle.

During the 1930s, not only did Stanley's condition stabilize, but he experienced more normal days than psychotic episodes. Always an avid reader, Stanley enjoyed a library that housed thousands of books and magazines.

C O P Y

LAST WILL AND TESTAMENT

15 May 1954

I, Stanley McCormick of the city of Chicago, State of Illinois, United States of America, now temporarily sojourning in Geneva, Switzerland, being of sound mind, memory and understanding, do make, ordain, publish and declare this to be my last Will and Testament.

1. I direct my Executrix, hereinafter named, to pay all my just debts and funeral expenses.

2. I give, devise and bequeath unto my wife Katharine Dexter McCormick all my property, real, personal and mixed of what nature soever and wheresoever the same shall be at the time of my death.

3. As Executrix of this my last will and testament I nominate and appoint my wife Katharine Dexter McCormick who shall not be required to give Bond for the faithful performance of her trust.

4. I hereby revoke all former wills by me made.

In witness whereof I have hereunto set my hand and seal at Geneva, Switzerland, this fifteenth day of September in the year One thousand nine hundred and four (1904).

Stanley McCormick.   L. S.

Signed, sealed, declared and published by Stanley McCormick, testator, as and for his last will and testament in presence of us and each of us, who at his request, in his presence and in the presence of each other have hereunto subscribed our names as witnesses:

Horace Lee Washington	) Department of State) Washington - D. C.
Louis H. Munier	) 8 Chemin Rieu) Geneva, Switzerland.
Felicien Vullié-Termet	) Quai du Leman 29,) Geneva, Switzerland.

Stanley's last will and testament, made on the day of Stanley and Katharine's marriage in 1904. He gave his entire estate to Katharine and named her executrix. At the time of his death, Stanley's estate amounted to more than $35 million. (Courtesy Wisconsin Historical Society)

Dr. Gregory "Goody" Pincus, cofounder of the Worcester Foundation for Experimental Biology, was persuaded by Katharine to pursue development of an easy-to-use and reliable contraceptive for women.

In a rare public appearance, hobbled by acute arthritis, Katharine attended a Chilton Club meeting in 1958. (Courtesy MIT Museum)

Although quite infirm, Katharine made a short acceptance speech at the dedication of Stanley McCormick Hall at MIT in March 1963. At the end of her speech, she promised to build an additional wing to the new women's dormitory, startling the crowd. (Courtesy MIT Museum)

The two wings of Stanley McCormick Hall housed more than 300 women undergraduates, thereby tripling the number of women able to attend MIT. (Courtesy MIT Museum)

During the 1975 centennial honoring Katharine, a portrait of her was admired by the MIT president and McCormick Hall students. Her portraits
in the dormitories offered students a fleeting glance of the benefactress
who made it possible for them to attain their educational potential. (Courtesy MIT Museum)

The League of Women Voters
(continued)

Nineteen

Shortly after Katharine began therapy with Dr. Brill, NAWSA opened its Victory Convention, on February 12, 1920, at the La Salle Hotel, Chicago. The suffrage amendment was not yet part of the U.S. Constitution, but the delegate mood was bursting with optimism.[1]

As their first order of business, convention delegates formally agreed to reformulate NAWSA into the National League of Women Voters.[2] They adopted a constitution and bylaws, designated Washington, D.C., as national headquarters, and voted to elect a four-member executive board comprising a chair, vice chair, secretary, and treasurer. From the ten names selected by a nominating committee, the delegates chose four: Maud Wood Park, Edna Gellhorn, Marie Edwards, and Pattie Jacobs. The new board members were asked to agree among themselves the office each would hold.

Neither Mrs. Catt nor Katharine was selected by the nominating committee, but for completely different reasons. Following agreement of the League's constitution, Mrs. Catt called for "younger and fresher women" to lead the new organization; she refused leadership, except as "honorary chairman."

The *Boston Globe*'s front page headlined that the contest for the presidency of the League was between two former Massachusetts suffragists, Maud Wood Park and Katharine Dexter McCormick.[3] Nevertheless, the nominating committee did not select Katharine, much to the surprise of the delegates. In response to questions about the omission of Katharine's name, some members suggested it was due to her long-term allegiance to Mrs. Catt, and when Catt declined a leadership position, her action influenced people not to include Katharine. Other delegates believed it had more to do with Katharine's relationships with committee members. Where Park was perceived as gracious and tactful, Katharine was uncompromising and businesslike, likely alienating some people. A few of the more conservative members cited Katharine's position on social hygiene as a reason for their nonsupport. Katharine felt the defeat deeply. With Dr. Brill's support, however, she was able to maintain stable decorum throughout the convention. "Do you really want to be president?" Brill asked Katharine. She could not, unhesitatingly, say yes.

With Katharine chairing the opening session, a special tribute was made to Reverend Shaw, who had died the previous July. In her brief speech, Katharine praised Shaw for her "transcendent gifts," and called for a moment of prayer, exactly as Shaw had done at the beginning of each of the twenty-eight conventions she had opened.

Katharine then made a welcoming speech, considered by many to have been the most animated and emotional she had ever made at a convention during her tenure as a NAWSA officer. Starting slowly and quietly, her voice grew louder, her words more pronounced with each phrase until, at the end, she was nearly shouting at the audience.

When we met at St. Louis a year ago in the 50th annual convention of our association, we knew that the end of our long struggle was near. There is no power on this earth that can do more than delay by a trifle the final enfranchisement of women. The enemies of progress and liberty never surrender and never die. They are still active, hysterically active, over our amendment. It does not matter. Suffragists were never dismayed when they were a tiny group and all the world was against them. What care they now when all the world is with them? March on, suffragists, the victory is yours![4]

Inspired by her words, delegates cheered and applauded. It was to prove her final appearance on the podium for both NAWSA and the League.

Finally, Katharine called for a resolution honoring President Wilson, declaring "that the gratitude of the convention be expressed to the President for his constant cooperation and help."[5] A wildly enthusiastic crowd unanimously passed the resolution. Apparently, the moment's exhilaration made delegates forget the contentious issues encountered between NAWSA and Wilson.

When Mrs. Henry Wade Rogers, NAWSA treasurer, gave her report, she recalled Katharine's previous work, noting her efforts to increase the organization's funds from $43,000 in 1914 to more than $97,000 in 1920. She concluded the report by stating: "I succeeded, with trepidation, Mrs. Katharine Dexter McCormick's efficient service. You may not be aware that she and I are the only members on the present board who were members in 1914." Katharine was forced to stand up to acknowledge the delegates' applause.

In honor of NAWSA's "older workers," a "Pioneer Suffrage Luncheon" was held on the final day of the convention. Katharine was selected by the NAWSA board to preside over the festivities, the object of the gathering to "honor members for their long years of trial and sacrifice."

A deep sense of sadness and nostalgia pervaded the luncheon as members recognized that this meeting would likely be the last of the "love feasts" they had shared for many years. As Katharine listened to attendees' anecdotes of past successes and failures, she was reminded of her early suffrage activities at MIT and those adventurous and exciting recruitment trips through Massachusetts. Yet, there also remained the question of future commitments; conversations with Dr. Brill would, she hoped, clarify the direction of her efforts.

Immediately after the close of the convention, several hundred women remained to attend a political education school that Mrs. Catt had organized to train new voters all over the country, once the amendment was passed. Katharine, however, was conspicuously absent. She and Julia had returned to New York so Katharine could continue her discussions with Dr. Brill. A summer trip to Switzerland followed the conclusion of her therapy with Brill.

When Katharine arrived at the château, Josephine handed her a stack of cables from Bentley and Anita regarding a particularly violent episode that had occurred between Stanley and Dr. Brush. Bentley reported that Stanley had struck Brush and his nurses on a succession of days and had to be confined to his room in restraints. Stanley's being put in restraints always annoyed and dismayed Katharine. "Can't they find a more civil way to contain Stanley?" she commented to her mother.

Dr. Brush had indicated the apparent reason for Stanley's violent display: an article in a newspaper about recent social activities in Geneva in which Katharine had been mentioned.[6] The article described the latest in women's fashions worn during the recent horse races and reported that women were appearing in public with their legs stained with henna, in lieu of wearing stockings. The article further remarked, "Among the fashionable spectators was Mrs. Stanley McCormick." Of course, Katharine had not been in Geneva at the time, let alone ever been seen at the races.

Katharine immediately cabled Dr. Brush to find out who had sent the article and how it had "so easily slipped past the censors." Brush admitted that the clipping had been sent to Stanley by Nettie. To counteract this action, Katharine wrote Stanley, telling him she had not been in Geneva at the time, since she was working on IWSA issues. She expressed sorrow that he could not be with her to share her experiences. In his weekly report to Dr. Meyer, Brush reported that, after receiving Katharine's letter, Stanley returned to "a semblance of stability." (No one admitted responsibility for the incident and Katharine was too far away to press an investigation.)

Katharine returned to New York in late November, relaxed and refreshed. In the meantime, a number of significant political events had occurred, both good and bad for women.

In August, as expected, the national suffrage amendment had been ratified. In breathtaking fashion, the last state needed to pass the law, Tennessee, gave the amendment its approval, but not without some last-minute maneuvering and individual heroics. After the state senate had passed the amendment, antisuffrage politicians mounted a concerted effort to prevent a vote from taking place in the assembly. This included such actions as blocking the entrances to the assembly hall to deny a quorum. After some delay, a Tennessee assemblyman, representing a rural jurisdiction, finally cast his vote in favor of the amendment. Newspapers reported that he had been persuaded and cajoled by his mother to "vote for the women of our country."[7]

A week later, on August 26, 1920, in a brief ceremony in the U.S. House of Representatives, the Nineteenth Amendment was proclaimed part of the Constitution. Newspaper banners shouted that women had finally won the right to vote. Press coverage across the country put women in the news as never before. No other amendment to the Constitution had taken so long to secure, been resisted so ferociously, been fought for with untiring hope and determination, and, in the end, been so widely regarded as a national event of surpassing historical significance. Yet all of these heroic efforts had taken a toll.

The November national election brought Harding and the Republican Party to Washington, D.C., and resulted in Republican control of both the executive and legislative branches. The climactic event of the year had been the opportunity for more than twenty million women to vote. Yet less than half of those registered went to the polls, ensuring a Harding victory. For League of Women Voters leaders and long-term members of NAWSA, it was a serious embarrassment and a surprising reversal.[8]

Numerous reasons were offered for the low turnout: voter apathy; exaggerated hopes; the lack of a unified, one-issue campaign; and public criticism of the league by partisan women. The League of Women Voters, seemingly so vibrant a year ago, revealed the weaknesses of its organization.

When Katharine attended the IWSA board meeting in London in November, she and Mrs. Catt reviewed the league's situation. Neither was any longer intimately associated with the league, nor did they express any desire to be more involved. Mrs. Catt believed she had "given everything she had" to suffrage and now wished to concentrate on the issues of women's rights in the international arena. Katharine had already resolved to reduce her involvement with the league and to seek another venue for her energies. She agreed, however, to continue working with the IWSA, at least for the next several years.

When Katharine arrived in New York, a batch of letters from Riven Rock, Bentley, and Anita awaited her attention. Reading them quickly brought her up to date on the latest "crises." Bentley reported that Nettie had been diagnosed as suffering from mild dementia. Anita wrote that Cyrus Jr.'s wife, Harriet, was gravely ill, and her death appeared imminent. Dr. Brush gossiped that Dr. Hamilton had announced the opening of a practice in Santa Barbara but abruptly departed the city before the office was opened. No one seemed to know why he had changed his mind. McKillop complained about Dr. Brush's management. And everyone seemed to be fussing about how Stanley's Christmas gifts should be labeled. These issues always seemed to be raised prior to her visiting Riven Rock, Katharine noticed.

Upon her arrival in Santa Barbara, Katharine called the respective parties together in order to obtain an assessment of the current situation. Not surprisingly, she found no real crises; actually, everything seemed quite stable. Stanley was reported by Dr. Brush to be calm and functioning comfortably within his prescribed routine. McKillop's concerns had more to do with house and garden maintenance than with Stanley's care. Bentley and Anita would not be visiting Riven Rock until January to review the estate's expenses with Katharine, so they were of no immediate concern. Nonetheless, Katharine found two problems that troubled her and needed to be addressed.

First, when Katharine queried Dr. Brush about a series of tests for Stanley she had ordered months ago, she discovered that none of them had been administered, by order of Dr. Meyer. Upon review of the weekly reports prepared by Brush, Katharine observed that nothing in the program suggested any effort to "improve" Stanley's mental condition. Letters to Brush from Meyer had called for maintenance procedures only, to keep Stanley stable. When Katharine found that Dr. Meyer was planning to attend the meeting in January, she added to the agenda a discussion of his recent directions to Brush. In addition, she planned to present recommendations for the best psychoanalytic approach for Stanley, a debate sure to elicit controversy, since Meyer had previously argued strongly against Freudian techniques.

Katharine attacked the second issue immediately. Examining correspondence from previous months, she discovered further attempts at censorship. A discussion with Dr. Brush revealed that Meyer had suggested to him "the editing of letters," a suggestion with which Bentley concurred, to avoid a recurrence of Stanley's violent episodes of the past summer. Katharine was irate.

"Why had I not been consulted? Hadn't everyone agreed not to censor letters after last year's affair?"

Dr. Brush could only respond that he had been following orders. Katharine immediately sent cables to Bentley and Meyer, expressing her anger and demanding that all censorship cease. Bentley did not respond to her cable, deferring to Dr. Meyer.

Diplomatically, Meyer answered with an apology, citing the fact that the episode causing Stanley's violence had occurred while Katharine was out of the country and not available to consult as to all the details. He recommended that "some editing" was necessary to avoid inciting Stanley in any manner. Unable to obtain a clear explanation of the factors that caused Stanley's behavior, Katharine reluctantly agreed with Meyer's suggestion, but only as long as guidelines, which she would establish, dictated what information might be deleted. Still, Katharine remained uncomfortable with the situation, since she was unable to monitor closely all of the correspondence that passed between various parties and Riven Rock.

Dr. Meyer was keenly aware that the "problem" with Katharine would not go away as long as she sought to check correspondence, so he instructed Dr. Brush to be "especially careful" when handling her letters. Meyer also hoped that, by agreeing to Katharine's demands, she might abandon "her ideas concerning gland therapy and psychoanalysis for Stanley."

The guardian meeting in January 1921 began ominously. Stanley became aware of the arrival of the participants and retreated into his room, expressing a fear of "being bitten." Dr. Meyer requested that Dr. Brush be admitted only to "selected" portions of the agenda. Anita reported that Harriet was near death, thus she might be called back to Chicago before the meeting concluded. McKillop reported that Mrs. Brush was "acting strangely" and had recently stated a desire to leave Riven Rock.

Riven Rock's yearly budget was reviewed first, since it had continued to escalate even though careful attention was being paid to expenditures. The house needed redecorating; walls had to be erected along the creek to reduce possible flooding of the grounds; the Brush cottage required a new roof; and Dr. Brush had requested an increase in salary. Except for agreement on redecorating, the remaining issues were postponed, as usual, due to the group's inability to reach consensus.

Katharine decided to drop the request for gland therapy so as to concentrate on recommendations regarding the school of psychoanalysis to be employed for Stanley. She reported on the investigations of various psychoanalytic techniques and how they might be applied, and submitted a list of doctors who were currently available to accept Stanley as a patient. In a rare display of candor, Katharine also revealed her own discussions with Dr. Brill and how much they had helped her, hoping this would persuade Bentley and Anita to accept her recommendation. Instead, they deferred their decision, insisting that it had to be discussed with the McCormicks. Dr. Meyer, however, openly and critically opposed the use of psychoanalysis "at this time" and particularly derided the Freudian school, which annoyed Katharine.

"What don't you like about the Freudian school?" Katharine pressed Meyer.

"It will not get at the issues affecting Stanley," Meyer answered somewhat evasively.

"And what are those issues?" Katharine asked.

"They are the same as those uncovered by Kraepelin, Hoch, and Jelliffe," Meyer responded, "and as long as Stanley is unable to articulate his feelings, it is impossible to interrogate him."

"I believe you underestimate Stanley, Doctor. I believe, if he were given the opportunity, he would welcome the chance to talk to someone who was indeed interested in what he had to say." Katharine stared at Meyer intently as if challenging him to defend his position.

Bentley broke the silence by bringing up Mrs. Brush's comments about wishing to leave Riven Rock. If she did, Bentley pointed out, then it was likely Dr. Brush would leave too, and they would be faced with finding another doctor. What could they do to make Mrs. Brush feel more comfortable, he asked the group. Like most of the other issues, however, the decision was deferred until her condition could be better understood. Bentley promised to discuss the issue with Dr. Brush, as well as Mrs. Brush, if she was willing.

All pending issues were temporarily set aside when Harriet died after a long illness. Katharine traveled to Chicago to attend the funeral. She hoped to use the occasion to press Bentley and Anita concerning the unfinished January agenda. For the first time in thirteen years, she and Nettie shared the same room. For Katharine, the meeting brought back memories not only of the courtship with Stanley, but also of the conversations with Dr. Brill about the adversarial episodes with Nettie and their significance. Surprisingly, she felt no discomfort.

Although exceedingly frail and disoriented—Anita and Harold were at her side continuously—Nettie recognized Katharine, with a look of surprise that quickly changed to scorn. Raising her hand and shakily pointing a finger at Katharine, she shouted, "You're the woman who killed my dear, beloved son!" then broke down crying. Anita and Harold quickly assisted her out of the room. Katharine could only feel sorry for the old woman who never stopped hating her for "stealing" Stanley.

After the funeral, Anita took the opportunity to discuss with Katharine the recommendations of psychoanalysis for Stanley. She disclosed that Dr. Meyer had strongly opposed its use, particularly the Freudian approach, but that she wanted to explore the issue further. Katharine talked again about her own therapy and the insights it had produced, including those related to her personal conflicts with Nettie. Katharine attempted to "sell" Anita on psychoanalysis and, at the same time, reduce the tension between herself and the McCormicks, now that Nettie was infirm and out of touch. Yet, the extent to which she succeeded proved problematic. According to Anita's letters to Dr. Meyer, she was unconvinced by Katharine's "openness," noting that Katharine seemed to be more "focussed than she had been in previous years, for good or ill."

From Chicago, Katharine traveled to Cleveland, Ohio, to attend the League of Women Voters' first convention, opening April 11, 1921. Katharine was serving both as an IWSA representative and as a delegate from the Boston branch of the league.[9]

The announcement of the league's first annual convention had been sent nationwide to groups representing more than two million women, heralding the "exalting and holy crusade" that had finally endowed women with "power." Yet, at the same time, it asked women "how best shall we use this power?" Under questioning by the press, President Park indicated that several courses were open, but she refused (or was unable) to elucidate details. As the convention approached, views from congressmen were solicited regarding appropriate goals for the new organization. Suggestions, doubts, and outright hostility from many circles only sharpened the painful soul-searching for league leaders as they attempted to shape goals and objectives. After its first year, the league realized how difficult it had become to bear the torch of independence in the face of a continuous onslaught of partisan politics and, at the same time, maintain an effective level of membership, now severely depleted after passage of the suffrage amendment.

Nearly a thousand delegates, from forty-six states and nine women's organizations, attended the convention. President Park's initial address clearly reviewed their difficulties—meager financial support, a lack of efficient administrative machinery, internal disagreements over proposed programs, and attempts at establishing links with other interest groups. The barriers to acceptance were formidable, Park reported. The league was criticized for supporting "interventionist" legislation; efforts to train voters were viewed as an invasion of the rights of political parties; desires to inform themselves about candidates had been labeled "pestering."

Mrs. Catt's opinions regarding the direction the league should take served only to disrupt proceedings more. She casually suggested that the organization drop the word "women" and become the League of Voters. The notion clearly represented a dramatic change from her position when the league was being formed. "What is she thinking?" delegates wondered. In rebuttal, Katharine was one of the first of the delegates to denounce Catt's suggestion, calling it "counter-productive." Instead, she pushed efforts for the league to position itself as a civic organization.

President Park had asked Katharine to assist in building an operational structure, but she declined. After Mrs. Catt had expressed views that might jeopardize the already fragile organization, Park again turned to

Katharine asking for her guidance, and again Katharine declined, saying she was unable to help the league at this time. Near the end of the convention, when Mrs. Catt gave an extemporaneous speech on world peace, Katharine decided that her own interests and efforts lay in a direction quite apart from the league. Yet it proved difficult to pull away from the organization she had helped create.

Following the convention, Katharine met with Newton Baker, who had recently retired as Secretary of War, returned to Cleveland, and renewed his private law practice. She asked Baker to assume direction of all legal matters on her behalf, a proposal to which he readily agreed. It marked the beginning of an association that was to last for more than forty-six years, extending even beyond her death. It also introduced a more authoritative and uncompromising voice into "the battle of the McCormicks."

Baker's first assignment was to represent Katharine in all dealings with the McCormicks, their lawyers, and Stanley's doctors. Since Katharine planned to go to Switzerland for the summer, Baker would fully assume her responsibilities as a guardian. Within a matter of days, he was questioning Dr. Brush about censoring Katharine's letters to Stanley.

Baker's intervention had been initiated by a letter to Stanley in which Katharine mentioned having suffered from a strep throat that put her in bed for a week. Dr. Brush complained that Stanley had reacted negatively to the news, and Brush used this episode as an example to prove that censorship was necessary. Further, Brush had asked Dr. Meyer to support him, as part of his request to the guardians to allow censorship. Baker responded quickly, reminding both Brush and Meyer that the guardians made all final decisions and had to be informed about any proposed change in Stanley's care.

In the process, Baker uncovered another lapse in communication. It seems that Dr. Meyer had not supplied Brush with the entire family history, or with information on the early years of Stanley's illness.

In a terse cable, Baker questioned Meyer, "Why not?"

Meyer replied that he had not wanted to prejudice Brush's views before he was fully aware of Stanley's condition.

"But surely Dr. Brush became aware of Stanley's condition months ago," Baker rebutted.

On Katharine's orders, all data on Stanley were to be made available to Dr. Brush, although she confided to Baker that it likely would not change Stanley's care program, "because Dr. Brush is not equipped to administer the necessary techniques." Through Baker, Katharine also warned Meyer to make no decisions regarding medical activities at Riven Rock without consulting the guardians.

Baker also became involved in the debate regarding the redecoration of Stanley's residence and surrounding grounds. Plans had been made, discussed, and modified, and they now awaited agreement by the guardians.

When the McCormicks wanted to push through the alterations quickly, Baker informed them that final decisions could not be made until Katharine returned from Europe. In a letter to Katharine, Baker remarked about the incessant "confusion and indecision" he encountered as he attempted to negotiate with "that Riven Rock crowd."

Birth Control

Twenty

Before 1840, legal attention to abortion in the United States was minimal, because there was no medical way to determine whether a woman was pregnant until the fetus began to move in the womb. During this time, those seeking abortions were usually unmarried women from "better" families viewed as victims of male lust.

After the Civil War, however, when the status of women began to change, physicians began to experience pressure to perform abortions, which led them to institute a campaign to outlaw abortion at any stage of pregnancy. By 1880, thanks to the physicians' successful campaign, abortion was declared illegal. The culmination of the campaign against abortion occurred with the passage of the 1873 Comstock Act, a national "obscenity" law, in which all activities related to pornography, abortion, and contraception were prohibited.

The chief proponent of the bill, Anthony Comstock, had begun his career as a lobbyist for the New York Society for the Suppression of Vice. He soon became the spokesperson and combative evangelist against the "forces of evil," as identified and defined by Comstock himself, and obtained power to have offenders arrested. Comstock's power came from prominent New York businessmen who paid his salary, eminent physicians who had campaigned against abortion, and political and religious leaders who viewed Comstock's actions as "ridding society of the devil's disciples."

Comstock's public activities carefully masked the actual motivations of this group of men. In reality, they saw the declining birthrate, the spreading emancipation of women, the hedonism of popular culture, and the increasing influx of foreigners as significant threats to their Protestant value system, as well as to the stability and self-righteousness of a white, Christian, middle-class society.

However, these beliefs ran against the rapidly changing mores of the late nineteenth century. Both sexes were gaining control over parts of their lives that in the past had been resigned to fate or subject to specified rules of behavior. Due to the mass popularization of romantic love, people were beginning to consider casual, nonmarital sex. Nevertheless, the forces of suppression were formidable. When Comstock and his accomplices raided a so-called "den of obscenity," they always attracted front-page headlines.

In the early 1900s, as more and more women found jobs outside the home, relations between the sexes took on a new reality. A new standard of permissiveness became the basis for twentieth-century love. Sex and procreation were being viewed separately. As society became more urban and secular, there was an increased emphasis on material well-being and pleasure. Some manifestations of this movement were the growth of women's magazines, women's leisure-time activities, the development of beauty shops and the cosmetics business, and the expansion of the advertising industry. Still, protesters of the country's "declining" morals were not ready to concede that affection justified sex. Victorian attitudes, especially as practiced by the medical profession, as well as the influx of millions of immigrants carrying their own cultural mores against open sexuality remained barriers to new sexual expression.

At the time, those who publicly questioned the suppression of contraception included the civil libertarians, who pushed for the rights of individuals to manage their own sexuality, and the quality controllers (eugenicists), who sought to define the population problem as a need for more people of "the right kind." Ardent feminists, such as Emma Goldman, Margaret Sanger, and Mary Ware Dennett, became public promoters of the potential for erotic fulfillment against the male forces of sexual repression. Yet, the majority of middle-class and professional women still focused their energies on suffrage and equality in the workplace.

By 1920, Margaret Sanger had solidified her position as a leader of the birth control movement, heralding a new crusade on behalf of women's rights.[1] Beginning in 1912, as an organizer for the Industrial Workers of the World, she quickly became a radical journalist, paying special attention to the predicament of working-class mothers. After a series of confrontations with politically radical male colleagues, whose beliefs regarding women's reproductive rights she found to be fundamentally no different from those of men who advocated male supremacy, Sanger decided to concentrate all her efforts on women's issues.

As a first step toward distinguishing obscenity from contraception, Sanger openly defied the Comstock law and Anthony Comstock himself. Indicted for publishing "obscene" material in her monthly radical journal, *The Woman Rebel*, Sanger fled to England in 1914 to escape prosecution. She returned a year later with renewed vigor and traveled across the country urging women to control their own lives by establishing contraceptive centers. In defiance of the prevailing laws, she opened the nation's first birth control center, in the Brownsville section of Brooklyn, in 1916. Ten days later, the police closed the center and hauled Sanger off to jail.

Appealing her case, Sanger won a decision that opened a new strategy for her cause. While the judge upheld the Comstock law, he ruled that the law would not prevent physicians from prescribing contraceptives when medically necessary. Thus, instead of fighting the law, Sanger decided to seek out physicians to organize and direct birth control clinics under the direction of the American Birth Control League, an organization she founded in 1921. Sanger also discovered new support from well-to-do women whose activities to that time had been primarily directed toward suffrage and civil rights. Among these women was an already experienced and battle-tested suffrage leader, Katharine Dexter McCormick.

Katharine had first met Margaret Sanger in 1917, when Sanger was attending a Boston trial in which a young man had been arrested for distributing one of Sanger's pamphlets on contraception. Listening to Sanger testify in court and speak to the press outside the courthouse, Katharine was greatly impressed by Sanger's passion, dedication, and advocacy. Even at this early stage of her career, Katharine firmly believed that contraception was the key to women's freedom. Because of her commitment to NAWSA, however, Katharine was unable join Sanger's crusade.

During the summer of 1921, Sanger was planning the first American Birth Control Conference, to be held at the Plaza Hotel, New York City, in November. Her personal friend and supporter, Juliet Rublee, had begun developing a network of contacts among women professionals, clubwomen, journalists, and reformers to help underwrite the conference. Unlike Sanger's previous attempts at setting up conferences, this one was the first to acknowledge and, she hoped, capture the support of society's elite.

Sanger mailed flyers to more than 31,000 people. Each flyer included a contribution card and a questionnaire on the recipient's feelings about birth control practices. More than 5,000 responded, some with contributions, a response well beyond Sanger's expectations. Upon receiving the mailing, Katharine contacted Sanger and requested a meeting after her return to the States.

The meeting between Katharine and Sanger began with the usual courteous salutations but ended with the two disparate and equally aloof women sitting at a table, papers spread before them, eagerly discussing strategy and actions, as if they were planning the overthrow of a government. As different as their personalities and backgrounds were, both recognized a unique compatibility that centered on women's rights and freedom of choice. When Katharine left the meeting, she knew that she would assist Sanger in an effort that would quickly become their mutual crusade.

How could two women with such diverse backgrounds and personal experiences find themselves in such harmony as to unite their talents for a common, highly controversial cause? They were both fully aware that the battleground would be replete with risk, danger, defeats, and public maligning of their names; but the challenges did not appear to deter them. Both had already experienced such adversities and had managed them successfully. Together, they hoped to accomplish even more.

During this initial meeting, each woman quickly recognized the talents and abilities of the other, as well as how the other could support and bolster her own shortcomings. They found that they could freely discuss ideas and strategies and quickly agree upon actions. While the partnership was definitely pragmatic, it was also psychologically fulfilling.

Margaret Sanger perceived Katharine as a representative of the new generation of feminists. Katharine was a ranking member of the social upper class, providing entrée into high places and access to potentially large sources of money. Her knowledge and commitment to science and professionalism could be employed to attack the stereotype of women as emotional, irrational, and subjective. In Katharine, Sanger saw a highly engaged and determined woman, one who was not afraid to take on controversial causes. Katharine's talent for organizational planning would also be of benefit to the cause.

Katharine, in turn, was impressed by Sanger's unflagging commitment and charisma on behalf of the birth control movement. She saw Sanger as tough, political, and ruthless in her dealings with adversaries. Like Mrs. Catt, Sanger was a public relations icon for women's rights, but one who was much more focused with clearer direction. Sanger knew how to use people for her own purposes, but that did not bother Katharine, as long as the greater goal could be achieved. In addition, the growing birth control crusade appeared to be a good place to invest her funds. This could very well be the arena, she believed, where her vitality, talents, and abilities might best be utilized. As previously defined by Dr. Brill, it could be her "new love."

Sanger had recently collected a responsible group of people to underwrite and legitimize the birth control movement. Included on the conference's executive committee were physicians and social hygiene practitioners. The list of conference committee members included prominent physicians, university professors, social doyens, and judges, all endorsing Sanger's crusade. They included such names as Winston Churchill, Dr. Alice Hamilton, Theodore Dreiser, Mrs. Learned Hand, Mrs.

Maxfield Parrish, and Mrs. Stanley McCormick. Katharine volunteered to assist in organizing the conference and made a contribution for publishing materials. Since she was living at the Plaza Hotel, she also assisted in actual conference preparations.

Thirty-three scholarly papers on birth control and contraception were presented by physicians, social hygiene experts, and professors from the United States and England. Sanger opened the conference with an address welcoming the speakers and participants. The speech was largely calm and restrained, although she did include a brief tirade against the Catholic Church, a tactic that, near the end of the conference, would create serious repercussions.

It was obvious that Sanger was pleased with the conference agenda and positive press coverage. Examining the roster of committee members and renowned speakers, she was particularly delighted with the stamp of legitimacy that she and her cause were receiving from "socially powerful people," as one newspaper identified those in attendance. The organization's executive secretary, Mrs. Anne Kennedy, opened the conference by presenting the aims and principles of Sanger's fledgling organization. These were received by the audience with wholehearted approval.

The conference's concluding meeting was to be held in the city's Town Hall, highlighted by an address from Harold Cox, a former member of British Parliament and editor of the *Edinburgh Review*. His speech was titled "Birth Control—Is It Moral?" Moments before he was to speak to a crowded assembly, a phalanx of policemen rushed into the hall and forcibly removed him from the podium. The intruders claimed to be acting at the behest of Archbishop Patrick Hayes of nearby St. Patrick's Cathedral. Shouts of protest almost turned the gathering into a riot. Margaret Sanger was also taken by the police, but she remained uncharacteristically calm during the entire proceedings. Front-page newspaper coverage offered strong support for Sanger and strong protests against the "unwarranted" police action.[2]

The following day, the mayor's office, spurred on by protests from the ACLU and a number of prominent New York attorneys, opened an official inquiry. In the end, investigators blamed the action on a local police precinct captain; the Catholic Church was never linked to the episode.

A week later, Cox was allowed to speak at the Park Theater, with 1,500 people crammed inside and another 3,000 supporters milling outside. The police were in attendance, but this time merely as protection. Sanger closed the session by calling on physicians to support women, and she boldly announced her intention to raise funds to open a birth control clinic in the city. The event gained significant support from the national press, which recognized both Sanger's right to speak out on birth control and her newly achieved relevance brought about by the "socially powerful" people who confirmed the crusade.

Katharine had been in attendance at the aborted session and was part of the crowd that condemned the police, as well as the Catholic Church, for their actions. Swept away by the crowd, Katharine felt heightened excitement and enthusiasm, emotions she had not experienced for many years. She later wrote Stanley about the conference and its intoxicating vitality, telling him of her interest in the birth control movement and her conversations with Margaret Sanger. With obvious exhilaration, she ended the letter, "I am so happy now that I have cleared the ground and have a definite policy, along the most progressive lines, assisting women."[3]

A week later, Katharine met with Sanger to discuss and formulate a publications program. Sanger had hoped to publish a number of pamphlets on birth control and contraception, although their distribution remained illegal. She also sought funding for a book she planned to write. Katharine promised to underwrite the cost of the pamphlets.

Buoyed by the support she received from upper-class feminists, Sanger wanted to organize these women to help her cause. She and Katharine hypothesized that their power and influence could assist Sanger in two important strategic ways: by downplaying her own past activities and legal transgressions, and combating the increasing attacks against her by the Catholic Church and other religious groups. Through Katharine, Sanger believed, both these goals could be met, and she could obtain funds from this wealthy group of "progressive" women.

Quickly, Katharine embarked on a campaign to enlist socially prominent women through her contacts in NAWSA and the League of Women Voters, particularly among those who, like herself, remained activists but sought new challenges since their suffrage victory. She also tapped into her Boston and Chicago contacts, including Anita, to solicit funds. Katharine presented the argument that, by their joining Sanger's movement and supporting birth control and contraception, equal rights for women would be decidedly advanced.

Writing numerous letters, conducting meetings, and hosting many individual dinner engagements, Katharine preached "the cause." Unlike the League of Women Voters, the birth control movement provided a clearcut cause for women during the 1920s.

Katharine's arguments that the movement was "an instrument of liberation" drew increasing attacks from the Catholic Church, particularly in Boston, where the Church assailed the activities of the Dexter family, to Josephine's embarrassment. In spite of this, Katharine was not only able to form a coterie of birth control sympathizers, but also succeeded in obtaining funds to pay for Sanger's nationwide lecture tours in 1922 and 1923.

In 1922, Sanger had incorporated the American Birth Control League, a nonprofit organization, in accordance with New York laws. Katharine was selected as one of the organization's directors. In addition, Sanger began publication of the *Birth Control Review*. She had collected her own group of loyalists—Juliet Rublee, Frances Ackermann, and Anne Kennedy—to run the organization and publish the newsletter. Katharine donated the seed money to get the newsletter started. In the first year of the publication's program, more than 75,000 pamphlets, twelve books on birth control, and more than 15,000 copies of the *Birth Control Review* were distributed.

On January 1, 1923, the first birth control clinic in the United States (with the exception of the short-lived Brownsville clinic) was opened. Called the Clinical Research Bureau, under the direction of Dr. Dorothy Bocker, the clinic was positioned as a center for the medical study of contraception, supervised by physicians, in keeping with New York laws. The women who received examinations and contraceptives would be considered its research subjects. What better way to "objectify" its existence and mission, Katharine reflected in a letter to Julia Roessing.

Katharine's schedule for the summer of 1922 was filled with meetings and conventions. She was selected to be a U.S. representative at the Fifth Annual International Birth Control Conference to be held in London, July 10 to 14. Margaret Sanger was serving as chair of the conference, and Katharine would be one of the twenty-six U.S. delegates.

Katharine also planned to attend the League of Nations meeting in Geneva in September, as an IWSA representative. Her itinerary included scheduled visits to Rome, Milan, Antibes, and Paris, besides London and Geneva. Even for Katharine, it was a rather ambitious schedule, but she had a specific purpose. Katharine was plotting to commit a felony.

Since the opening of the Clinical Research Bureau in January, more women than could be accommodated had requested appointments. The already meager supply of contraceptives had quickly run out, and the bureau was desperately seeking replacements from all sources, primarily from outside the country, since the availability of contraceptives was greatly restricted within the United States. Some diaphragms were smuggled into the country from Canada with the assistance of bootleggers bringing in liquor, and it was rumored that pirates were bringing them in from unknown sources. Still, the amounts were well below those needed for the bureau to function effectively.

In Europe, by contrast, diaphragms were readily available in many countries, with the largest manufacturers located in Rome, Milan, Antibes, and Paris. Katharine developed a plan to purchase diaphragms in Europe and bring them into the United States. How their purchase and entry might best be accomplished would be up to Katharine.[4]

In late May, Katharine sailed for the continent. To carry the necessary wardrobe for a four-month trip through Europe, she traveled with eight pieces of luggage, three of them large trunks. Since she planned to purchase many of "the latest fashions," more trunks would necessarily have to be purchased for the trip home. Through IWSA contacts, Katharine scheduled meetings with contraceptive manufacturers. Her objective: smuggle as many diaphragms into the United States as she could carry, for delivery to Sanger's clinic. It was, indeed, an adventure filled with risk and danger, but Katharine was excited by the challenge.

In the guise of a French or German scientist, Katharine met with manufacturers and purchased hundreds of diaphragms, giving the château address as the delivery destination. There is no evidence to suggest how funds were gathered to pay for the diaphragms, but it is likely that Katharine paid for most of them herself.

By the time Katharine attended the League of Nations conference in September, the château had already received the ordered items. In the meantime, Katharine had purchased clothing and additional trunks in each of the cities she visited, requesting that they be sent to the château to prepare for her return to the States.

Katharine hired local seamstresses to sew the diaphragms into the clothing and pack the clothes securely into the trunks. She now had eight trunks, requiring two heavily muscled men to move and lift them onto wagons. Their transportation to Le Havre was smooth, with no questions coming from border guards, although French customs officials at the dock marveled at the large number of "fashions" Katharine had purchased.

"How could you possibly use all of that clothing?" they asked. "Oh," Katharine responded, "they will be put to good use." Flattering Gallic pride, she went on to relate how women in America so loved French fashions.

Based on her frequent trips to Europe over the years, Katharine had become a familiar figure to New York customs authorities. During previous trips, her passport had likely been stamped at one time or another by most of the officials. After all, they were welcoming back a member of the country's long-established and highly respected social elite.

Eight large trunks were carried from the ship. Had they been opened for inspection, the trunks would have revealed dresses, evening gowns, coats, and other garments, all carefully hung from padded hangers and swathed in layers of tissue to protect their exquisitely embroidered fabrics. Predictably, however, the trunks were never examined.

Katharine attentively guided the luggage through customs, all the while maintaining the haughty manner that customs officials expected from representatives of her class. Of course, each of the porters who assisted Katharine in her passage received a generous gratuity. Outside, moving truck laborers, Sanger employees, were waiting, ready to load the trunks for delivery. After the truck was loaded, it was driven to the bureau office and parked in the back alley to be unloaded. Katharine followed in a taxi. Katharine had returned with more than a thousand diaphragms, enough to supply the bureau for the remainder of the year.

Twenty-One

Upon her return from Europe, Katharine made a brief stop in Boston to visit her mother. Josephine presented her with letters she had received from Stanley, Anita, and Dr. Brush, the contents of which quite disturbed her.

For several years, Riven Rock/McCormick encounters had amounted to no more than minor skirmishes that required minimal attention. Based on recent reports from Newton Baker, however, as well as her own observations, Katharine sensed increasing stresses and pressures, caused largely by the perceived inadequacies of Dr. Brush and consequent impositions by Dr. Meyer. The letters signaled that serious disputes were on the horizon.

Katharine was also surprised to find her mother in a frail condition, suffering so much from arthritic legs that her mobility had been significantly reduced. Due to her increasing infirmity, Josephine asked her daughter to take over the Dexter family's business affairs, a domain that she alone had controlled for more than thirty years and that still included various real estate properties in Chicago and Michigan. Gathering together the files, accounting ledgers, and legal papers, Katharine sent them all to Newton Baker, with definitive instructions on how each specific aspect and parcel of the estate was to be handled.

As Katharine had anticipated, her mother pleaded with her not to involve the Dexter family name in her personal crusade with Margaret Sanger. "I don't care to be singled out by the Catholic Church as a rebel," she explained. "A number of my friends have asked me why you have associated yourself with the birth control movement, and I'm unable to give them a reasonable answer."

"Mother," Katharine replied, "tell them only that I'm devoting my efforts to women's rights and women's freedoms. That should be sufficient to satisfy their curiosity without falling into religious debates. I'll deal with any accusations from the Church," Katharine assured her mother. In fact, Josephine was concerned about negative charges that might be directed against the Dexter heritage.

One of the letters sent by Dr. Brush replied to Katharine's appeal to purchase a radio for Stanley. Afraid to agree to Katharine's request, Brush telegraphed Dr. Meyer for advice. "Wish your opinion. Would have S. understand that either nurses or myself be the only ones to operate it."

There is no record of Meyer's response. Two weeks later, however, Katharine had the radio installed. For Katharine, this episode represented another example of Dr. Brush's ineffectiveness and trivialization with regard to Stanley's care. There was no question in her mind that Brush had to be dismissed as quickly as possible. Hurriedly, she wrote to Bentley stating her concerns and recommendation.

In response to Katharine's prodding, Bentley wrote Meyer to solicit his opinion regarding Dr. Brush's competence. Since he did not wish to have Brush replaced, Meyer suggested that Brush's responsibilities be restricted to physician's duties, no longer to include those of estate manager. "Hire an estate caretaker, and Brush will be able to perform his physician's role more efficiently," Meyer suggested. Bentley agreed, and he promised to discuss the hiring of an estate manager with the guardians. "I will do the best I can," he promised Meyer. For the moment, Meyer's actions served to divert Katharine's efforts to remove Dr. Brush.

Because of Nettie's failing health, the guardians' meeting took place in Chicago; Anita, Cyrus Jr., Harold, Bentley, Newton Baker, and Katharine attended. Since reports about Stanley suggested he was stable, little discussion was devoted to his health. Instead, most of the conversation concerned Dr. Brush and Meyer's recommendation to hire an estate manager.

For hours, the group debated Brush's future and Meyer's suggestion. As often happened, however, no final decision was reached, despite Katharine's stating firmly that she wanted Brush relieved of his position. In the end, she was outvoted; Brush remained Stanley's physician and continued to supervise the estate. Nevertheless, Katharine was able to persuade Bentley to write Brush detailing his job description. Bentley also promised her to visit Riven Rock to monitor Brush's handling of these responsibilities.

Upon receiving the letter from Bentley outlining the guardians' decision, Brush voiced his displeasure at being ordered to continue managing the estate. Instead of being relieved of such duties, as Meyer had recommended, Brush had been assigned even more tasks to supervise. His letter to Dr. Meyer complained about the new arrangement and, in consequence, he threatened to resign. Brush never carried through on the warning; only Meyer was aware of his unhappiness.

Immediately following the guardians' meeting, Katharine traveled to Des Moines, Iowa, to attend the League of Women Voters' third annual convention (April 9 to 14, 1923).[1] The meeting proved disappointing to her. In addition, she came under fire from members of the board for her involvement in the New York branch's actions regarding birth control. Moreover, a number of rancorous exchanges with Mrs. Catt made her wish she had not attended.

Each day's sessions revealed the league's continuing internal conflicts. As had occurred at previous conventions, Mrs. Catt's appeals to the delegates to debate issues not listed on the agenda only confused the organization's objectives and goals. Among her recommendations was a suggestion to invite men into the league. It inspired loud boos and hisses from the delegates.

Of course, President Park strongly disagreed. "If the League has a special purpose," she declared, "women must choose their own path, use their own techniques, and fashion their own political role." In addition, Katharine openly expressed her agreement with Park, to Mrs. Catt's chagrin. "What was the League formed for," as she pointed to Mrs. Catt, "if not for women to have a public forum." Katharine went on to remind Catt of their original reasons for organizing the league, "to keep women active in the political process."

Later in the convention, Katharine spoke on behalf of birth control when the Child Welfare Committee met to discuss the resolution. "This resolution must be passed, because of the necessity for us to confront this vital social issue," she implored the delegates, "and to demonstrate support for the movement itself." After considerable debate, in spite of Katharine's appeals, the committee defeated the resolution.[2] Katharine could not hide her anger at their actions and expressed disappointment at the delegates' "regressive thinking." In response to her accusation, a number of the committee members openly voiced their disapproval of Katharine's "tactics" with the New York branch to support Senator Rosenman's bill. At that moment, Katharine came close to resigning from the league. She became even angrier when she met with Mrs. Catt to discuss IWSA affairs.

Not surprisingly, Katharine received a cool reception from Mrs. Catt. She was stunned when Mrs. Catt informed Katharine that she was resigning from the IWSA to devote her energies to world peace. In fact, Catt had already drafted a letter and was about to mail it to the international board.

Taken aback by Mrs. Catt's decision, Katharine realized her tenure on the board would come to an end as well, since a new president would select her own officers. Thus, Katharine decided it was appropriate for her to resign the position of corresponding secretary. Unlike Mrs. Catt, Katharine chose to retain membership in the IWSA and, likewise, the League of Women Voters, because she believed it was necessary to keep informed of issues promoted by these organizations.

Nonetheless, this would be the first time in many years that she did not hold an official position in any woman's organization.[3] Although sorry about this turn of events, she seemed relieved. Fewer responsibilities and time commitments would free her energies for the birth control movement and Stanley's care.

In May, with an ambitious itinerary, Katharine sailed for Europe, her primary purpose to purchase diaphragms for Sanger's bureau. On this trip, she purchased more than she could safely bring back in her luggage. Katharine persuaded a ship's captain—money was undoubtedly exchanged—to transport boxes of diaphragms, carefully disguised in cosmetics cases, to a Canadian port. There, they were transferred to liquor smugglers, who carried the contraband across the border into one of the warehouses controlled by Noah Slee, Sanger's current husband and owner of the Three-In-One Oil Company, and ultimately to New York and the Clinical Research Bureau.[4]

When Katharine returned to the States in early December, she carried diaphragms not only in the linings of clothing, but in Christmas gift packages as well. As in previous years, customs officials did not inspect her luggage.

Katharine's summer of purchasing contraceptives had been briefly interrupted by a major crisis at Riven Rock. After a lengthy illness, Nettie McCormick died in Chicago, on July 5. Katharine received a cable from Bentley announcing Nettie's passing and plans for the funeral. Then, she heard nothing for three weeks. Who would inform Stanley of his mother's death, she wondered. What would they say? How would he respond? Katharine cabled Dr. Meyer regarding her concerns. "There may be something acute to require your presence," she informed Meyer.

Due to her concern about Dr. Brush's ability to convey such emotionally charged news, Katharine suggested to Meyer that McKillop tell Stanley. Meyer agreed and also pointed out that if Brush told Stanley, Brush might incur a violent reaction from Stanley. Meyer promised to help McKillop prepare the information for Stanley.[5]

At an appropriate moment, McKillop told Stanley of his mother's death. Afterward, McKillop reported that Stanley seemed to accept the information well; his only response was to order flowers for her funeral. To the guardians, Dr. Brush reported that Stanley seemed unusually calm since receiving the news.

Two weeks later, Katharine received a letter from Stanley. It had been written to her shortly after he had been informed of his mother's death.

Enclosed was a poem, the first he had written since their honeymoon, Katharine noted, and it came as a complete surprise.

Thoughts of a Young Tiger

I'm going on
I know not where
I'm going on
Where there was care
How good a job
Well done to dare.
I'm going on
Rest well assured
I know not what
Moment t'will be
Where fears around
Are crystalized.[6]

Katharine was simultaneously astonished and excited. She immediately sent a copy of the poem to Dr. Meyer to obtain his appraisal. "The enclosed poem came this morning from Stanley," she wrote. "It is the first straight speaking 'from the heart' that he has done."

Dr. Meyer responded with caution. Yes, it was indeed encouraging to hear from Stanley so soon after his mother's death. Yes, the poem had something to do with Nettie's death. Yes, the letter offered some insight into his feelings about being sequestered at Riven Rock. "Nevertheless," Meyer warned, "do not take this composition as an indication that Stanley is recovering his sanity. We'll have to monitor him closely the next few months to observe any aftereffects," Meyer concluded.[7] Neither Dr. Brush nor the McCormicks were ever informed about the poem.

Dr. Meyer's assessment of Stanley's behavior proved to be correct. As relevant as the poem had seemed to Katharine, Stanley's subsequent behavior shattered her optimism.

As a result of her activities with Margaret Sanger in New York, Katharine was unable to attend Riven Rock's Christmas festivities. Stanley seemed to sense her absence. Although he received gifts from Katharine, he claimed that she had not been thinking about him and had even forgotten his birthday. In a moment of anger, he ordered Dr. Brush to send Katharine a telegram:

Dear Mrs. McCormick:
    I divorce you.
    Yours truly,
    Stanley R. McCormick.[8]

A second telegram Stanley dictated went to Bentley's office.

Dear Sirs,
   I have just divorced my wife.
   Yours very truly,
   Stanley R. McCormick.[9]

Dr. Brush had no choice but to send the telegrams, following the orders given him about censorship. Nevertheless, he found himself unable to handle the volatile situation, let alone its implications, so he quickly wired Dr. Meyer for guidance. Meyer instructed him to retain the letters, but his wire to Brush came too late; the messages had already been sent.

Taken aback by Stanley's telegram, Katharine felt some guilt about not personally visiting Riven Rock. Instead of consulting Dr. Meyer, this time she turned to Dr. Brill for his analysis of the situation. Brill was quick to point out that Stanley, having shed one of the protagonists of the "battle" for his possession (Nettie), was now making an attempt to rid himself of the other. "It is a momentary reaction that will soon pass," Brill advised.

In contrast, Dr. Meyer saw this episode as an opportunity to reintroduce his proposal to Katharine to divorce Stanley, which, of course, would relinquish her control over him. Meyer alerted Bentley, who in turn informed Anita. But no one could agree on specifically what should be done about the situation. When the guardians met in February, Stanley's telegrams were never mentioned.

According to Nettie's will, Stanley was the recipient of all her household goods from the McCormick mansion on Rush Street, a rich array of furniture, rugs and tapestries, dinnerware, and family ephemera. While the family agreed he could do little about its disposition, they felt he should be consulted. "But how?" Katharine asked.

After much debate, as well as Dr. Meyer's advice, it was finally agreed that Dr. Brush would tell Stanley about the items and relay his reactions to the guardians. Still, the McCormicks were hesitant and worried that such a discussion might cause Stanley discomfort and possibly trigger a violent reaction. Final resolution of the problem was never revealed, although family letters suggested that Stanley was never approached about the disposition of his mother's household goods.

The question of endocrine testing had come about through a series of letters between Katharine and Dr. Meyer. She had written Meyer citing the results of a number of endocrine studies on mental patients in recent medical journals, which suggested that there appeared to be a relationship between chemical imbalance and mental disease. "Such knowledge could contribute to patient recovery," Katharine argued.[10]

Much to her surprise, Dr. Meyer did not disagree. In fact, his response persuaded Katharine to contact a number of doctors to determine what tests could be safely administered to Stanley. Among those contacted was Dr. Timme, a renowned endocrinologist who also happened to be a colleague of Meyer. In a letter to the guardians, Timme suggested that Stanley would likely be a good subject for testing. Meyer was reluctant to intercede between Timme and Katharine and instead requested that the guardians discuss the matter.

Since Meyer did not lobby against the evaluation, the McCormicks agreed to proceed with the tests, as long as Meyer supervised them. Katharine was pleased. After years of being stonewalled, she had finally obtained clearance for Stanley to receive an endocrine evaluation.

Unfortunately, the collaboration between Katharine and Dr. Meyer was interrupted when, in a letter to Katharine, Dr. Brush casually mentioned Stanley's divorce correspondence and Meyer's involvement. In panic, Brush cabled Meyer to help him out of this situation. Meyer was now forced to tell Katharine of his advice to the McCormicks following the episode and offered her his "interpretation" of why he had made the suggestion that Katharine divorce Stanley.[11]

Although Katharine was now made aware of Meyer's duplicity, she chose to set aside the issue since planning for Stanley's endocrine tests was more important. She did not, however, forget the deception. Dr. Meyer must be relieved of his consultancy, Katharine decided, as quickly as she could orchestrate it.

With little difficulty, Katharine persuaded Meyer to talk to Timme; when that was accomplished, she pressed to have Timme visit Riven Rock. "I am very anxious to have the endocrine viewpoint brought to bear on Stanley's case," she explained to Dr. Timme, "and hope there is some way of adding it to his present treatment."[12]

Dr. Timme agreed to visit Riven Rock in July; Dr. Meyer would also attend. Since Katharine was leaving for Europe in June—another diaphragm purchasing trip—Newton Baker would serve as her representative. Prior to the departure, Katharine wrote Meyer; the letter outlined Timme's mandate and Meyer's role to expedite it. "I am very anxious he [Timme] should have abundant opportunity to see and study the patient in any way he may think desirable." In other words, Meyer was not to interfere in Dr. Timme's examination, in any manner.

For a full week, Dr. Timme examined and tested Stanley. According to his report, Stanley was "extremely cooperative throughout." Timme's report concluded that Stanley was indeed suffering from "some endocrincopathy."

"This lack of balance is shown in his biochemistry," Timme wrote, "and his treatment must consist in endeavoring to overcome his present disturbance." Timme cautioned, however, "Even though the original cause may be removed, we have no means of being assured in advance to what extent this fixation can be diminished."[13]

After obtaining the report, Dr. Meyer wasted no time in finding out from Bentley when Katharine planned to return from Europe, giving as his excuse, "I am anxious to take up the question of the control work on the endocrine possibilities." Instead of waiting, however, Meyer ordered separate evaluations to determine the effects of endocrine treatments on Stanley. "I am going to take some steps to start some control investigations," he wrote Bentley. "I cannot feel satisfied without getting some work started before Mrs. McCormick's return."[14]

By initiating these actions, Meyer began his attempt to undermine the endocrine approach. Bentley was confused and wondered why Meyer was so insistent on initiating evaluation. Could he not wait for Katharine to return?

Unfortunately for Katharine, her summer had not proceeded as planned. Shortly after arriving at the château, she became ill and was diagnosed as suffering from a strep throat, keeping her at home, in bed, for three weeks. After two weeks of travel, Katharine experienced a relapse and was forced to remain in bed another two weeks, much to her dismay. The attending doctor recommended more rest and pointed out rather bluntly that, at almost fifty years of age, Katharine maintained too heavy a schedule. His advice was treated with disdain.

Nevertheless, Katharine's illness prevented her from making the planned round of cities to purchase diaphragms. When she returned to the United States in October, she brought back less than half of what had previously been smuggled in. Katharine was also chagrined about her recent illness—she had not been bedridden for more than twenty years—and resolved to take action to protect her health. Beyond that, she also made a number of other personal decisions.

First, Katharine moved from the Plaza Hotel to 640 Park Avenue, an apartment that provided more room and was more comfortably furnished. Along with the maid and cook, she employed a live-in secretary, a young college student. Then, she resigned membership in the IWSA, citing her increased activity with the birth control movement, but offered her services at future conventions. At the same time, Katharine's activities with the Clinical Research Bureau would have to be temporarily curtailed, because of her additional responsibilities in dealing with Stanley's care. With regard to her personal health, Katharine embarked on a papaya diet and daily, vigorous walks.

When Katharine learned, via Newton Baker, of Dr. Meyer's recent decisions, she immediately recognized that Meyer's control tests had been undertaken to discredit any future endocrine treatments. To better understand Meyer's aims, she wrote Dr. Brush and asked for a full report on Stanley's behavior and his observations on the results of treatments since July.

Brush responded by telling Katharine that Stanley had reacted badly to

Dr. Timme's testing (the opposite of what Timme had reported).[15] Brush noted both improvements and problems: Stanley seemed to be more accessible; his letter writing had become more coherent; his posture and gait had improved. On the negative side, Brush wrote, Stanley's tenseness had increased and masturbation had "certainly increased." Finally, with an uncharacteristic plea, Brush asked, "What can I do to bring more care into Stanley's life?"

Surely, Dr. Brush had not shared this letter with Meyer, Katharine thought. But neither did Brush make any references to Meyer's antipathy toward possible endocrine treatment and his actions regarding Stanley's testing, information he surely must have been familiar with.

Without waiting for further explanations, Katharine contacted Meyer directly. "I am asking two additional endocrinologists to examine Stanley and recommend treatments." She apologized for "failing to make clear my intentions" regarding Stanley's care, but that "any plan of examination will be decided by me."[16] Meyer did not respond to Katharine's directive.

The already sensitive situation was further exacerbated by a somewhat muddled letter Stanley sent to Katharine.

Decided Harvester undesirable situation too late for my success; ignorant of situation when asked you to be my wife. Impossible continue, request freedom.
    Stanley Robert McCormick[17]

Dutifully, Dr. Brush sent a copy of the letter to Meyer. Meyer, in turn, wrote Katharine, acknowledged having seen Stanley's letter, and suggested the patient seemed to be reacting to some "unknown stimulus"— the endocrine testing, Katharine believed his meaning to be. When Katharine pointedly asked Brush and Meyer why Stanley had written the letter, they were unable, or hesitant, to give an explanation. McKillop, however, volunteered an answer. He believed that Stanley had become angry with Katharine for not informing him of her return to the States the previous month. The episode disappeared as quickly as it had surfaced.

In the meantime, Dr. Timme had become increasingly aggravated by the lack of confidence Meyer had expressed regarding his tests. Following Katharine's suggestion, he settled for a joint conference to develop plans for evaluating Stanley. In accordance with Katharine's directives, the new endocrinologists, Drs. Rowe and Lawrence, administered tests. This time, however, the tests took a number of weeks to complete because Stanley often refused to cooperate. Urine tests and X-rays were particularly difficult to administer, and when they were completed, there was some debate about their reliability. Meyer questioned every step of the analysis.

The entire endocrine evaluation seemed on the verge of breaking down. Dr. Brush stepped in to explain to Katharine the "unnecessary delays," five months having passed since initiation of Timme's tests. Brush promised to complete the task. Nonetheless, in another of his now familiar gaffes, he expressed doubt about any positive results.

Exasperated with Brush's explanation, Katharine told him bluntly that she found his report so unsatisfactory that, in the interests of reliable testing, she was ending all such activity "for the time being." Everyone but Meyer agreed, since he wanted to prove the tests unreliable.

Simultaneous with the impasse on endocrine testing, Anita announced that Dr. Kraepelin planned to tour the United States during the summer. "Wouldn't it be fortuitous if he could examine Stanley as he had done in 1908," she suggested, "and give the guardians an updated report." Only Dr. Meyer objected. He wrote Bentley, advising that Kraepelin's visit be limited to observations of the patient, because anything more "would tend to detract from current efforts. I shall regret any complication at this juncture."

Katharine, Anita, and Bentley chose to ignore Meyer's argument and invited Dr. Kraepelin to examine Stanley. Katharine particularly saw this as an opportunity to diminish Meyer's involvement in Stanley's care. When Meyer received the news, he wrote Anita, restating his views and revealing his personal opinions about Dr. Kraepelin. He accused Kraepelin of having no interest in seeing Stanley other than to obtain access to the McCormicks to solicit funds for his institute. Meyer's real objections, however, were revealed in the last paragraph of his letter:

In view of the fact that Mr. Bentley turned down my request for support of the catatonia research, I regret somewhat that money should be diverted in the direction of someone who hates this country and who really will not have anything to contribute to the solution of our immediate problems.[18]

Unexpectedly, Anita shared the letter with Katharine and Bentley. Katharine, in turn, showed the letter to Newton Baker, who warned her of the implications of Meyer's continued interference. Regarding the events of the past year at Riven Rock, Baker also expressed the opinion that he "had never before dealt with such bellicose and indecisive people."

Together, the guardians agreed that Dr. Meyer had clearly overstepped his consulting role. Katharine prepared a letter, which Anita and Bentley also signed, expressing dissatisfaction with Meyer's supervision of Stanley and with his consultation. In what was clearly a devastating indictment of Meyer's competency, the guardians concluded, "From the layman's point of view, we find no recognizable improvement in Stanley."

Receipt of the letter convinced Meyer that his supervision of Stanley would likely be terminated. Nevertheless, given the manner in which the guardians solved problems, he believed it would take them some time to discuss and decide on the process of termination. In the meantime, he decided to extend the lucrative arrangement for as long as he could manage.

On April 25, 1925, almost seventeen years to the day since his previous visit, Dr. Kraepelin arrived at Riven Rock to examine Stanley. Upon completion of the two-day examination, he issued two brief reports to the guardians: the first was a summary of Stanley's current condition; the second was an analysis of Stanley's mental state, comparing it to the 1908 examination.[19]

According to Kraepelin's observations, Stanley was able to carry on a fairly well-connected and relevant conversation upon topics of the day. His irritability and temper had lessened. He was more willing to accept guidance from those around him, particularly his nurses. He no longer soiled his bed; his sleep, bodily functions, and appetite were "on a very good level." All in all, Stanley seemed to enjoy his daily regimen.

On the negative side, Stanley remained tense and overactive. He was still unable to complete tasks. Guards continued to prevent him from running away or striking the nurses.

As for the comparative analysis of Stanley, Dr. Kraepelin's report was quite negative. "I regret to have to state that the further course of the illness has corroborated the diagnosis made seventeen years ago, viz., that of a severe catatonic process," Kraepelin judged. "The profound catatonic manifestations are still present in pronounced form."

Upon reading the report, Dr. Meyer quickly responded. In defense of his supervisory role, "The situation concerning Stanley McCormick is very complex," he stated. Meyer referred to the replacement of doctors and the guardians' constant interference. He specifically pointed out Katharine's demand for "far more experimentation than has been deemed advisable." Then, in a brief letter to Kraepelin, Meyer advised him not to be hasty about his conclusions in the case.

A few days later, at her request, Dr. Kraepelin met with Katharine to report his observations. Beyond the written report, he told her that Stanley had demonstrated "mental deterioration." Further, he opined that Stanley should be granted more interaction with his family, including Katharine, to relieve his loneliness. "Dr. Kraepelin," Katharine revealed, somewhat annoyed, "I have not seen Stanley for seventeen years."

"Oh, no! Oh, no!" Kraepelin reacted in surprise.

"Would you have any objections to quoting your words to Dr. Meyer?" Katharine inquired.

"I will talk to Meyer himself before I leave the country," Kraepelin promised.

Instead, he wrote Meyer a letter. At the same time, Katharine reported to Meyer her conversation with Kraepelin. Not surprisingly, Dr. Meyer's response was antagonistic and deprecating.

"The note of Prof. Kraepelin is much more guarded than his conversation with you, in which he must have talked on the spur of the moment," Meyer wrote Katharine. "His real conception of mental disease is one of more or less fatalism concealed behind a profession of total ignorance of the real essence of the disease." He went on. "To me, this is absurd. It is explained only by the frequent lack of human contact with and solicitude for the patient."[20]

When Katharine specifically asked Meyer to explain his views regarding Kraepelin's examination of Stanley, he roundly criticized the psychiatrist's interpretation and reminded her of Stanley's improvement over the years. "I promise to prepare a complete report, putting all the facts together for the guardians," he declared. In closing, Meyer called Kraepelin's report "a misinterpretation of facts."

Katharine promised Dr. Meyer she would share his comments with Anita and Bentley. As far as she was concerned, however, this was just another example of Meyer's mishandling and defensiveness.

Waiting to receive Dr. Kraepelin's report, Katharine had postponed her annual trip to Europe. As she was preparing for the journey, she received a letter from Drs. Rowe and Lawrence regarding the results of the endocrine tests performed on Stanley. The results came as a complete surprise. The doctors reported they had found no endocrine disease, and thus no basis for endocrine treatment.[21]

Once again, Katharine delayed the trip to seek more information from the doctors. It proved a fortunate decision.

On June 29, 1925, shortly before 7:00 A.M., a major earthquake struck Santa Barbara, causing considerable damage to the city and surrounding areas. Riven Rock had suffered severely.

Twenty-Two

On June 29, near dawn, city engineer Herbert Nunn was awakened by an overwhelming stench of crude oil. From his house overlooking the beach, he saw oil seeping out of the sand across a wide expanse of the otherwise pristine beach. At the same time, personnel at the City Water Department noticed a distinct, uncharacteristic drop of pressure in all of Santa Barbara's water mains.

Santa Barbara residents rising before 6:30 A.M. quickly became aware of strange animal behavior. Dogs were seen running around in a bewildered fashion, some howling mournfully. Chickens were found huddled together in the corners of their pens. Cows and horses snorted and pranced and kicked uncontrollably in their pens. Cats crouched in seeming fear.

At Riven Rock, the day's usual activities had already begun. Stanley was awake; McKillop was helping him dress. Dr. Brush was in the kitchen seeing to the breakfast menu. Groundskeepers were already at work watering shrubbery and flowers partially dried out due to a continuing heat wave. A delivery truck from Santa Barbara was entering the estate, bringing the day's provisions.

At 6:44 A.M., the ground crackled, shuddered, and rolled as an earthquake of significant magnitude rippled through Santa Barbara from west to east.[1] The first shock lasted eighteen seconds—a "hard, jolting vibration," as most residents described the sensation. Many people were thrown to the ground or from their beds. After a brief lull, there followed a series of heavy rumbles and shakes, lasting from six to eight seconds each. By 7:00 A.M., the entire area was enveloped in a dusty, ominous quiet.

The initial shock had weakened structures; the following waves col- lapsed homes, stores, churches, and theaters throughout Santa Barbara's downtown. Railroad and telephone lines were down, disrupting services. A water reservoir dam in the hills above the town had disintegrated and sent forty-five million gallons rushing down the usually dry Sycamore Creek, through the center of town, sweeping everything in front of it to the ocean.

Amazingly, only twelve people were killed. However, the entire center of the town had been leveled, a grotesque scene of destruction that had never occurred in its history.

The area surrounding Riven Rock, significantly east of the epicenter, did not suffer such extensive ruin, although buildings were noticeably damaged, gates were torn from their foundations, creek walls had fallen, and paved paths had cracked. The only major damage found at Riven Rock was in Stanley's residence.

When the earthquake struck, the ever-alert McKillop quickly moved Stanley outside onto the lawn at the same time that groundskeepers began to congregate, many of them showing signs of panic. Dr. Brush and his helpers also escaped the house, and Brush was busy attempting to calm the personnel.

The house tower had sustained a sizable crack down its entire length. Both chimneys were now no more than piles of rubble, and thick dust filled the air, so heavy it was difficult to see beyond a few feet. McKillop reported that most of the windows in the house had been shattered and cracks were noticeable on most of the internal walls.

Stanley was later reported to have responded to the incident with rela- tively little agitation, although he did express sadness about the destruc- tion of his home. McKillop and Tompkins spent hours collecting what they could out of the damaged house and assisted Stanley into the rec- reation building, the least affected of Riven Rock's structures. The Brush cottage remained standing, but most of the household items inside had been disarranged or smashed. Mrs. Brush had become hysterical and re- quired sedation.

Dr. Brush reported the incident to the guardians by cable as quickly as he could, given the breakdown in communications. Actually, both the McCormicks and Katharine first learned about the earthquake in the newspapers; but information about Stanley's condition was delayed. Katharine had already embarked for Riven Rock even before she received the details of the cataclysm from Brush.

Prior to Katharine's arrival, Santa Barbara officials had activated emer- gency plans. Within three days, they were in operation, albeit in a nominal way. Only a few hours following the quake, debris-removal crews were already working, to hunt for trapped people and to clear streets. Additional police and fire personnel from Los Angeles had arrived to assist local authorities.

"Back to normal" became the town fathers' watchword. Food stores and bakeries were reopened in two days. Phone and telegraph communication had been sufficiently repaired to handle essential messages. State Street, the town's main business thoroughfare, had been cleared; and most businesses opened. Local newspapers, hampered by the lack of electricity to run their presses, managed to publish one-page extras and distribute them on street corners throughout the town. When McKillop picked up Katharine in Pasadena and drove her to Riven Rock, local roads had been cleared and rubble removed, revealing few signs of the quake.

When Katharine entered the estate, however, she was shocked to see the condition of the buildings and grounds. Although five days had passed since the earthquake, a pall of thick dust still hung in the air. She saw the main building in shambles and immediately recognized that it would have to be replaced. Other buildings had sustained less damage and could likely be repaired, she guessed. The grounds were already partially restored. From McKillop, Katharine learned that Stanley seemed to be enjoying his temporary quarters, joking with everyone about "camping out," although Brush had been instructed by Dr. Meyer to report at once any aftereffects in his behavior.

Katharine now assumed full control over Riven Rock's reconstruction. The main residence would require almost complete restoration. Was it worth it? She believed not and ordered plans for a new home to be built. Anita and Bentley were on their way to appraise the situation and assist Katharine. Altogether, within two weeks, a recovery plan had been prepared and refurbishing had begun. Through all of this activity, Stanley remained an interested, almost bemused observer. It would be more than a year before he would be able to move into his new home.

Since the availability of diaphragms had been curtailed because of a police crackdown on North American manufacturing sources, Margaret Sanger again had asked Katharine to purchase as many as she could smuggle in when she took her summer trip to Europe. Sanger's request came days before the earthquake struck Santa Barbara. Though her trip was delayed, Katharine promised to do what she could for Sanger, even though she planned a short European excursion and a return to Riven Rock in September. Directing all parties involved in the estate's reconstruction to keep her and Newton Baker informed daily, she prepared to sail from New York at the end of July.

The trip to the château and sojourns to various European cities would have been relaxing except for the flurry of cables and telegrams from Dr. Brush and Meyer, along with added commentary from Bentley. Katharine spent hours each day answering this correspondence; if she did not, she suspected, activities at Riven Rock would come to a halt. In agonizing

detail, Brush reported the construction of Stanley's residence and the numerous problems experienced with workmen. Katharine knew such self-
serving complaints to be an ongoing problem with Brush. After Katharine
had departed, Dr. Meyer visited Riven Rock to evaluate Stanley's condition. Bentley conveyed his observations of Brush's efforts, both positive
and negative, with his usual efficiency.

Not surprisingly, Dr. Meyer used Katharine's absence to obtain what he
described as "a full discussion of the facts" regarding the endocrine testing
program, in an obvious attempt to discredit them. He also pressed Katharine for further information on her conversation with Dr. Kraepelin,
which she refused to reveal, making no reference to it in her return letters.
Finally, in annoyance at his continual prodding, Katharine cabled Meyer,
telling him, simply and clearly, that "endocrine treatments are to be resumed immediately."

Along with her daily writing chores to the "Riven Rock crowd," Katharine also wrote Sanger, informing her of successes in purchasing diaphragms, all letters written in such a way that only Sanger understood.
At the same time, however, she informed Sanger that she would have to
withdraw from birth control activities "for some time," until the situation
at Riven Rock had stabilized. Enclosed in the letter was a $5,000 check in
support of Sanger's clinic.

Upon her return to the States—as usual, no problems with customs
officials—Katharine delivered the diaphragms, saw Sanger briefly, and
boarded the next train for Pasadena. A guardians' meeting had been
planned to update progress at Riven Rock and to allocate funds for its
reconstruction needs. When she arrived, Katharine discovered that work
on the new house had been stalled because county officials were bogged
down in paperwork dedicated to earthquake-related rebuilding. A quick
trip to county offices got construction at Riven Rock moving again.

The entire meeting, which was attended by Anita, Bentley, Dr. Brush,
Katharine, and Newton Baker, was taken up with Riven Rock's recon-
struction. Dr. Brush was assigned a new list of estate responsibilities.[2]
Bentley was to remain on the estate, ostensibly to assist Brush, but in
reality to see that he completed the tasks. After the meeting, Brush cabled
Meyer, complaining, "Am I a physician or a caretaker?"

No sooner was she finished with Riven Rock business than Katharine
headed for St. Louis to attend the sixth annual League of Women Voters
convention. Katharine had continued her membership and served as a
delegate from Massachusetts.

Although the league was now in its sixth year of operation, internal
and philosophical struggles, as well as financial deficits, continued to burden its national governing board.[3] Maud Wood Park, Katharine's old
friend, had retired from the presidency after four years, admittedly tired
but also satisfied that at least she had been able to hold the organization

together. She was frustrated, however, at being unable to establish the national board's authority and at the league's inability to attract new members.

Belle Sherman had been elected the league's new national president. During the early part of her reign, league directives appeared confusing to members. Debates about the role of the organization, which issues to embrace, and the division of responsibility between the national board and state branches continued to plague its leaders, and most of these debates remained unresolved. Sherman quickly discovered that pragmatic issues created more enthusiastic involvement and commitment than did philosophical issues. While Sherman continued to press for increased political education among women, it would take years before the issue would be embraced as a national goal. In 1924, only one woman had been elected to Congress, even though the league had sponsored a substantial get-out-the-vote effort. Lack of funds continued to plague the organization.

Choosing St. Louis as a site for the convention may not have been a good idea. St. Louis had been the location for the Jubilee Convention, the suffragists' final "hurrah" for having won the vote for women. Instead of the league's extolling the virtues of its suffrage heritage, however, the national board chose to sever all identity with it.[4] By 1926, none of the committee chairs had been in office in 1920, and only six out of thirty-six remained as state presidents. The convention attracted a smaller number of delegates than any of the five previous conventions, a total of only 311 women, and minimal press coverage. Forty-four states claimed they had league branches, but only twenty-four had functioning boards. Half of the delegates at the convention were controlled by five states, four of them representing the more conservative Midwest.

Further, the league reported its first debt since 1922. Its budget in 1924–25 had been $135,000, falling far short of its needs; significant program reductions would have to be made to balance the next year's books. Most of the league's funds had continued to come from wealthy supporters; their yearly donations had been keeping the organization alive. These days, however, this group of women was more likely to be supporting the growing birth control movement.

When Katharine raised the issue of birth control in a speech to the delegates, few listened to her pleas. When she appealed to members of the Health and Welfare Committee, Katharine could not even get them to recognize birth control as a league issue. They voted against supporting it, believing the league should not participate in such potentially contentious arguments. Nevertheless, at the conclusion of the convention, Katharine continued to show her support for the league by donating $5,000.[5]

Katharine shared with Sanger her frustration about the league regarding its position on birth control. "I was unable to get them to realize the relevance of the issue to their own cause," she wrote. Instead of responding to Katharine's concerns, Sanger asked if she would contribute money to Dr. F. A. E. Crew of the University of Edinburgh, who was planning to initiate research on pharmaceutical contraception.[6] It was like that, Katharine thought, with most of Sanger's letters, always asking for money. Yet this letter represented the first correspondence between Katharine and Sanger dealing with the possibility of a drug to prevent contraception.

After the convention, Katharine returned to Riven Rock, to find letters from Dr. Meyer protesting Dr. Brush's nonmedical responsibilities as caretaker of the estate, citing problems Brush was having with his wife as an excuse for his not paying "the necessary attention to Stanley" and as the reason for Brush's delay in conducting endocrine treatments. Katharine responded by reminding Meyer that the guardians continued to be "unsatisfied with his misplaced efforts." As Newton Baker noted to Katharine, the "battle" with Meyer appeared to be growing more contentious. Something would have to be done about it soon, he cautioned.

Dr. Meyer then asked Anita for a meeting to "clarify the issues." Meyer lamented: "It is a terrible cloud that my work is called unsatisfying." What would Stanley have been without the care he has been given? Katharine replied: "What, indeed."

Anita reported that Meyer seemed to have been jostled by the news. He claimed that he had never been treated this way and believed that "further understanding of my position is needed."[7]

"It is unfortunate that all has not been more open," Meyer continued. "I have no design. I have had to cross Mrs. McCormick, but I must on my judgement." Meyer also expressed his disappointment about the disagreement regarding endocrine treatments. "I wanted proof," he said, "but Mrs. McCormick wanted treatments."

During further discussion, Meyer brought up another problem he was having, one that involved Dr. R. D. Hoskins, a research endocrinologist at Ohio State University, who, according to Meyer, was talking to Katharine about the establishment of an endocrine research facility. "Why is Mrs. McCormick going behind my back to fund another doctor?" Meyer asked indignantly.

Actually, Katharine had planned to help develop the Hoskins project quite separate from Stanley or Riven Rock.[8] When she had heard of his proposal to establish an endocrine research lab, she requested that Hoskins develop a program "that would bring to bear the various laboratory resources and particularly such as offer promise from an endocrine point of view on the case of my husband." On what conditions would he be willing to direct such a laboratory, she inquired.

Now that Meyer had interjected the Hoskins project into his argument, it would require discussion and debate among the guardians and temporarily deflect the situation with Meyer, Katharine acknowledged. Meyer's comments were surely made in spite and would undoubtedly precipitate another round of those torpid, indecisive guardian discussions that Katharine so detested.

Hoskins dutifully submitted his plan to the guardians. It consisted of a five-year project, at the cost of $20,000 a year.[9] When asked his opinion by Anita and Bentley, Meyer balked at recognizing Hoskins's proposal and indicated he had little faith in Hoskins's ability to run the proposed laboratory. Bentley attempted to mediate, but failed. Meyer remained adamant about his opinion of Hoskins. "My doubts of Hoskins are great, in the light of the fact that Dr. Hoskins has hardly been one of those who have been the most creative and significant workers in the field of endocrinological biochemistry."[10]

Meyer also requested another meeting, this time with Bentley, to discuss the entire situation in detail. When Bentley shared the letter with Anita and Katharine, both expressed extreme displeasure with Meyer's arguments and especially his comments suggesting that Hoskins was somehow "unprofessional." They agreed it was time to tell Meyer he was no longer needed to supervise Stanley's care. Bentley was chosen to carry the news.

When Bentley met with Meyer, he outlined the guardians' position as regarded Stanley's care. Bentley noted Meyer's unswerving support of Dr. Brush, whereas the guardians considered Brush untrustworthy and untrained in psychoanalytic methods. This, the guardians considered, was one of the primary reasons that Stanley had been "losing ground." The guardians believed the situation could no longer continue.

Although Meyer disputed the allegations, he knew the effort was fruitless and recognized that his tenure as a consultant was coming to an end. Still, he fought the inevitable. Instead of resigning, Meyer waited for the guardians to dismiss him.

Katharine remedied that impasse with a letter to Meyer, telling him succinctly that "Stanley had not had a sustained attention and examination from you regarding that of the new psychology. For that reason, your services are no longer needed."[11]

Regarding the Hoskins proposal, Katharine decided to fund the entire project herself, apart from any guardian involvement, with Hoskins reporting to her. Thus, the Stanley R. McCormick Memorial Foundation for Neuro-Endocrine Research Corporation was born. (The reference to Stanley was soon dropped for tax purposes, on the advice of Newton Baker.) Dr. Hoskins was made director of the foundation, and he would remain in that position for more than twenty years. Katharine became president of the board of directors. The organization was the first of its kind in the United States to conduct research on the relationship between endocrinology and mental illness, particularly schizophrenia. Thirty years later, research psychiatrists would acknowledge and declare that a chemical imbalance in schizophrenics likely contributed to their illness, just as Katharine had originally speculated.

During the time the foundation operated, more than 350 studies were completed and published. Unfortunately, none of them served to help Stanley. During the 1940s, the foundation moved to Worcester, Massachusetts, and Hudson Hoagland, a friend of Katharine, took over as director. It is estimated that Katharine donated nearly half a million dollars to the foundation.

Now that the Meyer predicament had finally been settled, Katharine believed, efforts must be initiated by the guardians to find another doctor for Stanley, preferably one with a "modern" approach toward his care and possible rehabilitation. Katharine had not yet given up on Stanley's recovery, especially now that the "old affiliations" had finally been overthrown.

Dr. Kempf, the Trial, and the Aftermath

Twenty-Three

In June 1926, Margaret Sanger announced that she was taking a leave of absence from the American Birth Control League to prepare for an international conference scheduled for the following year in Geneva, Switzerland. Both she and Katharine believed that Geneva would be an excellent location for the birth control conference since it was the home of the League of Nations and offered a unique opportunity to educate delegates about the importance of population control. Katharine not only assisted Sanger in planning the conference and donated funds for its operation, but also offered her château for conference use. For her contributions, she was to have been in charge of the meeting's social programs.[1]

What surely had to have been frustrating for Katharine was that she could not attend the conference when it opened on August 31, 1927. A series of escalating disagreements about Stanley's care would demand her full attention and prevent her from leaving the country. These were but preludes to an emotionally charged confrontation with the McCormick family that in late 1929 would result in what the press labeled "the Freudian equivalent of the Scopes trial." National coverage of the trial proved so fascinating and seductive that it took front-page precedence over the country's stock market crash.

This compelling drama all began when the guardians initiated their search for a new doctor-in-residence for Stanley. Much of the responsibility had been assumed by Katharine, who promised to identify and screen possible psychiatrists, interview them, and report her recommendations to the guardians. At their annual February meeting, the guardians decided that, for the time being, Dr. Brush would be retained, to help ease the transition. They also acknowledged that a new psychiatrist would likely come at a high price, so additional funds were set aside to handle such an eventuality. Katharine returned to New York to begin her search.

Katharine quickly discovered that most physicians were reluctant to give up their practices and move to an "outpost" like California. Some were aware of the "bizarre" medical situation at Riven Rock and wanted no part of it. As a last resort, Katharine asked Dr. Brill for recommendations; he suggested two psychiatrists, both world famous in the field, who might consider the challenge: Drs. Edward Kempf and William A. White. Katharine immediately contacted them for meetings.[2] To her surprise, Dr. Kempf seemed eager to discuss the assignment with her.[3]

Dr. Kempf and Katharine quickly came to an agreement, subject to the guardians' approval, by which he would become resident psychiatrist, on a yearly contract of $120,000. His responsibility would be solely therapeutic, with estate management assigned to another person. His work would begin in June 1927, after a visit to Riven Rock in May to meet the patient and gain familiarity with the environment. Although it meant a leave of absence from his practice, Kempf appeared ready to embrace the challenge.

Since he was deeply involved in hospital work at St. Elizabeth's in Washington, D.C., Dr. White was reluctant to relinquish his position. As an alternative, Katharine persuaded him to supervise Kempf in his work, conferring with him and occasionally examining Stanley to corroborate Kempf's analysis and Stanley's progress. For a fee of a reported $6,000 a year plus travel expenses, White accepted, and promised to join Kempf in the trip to Riven Rock.

When Katharine convened with the guardians, she was met with Bentley's resignation. He claimed to be "worn out," but rumors suggested he was exasperated with battling Katharine on behalf of the McCormick family for so many years. Harold was elected to take his place, and the guardians decided to give themselves a new name, the Personal Care Board. Their first act was to accept Katharine's recommendation of doctors to care for Stanley, since they seemed highly qualified. Their second act shocked Katharine.

Using the excuse that a calm and orderly transition would be beneficial to Stanley, Anita and Harold voted to have Dr. Meyer work with Kempf and White to explain the history and procedures necessary and help him understand the patient more fully. Katharine said nothing about the decision but later unloaded her frustrations on Newton Baker. "So we fire Dr. Meyer, and yet he continues to annoy us," she lamented. "What is he likely to tell the doctors?" Baker advised Katharine that nothing could be done about the decision except for her to monitor closely Meyer's interactions with Kempf and White.

Unknown to Katharine, Dr. Meyer had continued to maintain close touch with all activities at Riven Rock. Although Dr. Brush knew Meyer had been terminated, he continued to write weekly reports to his mentor, detailing everything that had taken place at the estate. In addition, Anita had hired Meyer as a consultant in the case of Mary Virginia, for a fee of $20,000 a year for five years. He was promised additional money for assisting Kempf and White.

In May, Drs. Kempf and White, Anita, Harold, Dr. Meyer, and Katharine visited Riven Rock. After Kempf met Stanley and toured the grounds, one of his first decisions was to remove the bars from Stanley's windows. Another, of greater significance, was to initiate a program whereby Stanley would meet with his female relatives, including Katharine. Kempf declared his firm belief to the guardians that family ties were an important part of the therapeutic process. In fact, he suggested that Katharine write Stanley, informing him of the changes in his care program. With obvious enthusiasm, Katharine embraced the assignment.[4]

To begin her letter to Stanley, Katharine apologized for not having written more often or with more feeling, explaining, "They [the presiding doctors] directed me to write very little and to make that little as impersonal as possible."

"I am writing today," she went on, "to tell you that all this situation is now changed and that for the first time since your illness I am able to write frankly and fully." Katharine went on to tell Stanley that she had become "thoroughly discontented with the way your case was being directed." She mentioned that, while Dr. Meyer "was a fine man, he belonged to the old school of psychiatry." She disclosed that Drs. Kempf and White were now going to work with him, outlined both their extensive resumes, and assured Stanley that they believed his case "to be curable."

Dr. Kempf, however, was not entirely satisfied with the allusions Katharine had made in the letter and shared his reactions with White and Meyer. Meyer took this opportunity to warn Kempf about Katharine and her "constant interference with the physicians." In a handwritten, private letter to Kempf, Meyer called Katharine an "unacceptable mate" to Stanley, causing Stanley's collapse into "a state of very disturbing emotional turmoil."[5] He related Katharine's interest in endocrine treatments and her efforts to get them started "against everyone's wishes." He accused Katharine of wanting "exclusive control" over Stanley and warned Kempf that she would hamper or fire any physician who didn't agree to her demands. Meyer also succeeded in persuading Kempf to retain Dr. Brush to assist him (and so keep Meyer closely apprised of the activities at Riven Rock).

In late June, Dr. Kempf arrived at Riven Rock and began daily discussions with Stanley to gain rapport and better understand his ability to articulate his feelings. No other doctor had talked to Stanley in this manner, let alone acknowledged that he was even "accessible." Within a matter of days, the doctor/patient relationship seemed to reap rewards. In his report to Katharine, Kempf informed her that a good deal of Stanley's "nervousness" had to do with his beliefs regarding her feelings about sex. Could he talk to her about the subject? Without hesitation, Katharine agreed.

In great detail, she related her experiences and frustrations early in the marriage, explaining to Kempf her naive approach toward these feelings, until they were later explored and understood under Dr. Brill's guidance. "I was so interested, and feeling so strongly all the time about sex, and desiring sex so much, I really understood almost nothing about sexual feelings themselves—in fact could scarcely have any at all—because of having been so repressed and inhibited all my life as the result of my up-bringing."[6]

Kempf suggested she share these feelings with Stanley to persuade him to discuss the issue more freely, which she did, addressing her husband as she had not done since he was placed in a hospital: "my dearest heart." She related to Stanley her conversations with Kempf and asked him to "talk with Dr. Kempf as freely as possible" and "not hold back a single detail that you can remember." She signed the letter, "I love you, darling heart."[7] Stanley, however, did not answer Katharine's letter, raising doubts in her mind. Maybe she had gone too far in revealing her inner-most feelings to Dr. Kempf, Katharine thought. Indeed, she now felt quite vulnerable.

Stanley's first unfettered walk in the yard soon turned to running, with McKillop and Kempf by his side. When he finally stopped, exhausted, he exclaimed excitedly, "This is great, Dr. Kempf." To help reduce Stanley's "feelings of humiliation," Kempf instructed the nurses not to hold him up when they walked around the grounds. A renewal of afternoon automobile rides often included amusing elbow horseplay with the nurses, "elbowing my way through life," Stanley explained to Kempf.

Kempf then introduced sketching to Stanley. At first hesitant, Stanley soon was outside, avidly drawing trees and clouds. According to Kempf, Stanley's inhibitions seemed to be receding as he increased his sense of personal freedom.

When Kempf told Stanley that he appeared ready to receive Katharine and Harold, Stanley, apparently frightened, left the room and remained silent for hours. The next day, however, he told Kempf that he would be delighted to see them.

When Katharine and Harold arrived, Kempf gave them instructions on what to say and how to behave. She and Stanley had not talked to or touched one another for twenty years. Katharine was so apprehensive that she nearly backed out. She appeared nervous, but Kempf assured her that, though the meeting might be awkward, "We have to start somewhere."

Although generally uneventful, their initial meeting proved more hysteric than historic. When Katharine and Harold walked up the steps of the house, the nurses ceremoniously unlocked the front door. Stanley stepped forward at once, stopped, looked at his visitors, and exclaimed excitedly, "This is Katharine!" Instead of any further greetings, however, he ran past the guests, through the door, and out onto the front lawn. With cool dispatch, the nurses caught him and brought him back into the house, where Kempf calmed him. A few minutes later, Stanley asked to see Katharine. Together, they sat in the parlor, but conversation was difficult. When Katharine left, Stanley gave her a formal "good-bye." Katharine sobbed all the way back to the hotel, admitting her joy at once again being with Stanley and her sadness remembering their early years together. Kempf, however, was ecstatic with the results of this first meeting.

During the days that followed, the meetings went much better. Stanley and Katharine talked of his drawing and the books read to him by Dr. Brush. Upon Katharine's departure, he kissed her formally. When he apologized for his action, Katharine assured Stanley that "the act had been well-received."

During July and August, Katharine and Harold made daily trips to see Stanley, and Kempf reported they were "giving very helpful assistance." Kempf then planned a beach outing, in response to which Stanley, aware of the significance of the event, pointed out that this would be his "first vacation outside the walls." Katharine then asked Kempf whether she might include her visitor, Julia Roessing, in the party. Kempf reluctantly agreed, but he warned Katharine of Stanley's possible reaction to a perceived "rival."

Successive beach parties saw Stanley relaxing to the point where he wore bathing trunks and enjoyed wading in the water. Stanley now seemed quite comfortable eating with other people and enjoying the outdoors. At the end of each evening's activities, he warmly kissed Katharine good-bye.

On their way back to New York, Katharine expressed to Julia her excitement and delight about Stanley's improvement and "the chance to actually be with him again." Julia had not seen Katharine so cheerful in years; but she wondered how long this idyllic situation could last, given the years of family friction.

Shortly after her return East, a satisfied and confident Katharine sent a proposal to Dr. Kempf regarding endocrine treatment along with a brief explanation of Dr. Hoskins's plans to conduct endocrine research, suggesting they might be coordinated in some fashion. Kempf had just returned to New York to close his office, and he recommended a meeting with Katharine, Harold, and Dr. Hoskins to discuss Katharine's proposal. The meeting became the catalyst for increasingly acrimonious arguments between Katharine and Dr. Kempf.[8]

First, Kempf felt that his work and Dr. Hoskins's research could not be combined because their objectives were so different. Regarding the use of endocrine treatments for Stanley, Kempf told Katharine, "Mrs. McCormick, I am unwilling to have anything in the way of glandular therapy introduced into the case at present, fearing it would affect adversely, by interruption or delay, the course of my psychoanalysis."

"While I appreciate the fine work you are doing, Dr. Kempf," Katharine replied stonily, "I am totally unable to see why the glandular treatment could not go on at the same time with the psychiatric."

Hoskins supported Katharine's argument, believing that such therapy could do no harm and, certainly, there was a chance of its success. However, Dr. Kempf rejected their entreaties outright and reminded everyone that he was in charge of the case; his position on the proposal was final. Katharine became so agitated with Kempf's response that she left the room.

A week later, Katharine received a letter from Kempf, apologizing for his decision but reaffirming his position regarding endocrine treatments for Stanley. What followed in the letter put Katharine in an even greater temper.

"In order to protect the patient during this most sensitive period of psychoanalysis, I am reviewing all correspondence sent to Stanley," Kempf wrote. In addition, he went on to suggest that, in future visits to Riven Rock, Julia Roessing should not accompany Katharine, "so as not to disturb the patient, as we are now embarking on a number of sexual matters."

Katharine quickly responded to Dr. Kempf with a telegraphed order. "I forbid you to interfere in any way with my correspondence with Stanley without my formal permission."[9]

In light of what she considered to be Dr. Kempf's intransigence, Katharine consulted with Newton Baker regarding what recourse she had to oppose his decisions. Baker told her she had no grounds to rebut him about Julia, but the contract with Dr. Kempf clearly stated that the guardians were in charge, not Kempf, as he had claimed.

Katharine immediately dispatched a telegram to Anita and Harold, indicating the withdrawal of her signature from Kempf's contract.[10] She followed with a letter to them outlining the reasons for retreating from her original support for Kempf, pointing out his "unwarranted decisions" and "arrogance in his belief he is in complete charge of the case."

Katharine was fiercely determined. "The physicians are employees of ours," she reminded Anita and Harold, "and we are in charge of Stanley's care."

In addition, she attempted to clarify her relationship with Julia Roessing by mentioning their friendship in the suffrage movement since 1910 and that "she is a warm friend of Mr. and Mrs. Newton Baker,"[11] as if she needed to legitimize the woman's social standing. In defiance of Dr.

Kempf, when Katharine visited Riven Rock at Christmas, she brought Julia. In apparent retaliation, Kempf accused Julia of asking the nurses unwarranted questions about Stanley. The holiday festivities were strained, yet this was the first time since Stanley's hospitalization that the entire family had celebrated New Year's Eve together.

The Personal Care Board's meeting in February 1928 simmered with tension and enmity. In his report of Stanley's progress since the previous June, Kempf complained about Katharine's "interference." In turn, Katharine delineated her reasons for removing her signature from Kempf's contract and argued to have him fired. Nonetheless, Anita and Harold voted to retain Kempf because Stanley seemed to be improving.

Kempf's report was, indeed, quite encouraging.[12] He had brought in a female nurse and housekeeper because Stanley's sexual fears had diminished. Extensive dental work, long delayed, had at last been completed, due primarily to Stanley's increasingly cooperative attitude. With no apparent problems, Stanley was periodically being taken into Santa Barbara to see the sights. Stanley's ability to talk, read, walk, enjoy companionship, and engage in conversation had all improved. Most important, his attitudes toward family members had become more trusting and loving.

Yet Kempf did include in his report his opposition to endocrine treatments and noted Katharine's rigidity regarding his examination of Stanley's mail: "Her refusal prevented me from protecting Stanley from disturbing suggestions and subjects which may cause excitement, depression, or confusion." He also mentioned the episode of Katharine bringing Mrs. Roessing to Riven Rock. "In the future, if Mrs. McCormick would cooperate with me more closely," Kempf concluded, "a more successful administration of Stanley's environment would take place."

In response, Katharine condemned Kempf's arrogance; she could not tolerate the censorship of her letters to Stanley. "Dr. Kempf no longer has my support," she stated, "and I wish him to be terminated." Anita and Harold said nothing, and the meeting ended without discussion of the usual budget planning for the coming year.

After the meeting, Baker asked Katharine why, if Kempf seemed so successful with Stanley, she wanted him fired. "It is not just his attempt to intimidate the Personal Care Board that bothers me," Katharine replied, "but . . . his insistence that Stanley has so dramatically improved."

"I believe you should give him more flexibility, Mrs. McCormick, since he has helped Stanley more than any other doctor," Baker advised.

"Thank you for your advice, Mr. Baker, but after seeing Stanley almost daily for two months, he seems to me to be getting no better. I am particularly concerned over this lack of adequate attention to his physical condition."

"You mean Kempf's refusal to conduct endocrine treatments?" Baker asked. "Or are there other matters troubling you?"

"That Kempf's therapy should be allowed to dominate the situation to the exclusion of the physical seems to me incomprehensibly negligent. It is my intention to urge the utilization of every possible means of helping Stanley," Katharine declared defiantly.

Later, after reviewing the meeting and his conversation with Katharine, Baker wondered what other issues were weighing on her that seemed to have produced such uncharacteristic anger against Kempf. Baker believed the situation would only worsen.

Baker's prediction proved correct. Between February and June, when Kempf delivered his next appraisal of Stanley's progress, the conflict between him and Katharine escalated. When Anita praised Kempf's "powers" and Stanley's renewed socialization with the family, Katharine responded with disdain. "For twenty years, I allowed myself to be persuaded that it was better for Stanley not to see me at all. The actual fact is that his resocialization, which is the only recent improvement apparent in his case, is coincident with his renewed contact with his wife and family."[13]

When Kempf reported that "the patient was doing much better since the family was away from Santa Barbara," Katharine's answer was passionately accusatory toward both Kempf and the board. "I am quite unwilling to accede to such isolation for Stanley, as I cannot believe it is conducive either to his best interests or to his happiness—in fact I believe it to be just the opposite."[14]

In September, Anita and Harold renewed Dr. Kempf's contract and salary for another year. Katharine again voiced her opposition to Kempf, and she threatened to obtain a petition to gain sole custody of Stanley. Anita and Harold were stunned. When they protested her warning, Katharine averred that she was prepared to go to trial, if necessary, to gain custody. Having announced her intent, Katharine collected her papers, rose from her chair, and exited the room. Anita believed that "war had just been declared," but she too was left confused by Katharine's belligerent attitude.

For the next several months, Katharine and Newton Baker huddled frequently to plan strategy and prepare legal documents. Petitions and counterpetitions were filed; letters, Riven Rock records, and doctors' reports were submitted to the probate court in Chicago. Court-appointed conservators were rejected by both parties. Proposed hearings were delayed and dismissed. Each side worked diligently to gain the upper hand before the trial date was set and the location decided. Baker's efforts were directed toward moving the trial from Chicago, which he believed would favor the McCormicks, to Santa Barbara, Stanley's residence and site of the court where he had been adjudged insane. Charges and countercharges continued throughout the summer of 1929, seemingly with no resolution in sight.

Then, at the end of October, the probate court announced it would hear the case in Santa Barbara, beginning the following month. The

McCormicks attempted to block the order but failed. Each side now gathered all its legal forces to prepare for the confrontation. Depositions were collected, expert witnesses subpoenaed, doctors' records duplicated, and witnesses selected for testimony.

During these preliminary skirmishes, no one beyond the litigants seemed to be much interested. Yet when the trial date was publicly announced—*McCormick v. McCormick,* to decide who held custody of an insane millionaire—newspaper reporters from across the country flocked to Santa Barbara to view and describe, as the *Chicago Tribune* tagged it, the "trial of the decade."

Asked by the press what they might expect in the trial, Newton Baker replied philosophically: "It is drama that might have been written by one of the great Russians, it seems to cast so deeply into life and touch so many issues of fundamental importance."

The press presaged the trial with its own interpretation of coming events. A headline read, "Rich Family Badly Split; Psycho-analysis Enters Fight for Control of Millions of Incompetent Stanley McCormick."[15]

Twenty-Four

As opening arguments were about to begin, the *Santa Barbara Morning Press* prepared for its readers a preview of the soon-to-be memorable trial.

It is to be a battle of some of the best legal, medical and psychological brains in the country, this difference over the care and treatment of Stanley McCormick, who, for the past thirty years, has spent his time mostly behind the walled estate of Riven Rock.

Money, according to court attaches, is not much of a matter in this hearing. The difference which has arisen between the brother and sister on one side and the wife on the other is in regard to what might cure or benefit the incompetent.[1]

According to the *New York Times*, the trial "will represent the largest custody case in the history of the country."[2]

Intent upon maintaining judicial objectivity for the upcoming trial, the California Superior Court enlisted Judge William Dehy, from a small, rural upstate county, to preside. Since it was claimed that Judge Dehy had little experience with high-profile cases, both litigants protested his appointment. In spite of these challenges, the Superior Court claimed that Judge Dehy was "the correct man for the job." Many observers, however, believed that the judge would find himself "in over his head" and his inexperience could likely throw the entire judicial process into turmoil. Dehy's first decision appeared to confirm their trepidations.[3]

The day before the trial was to begin, the judge declared that all sessions would be conducted "behind closed doors," barring the press and interested spectators from the courtroom "for the duration of the trial." Dehy

had responded to a motion made by Oscar Lawler, the McCormicks' attorney, to seek privacy for the entire hearing, claiming that "any publicity
given to the proceedings would be disastrous for the McCormick family."
The attorney also suggested that any crowd in the courtroom might disturb the ward if he were to appear there, although everyone knew that
Stanley would never testify. Further, Dehy ordered that transcripts of the
proceedings be made available only to attorneys of record and that no
witnesses could publicly divulge the contents of their testimony.

Not surprisingly, newspaper and news service representatives swamped
the judge with demands for an open court and "free speech" and accused
him of illegal censorship and poor judgment in dealing with an important
public issue.

Pressure on the judge came from many sources, including members of
the State Supreme Court, and he reversed the decision the following day.
When the doors were opened, newspeople and interested parties scram-
bled into the courtroom en masse. In a formal statement regarding his
new decision, Judge Dehy stated that "as a general rule the court's business should be the public's business," which elicited a loud cheer of approval from the crowd.

Representing the McCormick family were Oscar Lawler, of the Los An-
geles firm of Lawler and Degnan; John W. Heaney, of Heaney, Price and
Postel, from Chicago; and eight medical experts, including Dr. William
White. Katharine was represented by Newton Baker and Paul Patterson,
Cleveland; Walter K. Tuller, of O'Melveny, Tuller and Myers, Los Angeles;
and six medical experts.

Reports, depositions, and letters accumulated over the twenty-three
years of Stanley's hospitalization, consisting of more than 64,000 pages of
material, were submitted to the court for examination. Twenty-seven witnesses were scheduled to testify, of which fourteen were expert witnesses
from the medical profession. Among interested parties slated to present
their sides of the argument were Anita; Harold; Cyrus Jr.; Drs. Kempf,
Meyer, and Brush; nurses McKillop, Tompkins, and Margaret Gleason;
and Katharine.

In his opening statement, Newton Baker presented his view of the key
issues of the case: (1) the dismissal of Dr. Kempf because of his attempt,
by psychoanalysis of the ward, to alienate Stanley's affection from Katharine, and (2) the transfer of sole custody of the ward to Katharine from
the McCormick family because of their inability to deal with the ward's
medical issues. Attorney Lawler, in contrast, stated that "the only issue in
this case is whether Stanley McCormick is getting well."

Seated in the audience was Julia Roessing, already labeled by the press
as "Mrs. McCormick's constant companion."[4] She, along with Katharine
and the attorneys, was housed at El Mirasol Hotel, where strategy meetings would be held both before and after each day's testimony. Observers

noted that the conference room in which they worked resembled a "government war room."

The first witness to testify was Dr. L. W. Barder, professor emeritus of Johns Hopkins University Hospital and an authority on endocrine glands. His testimony covered the history of endocrinology, the development of endocrine tests and treatments, and the current state of the discipline. Attorney Newton Baker attempted to emphasize the importance of endocrine treatments for Stanley, while Attorney Lawler, in his cross-examination, endeavored to have Dr. Barder admit the lack of research in understanding how such treatments worked. Barder's testimony occupied the entire first day of the hearing, and his use of obscure medical language caused many of the spectators to lose interest.

The second day of testimony produced heated accusations between Baker and Dr. Meyer, the next witness, as well as between Baker and Lawler regarding the current state of Stanley's health. Dr. Meyer reported, with confidence and apparent professional pleasure, how Stanley had so favorably responded to Dr. Kempf's treatment. He went on to relate in detail the history of Stanley's illness, the various methods used in his care, and the continuous battles between the McCormick family and Katharine. His story included a brief history of psychology, as he described the various theories of several schools.

In the afternoon session, Baker prodded Meyer to reveal his personal feelings about Freudian psychology, getting him to admit his "uneasiness" with the approach. "Then why did you sanction it?" Baker asked.

Baker also made Meyer reveal the specifics of his financial relationship with the McCormick family since 1908 and Anita's subsequent hiring of Meyer as a consultant. Baker questioned Meyer's objectivity in the case in light of his being so "wedded" to the McCormicks.

Following Meyer, Dr. Kempf was briefly brought to the stand to determine if Judge Dehy could visit Stanley. "Without a doubt," Kempf answered, "in a few days, as soon as he has digested the idea."

The second day's testimony ended with Dr. White, who defended Kempf's techniques "since they helped the patient." Baker prodded White to explain Freudian theory and its emphasis on sex. To everyone's disappointment, the discussion had to be continued later.

Except for Newton Baker's assault on Dr. Meyer's credibility and Dr. White's interpretation of Freudian sex, a sleepy courtroom yawned over the technical and medical details of Stanley's long-term care. Through these long hours of discussion, Katharine was observed to be almost unmoving, except when she leaned forward to make notes on a small pad.

Baker began the third day's cross-examination of Dr. White by asking him to tell the court about his involvement with Dr. Kempf and Stanley, and the justification for a salary of $11,000 a year. Reacting nervously to

Baker's pressing questions, White admitted that his visits to Riven Rock had been infrequent.

"How infrequent?" Baker asked.

"Twice in the last year," White answered. Moreover, White admitted that his evaluations of Stanley's progress derived primarily from Kempf's reports.

Baker then produced a recent book, written by Dr. Kempf, which interpreted the sexual significance of a number of famous paintings, including pictures of English cathedrals. With sarcasm in his voice, Baker asked White if he agreed with Kempf in comparing these pictures to the female body. White admitted that he had not read all of Kempf's book, even though it was dedicated to him. He also admitted the book had been given to Stanley.

"Despite the grave sexual aspects of his illness?" Baker questioned. A brief but audible collective gasp spread through the courtroom.

Lawler objected strenuously to the interrogation but his objection was denied by the judge.

Much to Dr. White's discomfort, Baker continued the attack. "So Dr. Kempf goes through the world finding sex in the sunshine, flowers, moonlight, art galleries, and even in churches. Correct, Dr. White?" White did not answer.

"He sees sex significance in everything," Baker continued. "And this is the physician you want to continue in charge of Stanley McCormick, whose mental illness has so many grave sex aspects." Again, Dr. White did not answer.

As if he wished to save White from further embarrassment, Judge Dehy adjourned the court for the weekend. Members of the press were seen running to telephones to report the day's results.

On Monday, Baker continued his cross-examination of Dr. White. His objective: to demonstrate White's claim that Stanley had improved to be "misleading, if not entirely false." When Baker asked White why Stanley had recently attempted to run from the estate, the doctor replied that the patient believed he was late for lunch.

"Outside the estate gates?" Baker questioned.

"The patient often gets confused. It's a normal part of his illness," answered White.

White then attempted to counter Baker's interrogation by boasting that Stanley was now sketching and painting and that female nurses had, for the first time, been introduced into the household. Under further questioning, however, White mentioned that one of the women nurses had been struck by Stanley and had left Riven Rock.

That afternoon, a series of expert witnesses began to testify on behalf of or in opposition to the use of Freudian psychology. Having examined Stanley, some claimed the patient was stable and improving; others claimed he was incurable and continued to experience impulsive behavior. Testimony from this array of doctors continued for almost the entire week.

Newspaper coverage paid little attention to the testimony of the expert witnesses, partly because they used incomprehensible medical terminology and partly because they offered little real information about issues of the trial. Reporters considered the time devoted to these people "dull and boring." Some even absented themselves from the courtroom.

The next two days were as dramatic as the previous had been tedious. McKillop, Stanley's longtime nurse, and Roscoe La Source, chauffeur since 1914, provided riveting details of Stanley's private life, from the days he had been transported in his private railroad car to Riven Rock until the day when the bars had been removed from the windows of his room. Reporters diligently recorded every word of their compelling stories.

McKillop went into great detail explaining Stanley's sequestered life, how the nurses dressed him each day, cared for his teeth and hair, and cut his food. He told of how Stanley had shown improvement in 1917, taken walks, played croquet, and even shown interest in the war. McKillop testified that the patient lived mainly in a bedroom, 20 feet by 30 feet, with an attached sunporch. All doors and windows had been barred, and the only furniture in the room consisted of a brass bed bolted to the floor. Three male nurses were on duty during the day, and two at night.

"He had to be cared for much as a child in those early days?" asked Lawler.

"Yes," replied McKillop. "He had his good and bad days."

"And no women were allowed to see him until Dr. Kempf took over?" asked Lawler.

"In 1918, Mrs. Blaine pushed him around the house in a wheelchair; and Mr. McCormick's mother visited the estate once," McKillop related. "But Mr. McCormick was in such an excited condition, he was not allowed to see her. She stood behind a door and watched him."

"And neither Mrs. Blaine nor the patient's wife saw him until 1927. Is that correct, Mr. McKillop?"

"That is correct," McKillop answered.

Roscoe La Source told how a greater amount of freedom had been granted Stanley since Dr. Kempf's arrival, how the patient had made visits to downtown Santa Barbara and taken part in beach parties with his wife. Under Baker's questioning, La Source revealed that the beach parties had occurred early in Dr. Kempf's tenure; during 1928 and 1929, however, Stanley's wife had not been allowed on the estate.

Back on the stand, McKillop testified that Stanley still struck at nurses on occasion, that he sometimes still had to be fed, and that he often refused to leave the shower and could be removed only by force.

"So how would you classify Stanley's condition at this time?" Baker asked McKillop.

"Mentally, there hasn't been much change, but physically, he is generally better. There has been a general softening, an easing up," replied McKillop.

When Lawler questioned McKillop, he could not get him to change his statement. Lawler then informed the judge that he wished to treat McKillop as a hostile witness. The judge, however, refused.

Reactions to McKillop's testimony ranged from gasps of surprise to groans of sorrow as he described Stanley's life. Katharine, who had remained impassive during previous testimony, could be seen raising a handkerchief to her eyes. During McKillop's entire recitation, her pain was clearly perceptible.

The following morning, Judge Dehy traveled to Riven Rock to see Stanley and spent half an hour with the patient. Dr. Brush was present, as were guards, stationed outside the room. Later, the judge had little to say about the encounter. "McCormick acted like a normal person and carried on an intelligible conversation regarding football and motoring," he noted. "It was a pleasant and ordinary visit." When reporters asked the judge whether he believed the patient was insane, Dehy declined to answer.

While the judge took a short trip back to his home district to attend to several cases there, both sides in the dispute held long sessions to plan strategy. Reporters believed that, at this point in the trial, Stanley's improvement seemed in doubt and Dr. Kempf's reliance on Freudian sexual analysis appeared questionable. Still, Dr. Kempf had not yet testified, nor had any of the McCormicks.

Reporters also spent their free time attempting to interview anyone who might have had some association with the "Riven Rock crowd"—delivery truck drivers, gardeners, hotel managers, and neighbors. What they usually found was "old news" to locals but obviously of titillating interest to readers in other parts of the country.[5] One rumor that received attention suggested that the real reason Katharine had accused Kempf of alienating her husband's affection was because the physician had been secretly bringing in women to "entertain" Stanley. None of this potentially scandalous, albeit unconfirmed, information was ever brought up in court.

Katharine, Anita, Harold, and their respective lawyers maintained a pretense of civility throughout the trial. Each morning before the trial opened, Katharine greeted and shook hands with Anita, Harold, and Attorney Lawler. At the end of each day's hearings, Anita and Harold shook hands with Katharine and Newton Baker and wished them a pleasant evening. To reporters, their actions seemed surreal, considering the animosities exchanged during each day's testimony.

When the trial reopened, Lawler recalled McKillop to the stand in an attempt to impeach the witness, since Baker, in a previous session, had turned the nurse's testimony to Katharine's advantage. The questioning devolved into a shouting match.

"He used excuses to get out of walks," McKillop explained of Stanley's behavior.

"What do you mean?" asked Lawler pointedly.

"Well, he didn't want to go, and we forced him on occasion."

"You don't do that now?" asked Lawler acidly.

"Yes, we still do," McKillop responded, with some annoyance.

"With the doctor's knowledge?" the attorney inquired loudly.

"Yes, with the doctor's knowledge," McKillop shot back.

At this point, Judge Dehy deemed it advisable to adjourn the trial for the day, since McKillop "could offer no further information."

Across the country, Sunday newspapers ran feature articles about the trial, under headlines such as "Wife of Mad Millionaire Fights to See Him," "Guards Bar Gates to Palatial Retreat in California on Doctors' Orders," and "Guardians At War Over Mad Millionaire." Added to photos of the people involved in the trial were pictures of Cyrus McCormick, Stanley's deceased father; the heavy iron gates of Riven Rock, "behind which Stanley McCormick was jailed"; and Sigmund Freud. Each article outlined the entire story of Stanley's madness, the famous doctors who had treated him, and the current debate over whether Freudian psychology had been beneficial or harmful to the "incompetent patient." The stories could not have been told in more sensational fashion.

"A little boy nobody understood," pitied the *Chicago Daily Times*.[6]

"Stanley McCormick, while having every luxury that money could buy, failed to receive the sympathy and understanding his retiring nature craved," reported the *Los Angeles Times*. "For 23 years now, he has been paying the price of his parents' folly."[7]

The *New York Graphic Magazine* revealed that "the controversial sexual psychology of Sigmund Freud" was the real cause of the fight between members of the McCormick family.[8] By the end of November, nearly every reader in the country knew about the trial, the opposing parties, the "poor" patient, and the principles of Freudian psychology.

It was now Katharine's turn to testify. She began by explaining her effort to surround Stanley with professional doctors who could administer the best of care and also discuss issues of the day. When asked about her recent observations of Stanley, she declared, "I have watched the psychoanalytic treatment for the past thirty months, and it is doing no good. My husband, I would say, in the past few months, is regressing. His memory is beginning to fail. He cannot apply himself with the same effort now as he did in 1927 and even in 1928."

Attorney Lawler began his cross-examination of Katharine by introducing doctors' reports and letters to show that Katharine had been in accord with all aspects of Stanley's treatment. In this effort, however, he ran out of time.

Anita was next on the agenda. She began her testimony by relating how close she had been with Stanley and describing the family's efforts to assist in his care. Lawler read letters and reports between the guardians and asked Anita to verify them. He then introduced a letter from Katharine, stating that the board "was most fortunate to engage Dr. Kempf. Stanley needs him all of the time."

When Lawler asked about Stanley's current condition, Anita touchingly replied that "Stanley's better, oh, so much, so much better." She went on to describe the recent interactions she and Harold had had with their brother. On the stand, Harold confirmed Anita's observations. In another brief appearance, Dr. Kempf testified that his patient "showed such improvement under psychoanalysis that the treatment should be continued."

Anita concluded the day's testimony, relating the emotional meeting she had held with Stanley the previous day. With tears in her eyes, her words choking in her throat, she murmured, "Stanley seemed wonderful to me. He was there with me. It was my brother. There was no veil, no film between us."

For the next two days of the trial, Dr. Brush and a series of expert witnesses described Stanley's progress and the perceived benefits of Freudian psychology. Newton Baker did not even bother to cross-examine them, wanting to conclude their testimony as quickly as possible.

It was now Dr. Kempf's turn to testify, and he performed the task with shocking descriptions and stirring pathos. He began by telling the story of a handsome, intelligent, sensitive man who had been treated as a boy; a boy who had been treated as an invalid; an invalid locked away for twenty years in a bare, barred bedroom, amid a vast, richly endowed estate—all this because of the way his mother raised him. "Stanley's madness was due in large measure to the dowager Mrs. McCormick herself," Kempf explained. "She ruled with an iron hand and could not bear to be separated from her youngest son."

Kempf then went on to list the causes of Stanley's illness as he interpreted them:

His stern puritanical home life under "The McCormick" (as Nettie was called)

Seductions by his nurse when Stanley was a child (luckily the nurse, Marie, had already died)

His thwarted ambition to be an artist

Family resistance to his marriage

His inferiority complex

Kempf refuted the claim that Stanley suffered from any form of dementia praecox. "If we consider the entire picture of his life, all its stresses from childhood until his illness—such as the strict puritanism of his home—all these made his sex traumas abnormally severe." Kempf defined Stanley's illness as "malignant neurosis."

Kempf's hours-long testimony included vivid description, heart-wrenching detail, and pompous self-congratulation. He described how "poor" Stanley had been mistreated by various doctors—frequent ice baths, days of isolation, debilitating physical restraints; how Stanley was forced to sit in bed, in silence, waiting to be fed and dressed; his violent acts and fits of crying, manifesting frustration at his inability to tell anyone how he felt. Kempf boasted that the Freudian method was "saving" Stanley. "Certain fears have been greatly reduced by the analysis so that they are neither so persistent nor severe."

Under cross-examination, Baker accused Kempf of preparing infrequent and incomplete reports to the guardians. He challenged Kempf's claims about Stanley's improvement, since no family members had been allowed to visit Stanley during the past year. Kempf avoided argument by repeating his claims.

Concluding his review of Kempf's testimony, Baker told the court that he felt somewhat sorry for Dr. Kempf. "Freud gave the world a gift in the statement that a very substantial part of the mental disability of the world had its origin in thwarted or defeated sexual psychology. If I were to make any criticism of Dr. Kempf, I would say that he became so enthusiastic when the world was enthusiastic that he had been unable to lose his enthusiasm as fast as the rest of the world."

On the nineteenth day of the trial, Katharine was again called to the stand by Lawler. Letters were read into the record telling of her initial enthusiasm for Dr. Kempf's methods. Details of the first time she saw her husband in twenty years were also revealed. "Everything is going wonderful," she had written her mother.

Lawler attempted to force Katharine to agree that Dr. Kempf possessed a fine reputation as a psychoanalyst. The best he could do was to get her to say, "I understand he was agreeable to all."

Expert witnesses followed in succession, supporting Katharine's claims, all of them suggesting that Dr. Kempf "may have accomplished all the benefit possible," but that much more was needed. On behalf of Katharine, Dr. Orbison had examined Stanley and now stated to the court that "my visits to Riven Rock have convinced me that McCormick is deriving no benefit from psychoanalytic treatments. In fact," he continued, "McCormick told me that he does not like the treatments and does not believe that they are doing him any good." With the dueling claims and counterclaims regarding the current state of Stanley's health, reporters sensed a legalistic impasse.

For the next two days, Katharine was on the stand. She told the history of her relationship with Stanley and her twenty-five-year quest to cure her mentally afflicted husband.

In a calm, kindly manner, yet one that unavoidably revealed her emotional strain, Katharine told of her schooling at MIT, the stormy courtship with Stanley, and his fateful trip to the mental hospital in Boston. She talked about Drs. Hamilton, Kraepelin, Hoch, Jelliffe, Brush, and Meyer, and, finally, Dr. Kempf, and her indefatigable efforts to find a cure for Stanley. She related her initial acceptance of and later dispute with Kempf, beginning with his denial of endocrine treatments and her subsequent request to the guardians to fire the physician. Katharine revealed that she had brought Mrs. Roessing with her to Riven Rock "when Dr. Kempf suggested I bring a friend with me."

Attorney Lawler began his cross-examination of Katharine by attempting to prove that Mrs. Roessing had been one of the instigators of the argument between the guardians. Judge Dehy, however, instructed Lawler that his questions were not germane to the case.

Lawler then questioned Katharine on why she had refused to meet with the guardians the past year. "I did not recognize any Board of Personal Care after I employed counsel in 1928," she answered. When Lawler accused Katharine of not making any effort to discuss the issue with the other guardians, she admitted not having made an effort, on the instructions of her attorney.

Ending her account, Katharine stressed the need for Stanley to obtain not only psychological but also endocrinological treatments. When Judge Dehy asked Katharine what she specifically wanted for her husband, she stated three requirements: the immediate discharge of Dr. Kempf; a thorough medical probe of Stanley's glands; and an "open house" at Riven Rock, with Stanley able to entertain all his relatives and friends. At the conclusion of Katharine's testimony, everyone slowly filed out in silence.

To everyone's surprise, the trial opened the next day with Newton Baker resting his case. In summation, he stated "that there is no animosity between the guardians, but that the disagreement is entirely an impersonal one, involving theories of psychological and physiological treatment." In response, Attorney Lawler also rested.

The case was now in Judge Dehy's hands. Reporters generally agreed that neither side would score a decisive victory. While they believed that Dr. Kempf would be released, they did not expect the court to grant Katharine exclusive control of her husband.

As they analyzed the case, the press opined that the hearing was probably the most expensive guardianship dispute ever argued in an American court. Legal fees alone were estimated to exceed $350,000, and the many specialists who had served as expert witnesses would receive an almost equal amount. Due to the voluminous transcripts and the length of trial, court costs would reach five figures.

Since all of these expenses were to be paid out of Stanley's estate, they had to be approved by Judge Dehy. Ironically, since the judge was paid in accordance with the population of the county in which he had been elected, Dehy himself would earn only $5,000 for his efforts.

On the morning of January 17, 1930, Judge Dehy alerted all parties that he planned to deliver his decision that afternoon. When he entered the courtroom, it was packed. Spectators overflowed into the hallway in restless anticipation of his verdict. On one side of the room were Anita, Harold, and Lawler. On the other sat Katharine, Julia Roessing, and Newton Baker.

Dehy began by reciting a brief history of Stanley's affliction, drawing the conclusion that he "had never made any marked improvement despite the best efforts of all medical science." He characterized the proceedings to settle the differences as "unique." He had come to the conclusion that there was no fraud or negligence apparent on the part of anyone involved in the case, only "an honest difference of opinion."

"We do not know where hope lies for the ward. No one seems to know," the judge declared. "His plaintive call for competency has not been answered. His case has baffled the best medical experts for years. At the present, it is evident that more careful and constant attention should be given to his physical health and well-being."

Where is Dehy going with this recitation, the audience wondered. The litigants could be seen shifting nervously in their seats. Reporters shared quizzical looks as Dehy spoke; and as he went on, everyone's puzzlement seemed to intensify.

Judge Dehy declared that he found "no breach of etiquette, of misconduct, or inefficiency" on the part of Dr. Kempf; and he complimented the psychoanalyst on his work. The judge also paid high praise to the Personal Care Board for the manner in which they had handled the affairs of their incompetent relative.

The judge went on to point out some of the difficulties Dr. Kempf faced caused by the lack of cooperation he had received, then hastened to add that he believed the patient had received all the value that he could expect from the treatment. "But the ward's treatment should not be changed too abruptly," Dehy cautioned. "This is an administrative matter to be worked out by those charged with the care of the ward, guided by the judgment of competent and experienced medical advisers."

Those in the audience now saw what was coming. To this point, Katharine had remained impassive.

"Considering the nature of the case," the judge announced, "the court is not yet ready to place its care and responsibility on one person, alone, as guardian." Reporters could be seen breathing a collective sigh of relief.

The McCormicks smiled and sat up straighter in their chairs. Katharine slumped slightly, hiding her face; and Julia took her hand. The judge, however, had not yet completed his statement.

"In conformity with these views, it is the opinion of the court, in the matter of the contract with Dr. Kempf, it should continue to February, 1930; that then, or as soon thereafter as proper and necessary arrangements can be made, the psychoanalytic method of procedure now being administered to the ward shall be discontinued."

A spontaneous shout of approval burst from the assembled. Nearly everyone seemed to be in agreement that Freudian psychology had lost! The McCormicks were duly surprised at the decision, while Katharine squeezed Julia's hand in triumph. Flash photos were snapped all around until Dehy called a halt, telling those assembled in the courtroom that he was not yet finished with his verdict. The spectators again became quiet. What more could he add?

"Instead of any removal of guardians," Dehy went on, "two proper persons should be appointed to said board of guardians to serve thereon with the present members of the board, until the further order of the court." Reporters were taken aback by the announcement. Both Katharine and the McCormicks were obviously chagrined and, by an exchange of glances, shared their mutual disappointment with Dehy's ruling.

When the court adjourned, Katharine rather coolly received the compliments and handshakes proffered by Anita and Harold. Yet when she left the courtroom, Katharine appeared numb.

Most newspaper headlines proclaimed a "divided victory" and a "compromise." Only the *New York Times* reflected Katharine's actual feelings: "McCormick's Wife Loses Ouster Suit."[9]

Katharine firmly believed she had lost the case, and she grew deeply depressed over the result. She had not felt so crushed since Dr. Putnam had taken Stanley to the hospital, twenty years before. She had publicly gambled in order to gain total control of Stanley's care, and she had failed. She felt a profound sense of frustration and sadness.

Later, Katharine conceded to Newton Baker that she had been bested and there now appeared little hope that she would ever gain custody. Baker had to agree with her assessment. Even more depressing, however, was Katharine's realization that, based on the sheer weight of testimony regarding Stanley's mental condition, he would probably never, ever recover his sanity. She could no longer deny the reality of the situation, as she had done for years.

Katharine retired to her room, ostensibly a defeated woman. Nor could the presence of Julia or Newton Baker relieve her pain. She felt old, tired, overwhelmed, and faced with the stark, undeniable fact that Stanley was "a hopeless case."

Twenty-Five

Legal observers generally agreed that Judge Dehy's trial decisions solved little. "Just about where they were at the start," one well-known lawyer declared. Other lawyers following the trial offered less generous evaluations. They believed that Dehy had almost completely failed to grasp the essentials of the case. The addition of two members to the board would definitely furnish Anita and Harold with a majority while robbing Katharine of her power. They predicted that in the future the board's new composition would precipitate even greater confusion and indecision.

When the guardians met shortly after the court's decision, their discussions reflected the quandary in which they had been placed. Two additional guardians had to be selected; but who would these be, and from where would they come? Who was going to replace Dr. Kempf? What kinds of new controls would the Chicago Probate Court put on Riven Rock operations? There were more questions than answers, and the guardians were at a loss as to where to begin. Katharine and Newton Baker attempted to lead the discussion, but it quickly degenerated into arguments about what Judge Dehy's decisions actually meant.

Amid this confusion, however, two decisions were made. First, Dr. Brush would retain his position, temporarily; second, the guardians agreed that an estate business manager had to be hired.

Katharine came away from the meeting dejected. She expressed frustration at the meeting's lack of results, and she and Baker agreed that nothing constructive would be accomplished in the near future, not until the new guardians were selected and a physician was hired to care for Stanley.

Katharine's gloom was displayed in other ways as well. She was not eating properly and had lost weight. She neglected personal care; her use of makeup was erratic. Her clothing appeared out-of-date or inappropriate. She had given up exercising, and her frequent letter writing had dwindled to short notes and telegraphic brevity. While Newton Baker was seen at Katharine's side on most public occasions, Julia Roessing had evidently disappeared.

In discussions with Baker, Katharine expressed a desire to continue fighting for Stanley's custody, if only to make people aware that she had not given up the quest. Baker suggested the effort would be a waste of her time and money. "Concentrate on selecting the new guardians," was his advice, "and make them aware of your concerns."

For the original guardians, the entire summer of 1930 consisted of seeking new guardians, a new physician, and an estate manager; reconstructing Stanley's theater building (where sound motion picture equipment was being installed); and attempting to resolve increasing dissension between Dr. Brush and the nurses McKillop and Tompkins. None of these activities helped to improve Katharine's demeanor, and she continued to express her resentment toward the legal system every time that one of her requests was denied.

In the meantime, Dr. Brush continued to write weekly letters to Dr. Meyer, keeping him informed of Riven Rock activities and Stanley's condition. Meyer, in turn, communicated with Anita, regarding not only the health of Mary Virginia, but also his suggestions for the selection of new guardians. With the departure of Dr. Kempf, Brush was now on his own and very uncomfortable with the prospects. "Just now, I am in a considerable quandary," Brush wrote Meyer, "as to the best course to follow with Stanley. I have worked out a sort of a program, which I'll send to you; for I would welcome your comments."[1] Meyer was more than pleased to respond to Brush's requests.

When the guardians met in August, they had compiled a list of prospective additions to the board, but predictably, they found they could not agree on the nominations. Instead, they asked Judge Dehy to appoint the new guardians, which he did quickly, selecting the deans of the Stanford and University of California medical schools, Dr. William Ophuls and Dr. Langley Porter, respectively. Each was to receive $15,000 a year for his board participation.

The doctors, in turn, recommended and obtained agreement from Anita and Harold, with Katharine abstaining, to establish a board of consultants to supervise Stanley's care. The consulting board comprised Dr. W. W. Boardman, an internal medicine expert; Dr. Milton B. Lennon, a neurologist; and Dr. Robert Richards, a psychiatrist and Riven Rock's new resident physician for one year, at $30,000. In addition, the guardians hired

Col. Joseph H. Bernard as Riven Rock's business manager, at $20,000 a year. Everyone was now in place.

The new Board of Guardians' first issue dealt with family visits to Riven Rock. After much debate, they were unable to reach an agreement, as Katharine pushed to have visitations begin immediately. When Ophuls and Porter disagreed, Katharine sent a petition to the probate court to have their voting rights nullified.

A new battle broke out when Katharine discovered that Dr. Brush, upon Meyer's recommendation, had given Stanley a transcript of the trial testimony. Enraged, she demanded that Brush be summarily fired, and she accused the new guardians of overlooking a critical issue that seriously affected her husband's mental health. When an investigation revealed that Brush had also shared with Stanley Katharine's trial testimony, she demanded swift retribution. While the guardians agreed with Katharine about the possible negative effects on Stanley, they nevertheless voted to retain Brush. She appealed to Baker to take legal steps against Dr. Brush.

At the guardians' next meeting in the spring of 1931, they agreed to dismiss Dr. Brush, likely because of Baker's threat to inform the probate court of Brush's indiscretion. Dr. Richards's excuse for terminating Brush suggested that, since a business manager for the estate had been hired, Brush's job had become redundant. With Brush's discharge, Dr. Meyer had lost his "spy" at Riven Rock; and his influence on Riven Rock operations was finally ended.

Dr. Richards, however, also requested that the guardians remove McKillop and Tompkins for what he labeled their "lack of cooperation." Katharine immediately came to their defense, pointing out their longtime loyalty and devotion to Stanley. "Where else would you find such devoted people?" she inquired of the guardians. After considerable debate, the guardians requested that Katharine talk to the nurses to "improve their relations with Dr. Richards." Again Katharine was exasperated by the guardians' failure to agree on a timetable for family visits to Riven Rock. Before concluding, they did vote on a Riven Rock budget of more than $125,000 for the year.

Since she would not be able to see Stanley at Christmas, Katharine decided to remain in Boston. Josephine was increasingly feeble and required constant care. Katharine's presence in Boston gave the two an opportunity to discuss the situation with Stanley and the McCormicks. Josephine bemoaned the ill-fated marriage, especially since it had failed to produce a Dexter heir, and now she worried that "the Dexter line was to be made extinct." For her part, Katharine expressed pessimism about the unpleasant events since the trial, particularly in that she felt even more cut off from Stanley. She shared with her mother her intent to file a petition to dissolve the Board of Guardians, another attempt to gain sole custody.

A brief note from Margaret Sanger—it seemed like years since Sanger had written Katharine—momentarily diverted Katharine's attention from Stanley to birth control.

Sanger had asked Katharine to entertain Mrs. Donald McGraw, who was in charge of legislative lobbying in Washington, D.C., on behalf of birth control.[2] Katharine was unable to meet with McGraw but sent her fifty dollars to "be of assistance to Mrs. Sanger."

The Board of Guardians meeting in early 1932 quickly agreed upon a budget for Riven Rock of $133,000 and commended Col. Bernard for his handling of business affairs at the estate. Still, the issues regarding Stanley's care remained unsolved.

"For almost two years now," Katharine claimed, "nothing has been done to help Stanley." She maintained that he had been "in limbo" and that Dr. Richards's "maintenance" approach had actually been detrimental to her husband. "He has gained weight," she declared. "He walks less. And he writes less often," she noted, "often telling me how lonely he is. What are we doing to treat these issues?" she inquired of the physicians at the table.

When none of the physicians replied, Katharine moved to discharge Drs. Boardman and Lennon for "contributing nothing," and she admonished Drs. Ophuls and Porter for hiring Dr. Richards to supervise Stanley. The meeting disintegrated into name-calling and accusations, with the doctors chagrined by Katharine's charges and Anita and Harold unable to regain control of the discussion. Relentless, Katharine continued to demand that changes be made.

Katharine then questioned why a board of consultants was even necessary. "What have they actually contributed? Stanley has not improved in twenty-five years under the care of six psychiatrists, and these men are no better," she stated forcefully. "Why don't we have an internist instead of a psychiatrist?" The meeting ended in disarray.

Immediately after the meeting, Katharine petitioned the probate court to dissolve the Board of Consultants, and she requested that all decisions be made by unanimous votes.

Katharine rented an apartment on Lake Shore Drive in Chicago within easy walking distance of the court's building, so she could personally deliver her demands. Soon, she was seen haunting the court offices. Employees wondered who this "old woman" was, she who so often confronted them. Her frequent visits helped to influence certain court administrators to be "out of the office" whenever they were alerted of an upcoming visit.

Their strategic absences were not lost on Katharine—"just like the legislators when we were lobbying for the women's vote," she wrote her mother—and she demanded that specific people be present or she would bring a complaint to higher court officials. Not surprisingly, each of her numerous petitions was rejected.

In response to her persistent efforts, the probate court ordered an independent physician, Dr. Lewis J. Pollock, chairman of the department of medicine and mental diseases, Northwestern University, to examine Stanley, evaluate his care program, and assess his environment. Dr. Pollock's results were presented to the court and the guardians in December 1932.[3]

Dr. Pollock began his report with kind words about the physical environment in which Stanley lived, "sunny, comfortable, decorated in good taste, and has the appearance of a well-appointed home." He praised Col. Bernard for his renewal of Riven Rock, "for the intelligence and devotion, order and economy with which he has carried out the plans and policies of the Board of Guardians." Pollock's analysis of the therapeutic situation suggested that Stanley was receiving good care, noting that he "has become more accessible, inclined to talk much more of personal things, and the new regime has permitted the patient to better control his complexes."

In contrast, however, Dr. Pollock revealed "an atmosphere of dissension, suspicion, and resentment" at Riven Rock "among employees, administrative groups, and members of the family." Pollock stated flatly that "no mentally ill patient should be treated in such an atmosphere." He blamed these results on the lack of a "decisive, fearless, and courageous administration." In other words, the Board of Guardians had become a management handicap.

Members of the Board of Guardians were embarrassed by the report. Katharine, however, used the report as a means to press the probate court to review her petitions again. For more than two months, the court demurred, before finally rejecting her requests once again. Nonetheless, to streamline the decision-making process—the weak point identified in Pollock's report—the probate court set up a three-person conservator group with final decision-making power. The group consisted of the Continental Illinois National Bank (holder of Stanley's estate), Harold, and Katharine.[4]

As a result of this change, Dr. Ophuls resigned, claiming failing health. Dr. Porter's yearly stipend was reduced. The Board of Consultants was dismissed as being redundant. Yet Katharine's petition to fire Dr. Richards was rejected. Still, the entire governing body had been reduced in size, their responsibilities clarified, and the decision process simplified, to Katharine's satisfaction.

Newton Baker expressed some amazement at the outcome of Katharine's persistent lobbying campaign, although both acknowledged that Dr. Pollock's report had been the catalyst for change. "Katharine," Baker complimented her, "now I understand better how women got the vote." "However," he advised, "I recommend you give the new group an opportunity to function before you decide to use the petition process again." Katharine promised she would cooperate.

Birth Control (continued)

Twenty-Six

Margaret Sanger had worked hard to transform her public image from street radical to uptown reformer. Partly due to her association with the medical profession and partly due to support from the social elite, her standing had been elevated and her public persona legitimatized. Donations and contacts had helped Sanger to buy her way into the political process.

In 1931, in one of her first forays into Washington, D.C., politics, Sanger sought congressional sponsorship for a birth control bill. She persuaded seventy-nine-year-old Massachusetts Republican F. H. Gillette to carry the bill to committee. Like the other previous measures, this bill was summarily killed. The Catholic Church had mounted a campaign to suppress the bill and, for that matter, any legislation related to birth control. Sanger lobbied hard to initiate legislation and obtain sponsorship for new bills, but she was thwarted at every turn by the Church. At the time, it seemed that no such legislation could ever survive the scrutiny of the Church.

During the early 1930s, the effects of the Depression suppressed birth control activity in the United States, so much so that Sanger left for Europe, where such actions were considerably more acceptable. In 1932, however, the election of Franklin Delano Roosevelt enthused the movement; Eleanor Roosevelt had once served on the board of the American Birth Control League. Nonetheless, Sanger's attempts to meet with the president failed. So, when Secretary of Labor Frances Perkins launched a campaign extolling the virtues of working women, Sanger argued publicly that birth control could serve as an important means to help women combat the economic burdens of the Depression. The Church blocked that gambit by reminding the president that practicing Catholics had been, and remained, one of his most important constituencies. Congress was so busy pulling the country out of the Depression that it had no time for birth control.

Thanks to an introduction by Carrie Chapman Catt, Katharine met with Secretary Perkins and pled the need for birth control measures. The meeting cemented a friendship with Perkins, who promised to help, although she warned that the Church was a formidable opponent.

In 1934 a bill legitimating the mailing of contraceptives reached the Senate Judiciary Committee and, to everyone's surprise, was sent to the Senate floor for debate and a vote.

Since it was considered a minor bill amid a crunch of more than 200 others, the measure did not appear on the agenda until the final day of the session. In the confusion of the day, the contraceptive bill was read three times and, without debate, passed on a voice vote. For a brief, joyous moment, advocates of the bill were astounded that the bill had been passed. Their elation lasted but a few minutes.

By unanimous consent, the bill was hastily recalled by Senator Pat McCarran of Nevada, a prominent Catholic, and tabled. Since not even the senator carrying the bill voiced opposition, the bill died. Joy turned to frustration at the action of the Senate; yet, as one senator explained to the bill's sponsors, "That's politics." Still, the fact that a birth control bill had nearly won approval heartened advocates.[1]

The following year, another birth control bill reached a committee and again was tabled. In 1935, a frustrated Sanger visited India, where Mahatma Gandhi sought ways to limit his country's population explosion. Sanger next traveled to Japan to promote her crusade to more willing governmental ears.

While she was out of the country, however, a three-judge court of appeals panel in New York ordered the release of contraceptives for mailing, in a trial that had been simmering for some years. For the pro–birth control forces, it was a landmark decision, and Sanger turned the victory into a public relations campaign. Magazines like *Time*, the *Nation*, and *Life* hailed "the emergence of the birth control movement into the bright light of scientific acceptance and friendly publicity."[2]

Of even greater significance was the endorsement of contraception by the American Medical Association at its 1937 annual convention. After years of voting the issue down, the AMA suddenly reversed itself and gave its approval to artificial contraception. Granted that birth control remained under strict medical supervision, contraception became an element of normal sexual hygiene in married life. Unfortunately, due to various state laws, the edict applied only in New York, Connecticut, and Vermont. When the Massachusetts legislature attempted to pass a law allowing for physicians' dissemination of contraceptives—Katharine had led a contingent of lobbyists to testify on behalf of the bill—it was defeated, thanks to the pressure of the Catholic Church. Interestingly, in many cases those legislators speaking against the bill were the same ones who had spoken against women's suffrage. It struck Katharine as ironic that the women's battlefield had not changed fundamentally in two decades.

Katharine's activities were limited, but she did donate money to Sanger's ABCL and to legislators carrying bills through Congress. Finally, at the beginning of 1937, when Katharine believed the Riven Rock situation had become "routine," she telephoned Sanger saying she was ready to return to the "birth control wars."[3]

Over the past four years, Riven Rock had been transformed from a sea of troubles to a calm venue for "Stanley's peaceful walks in the park." Under considerable pressure from the conservators, Dr. Richards had resigned his position as Riven Rock's resident physician. In his resignation letter to the board, he protested that his work had been compromised "by interfering forces," which prevented him from performing his responsibilities "in a meaningful manner." In other words, Katharine had succeeded in making his position untenable.

The guardians voted to have Dr. James Campbell replace Richards, although Campbell had no psychiatric training. Katharine voted against hiring Campbell and asked Newton Baker to assist her in removing this "unqualified doctor." Six months later, Dr. Campbell was asked to "step down," and the search for a competent physician began once again. In the meantime, throughout these personnel changes, Stanley's condition remained stable. From McKillop, Katharine learned that Stanley had experienced some brief violent episodes, all of which had been handled judiciously. According to McKillop, Stanley had directed his hostility more toward objects (an auto, a flower garden) than toward people. He tired easily, said McKillop, and when tired was more likely to "lash out." Still, he was reported to be in good condition.

A month later, the guardians hired Dr. Ernest Russell, a psychiatrist who had maintained a well-respected practice in Santa Barbara. Again, Katharine voted against the selection. Within a month of his employment, however, she changed her mind. Russell's weekly reports were concise and informative. Col. Bernard reported that routines at the estate had "settled down," and Stanley responded well to Russell's care and attention. Best of all, Dr. Russell informed Katharine and the McCormicks that they could now visit Stanley.

To assist Dr. Russell as his secretary, Col. Bernard hired Gertrude Calden, who had worked in a similar position at a local hospital. Calden had no problem accommodating to Stanley, nor he to her. Dr. Russell and Calden would work together for fourteen years, both of them remaining at Riven Rock until Stanley's death.[4] After Stanley's funeral, Calden would receive a letter of thanks and a month's salary from Katharine. Russell would return to private practice in Santa Barbara.

For the next two years, the situation at Riven Rock proved stable, with few crises. Stanley's routine had been firmly established by Dr. Russell, and the patient adhered to it with remarkable reliability. Typically, he was allowed to rise in the morning of his own volition. More often, now, he dressed himself and was shaved by one of the nurses, which he enjoyed. Breakfast was prepared by a dietitian. Three women, picked up from and returned to their homes each day, were employed to cook. After Stanley took a brief morning walk, a small musical group, led by Raymond Eldred, would play for him in the theater building. Like the food preparers, the musicians were transported to and from the estate each day. Katharine had initiated this entertainment, as well as occasional visits by a minister who read poetry to Stanley.

After lunch, Stanley would rest and sometimes read. A large library had been accumulated, consisting of history books, humor books, and Princeton publications, and a local newspaper was delivered each day. Afternoons or evenings were often times to show movies in the theater; Stanley enjoyed movies of all kinds. Some evenings, he would share the movies with Dr. Russell's daughter and other employees' children, in whose company he appeared to take pleasure.

Several times a week, Stanley and Dr. Russell discussed his feelings and whatever happened to be on his mind at the time, in a relaxed, freewheeling manner. Their rapport had developed rapidly, and their deepening friendship made Stanley feel at ease and comfortable; he had no problems openly discussing his sentiments. A conservative doctor when it came to psychiatric methods, Russell dealt with practical issues and Stanley's behavior each day in a calm, consistent manner.

After dinner, Stanley would walk on the estate with one of the nurses and, after a snack, retire early. Stanley was able to receive letters from family and old friends, although he rarely wrote letters himself. Letters from Katharine, Anita, and Harold were friendly and newsy. For her part, Katharine often wrote of her activities with Margaret Sanger and birth control. All incoming mail was still checked to ensure that nothing would upset Stanley. Yet Katharine offered no objections to this arrangement, under the current more agreeable circumstances.

When Katharine came to visit Stanley, she stayed at the El Mirasol Hotel in a cottage reserved exclusively for her use. Each morning, she called the doctor to find out if she would be allowed to visit Stanley that day. If the doctor agreed, a few hours that afternoon would be set aside for the meeting. These encounters were amicable, if not affectionate. Often, they shared music or movies. When they parted, Stanley hugged Katharine, and she kissed him on the cheek. After each meeting, Katharine reported to Dr. Russell, and they shared their observations of the day. In fact, Stanley's condition had become so routine that Katharine considered leaving Chicago and moving to Santa Barbara so she could visit her husband on a regular basis.

Katharine had indicated to Sanger that she was ready to donate money and pursue possible research projects leading to new and improved means of contraception. Sanger responded by giving her a list of various projects in which she might be interested. "Or," Sanger wrote, "can you give me a more definite idea as to what you yourself had in mind?" In any case, Sanger reiterated, financial assistance would always be greatly appreciated.

While Katharine was considering a three-year project undertaken at the University of Pennsylvania dealing with possible contraceptive "immunizations," she received a frantic call from 393 Commonwealth. Her mother had turned gravely ill. Katharine was urged to return to Boston immediately.

Katharine found her mother bedridden by ailments doctors were hard-pressed to diagnose. "After all," they reported, "she is ninety-one years old and has been suffering from arthritis for years." There was no doubt in Katharine's mind that her mother required her full attention, since Josephine needed twenty-four-hour care and adamantly refused to enter a hospital. She wrote Sanger in April, apologizing for her inability to involve herself more fully in the movement. "I have been much occupied over my mother's ill health," she wrote, "and must stay in Boston indefinitely."[5]

"As you know, I am deeply concerned over the research aspects of the birth control movement," Katharine declared, "and wish very much I could enter that field in a definitely constructive way. Unfortunately, I cannot at present. When I talked to you last over the telephone, I had hopes that I might get into it positively, but since then I have had to recognize that I cannot do so yet. I am very sorry." Included in the letter was a check for $1,000. Katharine promised to keep Sanger informed.

Unfortunately, Josephine lingered for almost six months in a gradually deteriorating condition. While Josephine received full-time care, it was Katharine who had to deal intimately with a person whose mind and body were expiring before her eyes. Newton Baker visited often, primarily to set Josephine's estate in order for probate, but also to monitor Katharine's own state of mind, which was of great concern to him.

On November 16, in the early morning, Josephine died in her sleep at 393 Commonwealth Avenue, her home for forty-two years. Doctors attributed her death to arterial sclerosis and heart disease, but it seemed to Katharine the death of an old woman whose body could no longer function. At Josephine's side were Katharine and the night nurse. Both the doctor and funeral director were immediately called. Through all of the preliminary arrangements, Katharine was not seen to cry, but when she met with the funeral director, it was obvious she had been mourning.

She wrote Stanley a long letter informing him of Josephine's death and reminiscing about her mother's longtime commitment to the Dexter heritage and her desire for an heir. "I am deeply sorry we were never able to make her happy," Katharine confessed. That part of the letter was never shared with Stanley.

The funeral took place two days later in Chicago, at Graceland Cemetery, where Josephine was buried in the Dexter family plot, between Wirt and Samuel. Anita and Harold attended the funeral and courteously shared their sorrow with Katharine. The announcement in the *Chicago Tribune* seemed appropriate; both Josephine's husband and daughter were prominently mentioned.

Mrs. Wirt Dexter, mother of former suffrage leader Mrs. Stanley McCormick, of Chicago, died today at her home, 393 Commonwealth Avenue. She was married to Wirt Dexter, noted Chicago lawyer. Her home in Prairie Avenue was used as a central administrative building after the Chicago fire of 1871. Her husband was chairman of the relief and refugee committee. She was a charter member of the Fortnightly club in Chicago, the Chilton club in Boston, and the Colony club in New York City.[6]

Katharine wrote Sanger of her loss and again apologized for being unable "to help you more than I do." Because of the size of Josephine's estate, the probate process had to be extended, and Katharine hoped that Newton Baker would complete the paperwork in a timely manner. In fact, Baker was planning to visit Katharine immediately after the Christmas holidays. Unfortunately, before he could meet with her, Baker suffered a heart attack and died.

Due to the recurrence of a heart condition that had confined him a few months before, Baker had been put to bed a few days before Christmas. On Christmas day, he was visited by his law partners and four grandchildren. "He was feeling fine," Baker's partner related. "He was very cheerful and remarked that he felt very much better." A few hours later, however, attended by his son and nurse, Baker lapsed into unconsciousness. Mrs. Baker was quickly summoned and arrived moments before her husband died without having regained consciousness.

Katharine was notified by telegram of Newton Baker's sudden death. Shocked by the news, she collapsed in a chair and sobbed quietly for some time. It was a deeply felt loss for Katharine; Baker had been in charge of her personal affairs and had come to know her as no other man ever had. Soon, she instructed her secretary to make arrangements for her to attend Baker's funeral in Cleveland, so that she might pay her respects to a dear friend and trusted advisor.[7]

Baker had been a renowned lawyer and politician in Cleveland for many years. Following the elaborate funeral services, Katharine was taken aside by William Bemis, one of the law firm's partners, who announced that he would now be overseeing her affairs. Katharine knew Bemis to be an affable gentleman and, at the same time, a tough, uncompromising negotiator. Bemis would serve as Katharine's lawyer and confidante for the rest of her life.

With Bemis at her side in probate court, Katharine secured her mother's estate, valued at more than $10 million. Real property in Chicago and various Michigan towns comprised most of the estate, along with the château in Nyons. Katharine's first act was to donate $1,000 to Sanger's ABCL. Sanger's secretary responded—Sanger was at home in Tucson, Arizona, recuperating from a gallbladder operation—by thanking Katharine for "your valued assistance at this time."[8]

Shortly afterward, Sanger asked Katharine to become involved in a project that promoted birth control services as part of a state's health program. Characteristically, she also appealed for $5,000 to fund the project. In response to the request, Katharine reminded Sanger that her primary interest was in conducting contraceptive research: "If later on I can help you financially along these lines, I will advise you."[9]

When, in 1938, Sanger announced that the ABCL was about to form a Citizen's Committee for Planned Parenthood, Katharine was one of the first to offer her services.

Twenty-Seven

As Katharine gazed out the train window at the passing panorama of sprawling farms, small towns, and occasional forests, her mind reached back to those times when she and her suffrage colleagues had descended on the Capitol to preach passage of the women's vote amendment. It seemed only a few years ago, but it was actually two decades earlier that women were battling Congress to, at long last, recognize women's political rights.

Now, she and a coterie of birth control advocates were on their way to Washington again, this time to plead for public funding of contraceptives. Although they had been warned of congressional opposition, the women nevertheless believed their commitment important enough to make the trip to champion their cause. Even in defeat, the opportunity to educate legislators about birth control could be a major accomplishment.

Actually, the trip was a failure. Advocates of birth control were frustrated by their inability to obtain commitments to act from members of Congress, even those sympathetic to the cause. None would stand up to entrenched Catholic opposition. When Katharine visited the state legislatures in New York and Massachusetts, thanks to Averill Harriman's assistance, the results were little different. Yes, legislators admitted, the issue was important. No, they would not be willing to fight for it on the chamber floor. For all the activity that the Citizen's Committee for Planned Parenthood generated during 1938 and 1939, it had almost nothing to show for it.

The year 1939 also saw Katharine close up 393 Commonwealth to move to Santa Barbara. She had found a house that suited her within walking distance of the downtown area, on Arrellaga Street. The building was old and in need of repair, having been constructed sometime between 1881 and 1884. A document dated 1898 described the building as a wooden two-story structure with a number of outer buildings.[1] The fact that it had survived the 1925 earthquake was obviously a plus. As soon as she arrived in Santa Barbara, Katharine began planning additions and refurbishments to the structure.

Records stated that Col. Bernard, Riven Rock's business manager, owned the property, but he was Katharine's employee. Actually, through the efforts of William Bemis, the title had been set up in this manner to avoid zoning laws and taxes and to keep Katharine's name out of the transaction. Bernard was put in charge of rebuilding the residence, under Katharine's supervision and subject to her agreement. Documents that revealed personal conversations by members of the city's Planning Department suggested that Katharine resided at the El Mirasol Hotel until after Stanley's death in 1947. In reality, Katharine lived in the Arrellaga Street house from 1940. According to the architect's wife, a large gymnasium, an exercise room, a special bathroom, and a chamber for water therapy were added to the original structure, in the hope of transferring Stanley from Riven Rock. One can only conclude that Katharine continued to believe that Stanley would recover sufficiently to someday leave the confines of his gilded estate.

Settling into her new home, Katharine initiated a strict daily regimen, with a noticeable emphasis on physical fitness.[2] Early each morning, she could be seen walking briskly along neighborhood streets, eyes forward, arms vigorously in motion, wearing a tight-fitting beige hat, a long dark coat reaching down to her ankles, and black walking shoes. A dietitian prepared her meals, which included fruits (especially papaya), vegetables, and dairy products. Mornings were taken up with correspondence, which was considerable, and the daily call to Riven Rock regarding a possible afternoon visit with Stanley. When she was unable to see Stanley, Katharine devoted her time to the latest reports of medical research and birth control activities. Most evenings were spent at home alone.

Gertrude Calden, secretary to Dr. Russell, had the opportunity to observe Katharine's behavior over a period of several years. She described Katharine as a highly dedicated, loyal, responsible idealist. "She lived what she thought was her duty," Calden recalled. "She only saw tension with men, and they were afraid of her." Calden admitted she rarely saw Katharine smile, yet she knew Katharine was sensitive to people's feelings and needs. Katharine's generosity to issues she believed in "was unbounded." She did all she could to honor Stanley, Calden said, but seemed resigned to Stanley's circumscribed future.

On rare occasions, Katharine was seen at the Lobero Theater, alone, to enjoy plays or listen to classical music. She sometimes attended teas given by members of Santa Barbara's social elite. In general, Santa Barbara society regarded Katharine as an "odd woman" who undoubtedly carried a heavy burden. Few were aware of Katharine's involvement and participation in women's issues. Through these social events, Katharine became interested in the establishment of the Santa Barbara Museum of Art.

A major leap in Santa Barbara's artistic milieu had begun to take shape in the late 1930s.[3] A group of artists and art patrons shared the goal of founding a city art museum. In 1937, a former post office building was suggested as the site for the new museum. Through the dedicated efforts of a variety of people who had committed themselves to strengthening the city's cultural base, the realization of this goal progressed. Although she was but a recent resident of Santa Barbara, Katharine became one of the prime movers behind the launching of the art museum.

The museum held its official opening on June 5, 1941, with an exhibition entitled "Painting Today and Yesterday in the United States." Visitors noticed two focal points of the renovated facility. One was a skylighted courtyard beyond the entrance, a gift from one of the museum's primary benefactors, Wright Ludington. The other was a large, high-ceilinged viewing room, called the McCormick Gallery, named for Stanley McCormick.

As one of the founders, Katharine had given $7,500 to assist in remodeling and another $300,000 to inaugurate the largest gallery in the museum in Stanley's honor. A year later, Katharine donated another $54,000 to expand exhibition space. The new museum's first year of operation was a notable success and laid the foundation for future accomplishments. Katharine remained a member of the museum until her death, giving generously to various endowment funds. In her will, she gave her home and her collection of Impressionist paintings—those she and Stanley had purchased in Paris on their honeymoon—to the museum, all in Stanley's name.

In 1940, birth control suddenly became a public issue when Eleanor Roosevelt announced that she favored "planned families." Following her husband's unprecedented third-term victory, she felt less constrained and called for a meeting with birth control and government representatives at the White House. The result of this meeting, as well as others that followed it, was the initiation of a number of projects in which Sanger was already associated.[4] One of them, called the Negro Project, was a "unique experiment in race-building and humanitarian service." Below the horizon of public awareness, a series of state-initiated family planning programs were approved, but the war interrupted their operation. Although Katharine was informed of these activities and invited to participate, she declined because they seemed to sidestep the issue she envisioned as the most important for women's freedom—contraception.

In fact, once the war began, U.S. public health programs distributed nearly 50 million condoms a month to the military. The program, however,

did not include women. The navy inexplicably canceled distribution of
two films for women, one on sexual hygiene and the other on birth control.
Birth control advocates protested, but to no avail.[5]

Although rivalries within the birth control movement had persisted for
years and frequently undercut its energies, Sanger recognized that the
movement had to unite its various groups to promote legislation and fight
the Catholic Church. To do so, she negotiated a merger between her clinic
and the American Birth Control League and obtained the cooperation of
other birth control organizations. Together, they formed the Birth Control
Federation of America. After months of negotiation, people who had for-
merly resented Sanger and her tactics now recognized that without her
name the movement could not grow and develop. To run the new organization, a committee was formed, consisting of Margaret Sanger, honorary chair; Dr. Richard N. Pierson, president of the board of directors;
and D. Kenneth Rose, national director.[6]

Sanger and Katharine were quick to notice the ascendancy of men in
the movement, but the argument offered for why men had to lead was,
indeed, true: the groups upon which the advancement of birth control
depended were controlled by men—in Congress, on public health boards,
and in the AMA. Ironically, as the new leaders attested, the birth control
movement would be taken seriously only if men were in charge. Moreover, the image of the organization would have to be changed as well;
"birth control" was too controversial a phrase.

In the meantime, Sanger had inaugurated a citizen's initiative challenging Massachusetts's restrictive birth control law. She could not have chosen a tougher challenge, and Katharine had warned her of the Church's
influence in the state. Yet Sanger's group helped to collect more than fifty
thousand signatures for the initiative petition that, in referendum form,
was placed on the ballot in 1942. During the campaign, birth control advocates and Church followers engaged in a heated battle, one that sometimes reached the streets with demonstrations and marches.

Katharine gave money for publicity, and she often spoke at assemblies
and appeared in marches to promote the referendum's cause. It was not
surprising, then, that her name reappeared in Boston newspapers as "that
Back Bay matron" whose suffrage activities had now become identified
with the birth control movement. "Shame on you," they said.

Initial polls indicated that support for the referendum was in the lead.
However, the archdiocese of Boston mounted an extensive campaign to
defeat the initiative, claiming that the new law "would establish state
control over childbirth and legalize abortion." To no one's surprise,
Church forces handily defeated the referendum. Birth control advocates,
incensed by the loss, blamed state legislators for a lack of support, which
certainly was a fair argument. Fearing the Church, most legislators had

separated themselves from the referendum campaign by becoming conveniently unavailable for speeches and meetings.

The new Birth Control Federation of America—led by Rose and controlled by him through a vote of members he engineered—now claimed to be in favor of child spacing. What had happened to its position on limitation, Katharine wondered. Rose even changed the organization's name to the Planned Parenthood Federation of America.[7] Sanger strongly objected to these decisions, as did many longtime advocates of birth control. But she and her followers no longer held decisive power. Sanger felt that the original crusading spirit had given away to caution, bureaucracy, and caretaking. She was further angered when the PPFA's new board adopted a policy to avoid religious controversy and, instead, emphasize only the health and social values of family planning. Since it was wartime, the board did not want to be perceived as unpatriotic by encouraging a low birthrate.

Still, committed to the spirit of the organization, Katharine donated $5,000 to the PPFA, because she believed it was the best available vehicle to promote her own agenda.[8] She made frequent visits to Rose, arguing for the initiation of contraceptive research. He promised to look into the issue, but nothing came of these meetings. In fact, Katharine's visits became so discomfiting to PPFA officers that they often made themselves absent when alerted of her coming.

During and immediately after the war, the PPFA positioned itself as an organization devoted to strengthening the family. This policy became Katharine's primary argument with the group. She believed it should be the woman in the family, not the family itself, and particularly not the patriarchal male, who held the key to reproductive control. PPFA testified for planned child spacing and family size. Katharine countered that women should be able to maintain unilateral control of the biological consequences of their sexual expression, whether it occurred within or beyond the family, a radical opinion at the time. Thus, they must be provided easy access to contraceptives. Their debate continued for almost a decade, although Katharine continued to donate money each year to PPFA, with her stipulation that the donation go specifically to research projects devoted to contraception. The extent to which the monies were allocated in this way is not known; PPFA never gave Katharine an accounting.

The war years found Katharine spending most of her time in Santa Barbara, visiting Stanley and engaging in long-distance efforts to promote birth control, primarily through donations. Frequently during summer months, Sanger, now mostly retired, visited Katharine, and the two engaged in long discussions about birth control strategy. The meetings helped Sanger plan her travels and speeches for the coming year and reinforced Katharine's belief that the only way that women would be fully free of male domination was through their personal control of the contraceptive process. In 1944, when, with Sanger, she celebrated her sixty-ninth birthday, Katharine vowed it was her "duty" to continue the fight for women's freedom.

In the meantime, visits with Stanley continued, and Katharine's daily routine became something of a fixture in local lore.[9] People claimed to set their watches by her walks. When the big blue Packard luxury sedan was seen on the road leaving Santa Barbara, everyone knew that Katharine was on her way to visit Riven Rock. The estate itself now sponsored flower shows each summer and gave awards for outstanding floral displays. Stanley was often seen at these shows but never participated in them. After the Museum of Art was opened, Katharine often met with the architects and was seen at the museum supervising construction of the new McCormick Gallery. During this same period, Katharine made a gift of $100,000 to Princeton University, in Stanley's name, for construction of a new dormitory.

During these years, Stanley's condition appeared to have improved. He met with visitors more frequently and suffered "difficult days" less often. According to Gertrude Calden, the only time Stanley became violent was when he believed that someone had lied to him. Other than that, Calden described Stanley as intelligent, generous, warm, and quiet. He was aware of his environment and his confinement, she recalled.

Yet he seemed to be content with the situation, Calden believed. When Stanley was offered the opportunity to leave Riven Rock, if only for brief periods, he declined, admitting that he was afraid.

For a time, it appeared that Katharine and Anita had become more friendly. They corresponded often, and their letters had more to do with newsy items than anything concerning Riven Rock. Of the five McCormick siblings, only Anita and Stanley were still alive. Cyrus Jr. had died in 1936, Mary Virginia in May 1941, and Harold the following month. After Nettie had died, the McCormick estate had been divided equally among the five children, even though two of them were under legal guardianship. When, in turn, each sibling died, his or her estate was equally divided among the remaining members of the family. At this point, Stanley and Anita shared an estate of many millions of dollars, the true extent of their wealth unknown even to the guardians.

In 1946, however, a strange disagreement arose between Katharine and Anita. Anita complained that Katharine had been visiting Stanley too frequently and was responsible for "some disturbance" in his demeanor. Although Dr. Russell reported no such problem, Anita went to court to reduce Katharine's visitations. Katharine asked Bemis to investigate Anita's allegations, only to find that they had emanated from the ever-present Dr. Meyer.[10]

Meyer had remained a consultant to Anita on behalf of Mary Virginia.

Although Mary Virginia had died in 1941, Meyer, at Anita's request, continued to correspond with her, offering advice on various matters. When Anita expressed concern about Stanley's frequent colds, Dr. Meyer suggested that they might have been brought in from the outside, and Katharine was singled out as a possible carrier because of her frequent close contact with Stanley.

The court, however, refused to take a position, telling Anita that the issue was a matter for the guardians to discuss. Nonetheless, the incident caused a chill between Katharine and Anita that was never resolved. Stanley's illness instigated the final break in relations between Katharine and the McCormicks. Under the veneer of Victorian civility, the mutual animosity remained as bitter as it always had been.

In 1946, just prior to the Christmas holidays, Stanley became ill with what first appeared to be a stomach ailment. His discomfort necessitated a quick trip to Riven Rock by Dr. Kofod, the local physician who attended to Stanley's general health. He diagnosed Stanley's illness as a chest cold and gave the nurses appropriate medications and instructions. It was decided that the holiday festivities would take place nonetheless, with Katharine and Anita—they had called a temporary truce for the holidays—organizing the party and exchange of gifts. While Stanley did not participate in the gift exchange, he gave Katharine a large assortment of flowers taken from Riven Rock's lush gardens and had them arranged in an elaborate bouquet. Katharine removed one of the roses to keep as a remembrance of the occasion, as she had so often done with Stanley's gifts.

For two weeks, Stanley appeared to return to normal health and to be occupied with his usual routines. Then, with no warning, he began coughing heavily, vomiting food, and complaining of severe weakness. Dr. Kofod was quickly called and, upon examining the patient, declared that Stanley was suffering from pneumonia. The prognosis was not good. Consulting physicians believed that Stanley should be removed to a hospital, but he refused to leave the estate.

For two days, Stanley alternated between coughing spells and fitful sleep. Kofod detected increasing congestion in his patient's lungs, and he reported his observations to Katharine. Though Katherine attempted to feed him, Stanley refused even liquids. She remained at his side the entire time.

On January 19, 1947, at 4:45 P.M., seventy-two-year-old Stanley Robert McCormick died. The death certificate attributed his death to pneumonia; it also indicated that he had suffered for years from arteriosclerosis and nephritis.[11]

Stanley had lived in seclusion for more than forty years in a sumptuous, walled estate, where a corps of doctors and nurses attended him at all times. After a seemingly bright future had been aborted by mental disease, his only fame derived from lawsuits over his custody and the vast amounts of money spent to care for him. "Many Americans must have wondered about the justice of their country's economic system," said the *New York Times* in its obituary of Stanley. "After a lifetime of inactivity and unproductivity, the youngest reaper left an estate worth in excess of $36 million."[12]

Katharine was resigned, almost sad, as she collected the few artifacts Stanley had kept in his bedroom and the few drawings he had made while under Dr. Kempf's care. She could clearly remember the previous times she had been present at life's last moment. Now, she thought, the last of the men she had loved was gone. Moreover, save for William Bemis, there was no one around to offer her comfort and solace.

With the assistance of Dr. Russell and Gertrude Calden, the necessary people were called, the requisite arrangements made. Funeral services were to be held two days later, at the Unitarian Church in Santa Barbara, after which Stanley's body would be shipped to Chicago for burial in the Mc-Cormick family plot. At the funeral, the Reverend Berkeley B. Blake, the minister who had often read poetry to Stanley, presided. Friends had been requested not to send flowers. No psalms were sung. Only a few words were spoken by Blake, on behalf of the "tortured soul of the deceased."

Katharine herself had assumed the responsibility of writing Stanley's obituary. It was a long treatise in the *Santa Barbara News-Press*, detailing Stanley's life and accomplishments in spite of his infirmity. An unacquainted reader would have thought the obituary was a public relations release for a corporate executive. Readers might also have been struck by detailed revelations of the McCormick finances and Riven Rock expenses.

Stanley R. McCormick, 72, who has lived on his famed Riven Rock estate in Montecito since shortly after the turn of the century, died late yesterday after being stricken with pneumonia.

Funeral services will be held tomorrow afternoon at 4:15 at the Unitarian Church, with Rev. Berkeley B. Blake officiating. Friends have been requested to omit flowers. Interment will take place in Chicago.

Mr. McCormick, whose wealth was bestowed generously on many charities and worthwhile institutions in Santa Barbara, was the fifth child of Cyrus Hall McCormick and Nettie Fowler McCormick. The father's invention of the harvester laid the groundwork for the great McCormick fortune.

After his health broke and he moved to Santa Barbara, opening up Riven Rock, the estate became an important cog in the economic progress of the community.

Mr. McCormick was born in Chicago, Nov. 2, 1874. He was educated by tutors in his early years and then went to Browning School in New York where he prepared for college.

He entered Princeton University in the fall of 1891 and graduated *cum laude* with his class in 1895. After college, he went abroad with his widowed mother and made a tour of Europe. While abroad, he studied art for several months in Julian's studio in Paris; and friends said he showed a marked proficiency in both drawing and painting.

Mr. McCormick married Katharine Dexter of Boston in Geneva, Switzerland, on September 15, 1904. After a year spent abroad, he returned to Chicago to live and was appointed comptroller of the International Harvester Co. An increasing disposition to nervous disorder prevented his continuing in this post; and in 1906, upon becoming seriously ill nervously, he resigned it.

It was about this time that he came to Santa Barbara. Stanley's increasing disability, both mental and physical, culminated in an acute pneumonia, which attacked him Friday, and to which he succumbed late yesterday.

His Riven Rock estate is a beautiful 90-acre woodland area with lavish gardens and a 16-room home. Here, for 40 years, he lived the life of a country squire, showing great interest from time to time in world affairs, motion pictures, music, art and radio. For many years, a Santa Barbara orchestra has played concerts there regularly. Maintained for him at Riven Rock was a magnificent library and fine-art collection.

He had moved to Santa Barbara after the Chicago courts, following his breakdown, placed his share of the McCormick fortune under guardianship. The last time his estate was evaluated, it was worth $50,000,000. Under the guardianship, the estate prospered, the income from it one year, 1943, being $3,246,905, according to the report of conservators to the probate court in Chicago.

The same report showed the maintenance of Riven Rock that year cost $115,518 and that Mr. McCormick's medical care cost $108,111.

The benefactors to this community and others from the estate were many. Once a check went to Princeton University for $100,000 to help solve the housing problem of the institution. Another for $70,000 went to the Santa Barbara Museum of Art.

The famed gardens of Riven Rock have been a pillar of the annual Santa Barbara Flower Show. Mr. McCormick's skilled gardeners developed rare orchids and other varieties in greenhouses and experimented successfully in water culture. All of these experiments were made available to local gardeners. The estate gave freely from its gardens, of the service of its gardeners, and financially to help the Flower Show.

Mrs. McCormick, who survives, also is a patron of the arts and prominent here in civic benefactions. Mr. McCormick is also survived by one sister, Mrs. Emmons Blaine of Chicago.[13]

The lengthy obituary by Katharine appeared to make one last attempt to elevate Stanley's life into one that might be deemed honorable and respectful. Yet there seemed to be no separation between Stanley the corporation and Stanley the person. Was it psychological need, family duty, or guilt that drove Katharine to write such a treatise? Likely, all three played a part.

Within a few days of Stanley's burial, the McCormick family, led by Anita, were in court to claim Stanley's estate. It appeared that another prolonged battle over Stanley was about to commence. A probate clerk, however, promptly settled the matter with an amazing discovery.

Probing through a safety-deposit box full of Stanley's papers, dating back more than forty years, the clerk found a single sheet of hotel stationery, now crumpled and yellowed, stuck between the pages of Stanley's meticulous financial records of his and Katharine's honeymoon.

"I hereby bequeath my entire estate to my wife, Katharine Dexter McCormick," Stanley had written. "I also make her the executrix of the estate. Signed, Stanley R. McCormick."[14] He had written the document on September 15, 1904, the day he and Katharine were married.

Anita was shocked—the more so when her lawyers informed her she could not contest the document. Katharine had inherited more than $35 million, which included 31,900 shares of the McCormick-owned company, International Harvester.

Twenty-Eight

Margaret Sanger knew it was coming, sooner or later. Yet when she received the January 22, 1952, letter from Katharine, it nevertheless excited her, like a "call to arms," she recalled.[1]

"I am feeling pretty desperate over the research end of our work," Katharine wrote, "and I sent all I could to the memorial fund to Doctor Dickinson last month, but it does not make me feel any better about the vitally constructive efforts necessary to achieve a fool-proof contraceptive, which is the main end I hold in view at present, and over which I chafe constantly."

Katharine believed she could now focus her full energies toward solving the contraceptive dilemma. It had taken her almost five years to settle Stanley's estate and deal with the overwhelming inheritance taxes. The federal and state governments had claimed taxes amounting to more than $21 million.

Her first action, divesting International Harvester stock, was no easy matter. An outright sale of Katharine's total holdings would have jeopardized the company's cash flow and bank obligations, to say nothing of the stock market. The best Katharine could do was to sell off small portions of her equity each year for several years.

To divest all of Stanley's property, including the Riven Rock estate, proved even more difficult. Because the value of the properties had increased substantially over time, additional taxes had to be paid due to profit from a sale. The Internal Revenue Service also charged interest on taxes past due, those not completely paid off in one year, and given the constraints of her financial situation, Katharine sometimes was unable to meet her annual obligations. Each year's efforts required Katharine and Bemis's full attention and included numerous trips from Santa Barbara to Boston and Chicago.

The sale of Riven Rock represented Katharine's most difficult task. The buildings had been closed and most of the employees dismissed. Only a skeleton crew remained to maintain the estate. Finally, in December 1949, Riven Rock was sold to Thomas G. Markley of Baton Rouge, Louisiana, a real estate developer. The following September he turned the estate over to P. H. Philbin, who subdivided the property into thirty-four parcels and put them up for sale. Riven Rock had become such an encompassing part of Katharine's life that she found it very difficult to sign over the estate's ownership; it was almost impossible for her to keep the pen steady as she signed the deed.

In November 1948, Sanger wrote Katharine asking for funds, this time for the Massachusetts branch of PPFA, which was lobbying to change state law regarding the dispensing of contraceptives. While Katharine acknowledged that "nothing is more important than birth control," she had to decline. "I can do almost nothing on outside charitable contributions until the overwhelming demands of the confiscatory inheritance taxes on my husband's estate are paid. This matter has been much delayed, and I do not yet know when it will be finished."[2] The proposed state law was defeated due, in part, to a last-minute $300,000 publicity campaign sponsored by the Catholic Church.

Two years later, apparently in an improved financial situation, Katharine inquired of Sanger "two questions that are very much with me these days." She wanted to know where financial support was most needed for the birth control movement and what the prospects were for birth control research. "And by research I mean contraceptive research," she explained.[3]

An enthusiastic Sanger answered by suggesting Katharine donate money to the Committee of Contraceptive Research, part of the National Research Council, which was funding projects in England and Germany. But Katharine sought U.S. projects exclusively and was disappointed to find that little research seemed to be under way in America. Of importance to Katharine was Sanger's appraisal of the PPFA. "They had abandoned the project of getting our Public Health units to use contraceptive supplies. As I see the PPF," Sanger observed in her letter, "they are marking time and just holding their own."[4]

Again, Katharine had to decline donating money when Bemis alerted her that new federal taxes would impose further restrictions on her funds. Replying to Sanger, Katharine stated, somberly: "Unfortunately our estate, which was terribly crippled by the inheritance taxes of over eighty-five percent, will again suffer from the new ones about to be imposed." Still, she expressed her concern and impatience in getting back into the movement to meet "the overwhelming necessity as soon as possible, now too long delayed, as we both know." Frustrated that she could do so little, Katharine nevertheless sent Sanger a check for $5,000 for her own use, plus $1,000 to PPFA.[5]

Throughout the spring and summer of 1951, Sanger was spending much of her time in Europe, and correspondence between the women was limited. During this same period, Katharine was engaged in fighting the "inheritance wars," as she described them, in Chicago and Santa Barbara. She also traveled to Nyons, Switzerland, in the hopes of selling the château. In a continent still economically ravaged by war, she found no serious buyers. It had been her first visit to the château since her mother died, and she expressed considerable discomfort about the trip. "Europe is terribly changed, and travel very onerous," she told Sanger. "How do you do it?"

In October, when Sanger wrote Katharine of her most recent adventures, she mentioned work by two European contraceptive firms. The companies were testing a powder that, mixed with water, could be applied by sponge or cotton wads. The products were already being shipped to India and Japan. In response to Sanger's description, Katharine replied that "my greatest worry is over the lack of easy and adequate contraceptive means in the U.S."[6]

It was four months later that Sanger received the fateful letter from Katharine, the one she had been anticipating for some years. She responded speedily. "I appreciate your feeling regarding a fool-proof contraceptive. Everyone agrees that a simple, cheap, harmless contraceptive must be found soon, very, very soon."

In January 1952, on her way to the Far East, Sanger stopped in Santa Barbara for a brief visit with Katharine. They talked at length about the possibilities of sponsoring contraceptive research. Sanger had already approached the Ford Foundation, but it had refused her request because of the controversy surrounding contraception. Where else could they go, the women wondered.

A month later, Sanger scribbled a brief note that mentioned the work of Dr. Gregory Pincus.[7] She had met Pincus at a dinner two years earlier. At the time, he was studying the utilization of hormones as a measure for the control of fertility in rabbits. Katharine was already familiar with Pincus's work, having read his articles in recent medical journals, and she had also talked to her old friend Hudson Hoagland, who had partnered with Pincus to form their own laboratory in Worcester, Massachusetts. She promised Sanger that she would try to visit the laboratory when she returned to Boston in May.

Arriving in Boston, Katharine immediately contacted Dr. Hoskins, who had supervised Katharine's endocrine lab from 1927 to 1947, to arrange a meeting with Dr. Pincus, which Hoskins promised to do. In a June 20 letter to Sanger, she reported an appointment "in Shrewsbury, at the

Worcester Foundation, with Dr. Hoagland next week." She expressed excitement about the meeting and what she hoped to find there.

Unfortunately, the meeting did little to fulfill her expectations. Dr. Pincus did not attend, nor did Katharine learn much about his current hormone research, although Hoagland promised to send her details of their latest projects. Katharine was also somewhat disappointed at the lab's facilities and resources—one small building, a few working lab areas, and a small staff of researchers, though one was Dr. Min-Chueh Chang, one of the leading experimental biologists in the country. Hoagland admitted the operations were on a tight budget but noted that Pincus was currently wooing a number of potential contributors.

Katharine became even more frustrated when she discovered that the PPFA had refused a $3,600 stipend to Dr. Pincus because the board was not "sold" on his work. When she attempted to question their decision, a meeting could not be set up, for "various reasons." Nor could she get back to Worcester to visit Pincus. When she finally succeeded in meeting with the PPFA board, along with delivering a promised donation, she requested that Pincus be given the money for his research. Hormones for rats, the board members protested. Of what value is that kind of research? They remarked that the board would have to visit Pincus's laboratory to see what he was doing with the money they had already given him. "You mean you haven't been to his laboratory yet?" Katharine asked in surprise.

Actually, the PPFA had been investing in contraceptive research, but board members wished to keep the activity quiet to protect the organization's public image. In April 1952, it gave $3,400 to Pincus for a study of the effect of steroid substances on contraceptive activity. A few months later, Dr. Chang reported that he had recently been able to inhibit ovulation in rats over a protracted period, using a progesterone compound. The results of the research were reported to PPFA in January 1953, at which time the Worcester lab requested another stipend to further study the use of progesterone. Chang talked about developing an oral contraceptive to inhibit ovulation in humans, but the PPFA board scoffed at the idea and expressed concern about possible side effects. Yet it also asked whether the process could be patented.

When Pincus replied that clinical tests could be undertaken and he foresaw no side effects, his grant was finally approved. It was the same grant that had previously been turned down, but Katharine had now persuaded the board that it should be funded. Yet she was very concerned about the seemingly indifferent manner in which contraceptive research was being funded and conducted.

"I am perfectly frantic over the research delays on contraception," Katharine lamented to Sanger, "but, of course, research is like that. I suppose one has to wait, but it is very hard to do so when the need is so urgent."

On a note of frustration, she concluded the letter, "It is pretty trying not to be able to *push it!*"[8]

Sympathetically, Sanger responded: "You are quite right in feeling as you do about research. In a few months, perhaps, we can go to see Dr. Pincus."

Sanger announced her plan to be in New York and Boston in June and suggested, "It would be such a pleasure to go with you to see Dr. Pincus." Telegrams and phone calls crisscrossed as Katharine, Sanger, and Hoagland attempted to make a firm date in June for all of them to come together.

They all agreed to meet on the afternoon of June 7, at the Worcester lab. To Katharine, this was not to be a get-acquainted meeting. Serious business was on her agenda.

Years later, in her book on the development of the birth control pill, Loretta McLaughlin described the meeting between Pincus, Hoagland, Sanger, and Katharine as setting "the stage for the debut of a new star—the world's first oral contraceptive." As for Katharine, McLaughlin described her as "a woman more strange and powerful than fiction could ever invent."[9]

The Pill

Twenty-Nine

Although Hoagland had forewarned him, Dr. Pincus was not entirely prepared for the meeting with Katharine and Margaret Sanger. He was quite taken aback by this first encounter.

They were no sooner introduced than Katharine declared, "I want a tour of your labs. Then, I would like to review the résumés of your scientists, particularly Dr. Chang. I also wish to discuss a theoretical timetable, if we agree to proceed with a project."

Even before Pincus could recover and respond, she continued. "Most important, I want to know how you feel about contraception; not just birth control generally, but how it particularly affects women."

Pincus must have answered Katharine's questions adequately and his labs and personnel must have passed her critical eyes because, at the end of the meeting, she wrote him a check for $20,000. "As start-up," she explained, "with $20,000 more to follow when we work out procedures and details."

Gregory Goodwin Pincus ("Goody" to his friends) was born April 3, 1903, in Woodbine, New Jersey, a member of a distinguished academic family. They had come to America from Russia in the late nineteenth century exodus to escape the oppression of Czarist pogroms.[1]

Gregory had matriculated at Cornell and majored in agriculture, with a special interest in apple growing. When he entered the graduate program at Harvard, genetics had become his primary interest. During his graduate years in Cambridge, he met and became close friends with Hudson Hoagland. Together, they received doctorates in 1927. In 1930, after two years of study in England and Germany, Pincus returned to Harvard as an instructor in general physiology.

Probably due to the strong wave of anti-Semitism that swept Harvard in the mid-1930s, Pincus was informed that he would not be reappointed to the faculty. Hoagland, who was teaching and doing research at nearby Clark University in Worcester, resolved to have Pincus hired at the school. The Clark administration agreed to his appointment. Unfortunately, they had no funds to support Pincus. On his own, Hoagland raised sufficient funds to grant Pincus a visiting professorship at the university. At the time, salaries for full professors did not exceed $5,000, and a research budget of $1,000 was considered remarkable. Battling the great hurricane of 1938, Pincus, his wife, and their two children, laden with their belongings, arrived in Worcester.

Successfully soliciting additional funding, Pincus soon attracted a number of young scientists to join him. Because of the lack of space in Clark's laboratories, Pincus's group first was assigned space in the basement of the science building. Later, they were moved into the "barn," in reality a commodious, three-story structure of Victorian vintage, which had to be painstakingly converted into laboratory space.

Located near Clark, the Worcester State Hospital had gained a reputation as a center for research on schizophrenia. In fact, in 1927 Katharine had established an organization known as the Neuroendocrine Research Foundation to conduct studies leading to a possible cure for Stanley. Though its offices were at Harvard Medical School, the foundation's program of research in schizophrenia was actually conducted at Worcester State Hospital, under the direction of Dr. Roy Hoskins. Hoagland was working with this group and, over the ensuing years, published many studies in which human subjects were used. At the time, there were no laws against the use of mental patients for scientific investigations.

Unhappy about their inability to work independently, Pincus and Hoagland discussed the possibility of establishing their own research institute, one that would be completely divorced from control by any university or college. In 1944, with more bravery than funds, they established the Worcester Foundation for Experimental Biology. It was founded without endowment or income, whether from patents, patients, or students. Nonetheless, due to Pincus's increasing abilities to obtain grants in the biomedical sciences and stipends from federal agencies, its success was almost immediate. In 1945, they moved to neighboring Shrewsbury, having found a residential estate for sale at an attractive price.

Staff were hired, eminent men with a variety of biomedical specialties, among them Dr. Hoskins and Dr. Min-Chueh Chang. Dr. Chang had received his bachelor's degree from the University of Peking and his Ph.D. from Cambridge University and had become an authority on the physiology of reproduction.

The cost of purchasing the property and hiring staff had exhausted the funds available to Pincus and Hoagland, so they could afford no support personnel. Scientists kept their own laboratories in order, cleaned their own chemical glassware, and performed clerical and household chores. Hoagland mowed the lawn, and Pincus did most of the animal caretaking. Within a few years, an increasing number of federal grants and experimental studies commissioned by commercial drug companies helped make the organization profitable. By the time Katharine met Pincus and Hoagland, the Worcester Foundation had become a well-known and respected, if not highly endowed, organization of skilled scientists making significant contributions in the field of steroid hormones.

Another colleague who joined Pincus and Chang once they began the pursuit for a female contraceptive was Dr. John Rock, an eminent Boston gynecologist. Although a practicing Catholic, Rock had already publicly called for the repeal of Massachusetts laws restricting physicians from providing advice on birth control. He was also a strong proponent of contraception. Coincidentally, at the same time that Katharine and Pincus were negotiating a contract, Rock was already giving his patients injections of progesterone, with the stated intent of helping them to become pregnant by predictably regulating their menstrual cycles.[2]

When Pincus and Rock met and exchanged descriptions of what they were doing, Pincus was astonished. While he was busy inoculating rabbits, Rock was administering a chemical contraceptive to humans. Immediately, Pincus asked Rock to join the team. Rock was not only willing, but was truly excited at the prospect of discovering a contraceptive that could solve and control the problems of fertility.

"Goody" Pincus was a hustler, a sociable charmer, and the life of the party with his stories and anecdotes on medical research. Without question, he was good at obtaining funds and grants; he had kept the foundation busy for years. When Katharine was introduced to him, Pincus quickly realized he had a potential bonanza in research money, although at the time, he was dubious that much would come out of such research.

Pincus was a devoted and loyal family man, his generosity extending itself to all of his relatives. Some years later, when cousins asked him for samples of the contraceptive pill—still in the testing stage—he cheerfully sent them a batch.[3] To his staff, he was a revered father figure.

On the business side, however, he was often hard-hearted, constantly manipulating deals and personnel toward a successful outcome. Pincus wanted to be a winner, and he went to great lengths to achieve that goal. At one press interview, when asked about his business practices, Pincus admitted to being amoral. "He was a politician at heart and enjoyed the feeling of importance," concluded the reporter.

From the very first, Pincus never felt entirely comfortable with Katharine; yet, in every interaction with her, he showed respect and responded promptly to her questions and requests. Initially, he was amazed at her scientific knowledge; their conversations could have been viewed as exchanges between two research scientists.

Katharine was much more than the traditional donor. She "knew the field," "spoke the language," and was unrelenting in her demand for details and rationale. For that reason, Pincus developed a sincere respect and admiration for her, although he often chafed at the amount of time he was required to spend in her presence.

Actually, while the entire project's activities were seemingly open to Katharine's scrutiny, there were a few items that Pincus kept from her. For example, early in the project, Pincus successfully negotiated with the pharmaceutical enterprise G. D. Searle to obtain progesterone by persuading the company of the commercial potential of a birth-control contraceptive. Shortly after, Pincus began receiving a monthly consultation fee from Searle.[4] Throughout the entire time of their association, Katharine never became aware of this affiliation. When Pincus went on speaking trips or to conventions, paid for by Katharine, he would purchase personal gifts and have them shipped back, adding extraneous costs to his travel expenses.[5]

Nevertheless, he was an innovative scientist with an ability to envision the ultimate success of projects. Had he not possessed these gifts, he likely would have rejected the challenge to develop the new contraceptive.

In contrast, Dr. Chang was a laboratory recluse. Rarely did he appear socially, and often, he did not even appear at meetings. His days were spent in the lab; working late hours and during weekends was characteristic. When he did discuss procedures and data with Katharine, he was highly articulate and responsive to her cross-examinations, although he admitted to having never met a woman like her before.

For Katharine, Chang's expertise and commitment to the project were admirable and honorable; she harbored no doubts about his results and conclusions, because he repeated tests innumerable times to ensure their accuracy. For that matter, Katharine often expressed envy for not being able to work in the lab herself. Still, it was Chang who was pessimistic about the project.

Dr. John Rock, true to his name, was a pillar of the medical profession in Boston. When this tall, good-looking, self-confident, fatherly man entered an examination room, women sensed that they were in the hands of the ultimate caregiver. His gynecological reputation was exalted, yet his beliefs about women's health were in direct conflict with those of the Catholic Church.

On one hand, Rock was a devout Catholic. Yet, the day before he was to be married by Boston's Cardinal O'Connell, he performed a number of cesarean sections, an intervention then forbidden by the Church. At confession, the priest refused to give Rock absolution, thus preventing him from receiving the sacrament of marriage the next day. The quandary was conveyed to Cardinal O'Connell, who immediately conferred absolution. Still, the cardinal's gracious act disturbed Rock, because the rules of the Church seemed arbitrary. The event marked the beginning of his confrontation with Catholic law on birth control and contraception. Ultimately, this confrontation would prepare Rock to be the spokesman chosen to appear before the FDA on behalf of the new birth control pill.

Dr. Rock and Katharine got along quite well, partly because of their shared backgrounds as Boston patricians, but also because of their strong, mutually held belief in the freedom of women to govern their own bodies. Some years previously, when Katharine had been assisting the Massachusetts League of Women Voters to lobby for the repeal of the law against contraceptive distribution, Rock had been the first Catholic signatory among a group of physicians to urge repeal.

In spite of his impressive credentials, Margaret Sanger protested when Dr. Rock was added to the Worcester Foundation team. In a letter to Katharine, she opined that Rock would not "advance the case of contraception." Katharine, however, defended the foundation's decision, telling her friend that Rock was a "reformed Catholic" who was able to separate religion from medicine. Sanger later changed her opinion of Dr. Rock to one of glowing admiration when she recognized the essential contributions he was making to the project.

The second meeting, held a week later, included Pincus; Hoagland; Katharine; and her intrepid lawyer, William Bemis. The object of this meeting was to lay the ground rules for operation of the project, the decision-making process, and a proposed timetable. Katharine had come to the meeting with an already drafted contract, so with Bemis explaining the details and making notes of changes to which everyone agreed, their business was quickly concluded. Katharine gave Pincus another check for $20,000 and agreed to improve the laboratories so the project could be speedily begun. The foundation's first-year budget was estimated to be $70,000.

During the meeting, Katharine again questioned Pincus regarding his commitment to women. Whereas a week before he had harbored doubts as to the success of the project, this time he expressed his belief that the goal could be reached and promised Katharine to do the best he could. His original opinion as to the time required for completion of the project, ten to twelve years, proved wrong, however. In two years a testable product would be isolated, and after four years of the most extensive tests ever made on a drug, "the pill" would be ready for presentation to the FDA.

A major mistake Katharine made in her initial agreement with the Worcester Foundation was to channel her contributions to them through the Planned Parenthood Federation, supposedly for tax purposes. Within months of the project's initiation, Katharine was at odds with William

Vogt, head of Planned Parenthood, regarding their reluctant allocation of funds to Pincus. Their argument would continue for the next eight months.

In the meantime, Margaret Sanger maintained her own rigorous schedule of national and international travel, spreading the gospel of birth control. Katharine and Sanger met only once during the next two years, but their correspondence was voluminous. Katharine penned her letters, often four to five pages in length. Sanger had her letters typed by her secretary, single-spaced, often running for two or three pages. The women had much to share.

Their letters were usually filled with personal, health-related topics: how Sanger was taking care of a cold or the inconveniences of Katharine's gastritis; "dutch uncle" recommendations from each about the need to rest and care for oneself; new remedies found for aches and pains. For Katharine, Sanger was the only person with whom she could share these intimacies. Sanger related in detail her many meetings and offered her observations concerning the people she met, optimistic that all of them would soon be espousing her dogma. She talked of birth control problems in the countries she visited and the assistance they desperately needed. Occasionally, she would hint to Katharine that a needy program might be worth a contribution. At the end of the letter, there would be a few paragraphs devoted to the Pincus project, Sanger responding to Katharine's update or her mention of interesting scientists whom she had met that might contribute in some way.

Katharine, in turn, attempted to keep Sanger up to date on the project and its almost daily manifestations, as well as her continuing problems with Planned Parenthood and her personal frustrations about "the slowness of progress." Midway through this period of correspondence, Katharine politely asked Sanger if it would be agreeable to her to be addressed as Margaret; she, in turn, could be addressed as Katharine. It was a welcome suggestion, one that Sanger cheerfully accepted. Past letters, always signed "Mrs. Katharine McCormick" soon gave way to "Katharine" and, later, just "KDM" or "Kay." At no other time, to no other person except Stanley and her mother, did Katharine sign her correspondence with such familiarity.

During the first few months after Katharine met with Pincus, he produced periodic progress reports, which tended to be brief and informal. Katharine was then traveling to Chicago and Santa Barbara and was consequently out of touch with the project's ongoing activities. In a September 1953 letter to Sanger, she expressed frustration at not being "on the scene," berating herself for her inability to participate in the project with Pincus and Rock.[6] "I haven't heard a word about the Pincus work and shall check up with him and Dr. Rock as soon as I get home and will let you know what I hear. I do hope they have not run into difficulties. There has now been time enough to get some sort of an idea as to how progesterone could function."

Sanger's return letter raised additional concerns for Katharine when she reported a rumor that Planned Parenthood had supplied Pincus with only enough money to support the work through January 1954.[7] When Sanger returned to the United States in November, she availed herself of Katharine's guest house in Santa Barbara for a brief rest. Katharine had already returned to Boston to tend to "necessary matters."

Katharine's letter to Sanger in Santa Barbara spoke of her meeting with Pincus and Hoagland, but it was concerned primarily with the problems at Planned Parenthood.[8] Vogt had visited Shrewsbury but had not talked to either Pincus or Hoagland. When Katharine questioned him, he indicated he would see them at a future Planned Parenthood board meeting. Still, he expressed doubts about the use of progesterone in the tests and, indirectly, the project itself. Katharine admitted to Sanger that she had nearly "exploded" in response to Vogt's remarks.

Yet there was good news from Shrewsbury: "As far as I have seen, there is nothing the matter with progesterone as an effective contraceptive, and Hoagland agrees with me that we should stick to an oral one, not branch into use of injections." Still, developing the oral progesterone was a key issue, which Chang was working on, literally, day and night. Rock's use of progesterone in a new experiment had run into problems, Katharine lamented, because a number of his patients had missed their scheduled appointments and "the whole experiment has to begin over again."

Nonetheless, she continued, "By the first of the year, the tests by Pincus and Rock on about seventy cases will have run for six months; and they expect to have a report then of what they have found so far."

In addition, the doctors had complained to Katharine about not having enough space to handle more cases, and she promised to see about providing the space and extra personnel they needed. For future testing, they had suggested that an experiment might be financed in Puerto Rico. Dr. Rock knew a doctor there who was interested in birth control and could offer "as many cases as five hundred," Katharine wrote.

Katharine expressed trepidation about testing "away from home," because of the need to maintain consistency and accuracy in the testing procedure. Nevertheless, the pressure to speed up the testing process surely meant their having to go outside the country.

For the next two months, Katharine was hard at work attempting to resolve some of the project's problems, or "holdups," as she called them. More working space was obtained by additions to the lab building, but construction would take months. New staff was being hired, but they had to be carefully and rigorously trained. When progesterone was found to be in short supply, Katharine had Pincus calling drug manufacturers to purchase larger quantities. It was not an easy task. Pfizer was a Catholic-influenced company, and it refused the order. Searle, which had supplied Pincus before, warned him that it wanted no part of experiments that might interfere with the menstrual cycle. Ironically, when Searle finally acknowledged Chang's success in isolating two effective compounds for contraception, one of which was a Searle product, Pincus got as much progesterone as he needed.

Dr. Rock was now very close to retirement and would be required to give up his position and practice at the hospital. So that Rock could continue to see patients and maintain his experiments, Katharine purchased a building directly across the street from the hospital and had it outfitted. When Pincus, Rock, and Katharine discussed the need for an increased sample population, Puerto Rico again was suggested as a possible site.

In February 1954, Sanger informed Katharine that Pincus and Rock had asked Planned Parenthood for more funds, and there had been vigorous debate about transferring the money to them.[9] "That is my money they are handling," Katharine responded incredulously, "and they had been given a directive about allocating it. What is going on in the Planned Parenthood Federation?" she asked Sanger.

The situation with Planned Parenthood could not continue, Katharine believed. She had to make some changes in the arrangement. She could not tolerate having money withheld from the project for any reason. Listing all of the reasons why she believed Planned Parenthood had not fulfilled its part of the plan, she concluded: "It appears to me that no one there is really concerned over achieving an oral contraceptive and that I was mistaken originally in thinking they were."[10] Her mind was made up.

"I believe that now I should give up trying to cooperate with the Research Committee of P.P. Federation and concern myself with the Shrewsbury laboratory work, endeavoring to make it advance as rapidly as such an investigation can."

There is no record of how Vogt or the Planned Parenthood board reacted to Katharine's decision, but they could not have been pleased. Within days, Katharine and Bemis met with Pincus and Hoagland to work out the details of working directly together on the project. Pincus would prepare a written report for Katharine every two weeks, apart from personal meetings and the usual daily phone conversations.[11]

In his first report to Katharine, Pincus expressed exhilaration that in Dr. Rock's testing with seventeen patients over a six-month period, none of the women had become pregnant. He and Rock again recommended that Puerto Rico be considered as a large-scale testing site.

In March 1954, Sanger wrote a long letter to Katharine, extolling the virtues of her friend Dr. Abraham Stone, who was in charge of the Margaret Sanger Research Bureau in New York.[12] She suggested that he be given the opportunity to conduct tests. According to Sanger, Stone had three endocrine scholars on his staff and the capacity to keep expert records. In fact, she had already asked Stone to get in touch with Pincus to discuss a possible arrangement. From her discussions with Stone, Sanger claimed that he could get "100 cases" quickly, and the total cost for all testing would be only $5,000.

Of course, this was Sanger's organization, and she had been trying for years to obtain funding for its continued operation, having already approached charities as disparate as the Commonwealth Fund and Doris Duke for donations. Katharine was fully aware of these connections but chose to let them proceed. After all, testing in New York was closer than in Puerto Rico. She stated her approval to Pincus, with the caveat "as long as all tests follow Pincus/Rock procedures." She then suggested that Pincus meet with Stone and plan for the initiation of testing at the Research Bureau. Unhesitatingly, Katharine committed to financing the entire investigation.

Further, she alerted Pincus that, when Sanger went to Japan the following month, she would be seeking to set up a testing station there.[13] If she was successful, additional sites would demand increased amounts of progesterone. "When can it be procured?" she asked Pincus, "and how fast can we get it delivered?"

To anticipate the possibility of working with outside testing sites, Katharine requested that Pincus write down in detail his and Rock's methodologies, so that others could follow them. Again, however, she stressed the absolute necessity for any supplemental testing to be scientifically acceptable and able to be readily integrated into the tests currently being conducted by Dr. Rock.

In response to her letter, Pincus agreed fully, promised to obtain the necessary progesterone, and said that he and Rock would personally monitor all testing.[14]

Upon hearing the latest developments from Katharine, including Dr. Stone's involvement in testing, Sanger reacted with pleasure, in her usual complimentary fashion.[15] "You act so quickly when your mind is made up. It is all very exciting and so wonderful that you and you only have pressed the button which has illuminated so many minds in this great project." Sanger promised to do her utmost while in Japan to sell Japanese officials on the idea of testing.

To no one's surprise, Sanger's enthusiastic proselytizing of the Japanese Ministry of Public Health and Welfare obtained a tentative agreement to participate in testing, but the Japanese expressed concern about where the progesterone would come from and who would pay for the research. To alleviate their concerns, Katharine suggested that, as a first step, one of the Japanese doctors be sent to Shrewsbury to become familiar with the procedures, the product, and Rock's testing before anything further was decided. She would pay for the doctor's expenses and time.

Events were now moving quickly toward implementation. Dr. Stone met with Pincus and received instructions on testing procedures. A check for $5,000 from Katharine followed shortly thereafter. A Japanese gynecologist was in the process of being selected to visit Shrewsbury, and Katharine requested a cost estimate from Japan, including doctors' salaries and testing procedures. Additional progesterone was ordered. Pincus contacted Dr. David Tyler in Puerto Rico to explore the possibility of testing there and asked Tyler what the costs might be.

A letter from Dr. Stone to Katharine thanked her for the funds "in this extremely important and valuable research work."[16] Stone went on to inform her of the actions he was about to take to initiate the testing process. A bit disturbing to her, however, was Stone's references to Pincus's work as "thus far uncertain" and his boast that he would personally carry on "the additional studies that are essential." I'll have to watch the Stone operation carefully, she thought.

At a June meeting with Pincus and Rock, concern was expressed about the availability of progesterone for Japan and Hawaii, another Sanger stop that had generated interest from local medical authorities. Actually, Katharine was more concerned about Sanger's evangelistic selling skills. She felt that the claims Sanger had made about the project and its ultimate success could very well attract premature attention. In fact, a minor episode in Japan had the press claiming that a new oral contraceptive had already been discovered, this based on comments Sanger had supposedly made in an interview. Luckily, lack of additional information prevented the story from mushrooming. At this point, Katharine wanted no one to know what they were doing. She was afraid that any adverse publicity reaching Massachusetts would wreck Dr. Rock's tests and could generate threats from the Church and state authorities. Such a scenario would mean disaster for the project.

The June meeting revealed both encouraging and disappointing news. Pincus reported that he had made a deal with the Syntex Corporation, or rather its branch in New York, Chemical Specialties, Inc., for as much progesterone as they needed now and for the foreseeable future. Dr. Stone had already received his supply. Hoagland revealed that initial testing in Puerto Rico, with a sample of 500 women, would cost $10,800 and could begin as soon as procedures were learned.

On the negative side, a Japanese doctor had not yet been chosen to visit Shrewsbury. Inoculations of progesterone in animals did not go well because they caused irritations, and the inoculations used by Dr. Rock had to be modified. Of the sixty women Dr. Rock had been treating for the past year, only thirty had generated data considered to be accurate, pointing out the need for expanded testing. Those thirty, however, had given "satisfactory contraceptive results"—in other words, no pregnancies!

Katharine's letter updating Sanger on the project's progress indicated her pleasure with Pincus's report.[17] With optimism, she wrote, "I do not see why we should not go ahead now as rapidly as we can. We need a multiplicity of cases," she declared in closing, "not only to show up any disadvantages in the use of progesterone, but also to demonstrate the scope of its effectiveness."

Unfortunately, Katharine's optimism was short-lived. When she heard of delays in both Japan and Hawaii, problems that would set back her proposed schedule, she did not take the news calmly. Comments to Pincus and a letter to Sanger voiced her displeasure and frustration. When she was informed that studies in Japan required further government approval, Katharine was convinced that testing in Massachusetts and in Puerto Rico would be the only way to accumulate sufficient samples and accurate data.

A hastily called budget meeting, slated to include Katharine, Bemis, Pincus, and Hoagland, detailed the required action on various projects during the coming months: $25,000 to the Worcester Foundation, for whatever was needed to speed up experiments; $5,000 for additional space at Dr. Rock's hospital, to add more subjects; $11,300 for Puerto Rico, for one year of testing; and, in another attempt to get the Japanese involved in the project, travel and living expenses for two Japanese doctors to come to Shrewsbury. To ensure the Puerto Rico project, Dr. Rock would travel there in October to assist in initiating the testing.[18]

As it happened, Pincus did not attend the budget meeting because he was speaking at a convention in Canada. His subject was clinical evaluation of progesterone effects on the menstruation-ovulation relationships in the human female. Actually, a good portion of the material derived from Dr. Rock's latest report on the thirty women in his experiment. When Katharine heard about Pincus's speech, she became upset about his public revelations dealing with the project. In a rare outburst of anger, she scolded Pincus for revealing so much of their efforts and made him promise that in the future, he would obtain clearance from her regarding his speechmaking topics.[19] She reiterated her concern—her fear—about any part of the project's attracting public interest. Luckily, few people heard Pincus speak, and fewer still understood what he was saying. No written material had been reproduced, and the topic seemed to disappear into the mass of convention material. Yet the episode surely exposed the increasing tension and nervousness that Katharine felt as the project progressed.

In late August 1954, Pincus, Rock, Katharine, and Drs. Tyler and Lee from Puerto Rico met to discuss the proposed testing. Tyler and Lee expressed great enthusiasm for the project and promised to begin as soon as they received the product. They were even more pleased with their budget allocation. Dr. Rock planned to return with them to assist in the initial efforts. Since the territory was predominantly Catholic, care had to be taken as to how and for what reasons the tests were being undertaken. It was decided best not to label the project a study of contraception, but to call it a study of the physiology of progesterone in women. All participants departed from the meeting confident that testing would proceed as planned.

Katharine's update of happenings to Sanger, now resting in Tucson with a lingering bronchial infection, covered the usual topics of health, both hers and Sanger's; Sanger's most recent international exploits; and, finally, activities dealing with the project itself.[20] Both of them were ailing. Katharine admitted to a recurrence of gastritis and specified her attempts to relieve the discomfort, ranging from beginning a restricted diet to ingesting large amounts of vitamin A and papaya. Significantly, there is no indication that, during her periodic gastric bouts, Katharine ever consulted a doctor.

Adding to the problems delaying progress at Shrewsbury was a devastating hurricane that pummeled Massachusetts and included the city in the swath it cut across the state. Hoagland informed Katharine that damage was light, the animal house having suffered the most. The next day, Pincus called Katharine to reassure her that the foundation had incurred little damage; the animal house could be quickly repaired. He also advised her that the Japanese gynecologist, Dr. Matsuba, had finally arrived. Pincus expressed confidence that testing in Japan could begin in the near future. He further suggested that a meeting be scheduled in November with all parties concerned, to review what had been accomplished during the past few months and what plans should be developed for the future. The most important news he kept for last.

"After considerable testing of rats and rabbits—200 separate procedures, according to Chang—he has isolated two blends of progesterone that work and can possibly be manufactured in pill form. For human application!" Pincus declared. He admitted, though, that the dosage factor had not yet been worked out.

Katharine gasped at Pincus's disclosure. "I am delighted with the news, Dr. Pincus," she responded. Pausing only long enough to catch her breath, she now sounded the trumpet: "Then there is no reason why we cannot begin testing in Puerto Rico immediately."

Thirty

Katharine celebrated her seventy-ninth birthday in the same way she had celebrated most recent birthdays—alone. Nevertheless, that very day she was meeting with Drs. Pincus, Hoagland, and Rock at Shrewsbury to discuss the latest project activities and outline financial needs for the next six months. Their meetings had become a ritual.

"What results have you to share from your latest tests?" she asked Rock. "What success has Chang achieved in his experiments on the new compounds?" And to Pincus and Hoagland, "What are your estimates for the funds we will need for the remainder of the year?" Pincus and Rock were fully prepared with answers, having become familiar with Katharine's constant requests for up-to-date, detailed, accurate information.

Since Pincus's announcement to Katharine of a breakthrough regarding the manufacture of a pill for human use, progress had unfortunately been slowed by a variety of factors: delayed delivery of progesterone; the on-and-off reports about participation by the Japanese; Puerto Rico's slow start because one of its administrators moved to another job; and the bureaucratic barriers raised by the city, blocking the construction of additional space for Dr. Rock.

Katharine was especially frustrated by the inability of testers to recruit larger numbers of women for the trial procedures and to keep those already in the program for a greater length of time. "The same old bottleneck," she deplored, "the difficulty in getting enough ovulating, intelligent subjects for the progesterone tests, I mean intelligent enough so they can be relied upon to carry out the procedure."[1] In spite of the current delays, Pincus attempted to reassure her about the future. "I think it is evident that things are beginning to happen," he replied, "and I am hoping that surely, though perhaps not rapidly . . . " (here Katharine frowned) . . . "our overall plans will begin to mature."

Nor did the holiday season offer any pleasure for Katharine. "I am a regular Scrooge when it comes to Xmas," she confided to Sanger. "The long stretch of holidays irritates me, as everything one wants to do is so held up. I shall be glad when they are over." Even the prospect of having to meet Pincus and Rock in two weeks "is very trying."[2]

The anticipated meeting offered little news. Chang was reported to be working diligently through batches of progesterone compounds to find a usable pill to administer to women; the animal house, under construction for more than a year, was finally close to completion; Rock's testing was moving along smoothly; and Pincus planned to visit Puerto Rico shortly to monitor their activities. Surprising news! Japanese doctors reported they were ready to begin testing and requested that progesterone be sent as quickly as possible.

Coincidentally, Sanger's International Planned Parenthood Federation (a separate group independent from the domestic organization) had scheduled its conference for October 24 to 29, 1955, in Tokyo, and she was actively soliciting top scientists and doctors to appear. Both she and an impatient Katharine believed it was now time to speak about the project and suggested that Pincus appear there, to reveal for the first time the nature of their endeavor. There was one caveat: enough progress had to have been made on the testing to claim preliminary success. To further entice Pincus, Katharine offered to pay for him and his wife to make the trip.

Katharine found the February meeting with Pincus and Rock to be full of "hopes." Rock had been testing two different compounds, and although they were still in the preliminary stages, both appeared to be working as predicted. Using a new pill formula, Rock had enlisted fifty women to participate in a test, the first human trials with an oral contraceptive. In the meantime, Chang had come up with a new compound, currently being tested on animals, that was ten times stronger than the one Rock was currently using. To Katharine, both Pincus and Rock expressed a strong belief that the compounds they were currently using represented the best prospects to date.

Initial testing in Puerto Rico, however, had become an "administrative flop," primarily because record keeping had not been accurate and, according to Dr. David Tyler, "the women ignorant."[3] The revised plan was to begin testing anew with medical students and nurses. Of concern to Katharine, Dr. Stone had not been in touch with Pincus for weeks, and it was feared his testing had failed.

When Katharine asked Pincus to attend the Tokyo conference and present a paper on the project, he expressed muted excitement about the opportunity. "But didn't you want to keep the project under wraps," he asked Katharine. "Dr. Pincus," she responded, "it is time to begin our campaign to make it known what we are doing." When she promised to finance the trip, he was convinced.

When Sanger received news from Katharine about the latest events, her response was apologetic, sympathetic, and complimentary.[4] She expressed regret about the initial testing in Puerto Rico but suggested that the new doctor, Celso-Ramon Garcia, would be a great asset. She apologized for Dr. Stone's not reporting to Pincus. According to Sanger's information, Stone had been having difficulties recruiting women for the test. She promised to "get some action" on the issue and was particularly pleased that Pincus had agreed to attend the Tokyo conference. In closing, Sanger's comments to Katharine were obviously written to buoy her spirits as well as her ego, something she often did in letters to Katharine. "You must rest your head peacefully each night," she said, "when you consider how much you have done to make all this work so successful. No single individual has done so much to bring this dream about." Katharine was rarely swayed by compliments, but such words from Sanger were always warmly received.

With Bemis working the local authorities, and after months of inconclusive negotiation, Dr. Rock's urgent request for additional space had finally been resolved. A new section to Rock's building had been agreed upon, adding office and lab space, but now at a cost of close to $100,000. Bemis and Katharine had already prepared for the expenditure.

Dr. Rock also informed Katharine that testing in Japan was to begin with animals; doctors there insisted on being completely comfortable with the results before using human subjects. "Even though they have the results of your tests?" she asked. "Pincus felt the testing of animals at this time was 'not valuable.' When will they start with human subjects?" Katharine wanted to know. Neither Pincus nor Rock could supply an answer. Further news from Puerto Rico indicated that testing had resumed, using a sample of twenty medical students and nurses. Yet these tests, too, proved to be short-lived.

When civic authorities in Puerto Rico discovered that the tests involved contraception, the project was stonewalled by a Catholic faction at the testing hospital. Support was withdrawn, and the project was forced to shut down. Luckily, Dr. Rock persuaded Dr. Garcia to leave Puerto Rico and join his staff in Boston.

The two failures in Puerto Rico proved profoundly frustrating to Katharine. For the first time, she wondered whether the entire enterprise was worth the effort. Revealing her personal feelings to Sanger, she wrote, "It is maddening that everything has to be so slow, so terribly slow."[5] Her dejection, however, was only momentary.

Her pessimism may have been brought to the surface by two other long-standing problems, dating back to the inheritance tax issues she had encountered following Stanley's death. One dealt with the original Dexter home in Dexter, Michigan; the other, the Château Prangins in Nyons, Switzerland.

Gordon Hall, the old Dexter mansion, had been sold after Katharine's grandmother, Millicent, died in 1899. In the 1930s, Katharine discovered that it was vacant and deteriorating. Emil Lorch, founder of the school of architecture at the University of Michigan, and U.S. Senator Royal Copeland, a Dexter native, persuaded Katharine to purchase her grandmother's house. Katharine hoped that once it was repaired, it would be used by the Dexter women's clubs. She paid Lorch to repair the damage and prepare the house for occupancy.[6]

In the early 1950s, however, with no prior notice, university contractors tore down the house's north wing, with the rumored tunnels used to hide runaway slaves during the Civil War, and gutted the interior. Katharine had forgotten to inform Lorch that, to help pay her estate taxes, she had donated the house to the university to make into faculty apartments. Lorch was disconsolate about the destruction of the classic interiors. He blamed Katharine's lawyers and the university for the house's demise. In fact, the lawyers had not informed Katharine of the university's proposed plans. Katharine was quite upset when she was told what had occurred, and she began legal action to reverse the decisions. The litigation went on for some years, however, and in 1955, Katharine gave up the fight. Today, the University of Michigan still rents a reconstructed Gordon Hall as apartments.

As for the château, it had become, in Katharine's words, "a white elephant," too large to be taken over as a residence and too expensive to be purchased by a school. Upkeep of the château had been costing Katharine thousands of dollars every year. The materialization of a possible buyer for the property found Katharine having to make a hasty trip to Nyons during June, only to witness the collapse of the deal. At the same time, an international summit meeting was about to open in Geneva, and Katharine offered the château as housing to the American delegation. Initially, they were delighted to accept the offer, but shortly afterward they turned down her generosity because the château was deemed insufficiently secure. Her efforts all for naught, Katharine returned to Boston with the château's future continuing to deplete both her mental energy and her finances.

Upon her return, she discovered that Dr. Stone's testing program had all but ceased, caused by his inability to recruit enough women. Moreover, those who had been recruited had not followed the necessary instructions. His earlier boasts aside, Stone now apologized to Katharine and offered to refund most of the $5,000 she had given him for the project. She refused his offer and thanked him kindly for his efforts.

She also found that construction of Rock's addition was moving at a very slow pace. Katharine's increasing frustration regarding the entire project again found its way into a letter to Sanger. "I do dislike to put money into bricks and mortar, rather than into brains and experiments; but in this exceptional case it appears necessary."[7] Regarding the slowness of testing and the inability to get women to follow the necessary procedures, Katharine asked Sanger, with exasperation, "How can we get a 'cage' of ovulating females to experiment with, this being our clinical bottle-neck."

To answer Katharine's plaint, Pincus came up with a plan to test patients at the nearby Massachusetts State Insane Hospital. Katharine agreed and entreated Pincus to "move ahead quickly."

Shortly thereafter, Pincus and Chang and their wives departed for Tokyo and the International Planned Parenthood Federation conference, carrying with them a speech intimating that a birth control pill was "on the horizon." Pincus and Sanger wanted Dr. Rock to accompany them, but Katharine vetoed their request, believing that, by letting Rock attend the conference, further time would be lost. "Rock cannot leave his work at this time," she declared, and the issue was quickly resolved.

At the Tokyo conference, scientists heard for the first time about a possible new and practical form of contraception. Pincus spoke of Worcester's work on animals and alluded to having begun preliminary work on women. Instead of the anticipated interest at the scientific breakthrough, Pincus's speech was received with apathy and detachment. Nor did the papers reprinted and distributed at the conference produce even a whisper. Pincus returned from Tokyo dejected that the speech had produced so little reaction; it was assuredly a blow to his ego as well. Rock, on the other hand, was relieved that the response had been so inconsequential, since he remained cautious about the testing results and any public reactions that might possibly alert the opposition, primarily the Catholic Church. In contrast, Sanger thought the conference "a huge success" and Pincus's paper a highlight. She expressed pleasure that news of the project had finally been made public.

With the Stone tests having been terminated, the tests in Japan not yet under way, and results from Puerto Rico "distant," only Dr. Rock's work remained as the primary source of data. Another brief display of self-doubt showed up in a letter to Sanger. "I have been so incensed over the delays that I am ready to abandon the whole matter."[8] Yet Katharine concluded the letter by expressing her eagerness for the next meeting with Pincus and Rock.

The meeting stirred Katharine from feelings of futility to elation. Rock reported on the isolation and trial of two pills, labeled 759 (from Syntex) and 4642 (from Searle), from which, after testing, he and Pincus would select the best-performing pill. Both were deemed acceptable, but 4642 seemed to cause fewer side effects. Pincus planned to visit Puerto Rico, monitor activities there, and introduce the use of the two new pill formulations. "I am very excited over this new prospect," Katharine confided in Sanger.

Pincus's report to Katharine in January 1956 was equally encouraging. Testing with both 759 and 4642 at the Massachusetts State Insane Hospital suggested that 4642 was better, although Rock wished to continue using both pills. He wanted to try both of them on all subjects until he was absolutely confident of their efficacy. Neither pill appeared to affect menstruation, and that was considered "a triumph" by Pincus.

Unfortunately, Pincus had to report another failure in Puerto Rico in the testing of medical students. Nevertheless, he planned to begin testing once again, this time through the Government Health Center. To their advantage, Pincus explained, the head of the U.S. Public Health Field Training Center and medical director of the Puerto Rico Family Planning Association, Dr. Edris Rice-Wray, was a strong advocate of birth control. Pincus said he would go to Puerto Rico to set up testing procedures. Before the initiation of testing in Puerto Rico, Pincus and Rock debated which pill to use—759 or 4642. In effect, deciding which pill to test could either make or break the project. Instead, Rock persuaded Pincus to continue to test both pills.

Financial commitments also had to be made to fund the next six months' work now that operational steps had been agreed upon. In total, more than $80,000 was budgeted, the bulk of it going to Dr. Rock and Puerto Rico. Katharine was adamant about those expenditures for testing. Another $20,000 was set aside for construction needs and conference travel. Yet, as their eighty-year-old "boss" was leaving the meeting, both Pincus and Rock noticed her pinched gait, the result of Katharine's arthritis. Together with her periodic bouts of gastritis, the doctors observed, Katharine had to have been battling chronic ailments constantly. Yet when asked about her health, she refused to acknowledge her debilities, blaming "the weather." Nor do records suggest any consultations with physicians.

Trial runs for testing in Puerto Rico began in February 1956. Full testing was initiated in April. This was the third attempt to obtain meaningful information to support and supplement Dr. Rock's work in Boston.

Participants were to be selected among residents of a public housing development in Rio Piedras, a suburb of San Juan.[9] The area was poor, with government housing likely the first real home for most of these people. A social worker, familiar with the tenants, was selected to recruit volunteers. Women coming to family planning clinics were asked if they would be interested in trying a new birth control pill. Most agreed, many women already having had several children and facing the prospect of sterilization.

Recruitment began slowly, but as the months passed and the women taking the pill did not get pregnant, word of mouth spread the news. Soon, the number of women coming to the clinic and asking to participate increased dramatically. Two factors were of concern to Pincus and Rock as the testing progressed: first, to extend the time each patient took the pills, so as to determine its long-lasting effects; second, to determine which of the pill formulations, 759 or 4642, would do the best job. The availability of 759 was uncertain, however, because of internal problems at Syntex. Rock's decision was to proceed with 4642 only until 759 was available to include in the testing. Rock was adamant that both be included in the field tests.

Questions such as whether extended use would alter the usual 50–50 ratio of boys and girls and what effect the contraceptive would have on the body after a woman stopped taking the pills were also critical. It was hoped that the Puerto Rico experiment would provide answers to these questions and demonstrate the efficacy of the pill to the scientific community and the FDA.

Field trials in Tenaco, Mexico, were also being explored, but Pincus waited for the selection of a doctor and the disposition of local authorities to embrace the project. Patients at the State Hospital had taken the compounds for six months without ovulation. Japan acknowledged receiving the shipment of progesterone but then announced they would work out their own program, at their own speed. Pincus, Rock, and Katharine were now convinced that the combined results of Rock's testing and the Puerto Rico experiment would be the only ones they could really depend on for accurate data.

Pincus's first report on May 18, 1956, was encouraging to Katharine. In Puerto Rico, 125 patients were now taking the pill. While there had been some dropouts, women interested in joining the project more than made up for the loss. Dr. Rock was adding fifty more women to his sample and requested additional clerical help to process the data. After a speech by Pincus in Chicago, local doctors expressed an interest in assisting the project, and the local Planned Parenthood branch—much more proactive than the parent group in New York—volunteered women for the project. Katharine was amused at the irony of the situation when she found that the offices of the Chicago branch of Planned Parenthood were in a building once owned by her father.

Now that Syntex was sold and the new owners expressed sympathy toward birth control, 759 would become available again. No word from Japan. Pincus and Rock now believed they had enough material to publish, to put the project before medical and scientific groups, likely in a fall issue of *Science* magazine.[10] In addition, an American Medical Association press release, in support of their article, would be published at the same time, thus providing further credibility. "Then the 'party' will be on," Katharine declared. "The fat will be in the fire, and everybody will begin to scream and contest your findings." Pincus and Rock, however, were no longer concerned about the possible negative consequences of publishing.

When the Catholic Church raised objections to the testing in Puerto Rico, Katharine was quickly informed. Condemnation of the project was coming from the combined forces of Catholic social workers, the pulpit, and the Catholic press. Their campaign was followed by a TV program that claimed the pill was physically dangerous.

Rather than respond to such propaganda, Katharine believed, the positive results of the testing would protect the project, and she was correct in her assessment. Once it was discovered that those women who dropped out of the test quickly became pregnant, there were no more problems recruiting volunteers. Katharine expressed amusement that the Church had outsmarted itself in its endeavor to prevent the project from continuing.

Unfortunately, Katharine's watch over the project was again interrupted by a forced return to Switzerland to deal with "château matters," tax problems that Bemis alone could not handle. "Keep me informed on all developments," she reminded Pincus as she departed.

Pincus's August report to Katharine told of "good news." He found that, with her out of the country, a recitation of problems would only serve to upset her. With an increased sample, Rock's latest data continued to show "stable results." Puerto Rico was looking better all the time; "no pregnancies from any women while they were taking the pill." The *Science* magazine article would be published in two months.

During this time, correspondence between Katharine and Sanger had dwindled considerably since both were traveling. What letters they did exchange continued the discussion of established topics: personal health (with Katharine admitting to some "minor" difficulties), Sanger's hectic activities, and Katharine's update on the project. Katharine announced she would return to the States September 21 and would "visit with Dr. Rock directly." Sanger did not, however, reveal to Katharine that she was now suffering from sporadic heart problems.

Together, Pincus and Rock presented Katharine with the latest information, realizing that, after being out of touch for some months, she would be very anxious to confer with both of them.[11] The reports from Puerto Rico continued to be good; so good, in fact, that both men admitted to surprise at the progress there. Over 200 women were now participating in the project. Only seventy-three had dropped out over a six-month period, and the figure had dramatically declined since the Church's failed media onslaught. Searle had guaranteed a continuous supply of Enovid, the name given to 4642. Although Rock continued to test with both 759 and 4642, the latter showed the greater success. Still, Katharine complained about the slowness of progress. In response, Rock pleaded the need for caution, not only to prove which of the two pills would perform better, but also to provide larger samples that would validate the current results. Katharine had to agree with Rock's view.

Katharine's letter to Sanger in Hawaii, where she had been confined to bed again after a strenuous foreign trip, described the Puerto Rico findings and reflected Rock's caution by indicating, somewhat apologetically, that "the tests may last for another year at least."[12] Yet the upcoming articles by Pincus and Rock in *Science* magazine were more thrilling to her. "I have been very moved and excited over the articles. They are the opening gun in the coming campaign." Sanger quickly responded with equal enthusiasm, believing that "the conspiracy of silence has been broken." Katharine had even suggested to Pincus that a public relations man be hired, but he believed it would not be necessary. "The word will quickly get out and speedily cross oceans," he predicted.

Returning everyone to the reality of business operations, Hoagland outlined budget needs for the coming six months. More than $110,000 had been spent during the second half of 1956. The following six month's expenses could exceed $120,000, due to expanded testing in Puerto Rico, and in another nearby site, the village of Humacao, and possible new testing in Haiti. In response to Hoagland's estimates, Katharine simply ordered Bemis to sell 3,000 more shares of International Harvester stock to cover the costs. Each time this was required, Katharine unhesitatingly agreed to supply the funds that were needed to carry the project further. Hoagland and Pincus could only stare with awe at the generosity of their patroness.

Katharine's usual update to Sanger revealed a gradually increasing optimism and excitement.[13] Results of the tests continued to be positive. Their ultimate goal was now clearly in sight. "I think we have gained the oral contraceptive we have been seeking and now it must be implemented as fully as possible. Nothing else matters to me now that we have got the oral contraceptive."

Results from Puerto Rico showed continued success, particularly with 4642. In addition, Dr. Clarence Gamble (heir to Proctor and Gamble), a strong activist for birth control internationally, revealed that his group was planning to initiate birth control testing in Puerto Rico. In support of his plans, Gamble cited the success of the Pincus/Rock tests; "no method failures" in seven months, he pointed out. In contrast, the Planned Parenthood Federation remained in denial and Vogt, its president, refused to acknowledge the success of the oral contraceptive formula.

Most exciting for Katharine, however, was Pincus's news that, prompted by his and Rock's persistent badgering, Searle had submitted a request to the FDA to approve Enovid as a treatment to regulate the menstrual cycle, using Dr. Rock's data as the basis to prove viability of the product.[14] With a minimum of debate, the FDA approved Enovid. By doing so, it unintentionally paved the way for the product to be ultimately licensed as a birth control pill.

Ecstatic, Katharine informed Sanger, "Of course, this use of the oral contraceptive for menstrual disorders is leading inevitably to its use against pregnancy; and to me, this stepping stone of gradual approach to the pregnancy problem via the menstrual one is a very happy and fortunate course of procedure."[15] Her reliance on Rock's methods and data collection was finally paying off, she said, and to Pincus's genius she gave "thanks eternally." That evening, for the first time in years, Katharine spent a leisurely evening out, attending a concert of the Boston Symphony.

To no one's surprise, plans for Sanger's upcoming conference of the International Planned Parenthood Federation ran into a major roadblock created by the national organization. Not only did the board want to delay the conference for two years, it also refused to allow either Pincus or Rock to speak. Frustrated, Sanger turned to Katharine to persuade the recalcitrant organization to change its decision. Katharine's efforts, however, yielded only increased animosity from Vogt and the PPF board.

The next meeting between Sanger and the program committee of the PPF did not go well either, despite the number of scientific people who spoke on behalf of a Washington, D.C., meeting the following year. In response, Sanger accused Vogt of "backhand behavior."

When told of the results of the meeting, Katharine responded, "I cannot understand what the members of that board are thinking about, unless they have passed out entirely. And that is the kindest thing one can imagine about them."[16] Still, Katharine promised to see what she could do about the seemingly untenable situation.

Dr. Rock's May report to Katharine was filled with uncharacteristic optimism, a rare expression from this usually conservative man.[17] "Work is progressing satisfactorily and safely," he said. "Continued experimentation here seems to show that any one of the several steroids used is effective in suppressing ovulation. Regarding the Mexico and Puerto Rico situation," Rock commented, "I have let the Mexican Indian Project lapse for the time being; for the Puerto Rico Project, as Dr. Pincus has doubtless informed you, is giving us as much information as we are able to absorb." Rock also alluded to the fact that he had been dispensing pills to unmarried women, for which he sought to "be forgiven for his sins."

Katharine's letter to Sanger the following month told of Dr. Rock's progress, as well as a recent conversation she had had with Pincus concerning the PPF. The organization had explained that its refusal to hold a meeting in Washington, D.C., was because all news emanating from the U.S. capital was viewed by the world as being the opinion of the U.S. government and was therefore open to misinterpretation. In other words, Pincus believed, the PPF wanted no discussion of birth control or contraception.

According to Pincus, based on the recent licensing of Enovid as a treatment for menstrual disorders, "4642 will shortly be put on the market and be available to MD's and to patients on MD prescriptions." At fifty cents each, the pill was expensive, but Searle believed the price would decline as use of the product widened.

An article on "the pill" appeared in the July 1957 issue of *Ladies Home Journal*. Pincus verified the report as "correctly written." Interestingly, the magazine reported few reader reactions to the story.

Pincus's latest report indicated that Puerto Rico was now testing 140 women, with not a single dropout, and testing in Humacao had begun with fifty women. Among women given the actual medication, control group data showed that patients were receiving complete protection against contraception. Further, Pincus said that he had obtained an agreement from Searle to supply the project with the additional number of pills needed for an enlarged sample. He also intimated that Searle's initial sales of Enovid had been so encouraging that the company's spirit of cooperation seemed to be swelling.

Budget matters were again the concern of Pincus and Hoagland. During the first six months of 1957, $114,000 had been spent, less than originally estimated. Yet they estimated the budget for the remainder of the year to be more than $131,000, again due to increased testing. Puerto Rico's needs alone accounted for more than $14,000. And what about the next year, Katharine asked. Pincus estimated that the project would require close to $230,000 for ongoing operations in 1958. Katharine merely turned to Bemis with a nod of her head. Bemis knew what to do.

Puerto Rico now had 200 women in the testing program, Pincus reported, including thirty-five who had been taking the pill since March 1956—twenty-one months—and had shown no physiological changes due to long-term dosage. Humacao had more than eighty on the pill. Circumventing Haitian bureaucracy, Dr. Laraque wanted to move ahead with testing; he already had records on seventy-three women.

To his obvious personal pleasure, Pincus told Katharine that, along with drug manufacturing companies approaching him for information, he has been "besieged with requests for study opportunities" at Worcester.[18] "Would you be interested in setting up a training station?" she asked Pincus. "Of course," he answered, "if we had the proper facilities."

Katharine's update to Sanger in January 1958 dealt primarily with the frustrating meeting that Pincus, Rock, and Garcia had had with the Planned Parenthood Research Committee, at which time they had explained Enovid and its recent successes. Questions to the three had been primarily related to side effects and long-term effects on patients. The doctors had successfully answered all such questions, using actual testing results. Still, nothing new had come out of the meeting. "P.P.F. is doing nothing about this, nor are any of the Foundations dedicated to human welfare," Katharine complained. "Shall we have to wait another fifty years for the implementation of this vast and essential reform?"[19]

Several years later, as a sidelight to discussing the latest news of the day, Katharine assured her friend she would continue to pay for Sanger's medical expenses, as she had done for years.[20]

Based on the increasing number of people requesting study opportunities at Worcester, Katharine suggested that Pincus develop an intern program whereby the theory, methods, and implementation of oral contraception could be taught. Without question, she would finance such a program. With this impetus, Pincus agreed to deliver a plan and list the people he believed would qualify for it. Katharine's request undoubtedly fed Pincus's ego, because he produced a proposal, including costs, within a week's time.

According to a copy of a Searle report that Katharine received from Pincus, costs for pills had already declined from fifty to thirty cents each, which suggested to her that the product was finding increasing acceptance among the medical profession. She also heard rumors that many doctors were already prescribing the pill to prevent pregnancies. If true, she wrote Sanger, this would hasten the overall acceptability of the product, "for the primary purpose we intended."

To Pincus and Rock, Katharine raised the question about abortion, in response to a recent *New York Times* article dealing with the large number of abortions in the United States and the Church's response to the problem. She feared that the Church might attempt to portray the pill as the "demon" responsible for increased abortions, although the argument seemed ridiculous to her. Still, they had to be prepared for such potentially frightening stories.

Vogt, and the PPF he represented, appeared deliberately to contribute to the volatile issue. Vogt took pains to voice his disapproval of the pill.[21] Moreover, in his annual report, he made the statement that, based on his discussions with Pincus and Rock, "There was no perfect pill, and very likely never would be one from progestins to be used as a contraceptive."

To Vogt's declaration, Katharine responded with letters to Pincus, Rock, and Sanger, "I have felt his hostility to 'the pill' before now, but have never seen it so clearly expressed. He must have known that his report on 'the pill' was false, so why make it!"[22] She pointed out that the Church would now publicly challenge the pill. "But I no longer have the slightest worry over the Catholics or any activities they might produce; you have so permanently defeated them."

The July 1958 report Pincus submitted to Katharine spoke of continued progress in Puerto Rico and Humacao, with additional small tests to begin in Nassau, Kentucky, and England. In London, despite adverse press by the *Times*, fifty women had been recruited to use 4642, although Pincus had doubts that the tests would offer any additional information to what they already possessed. Pincus planned to visit Puerto Rico and Haiti the following month. Would Katharine like to accompany him?

Of course, she would have loved the opportunity, but the ever-increasing pains of arthritis were making it difficult for her to walk. What a trip this could be, she thought, at the same time damning her infirmities. As if to emphasize her increasing debility, only days later, while attending a concert, Katharine fainted and had to be taken home by ambulance. Further, her secretary reported to Pincus that Katharine had been falling asleep in the middle of conversations and not realizing it. Yet, when Pincus raised the matter with her, Katharine refused to discuss it. Although Pincus advised her to seek medical attention "because the consequences might be serious," she did nothing about it. Her response to the situation was to exercise more and drink more tea. Both Pincus and Rock expressed concern about her obviously delicate health, but they were continually frustrated by her denials. She had recently observed her eighty-third birthday.

In late 1958, both Pincus and Rock received invitations to attend a major birth control conference in New Delhi, India. With Katharine's financial assistance, they planned to speak about the latest test results and boldly announce that they were very near to having a reliable oral contraceptive. Katharine hired a statistician to examine all the research findings in Pincus's and Rock's speeches to ensure that they were accurate.

At a stop in San Francisco, on their way to India, Dr. Rock was interviewed about the project. In response to a question about the Catholic Church's position on the pill, Rock publicly revealed that he was a practicing Catholic and believed the pill presented no threat to Church policies. While some people were surprised at his admission, official Catholic reaction seemed confused. The Curia obviously did not care for his statement, but it seemed hesitant to denigrate the eminent physician in any way. The episode served as a portent for challenges to come.

Hoagland reported that the budget for the first half of 1959 had now reached $144,000, of which $52,000 had gone to Rock's clinic and $20,000 to Puerto Rico. The budget also included a new category, public relations, funds for which were intended to be used to make copies of Pincus's and Rock's speeches and articles for distribution to the press, employment of a medical artist to illustrate all printed material, and the distribution of small bottles of Enovid to certain members of the medical profession, primarily because Searle had not yet fully committed to promoting the pill.

In fact, at that very moment, Searle was debating whether to plunge into or draw back from this obviously high-risk enterprise.[23] As success for the oral contraceptive was accumulating, Searle felt anxiety about public reactions and the possible interpretation that the product was "immoral." The company could invest in a product with the potential for returning countless millions for years to come but might suffer retribution for making a product that roused the ire of the public.

After much soul-searching, not to mention public opinion surveys, Searle finally committed itself to the production and distribution of the new oral contraceptive. Dr. Rock had chosen 4642 because it had clearly demonstrated a history of success in Puerto Rico. Laboratory and field test results could not have been more emphatic. As an additional test of the concept with the general public, Searle placed articles in the *Saturday Evening Post* and *Reader's Digest* explaining the pill and its purposes. It waited impatiently for what it believed would be a deluge of negative reactions. To the company's surprise, and relief, none came. What the articles seemed to convey to readers was the revolutionary idea that sex was now free from the unintended consequence of pregnancy and, perhaps even more important, free from the need for advance preparation and awkward precaution.

Thus encouraged, Searle began mass production and distribution of Enovid. Thanks to the tenacious testing and scientific evaluation of Rock, Pincus, and their colleagues, no medicine in history had ever been subjected to such extensive, laborious, and careful trials.

When Pincus and Rock returned from New Delhi, Katharine heard of their triumphs. They told of scientists flocking to meet them, collecting copies of their materials, and peppering them with questions about methodology. Their story had created an explosion of interest and had been rapidly communicated around the world. Pincus had been correct in his earlier assessment about the power of their message; it would, indeed, generate its own momentum. The societal implications were profound.

The news about Searle's commitment to commercial production of Enovid came at the same time as the revelations from New Delhi, and Katharine was thrilled with the result. Her elation was augmented by a note from Pincus reporting that 250 women were now being tested in Puerto Rico, 125 in Haiti, and 300 in Humacao, more than enough to prove the efficacy of the pill. To no one's surprise, testing in Japan never really materialized, and tests in England were thwarted by the costs of obtaining the product.

Katharine's excitement could be seen in her letter to Sanger, even to the point of telling an amusing story about a new slogan that she, Pincus, and Rock had formulated for the sale of Enovid in "backward Massachusetts." (Massachusetts proved to be the last state in the country to agree to the sale and distribution of birth control products, finally passing such a law in 1966.) "Take Enovid for the only true method!!" would surely "shake up" their adversaries, all agreed.[24]

During the summer of 1959, a series of meetings between Pincus, Rock, Searle representatives, Katharine, and Bemis centered on the timing of and strategy for submitting a request to the FDA for Enovid to be licensed as an oral contraceptive. Significant test results were now available, and the data had been checked innumerable times for accuracy. Questions about side effects, longevity of administration, costs, and Church opposition could be effectively answered, they firmly believed. But who would represent the group once the application was submitted and a date set for cross-examination? Actually, there was no doubt in anyone's mind: Dr. Rock would be the spokesperson to carry the battle. And all believed it would be a battle. Rock's knowledge, expertise, reputation, and "pedigree," they all believed, constituted the most potent weapon they possessed.

On October 29, 1959, Searle made its formal application to the FDA. When the announcement of the application was made public, Katharine was at once ecstatic, chilled, nervous, anxious, and triumphant. A tumult of emotions rushed through her like a flood.

Thirty-One

Shortly after Searle had submitted its formal application to the FDA for Enovid's approval, Katharine hurriedly wrote a note to Sanger. Intoxicated by the event, she waxed effervescent. "I do wish we might meet. So much has happened to talk about. I am bursting with excitement over it all. It just doesn't seem possible!"[1] Katharine's initial rapture, however, proved somewhat premature. The indefinite waiting period for the FDA's final answer instead diverted her emotions to anxiety and frustration. After months of waiting, those feelings were equally shared by Pincus and Rock.

In 1960, the year the pill was approved, the FDA's sole role in approving medications was to require they be safe and be manufactured with the utmost in quality control. For Enovid, the data submitted to license the pill consisted of results from 897 women, who together represented 801.6 woman-years and 10,427 menstrual cycles. FDA representatives had never seen so much confirming information for any medication. Even more important, the FDA was faced with a unique quandary. In all its years of approving medications, it had never before been asked to evaluate a drug that would be prescribed to treat healthy women, for longtime use. Coupled with stiff opposition from the Church and pharmaceutical companies, these key factors presented regulators with a dilemma. What to do about a drug whose approval might unleash "revolutionary" and controversial reverberations?

To delay a decision, the FDA had the authority to table the usual ninety-day application process for an additional six months. After the decision had been delayed twice, Rock was irate and believed some action had to be taken to speed up the decision-making process. Through Searle, a hearing was scheduled for late December 1959. Dr. Rock prepared to confront an irresolute FDA.

On a frigid day in December, the hearing took place in a wooden building erected during World War I as a temporary barracks. Located in the building were the offices of Dr. Pasquale DeFelice, the FDA's officer responsible for evaluating the pill. Standing in a cold hallway for more than an hour and a half, Rock and Dr. Irwin C. Winter, Searle's medical research director, waited impatiently for DeFelice to arrive.

Dr. DeFelice was a practicing obstetrician-gynecologist, having graduated from Fordham University, a Jesuit institution, and Georgetown Medical Center, a similarly Catholic-oriented school, although he was not yet board certified. He had been hired by the FDA in 1956 to deal with requests in his area of expertise. At thirty-five years old, DeFelice was young for the job and inexperienced in dealing with such a momentous decision. He was also a Catholic.

Rock was already irritated by the delay and, armed with his mandate to aggressively sell the efficacy of the pill, was more than ready to take on this "nondescript" young doctor. As Rock later recalled the meeting, "Can you imagine, the FDA gave him the job of deciding. I was furious."[2]

DeFelice was on the defensive from the beginning of the hearing since he had been the person responsible for twice delaying the decision. He was also in awe of Dr. Rock, "the light of the obstetrical world," as he put it. During the hearing, DeFelice brought up a series of issues, among which was the association between steroids and cancer. Rock presented data to show that no relationship existed between the two. He ended his presentation by stating, in a purposely sarcastic tone, "I don't know how much training you've had in female cancer, young man [he referred to DeFelice as "young man" throughout the entire hearing], but I've had considerable!"[3] DeFelice further attempted to argue that there had not been enough testing on the pill, but Rock's extensive data easily refuted the accusation.

When DeFelice hesitatingly raised moral and religious objections, particularly that the Catholic Church would never approve of the pill, Rock responded to the declaration with forceful, intimidating words. "Young man, don't you sell my Church short!"[4]

The hearing ended with DeFelice telling Rock that he planned to send the data to a number of consultants before making a final decision. DeFelice also requested Searle to conduct lab tests on 500 women to examine the relationship between pill use and blood-clotting mechanisms. Searle promised to do so, even though Rock had already presented evidence to suggest there was no such relationship. Searle's tests concurred, as everyone had expected. A revised application had to be submitted to the FDA because Searle wanted to license lower-dosage pills, 5 milligrams and 2.5 milligrams, as well as the 10-milligram pill.

When Rock reported on the results of the hearing, both Pincus and Katharine were unsure whether they had convinced the FDA or angered them. Rock expressed more confidence. He believed the FDA could not turn him down, since the data were so compelling.

The three then discussed the budget for 1960. Pincus had submitted a three-year budget to Katharine, one that included further testing and experimentation. Interestingly, his request now incorporated her recommendation about the pursuit of a male contraceptive. Katharine turned down the proposed budget, explaining that she wanted to wait for the FDA's decision before agreeing on new plans. She declared that they should continue to work on a budget divided into six-month periods, as they had done previously. For the first part of 1960, they agreed on a budget of more than $152,000.

On April 22, 1960, Searle received a letter from Dr. DeFelice, acknowledging that Enovid had been approved conditionally and that full approval would follow once examples of the final labeling had been received. Rock, Pincus, and Katharine were ecstatic with the news, hugging one another and sharing a bottle of champagne in triumph.

On May 11, 1960, the official notification for final approval of the oral contraceptive was received. It was almost seven years to the day since Pincus, Hoagland, Sanger, and Katharine had met to initiate the project. They discovered later that the FDA had sent a survey to sixty-one professors of obstetrics and gynecology, asking whether they believed the birth control pill should be approved. Fourteen of them were unable to reach a decision; twenty-six said yes; and twenty-one said no, two on religious grounds. Ironically, in the summary of the approval letter, deputy FDA commissioner Harvey had written, "Although we recognize the presence of moral issues, they do not come within the jurisdiction of the Food and Drug Administration."[5] Dr. Rock had won the war!

The celebration at Shrewsbury went on for an entire day, champagne and food (of course, paid for by Katharine) in abundance. New York Times headlines were plastered across the walls. The Times had called the approval of the pill "the most sweeping socio-medical revolution in history."[6]

This time, Katharine managed to contain her excitement. Relaxing in a chair, feet up on a hassock, displaying her best finery, she wore the look of victory displayed by a long-distance runner who crosses the finish line in record-breaking time.

The next morning, Katharine was awakened by a call from Pincus. He told her of threats the doctors had received and warned that, since Katharine had been mentioned in the newspapers as patroness of the project, her life might be in danger as well. That evening, under assumed names, Katharine and her secretary boarded a late train out of Boston's South Station, headed for an undisclosed location.

Final Years

Thirty-Two

Shortly after the announcement of the FDA's approval of the pill, Sanger jokingly asked Katharine what she planned to do now that the oral contraceptive battle had been won. Katharine quickly responded with a detailed letter and outlined her current, ambitious agenda.

What I am busy over is as follows:

1. Keeping on with the five branches of the Worcester Foundation oral contraceptive work, namely, a) Dr. Rock's clinical tests on his patients; b) the Puerto Rico and Haiti field tests on women; c) clinical tests at the Worcester State Hospital, with intensive laboratory testing and study of long-term effects; d) laboratory research at WFEB [the Worcester lab] to perfect Enovid.
2. Providing Shrewsbury housing for the fifteen post-doctoral fellows.
3. First plans for the women's dormitory at MIT. I am particularly happy to be able to provide a dormitory on the Tech campus for women students there. This has been my ambition for many years, but it had to await the oral contraceptive for birth control.[1]

Katharine also mentioned her increasing interest in the problems of world overpopulation and how the new birth control pill might help to combat it. "I am beginning to fear that, in the international field of birth control, it will be necessary to undertake male vasectomy as well as female oral contraceptives if we are to have any chance of getting ahead on the over-population situation."

No question, Katharine had decided to remain committed to Pincus and the Worcester lab, both in the testing program and in support of their new interns. Not only would funds continue to flow into these programs, but

Katharine also expressed a desire to remain closely attached in the scientific arena, which she succeeded in doing for the next several years.

Katharine's crusade to bring women's housing to MIT had actually begun in 1955, when Richard Gardner, a doctoral candidate, prepared a dissertation entitled "A Woman's Dormitory for MIT." Many of the features he recommended later appeared in the actual plans, such as kitchenette space, a housemother's suite, and space for sunbathing. Katharine had obtained a copy of this work and met with the MIT administration to lobby for women's housing. In return, they shared with her a copy of a 1959 planning document: "The Woman Student at MIT," which outlined the poor housing conditions with which women undergraduates had to cope, a primary reason why fewer than a hundred women were enrolled in 1959. The document went on to state the need for better women's housing, beginning with a building to accommodate 100 to 150 students, and specified the kinds of facilities necessary to meet students needs. Construction costs were estimated at $10,000 per resident; to accommodate 100 to 150 students, the project would require capital funds of $1 million to $1.5 million.

Katharine took it upon herself to make the proposal a reality. Surprised MIT officials, not having worked with Katharine before, were at first hesitant—their short-term plans had called for more men's housing—but when they came to realize Katharine's determination and the seriousness of her interest, they became willing participants in her plan.

While MIT admitted that the primary reason for the enrollment of so few women was the lack of adequate on-campus housing, the university had no currently pending plans to address the problem. Nonetheless, allocation of available building funds had already been directed toward the construction of men's dormitories. In her usual persuasive fashion, Katharine convinced MIT officials that the task of building a women's dormitory could be completed in a reasonable amount of time if sufficient motivation existed. To enhance their motivation, she promised to donate the necessary funds. Shocked officials took some days to comprehend her offer, but they soon came to the conclusion that a women's facility could comfortably fit in with their campuswide expansion program, even if not in the sequence they had originally envisioned. With William Bemis handling the negotiations for Katharine, the agreement was finalized, an architect was selected, and meetings were initiated to begin the construction process. MIT officials were at first surprised at Katharine's insistence on attending all planning sessions, but they soon understood her desire to participate. She had her own ideas as to what should be included in a women's dormitory, and "since she furnished the money to build it, she had her way."

Actual construction began in the spring of 1961 and was publicly announced in the newspapers. "The first on-campus dormitory for women in the history of Massachusetts Institute of Technology will be built with a gift of $1,500,000 from an anonymous MIT graduate, 'with a long-standing concern for the welfare of women students.'"[2] The announcement of the pledge underscored the reason for the new project: out of 3,600 undergraduates, there were only sixty-six women in the student body. (In her argument for the dormitory, Katharine had correctly pointed out that there were no more women on campus in 1960 than there were in 1904, a glaring example of the barriers faced by women who wished to become scientists.)

The dormitory was designed to accommodate from 120 to 150 women. In addition to the usual living quarters, the building would offer complete and self-contained facilities for study, recreation, and dining. The $1,500,000 pledge was the largest ever received by MIT with a specific designation for women.

As she always did when becoming involved in a high-profile project, Katharine had requested anonymity. But her visible participation in the planning process soon revealed that she was the donor. When she was identified in the press, articles spoke of her suffrage and League of Women Voters activities, as well as her lifelong efforts to find a cure for Stanley's illness. Nothing, however, was mentioned about her efforts on behalf of birth control and contraception. Apparently for self-protection, MIT did not want to be openly associated with anything relating to birth control since, in Massachusetts, laws against the dissemination and sale of contraceptives were still in force.

Throughout 1961 and 1962, Katharine remained a force on the building committee and saw to it that the dormitory would truly become a living environment for women. Above all, Katharine wanted to erase, as best she could, the derogatory image of women wishing to study "men's" subject matter. Even though MIT president Julius A. Stratton extolled the value of women's "contributions to scientific and technical progress," male students on campus continued the offensive practice of fondling the breasts on a bas-relief plaque of the school's first woman graduate, supposedly for good luck.

Some days were not as good as others for Katharine. Worsening arthritis had made it very difficult for her to walk or climb stairs. The early effects of dementia often caused Katharine to forget what she wanted to say. Through sheer force of will, however, she expressed her opinions and recommendations. When she did not feel well, meetings were held in her parlor at 393 Commonwealth. Katharine always dressed for the occasion, including hat and gloves—proper attire for business meetings, she believed. In spite of her increasing infirmities, Katharine continued to be a tough negotiator.

On October 7, 1963, Stanley McCormick Hall was dedicated. In her short but appreciative speech to the assembled, Katharine said, "Since my graduation in 1904, I have wished to express my gratitude to the institute for its advanced policy of scientific education for women. This policy gave me the opportunity to obtain the scientific training which has been of inestimable value to me throughout my life."[3] Before she was helped back to her seat, she surprised everyone by announcing that a second wing of Stanley McCormick Hall would be constructed in the near future.

Once the dormitory had been opened, Katharine also donated furniture and household items. Included was an elegant 1910 portrait of her, which was prominently hung in the "parlor."

Soon after the dormitory opened, Katharine initiated a weekly afternoon tea to offer students the opportunity to socialize. Invitations announcing the tea went out to all students, with the stipulation "hats required, gloves optional." In response, students arrived wearing all sorts of fancy hats and an assortment of gloves—baseball gloves, oven mitts, rubber gloves. The housemother was concerned that Katharine might react negatively to the students' interpretation of the tea's dress code. To her relief, Katharine was amused at their ingenuity and creativity.

Another episode had an air of mystery about it. A number of students came to the housemother asking about "that old woman, dressed in twenties clothes," who was often seen wandering through the halls of the dormitory late at night. "That's Mrs. McCormick," the housemother explained. "She built this dorm and is, kind of like, watching over it."

Construction on the new wing, built to house another 125 women, began in 1964 and was completed in late 1966. Katharine had little to do with this project due to her declining health and desire to remain at her Santa Barbara home. Dedication of the new women's dormitory wing was scheduled for March 1968. Katharine was again invited to speak at the dedication, but she never made it.

Meanwhile, Pincus returned from a symposium held in Copenhagen in late 1960 and boasted to Katharine that "Enovid was ahead of everyone else." He also reported that Searle was setting up testing projects in Ceylon; Bombay; New Delhi; and, once again, in Japan. Katharine became concerned, however, when Pincus told her that Dr. Rock had expressed a desire to return to his own practice; therefore, his budget allocation at Worcester would be eliminated.[4] Katharine immediately spoke to Rock. In spite of her efforts to convince Rock to continue with Worcester projects, the doctor declined, saying, in effect, that he had completed the job he had set out to do. Dr. Rock rarely saw Katharine after this parting, but they maintained a warm and respectful relationship. In 1963, Rock wrote a book, *The Time Has Come,* detailing his role in developing the pill and arguing that the conscience of the Church had more to gain by accepting it than fighting against it.[5]

Pincus also told Katharine that he had been chosen to receive the Laskar Award from Planned Parenthood in November, to honor his work on birth control. The award was given periodically to recognize outstanding achievement in family planning. The first Laskar award had been presented to Margaret Sanger in 1950.

Would Katharine attend the dinner as his honored guest? "Please attend," he begged her, "since your courageous faith has been the most responsible factor in the development of the work which is being recognized by this award."[6] Although she felt embarrassed by the attention given her, Katharine did attend the dinner and was duly acknowledged for her role in making the oral contraceptive a reality.

Because of her increased participation in the MIT dorm project, Katharine found less and less time to stay involved in Worcester activities. Still, when budget or progress meetings were held, Katharine managed to attend. The budget for the first half of 1961 came to more than $158,000, since testing in Puerto Rico, Haiti, and Humacao continued. Puerto Rico alone had 400 women in the project; and results had been spectacular, even with a reduced-dosage pill.

In May 1961, Margaret Sanger was honored at a New York dinner and symposium, led by Julian Huxley, at which her contributions to birth control and family planning were hailed. Sanger was quite ill at the time, her heart problems making it difficult to travel. Often, she was so weak that writing letters had become a chore. After the presentation, she offered a brief thanks and retired. Grant Sanger, her son, gave his mother's acceptance speech. Katharine was seated in the audience and warmly applauded her dear old friend.

In addition to honoring Sanger, the World Population Emergency Campaign, which sponsored the event, called for donations so it might be able to expand its overseas work. The audience gasped in surprise and wonder when Huxley announced that an anonymous donor had already provided $100,000 (it was actually $75,000) to the organization. Some days later, it was revealed that Katharine had been the donor.[7]

These days, Katharine could barely participate, but she could continue to donate. Additional funds went to Dr. Clarence Gamble and his work. Katharine also gave funds to produce two books on birth control, *The Complete Book of Birth Control* and *The Truth About the New Birth-Control Pills*, to be distributed to senior medical students in the United States and Canada. Within a year, more than 7,500 books had been distributed, and they had become required reading for these doctors-to-be.

Another attempt by Katharine to spread "the birth-control gospel" met with failure. She offered to fund a program at Massachusetts General Hospital to test Enovid. Nonetheless, administrators at the hospital refused the grant, saying they had "no pressing need" for the research program. In reality, they were afraid of expressing even tacit acceptance of the pill, fearing the disapproval of the Catholic Church and Massachusetts law.

The summer of 1962 found Katharine in Switzerland again. She hoped, at last, to shrug the château from her tired shoulders. The lack of buyers for her "white elephant" had been exacerbated by the new postwar economics racing across Europe; "old-regime" relics were of no interest at a time when sleek high-rises, fast cars, and shopping malls were being constructed in every city. The odds of ever profitably selling the château had turned against her.

For some time, Katharine had been weighing a proposal from Adlai Stevenson and Averill Harriman to donate the château to the U.S. government to house employees working at the Geneva headquarters of the United Nations.

The château had been owned by the Dexters—first Josephine, then Katharine—for sixty-seven years. Katharine had indelible memories of her youthful days of enjoyment in the gardens, her marriage with Stanley, and her later visits on behalf of Sanger's clinics. Seeing no other way to rid herself of the château, she agreed to the government's offer.

Yet because she could not bear to break away totally from the château, the government agreed to allow Katharine to build a small bungalow on the grounds, adjacent to Lake Geneva, where she stayed during the summers of 1963 and 1964. The bungalow remains today and the château itself continues to house U.S. employees.

When Katharine returned to Boston, her first task was to meet with Pincus to discuss the budget for the remainder of 1963 and examine the estimates for 1964. For the first time, Worcester's budget sheet showed sizable donations from other sources, including the Population Council, G. D. Searle, the American Cancer Society, and CIBA Pharmaceuticals, together topping Katharine's contribution, which currently amounted to $125,000. Katharine promised to give Pincus a similar amount for 1964. After that? Who could plan that far ahead, she said.[8]

Actually, Katharine's involvement with Pincus and Worcester had declined dramatically in 1964. Letters between her and Pincus were sporadic. They now included more about Pincus's speeches and articles than about actual research work being conducted at Worcester. Katharine's responses, likewise, were increasingly general, demonstrating her declining interest in Worcester activities.

Since returning to Santa Barbara, Katharine had taken on a new challenge—to open a Planned Parenthood branch in that city. Infirm, suffering now from bouts of vertigo, Katharine immersed herself in the project with the same zeal she had shown for all the others.

A visiting Planned Parenthood representative had met with a group of women who had dedicated themselves to promoting family planning, among them Katharine. In January 1964, Mrs. Miriam Garwood, a regional director of Planned Parenthood, stimulated Mrs. Katharine Gray and others to assemble a board of directors and establish a PPFA branch.

It was incorporated in April, with Mrs. Gray elected president. Katharine donated $1,000 to underwrite the group's initial activities.[9]

Up to that time, family planning advice and practice had been available at the County Hospital and the Visiting Nurse Association, but at a minimal level. When the new PPFA branch became an authorized affiliate, it became the primary outlet for the distribution of birth control devices. By 1965, the PPF of Santa Barbara had already served more than 3,000 women. Ninety percent of the contraceptive patients were taking the pill. Those participating in a research project sponsored by Searle received pills free for answering a few questions along with their monthly checkups.

In September 1965, the *Santa Barbara News-Press* announced a gift of $15,000 from Katharine, which paid for a lease and equipment for the PPF offices. In addition, Katharine and Mrs. Max Schott furnished the office space. When new quarters were needed to accommodate the rapid increase in patients, Katharine donated another $15,000 to guarantee rent. By the end of 1965, the PPF clinic was serving 385 patients a month, of which the vast majority were on the pill. Donations from Katharine also covered the hiring of a half-time nurse and yearly office rent. In the summer of 1967, she provided a gift of $60,000 toward clinic operations.

For months now, Katharine had been rarely seen outside, conducting her business through her secretary, Sara De Lancy. Also living-in was a full-time nurse, providing care for the ninety-year-old woman. In 1965, Katharine made only one trip to Boston, to receive an honor from the Massachusetts branch of Planned Parenthood. A more concise and laudatory representation of her crusades and her contributions could never have been made.

Katharine Dexter McCormick

Scientist, humanitarian, and lifelong champion of the cause of family planning: her devoted friendship for Margaret Sanger and her persistence in the cause despite attack and misrepresentation, give a pattern to inspire women today and tomorrow. Her training in biology, combined with an ability and willingness to support research, provided the greatest single impetus in the development of simple, practical methods of fertility control. She came forward at a time when large foundations were reluctant to touch this subject, and the attitude of government agencies was hands-off for political reasons. Her unflagging concern with this work made possible the results which today mark the difference between misery and happiness for millions of women in this world.

Katharine Dexter McCormick, because of her modesty, would disclaim any such tribute; but history will record her vital role in the most challenging area of human betterment, and we who have shared in her friendship and generosity must express in this inadequate way our heartfelt admiration and gratitude.

Planned Parenthood League of Massachusetts[10]

Assisted to the podium, responding almost in a whisper, Katharine thanked the group for "this profound honor." Ironically, less than a decade before, she had been battling with a reluctant PPFA board to accept the oral contraceptive as a new direction in family planning. Yet even in 1965, what Katharine had accomplished was, for most people, already ancient history.

Katharine's longtime compatriot, Margaret Sanger, died September 14, 1966, at age eighty-seven. During her last years, she had suffered with a bad heart and increasing dementia and had to be placed in a sanitarium. She, too, had quietly vanished from the world's stage. Katharine was not physically able to attend the funeral. Nonetheless, accompanying an immense wreath of flowers came a brief note of eulogy, so as to "always remember the great gift of humanity made by Margaret Sanger."[11]

In late 1967, Katharine was invited to attend the dedication of the new wing of Stanley McCormick Hall at MIT. Although she was now almost constantly bedridden, she, her secretary, and her nurse made the long trip by train to Boston.

A month before she died, James R. Killian Jr., chairman of the MIT Corporation, paid a call on Katharine. When he arrived, he was told that she would be slightly delayed in seeing him. Her staff had assumed that Killian would see her in her quarters, but Katharine decreed otherwise. She explained to Killian that she considered it inappropriate to receive an officer of MIT anywhere but in her reception room. She was brought down, properly dressed for the occasion, which naturally included hat and gloves. With an exquisite sense of decorum, holding fast against her infirmities, she met with Killian. The gesture, at once courageous and elegant, was characteristic.

Thirty-Three

In the early hours of December 28, 1967, Katharine died in her sleep, having suffered a stroke. She was ninety-two years old.

Funeral services were held in Boston, attended by friends and colleagues, including Drs. Pincus, Rock, Chang, Hoagland, and Garcia and representatives from MIT. Katharine's body was transported to Chicago for private services and burial. At the graveside services in Chicago were a number of McCormick cousins, representatives from the Chicago Art Museum, Contemporary Club, and Chicago Symphony, as well as William Bemis and his wife. Katharine's body was buried in the Dexter family plot, next to that of her brother, Samuel.

Katharine's obituaries were found in Boston newspapers, the *New York Times, Chicago Tribune, Los Angeles Times,* and *Santa Barbara News-Press.* If pictures were included with the stories, they were taken from the 1910 painting. Obituaries spoke of her graduation from MIT; her ill-fated marriage to Stanley, although very little was mentioned about her long-term efforts to seek a cure for her husband; and the diversion of her life toward humanitarian causes, such as suffrage and birth control. Mention was also made of her funding women's dormitories at MIT and art-related donations to the Chicago Art Institute and Santa Barbara Museum of Art. She was identified as the daughter of Wirt Dexter, the prominent Chicago attorney, and the wife of Stanley, the youngest son of millionaire Cyrus H. McCormick, inventor of the reaper. Except for mention in the Santa Barbara newspaper, no friends or colleagues were quoted talking about her career or contributions. Nor did the obituaries specify Katharine's lifelong efforts on behalf of women's rights.

Two months later, an article in the *Chicago Tribune* announced a Cook County probate court decision to name the Continental Illinois Bank and Trust Company as administrator of Katharine's estate, estimated at $35 million, $30 million in personal property and $5 million in Chicago commercial real estate.[1] Katharine's will, when made public, resembled a catalog of her crusades.

- $5 million to the Planned Parenthood Federation.
- $5 million to Stanford University to assist women seeking a medical degree.
- $1 million to the Worcester Laboratories, Shrewsbury.
- $500,000 to the Boston Symphony Orchestra.
- $500,000 to the Chicago Symphony Orchestra.
- $500,000 to the Chicago Art Institute.
- $100,000 to the College Club of Boston, including pictures that were to be hung in the new dormitories.
- Lesser amounts to the Chilton Club, Boston; Chicago Commons; Hull House; Chicago Historical Society; Contemporary Club, Chicago, including her mother's portrait; and the Law School of Northwestern University, including a bust of Wirt Dexter.
- Katharine's home at 393 Commonwealth, household belongings, and college papers to the Massachusetts Institute of Technology.
- Katharine's home in Santa Barbara and the Impressionist paintings she and Stanley had purchased on their honeymoon to the Santa Barbara Museum of Art.
- $100,000 to Franklin Dexter, a distant cousin, along with family portraits, silverware, and jewelry, which included her mother's engagement ring and Katharine's own engagement ring.
- Other donations in Santa Barbara, in increments of $25,000, to the Unitarian Church; Cottage Hospital; and Bruce Campbell Hopper, who lived in a cottage on the McCormick property.
- Sara De Lancy, Katharine's personal secretary, received $200,000 and many of her personal effects.
- Marie Louise Martinengo, Katharine's nurse, received $300 a month for as long as she lived.[2]

All donations were made in honor of Stanley, with one exception—the Katharine Dexter McCormick Library, to be housed at the Planned Parenthood Federation offices in New York.

Katharine received only two posthumous honors, both from MIT, in 1968 and 1975.

The first recognition came at the dedication of the second wing of Stanley McCormick Hall, on March 1, 1968. William Bemis headed the list of dignitaries honoring Katharine for her contributions. In his keynote speech, Bemis alluded to a number of Katharine's traits that had not before been revealed. "After Stanley's death," he related, "the responsibility for charitable giving fell exclusively on Katharine; and she made her own rules. One of her rules," he said, "was that she should support unpopular causes. Another rule was that the income from her property would be devoted to projects in which she could participate. Finally," he stated, "all projects, regardless of time or expense, had to measure up to her conception of what would be a fitting memorial to Stanley."[3]

Bemis concluded his remarks by pointing out that Katharine's "sense of dignity and self-respect was a quality, which she inherited from her tough-minded ancestors. In the Dexter tradition, love and respect for others was just as important as personal dignity."

John Killian, Katharine's last visitor, remembered Katharine as "a great lady, self-disciplined, steadfast in principle, decisive in judgement, firm in adhering to her own ideas and taste, and withal instinctively gracious and generous." Killian had obviously experienced all of these traits sitting across the table from Katharine when negotiations for the new dormitories were in progress and, like others before him, had been very likely irritated by her demands and decisions. After her death, these irritations were turned into admirable attributes.

When it was his turn to speak, Howard W. Johnson, president of MIT, proclaimed eloquently, "Katharine Dexter McCormick will always occupy a special place of honor and affection at MIT. I can confidently predict that generations of MIT students will come to know and love her for what she stood for and what she has done here."

Yet, in 1975, when MIT's women faculty were planning her centennial celebration, some school officials questioned why a person so little known should be awarded such an honor. This time, however, backed by the swell of a national feminist movement that occupied front pages across the country, Katharine received the recognition that had previously eluded her, confirming her contributions to women's rights. It was the first real, public recognition of the crusades to which she had committed her entire life.[4] Margery Resnick, a professor at MIT, former faculty resident at McCormick Hall, later summed up Katharine's life as that of "a woman whose intelligence, humor, grace, and independence of spirit allowed her to leave a mark on the world, while never ignoring the painful vicissitudes and responsibilities of her private life." Resnick concluded her speech by stating, "Her legacy is one of confidence and will to bring about further progress for women," to which hundreds of women in the audience stood in unison in celebration of Katharine's lifetime contributions.[5]

Since that time, little has been mentioned about Katharine except for excerpts from books regarding her involvement in the development of the birth control pill. The authors presented a distorted view of Katharine as an eccentric, rich widow dispensing her dead husband's money; they also denigrated her role in making the pill an accomplished fact. One wonders how much research these authors actually did, since they were unable even to spell her given name correctly.

An interesting and mysterious sidelight after Katharine's death: one year after her will had been probated and all beneficiaries paid, William Bemis abruptly resigned his position as a partner in his Cleveland, Ohio, law firm. It was later found that he had taken with him all of the materials pertaining to Katharine's activities during the previous thirty years. These materials have never been found. A lawyer at the firm, who had worked with Bemis, suggested that Katharine had made a pact with Bemis to retire, with a stipend from her, remove the materials, and destroy them. Mrs. Bemis, although elderly at the time of an interview, considered that just such an agreement might have occurred.

*   *   *   *   *

It is clear that the principle of self-realization for women was an integral thread in the fabric of Katharine's ninety-two years. In the personal sphere, Katharine battled for Stanley, to provide him the best and most humane treatment available, while investigating possible cures to restore his sanity. In the political sphere, Katharine battled for the right of women to vote and participate in the governing process. In the educational sphere, Katharine herself obtained a degree despite significant barriers and made it possible for other ambitious women to acquire a scientific education. Most important of all was Katharine's battle for women's sovereignty to determine for themselves whether or not to have children. All were illustrations of a particularly astonishing worldview.

At the beginning of the last century, the acknowledged achievement of a woman did not assure her acceptance as a self-determining equal, because a male-dominated society refused to recognize women as self-determining citizens. In response to this societal mind-set, Katharine became a dedicated advocate for women's rights. Her determination and commitment, while clashing with fierce opponents and overcoming sizable barriers, contrived to make things happen and carried her efforts to successful conclusions.

Today, Katharine's battle continues, even intensifies, as the same forces of repression she fought against for seventy years threaten women's rights again. One has only to examine recent news to understand the barriers and skirmishes that women continue to face.

- Many employers do not offer health insurance to cover contraceptives for women, while at the same time allowing Viagra to be prescribed for men. (*Los Angeles Times*, June 8, 2001)

- Giant retailer Wal-Mart was recently charged with discriminating against women in promotions, pay, and job assignments. Seventy-two percent of Wal-Mart's work force was comprised of women, but women filled only 10 percent of store management jobs. Besides this unfair treatment, women were also subjected to retaliation if they complained. "It's as if the last twenty-five years of progress for women never happened at Wal-Mart," said the women's lawyer. (*Los Angeles Times*, June 20, 2001)

- The San Bernardino County, California, Board of Supervisors banned distribution of the morning-after pill because it "might be promoting a form of abortion and encourage promiscuity among teens." Ellen Chesler, Margaret Sanger's biographer, responded to the councilmen's edict. "What we need is common ground in discussing women's choices about family planning. What we get is another blast of righteous moral indignation—one more amazing round in the explosive debate over choice that has poisoned America's politics too long." (*Los Angeles Times*, May 4, 2001)

- President George W. Bush decided to eliminate a special White House office on women's issues. He also signed a memorandum barring U.S. foreign aid to family-planning groups involved in any way with abortion. In fact, Bush's decision was aimed at preventing Congress from even voting on the issue. (*New York Times*, March 29, 2001)

- In the movie-making business, only 17 percent of the producers, writers, and directors are women. "Business as usual," replied a well-known male director. *USA Today* compared the salaries of men and women: as physicians, men made 35 percent more than women; as salespeople, men made 40 percent more than women. Female lawyers earned an average of $20,000 less per year than their male counterparts. (*Los Angeles Times*, June 8, 2001; *USA Today*, August, 2001; *New York Times*, July, 2001)

- Biomedical scientists are calling for research among women on all new medicinal products. Heretofore, the great majority of research to gain FDA approval had been conducted among males only. (*New York Times*, April 24, 2001) The New York State Assembly women's health care bill languished as time was running out on the legislative session. The problem: covering contraceptives for women. (*New York Times*, June 5, 2002)

- The Independent Women's Forum, a national research group, found on college campuses an atmosphere of "free-market sex, in which most of the consumers are males who see females as commodities." (*Los Angeles Times*, July, 2001)

So-called right-to-life and Christian Coalition groups target all women who favor abortion rights. Conservative members of Congress vote to curtail abortion spending. The Supreme Court position on *Roe v. Wade* is problematic.

The Catholic Church remains committed in its opposition to artificial birth control measures. To the Church, "unnatural" contraception is evil.

The dilution of affirmative action programs is directed as much toward women as toward ethnic groups. Opponents desire to block women's access to responsible jobs and adequate education, all in the name of "family values."

Hostility and aggression toward gay and lesbian groups is directly related to what some people believe should be the proper role of women in our society: a "return to the kitchen," if they had their way. Opponents have been winning the battle of public opinion and winning in the streets. They have been making headway in federal and state legislatures. Their sexist pursuits have already spawned violence—shooting doctors, bombing clinics, beating homosexuals.

In schools, these groups have aggressively sought to eliminate sex education, including information about contraception and sexually transmitted diseases, even AIDS.

Today, many men still refuse to acknowledge their responsibility for birth control. They either are uniformed, are misinformed, or stubbornly refuse to support their partners. There are no family-planning centers for men in this country mainly because men fear losing ultimate control of the relationship between themselves and women.

It is unfortunate that the advocates for women's rights, for women's equality with men—in the workplace, at home, and in politics—are on the defensive today. They are as poorly organized as they have been in thirty years. Unfortunately, the feminist movement is ancient history. Progressive women have no strong, visible personalities to lead them. They represent a morally divided and disengaged majority.

Katharine would never have allowed women to be seen and not heard. She would have continued her crusade on behalf of women, no matter the odds, no matter the obstacles.

It can only be hoped that her lifelong achievements—and she herself—may serve as a model for a few rare, brave women to lead the battle for women's independence in the twenty-first century.

Research Sources

GENEALOGY

Mormon Library, Salt Lake City, Utah
New England Genealogical Library, Boston, Massachusetts
Washtenaw Historical Society, Dexter, Michigan

DEXTER FAMILY

MIT Museum
MIT Archives/Special Collections
Massachusetts Historical Society
Boston Globe
Washtenaw Historical Society, Washtenaw County, Michigan
Chicago Historical Society
Prairie Avenue Association, Chicago, Illinois
Chicago Tribune

MCCORMICK FAMILY

McCormick Archives, State Historical Society, Madison, Wisconsin
Chicago Historical Society

Montecito Historical Society, Montecito, California

Dr. Adolph Meyer Papers, Johns Hopkins University Library, Baltimore, Maryland

KATHARINE DEXTER MCCORMICK

MIT Archives—class materials, letters

MIT Special Collections—donations, correspondence, dormitory material

Margaret Sanger Papers, Sophia Smith Collection, Smith College—correspondence 1928–1962; material related to suffrage movement, birth control movement, and development of the pill

Schlesinger Library, Radcliffe College—correspondence, material from Dennett Papers, Park Papers, Hamilton Papers

Planned Parenthood Federation—McCormick Library and Stone Library

Countway Library of Medicine—medical papers, correspondence

Santa Barbara Superior Court—court records, transcripts 1908–1947

Montecito Historical Society—material on Riven Rock

Personal correspondence:

Massachusetts Suffrage Association—Schlesinger Library, Radcliffe College

International Woman Suffrage Alliance—Library of Congress

National American Woman Suffrage Association—Library of Congress

League of Women Voters—Library of Congress

Margaret Sanger Papers—Library of Congress

Dr. Pincus Papers—Library of Congress

Dr. Rock Papers—Countway Library

McCormick Papers—McCormick Archives, State Historical Society

Dennett Papers—Schlesinger Library, Radcliffe College

Personal interviews:

Secretary to Stanley's doctor, 1934–1947

Son of gardener for Riven Rock estate

Son of former president of Planned Parenthood in Santa Barbara

McCormick Hall dorm housemothers from 1960s

McCormick Hall dorm students from 1960s

MIT women's studies professor

McCormick Papers archivist

University of California–Los Angeles women's studies professor

SUFFRAGE GROUPS AND LEAGUE OF WOMEN VOTERS

National American Woman Suffrage Association—Library of Congress, Smith
  College

University of California at Los Angeles

National Woman's Party—Library of Congress

Carrie Chapman Catt Papers—Library of Congress

Schlesinger Library, Radcliffe College

League of Women Voters Papers—Library of Congress

International Woman Suffrage Alliance Papers—Library of Congress

College Equal Suffrage League—Schlesinger Library

BIRTH CONTROL

Margaret Sanger Papers—Library of Congress

National American Woman Suffrage Association—Library of Congress

Dr. Pincus Papers—Library of Congress

Dr. Rock Papers—Countway Library

Worcester Foundation for Experimental Biology, Shrewsbury, Massachusetts

Personal interviews:

UCLA women's studies professor

Director, Worcester Foundation

MIT women's studies professor

Associate Editor, The Margaret Sanger Papers Project, New York University

Radcliffe College archivist

PHOTOGRAPHS

MIT Museum and Archives

McCormick Archives

National American Woman Suffrage Association

Montecito Historical Society

Santa Barbara Historical Society

NEWSPAPER ARTICLES

Chicago Tribune, 1890–1947

Los Angeles Times, 1929–30, 1947

New York Times, 1914–1920, 1929–30, 1947

Boston Globe, 1914–1920, 1929–30, 1947, 1964–67

Santa Barbara News-Press, 1908–1920, 1929–30, 1947, 1964–67

Abbreviations

MIT-A: MIT Archives, Cambridge, Massachusetts

RHS: Rye Historical Society, Rye, New York

MA: McCormick Archives, Madison, Wisconsin

AMP: Dr. Adolph Meyer's Papers, Johns Hopkins University Library, Baltimore, Maryland

SL-RC: Schlesinger Library, Radcliffe College, Cambridge, Massachusetts

HWS-LC: History of Women Suffrage, Library of Congress

MSP: Margaret Sanger Papers, Sophia Smith Collection, Smith College, Northampton, Massachusetts

PP-LC: Dr. Pincus's Papers, Library of Congress

Notes

ONE

1. A detailed examination of the Dexter ancestry can be found in N. McAllister, *Judge Samuel William Dexter* (Dexter, Mich.: Thomson-Shore, 1989). Information about the Dexter ancestry can also be found at the New England Historical Society, Boston, and the Mormon Library, Salt Lake City.

2. Sawislak, K., *Smoldering City: Chicagoans and the Great Fire, 1871–1874* (Chicago: The University of Chicago Press, 1995, pp. 4–5, 60, 75, 82, 92, 253–254, 269–270).

3. Sawislak, pp. 91–92.

4. J. Simmerling and W. Wolf, *Chicago Homes, Fact and Fables* (New York: McGraw-Hill, 1995), pp. vii-ix, 3–5.

TWO

1. Simmerling, for descriptions of the Prairie Avenue neighborhood and the homes of George Pullman, Marshall Field, and others.

2. McAllister, pp. 45–53.

3. Flexner, E., *Century of Struggle: The Woman's Rights Movement in the United States* (Cambridge: Harvard University Press, 1959). Chapter XV describes the various class levels of women who supported the suffrage movement in the 1880s.

4. A detailed description of Samuel's childhood, schooling, and relationship with Katharine can be found in *Funeral Services of Samuel Dexter*, May 7, 1894, MIT-A.

5. Biographical information on Wirt Dexter appeared in the *Chicago Tribune*, May 20–21, 1890; the *Dexter Leader*, February 4, 1987; and the *Chicago Times*, May 19, 1890.

6. Letters between Ellen Terry and Josephine Dexter, 1872–1875, MIT-A.

7. *Chicago Tribune,* February 17, 1872.

8. C. Callahan, "Etiquette and Dining in the Gilded Era," in *Prairie Avenue Cookbook* (Carbondale: Southern Illinois University Press, 1993), pp. 41–45.

9. Sawislak, pp. 76–78.

THREE

1. Special assessment for Wirt Dexter (deceased), Chicago Probate Court, year ending December 31, 1890.

2. Essays, circa 1893, found in papers given to MIT as designated in Katharine's will, MIT-A.

3. D. Deacon, *Elsie Clews Parsons: Inventing Modern Life* (Chicago: University of Chicago Press, 1997), pp. 22–25, 27, 29, 39–40.

4. Deacon, p. 25.

5. *Funeral Services of Samuel Dexter,* May 7, 1894.

6. Letter: KDM to Elsie Clews, January 5, 1895, RHS.

FOUR

1. Letters between Elsie Clews, Katharine Dexter, and Josephine Dexter, 1894–1896, RHS.

2. The Château de Prangins had been built by the French government in the early 1800s as a summer resort for the ruling royalty. While he was in power, Joseph Napoleon used the château as his summer home. Josephine purchased the château from the French government, eager to rid themselves of remainders of the monarchy.

3. Essay for English, Section 1, October 4, 1899, MIT-A.

4. Essay for English, Section 1, October 11, 1899, MIT-A.

5. Essay for English, Section 1, November 22, 1899, MIT-A.

6. Essay for English, Section 1, November 29, 1899, MIT-A.

7. "College Women's Suffrage League," *College Women,* November 24, 1900.

8. "College Women's Dramatics," *College Women,* April 25, 1901.

9. Details of Stanley and Katharine's meeting are found in Family and Personal History, MA.

FIVE

1. Family and Personal History, McCormick Archives, and G. A. Harrison, *A Timeless Affair: The Life of Anita McCormick Blaine* (Chicago: University of Chicago Press, date unknown), pp. 16–30.

2. Information on Stanley's early life can be found in Family and Personal History, Recollections of Ellen Hudson (nurse of the McCormick family), 1900; letters between Stanley and Harold, 1882–1889; and extracts from Cyrus McCormick Jr.'s diaries, 1874–1910; MA.

3. C. Stasz, *The Rockefeller Women* (New York: St. Martin's Press, 1995), pp. 103–105, 111, 124–125.

4. List of daily expenses, European trip, Stanley and Nettie McCormick, 1895–1896, MA.

5. Information found in Dr. Edward Kempf's analysis of Stanley, 1927–1929, "Report to the Personal Care Board on Mr. Stanley McCormick's Illness and Treatment, for June, 1927, to January 1, 1928," MA.

6. Extracts from Cyrus McCormick Jr.'s diaries referring to Stanley McCormick, 1897–1903, MA.

SIX

1. "Stanley McCormick—History of Courtship and Marriage and Onset of Present Illness," based on information obtained from Katharine and the McCormick family, McLean Hospital Records, MA.

2. Extracts from Cyrus McCormick Jr.'s diaries referring to Stanley McCormick, Harold's notes, January 26, 1904, MA.

SEVEN

1. *Chicago Tribune*, August 20, 1904.

2. "Stanley McCormick—History of Courtship and Marriage and Onset of Present Illness," McLean Hospital records, MA.

3. *Chicago Tribune*, September 20, 1904.

4. October 23, 1904.

5. Notes from Nettie McCormick's diary, November 4, 1904, MA.

6. "Stanley McCormick—History of Courtship and Marriage and Onset of Present Illness," p. 82, MA.

7. Extracts from Cyrus McCormick Jr.'s diaries referring to Stanley McCormick, April 29, 1905, MA.

8. Extracts, June 15, 1905.

9. Extracts, September 29, 1905.

10. Extracts, January 15, 1906.

11. "Stanley McCormick—History of Courtship and Marriage and Onset of Present Illness," p. 84, MA.

12. Stanley McCormick—History, p. 85, MA.

13. Stanley McCormick—History, pp. 87–89, MA.

EIGHT

1. An unpublished manuscript on the history of McLean Hospital by Alex Beam, of the *Boston Globe*, reports on the two years Stanley McCormick was treated there. See also: Extracts, pp. 88–89, MA.

2. Letter: G. A. Ranney to John Chapman, November 1, 1906, a report of Stanley's entire estate, MA.

3. Letter: Nettie McCormick to Dr. Billings, October 22, 1906, MA.

4. Letter: KDM to Cyrus Bentley, November 8, 1906, MA.

5. Excerpted from the papers of Dr. Adolph Meyer, AMP.

6. Dr. Meyer's report on Stanley McCormick, no date but likely in November 1906, MA.

7. Letter: Nettie McCormick to Harriet McCormick, January 10, 1907, MA.

8. A. H. Shaw, *The Story of a Pioneer,* (New York: Harper & Bros., 1915), particularly chapters 7, 9, and 11.

NINE

1. Letter: Dr. Hamilton to KDM and Anita McCormick, July 24, 1907, MA.
2. Letters: Nettie McCormick to Mrs. Hamilton, September 3, 1907, September 6, 1907, MA.
3. Letter: Dr. Hamilton to Nettie McCormick, October 10, 1907, MA.
4. Letter: KDM to Anita McCormick, December 26, 1907, MA.
5. A story of the history of Riven Rock can be found at the Santa Barbara Historical Society, in a magazine excerpt dealing with Montecito and Santa Barbara properties, chapter 3, "Riven Rock," pp. 251–258.
6. For a background and description of Dr. Emil Kraepelin and Dr. August Hoch's diagnosis of Stanley McCormick, see R. Noll, "Styles of Psychiatric Practice, 1906–1925: Clinical Evaluations of the Same Patient by James Jackson Putnam, Adolph Meyer, August Hoch, Emil Kraepelin and Smith Ely Jelliffe, Part II," submitted for publication to the *History of Psychiatry,* Cambridge, UK, December 1995.
7. Examination of Stanley McCormick, August 15, 1908, MA.

TEN

1. Letters describing the adventures of suffrage workers traveling through Massachusetts towns and villages are found at SL-RC.
2. Letter: KDM to Stanley McCormick, August 24, 1909, MA.

ELEVEN

1. Transcript of Stanley McCormick's insanity hearing, Santa Barbara City Hall, Court Hearings, June 1909.
2. Memorandum of Agreement between Katharine Dexter McCormick, first party, Nettie F. McCormick, Cyrus H. McCormick, Anita McCormick Blaine, and Harold F. McCormick, second party, and Henry B. Favill and Cyrus Bentley, third party, 1909, MA.
3. Telegram: Cyrus Bentley to Nettie McCormick, April 18, 1909, MA.
4. *Los Angeles Telegraph,* March 20, 1909.
5. *Chicago Evening Journal,* March 20, 1909.
6. *Santa Barbara Press,* April 9, 1909.
7. *Chicago Inter-Ocean,* March 22, 1909.
8. Letter: Anita McCormick to Dr. Meyer, March 12, 1910, MA.
9. Letter: KDM to Cyrus Bentley, April 18, 1910, MA.

TWELVE

1. Activities at the 1910 National American Woman Suffrage Association convention can be found in *History of Women's Suffrage,* pp. 286–287, HWS-LC.
2. R. B. Fowler, *Carrie Catt: Feminist Politician* (Boston: Northeastern University Press, 1986), pp. 51–53, 84, 108.
3. 1911 NAWSA convention, pp. 324–325, HWS-LC.

4. Ibid.

5. Letter: Carrie Chapman Catt to International Woman Suffrage Alliance membership, May 31, 1911, Carrie Chapman Catt Papers, Library of Congress.

THIRTEEN

1. Shaw, p. 320; letter: M. Cary Thomas, president of Bryn Mawr College, to Mrs. James Laidlow, March 6, 1912, recommending Katharine for the job of NAWSA treasurer, NAWSA Papers, Library of Congress.

2. 1912 NAWSA convention, p. 337, HWS-LC.

3. Series of letters between Nettie McCormick and Dr. Gustav Jung, October 1912, MA.

4. 1912 NAWSA convention, p. 337, footnote, HWS-LC.

5. Flexner, pp. 272–280.

6. 1912 NAWSA convention, pp. 338–340, HWS-LC.

7. Shaw, p. 317.

8. *New York Times*, April 23, 1913.

9. *New York Times*, May 4, 1913.

10. 1913 IWSA Budapest convention, pp. 862–868, IWSA Papers, HWS-LC.

11. *Boston Globe*, October 13, 1913.

12. 1913 NAWSA convention, pp. 370–375, HWS-LC.

13. 1913 NAWSA convention; report by treasurer Katharine Dexter McCormick with regard to financial affairs between NAWSA and the Congressional Committee, December 1913, HWS-LC.

14. 1913 NAWSA convention, p. 372, HWS-LC.

15. With Katharine's assistance, Dr. Hamilton's research on apes continued for almost ten years. See L. H. Marshall, "Early Studies of Primate Behavior in the U.S.A." (Elsevier Biomedical Press, November 1982), and G. V. Hamilton, "A Study of Sexual Tendencies in Monkeys and Baboons," *Journal of Animal Behavior*, September/October, 1914, vol. 4, no. 5: pp. 295–299.

16. 1914 NAWSA convention, pp. 418–419, HWS-LC.

17. Shaw, p. 317.

FOURTEEN

1. E. Chesler, *Woman of Valor: Margaret Sanger and the Birth Control Movement in America* (New York: Simon & Schuster, 1992), pp. 130–131.

2. Letter: KDM to Mary Ware Dennett, February 4, 1915, SL-RC.

3. Fowler, pp. 109, 121–131.

4. 1915 NAWSA convention, p. 457, HWS-LC.

5. 1916 NAWSA convention, pp. 484–489, HWS-LC.

6. F. F. Bushea, "Newton D. Baker Had Faith in Business Women," *Baltimore and Ohio Magazine*, May 1938, p. 20.

FIFTEEN

1. Letter: KDM to Cyrus Bentley, March 29, 1917, MA.

2. Letter: Dr. Hamilton to Cyrus Bentley, April 9, 1917, MA.

3. Letter: Dr. Brush to Dr. Meyer, April 13, 1917, AMP.

4. Letter: KDM to Dr. Hoch and Cyrus Bentley, July 3, 1917, MA.

SIXTEEN

1. 1917 NAWSA convention, pp. 527–543, HWS-LC.

2. Bushea, p. 20.

3. Summary of Jubilee Convention and Development of the League of Women Voters, p. 1, HWS-LC.

4. Condensed Minutes of the Jubilee Convention, St. Louis, Missouri, March 24–29, 1919, p. 8, HWS-LC.

5. Condensed Minutes, p. 8.

6. Discussion of proposed constitution, Women Voter's Conference, Jubilee Conversion Session, pp. 29–38, Library of Congress.

7. Summary of Jubilee Convention and Development of the League of Women Voters, p. 4, Library of Congress.

8. Ibid., pp. 4–5.

9. Ibid., p. 4.

SEVENTEEN

1. Letter: KDM to Dr. Meyer, October 6, 1919, MA.

2. Letter: Dr. Meyer to guardians, October 8, 1919, MA.

3. An example of these actions can be seen in the letter from Dr. Brush to Dr. Meyer, January 26, 1920, AMP.

4. Letter: Dr. Brush to Dr. Meyer, August 5, 1920, AMP.

5. Letter: Dr. Brush to Dr. Meyer, August 30, 1920, describing steps Katharine and Bentley took to eliminate censorship of letters between Katharine and Stanley, MA.

EIGHTEEN

1. Summary of the transcripts of the sessions between Katharine and Dr. Brill were found in AMP. Excerpts of Katharine's analysis were included in letters from Anita to Dr. Meyer and in guardian meeting notes, MA.

2. N. G. Hale Jr., *The Rise and Crisis of Psychoanalysis in the United States* (New York: Oxford University Press, 1995), pp. 67–68, 98, 104.

NINETEEN

1. 1920 NAWSA/League of Women Voters convention, pp. 596–615, HWS-LC.

2. Ibid., p. 601; Condensed Minutes of the Victory Convention, pp. 4–15, Library of Congress.

3. *Boston Globe*, February 12, 1920.

4. 1920 NAWSA/League of Women Voters convention, p. 597, HWS-LC.

5. Ibid., p. 600.

6. Letter: Dr. Brush to Dr. Meyer, October 11, 1920, AMP, describing the article appearing in the *Los Angeles Examiner* regarding fashions worn at the horse races.

7. Flexner, pp. 334–337.

8. L. M. Young, *In the Public Interest: The League of Women Voters, 1920–1970* (Westport, CT: Greenwood Press, 1989), p. 48.

9. Condensed Minutes of the 1921 League of Women Voters Convention, Library of Congress.

TWENTY

1. For an excellent biography of Margaret Sanger and the early history of the birth control movement, see E. Chesler, *Woman of Valor: Margaret Sanger and the Birth Control Movement in America* (New York: Simon & Schuster, 1992), and, regarding the history of birth control, L. Gordon, *Woman's Body, Woman's Right— Birth Control in America* (New York: Penguin Books, 1990, revised edition).

2. Chesler, pp. 200–205.

3. Letter: KDM to Stanley, February 20, 1922, MA. Whether the letter reached Stanley in the form it was sent is unknown.

4. Chesler, p. 431.

TWENTY-ONE

1. Young, pp. 71–77; Proceedings, League of Women Voters Des Moines Convention, April 9–14, 1923, Library of Congress.

2. Press release on Birth Control Resolution, League of Women Voters Convention, April 13, 1923, Library of Congress.

3. Katharine officially resigned her position in the IWSA at the end of 1923.

4. Chesler, pp. 254–255.

5. Telegram: KDM to Dr. Meyer, September 24, 1923, MA.

6. Letter: Stanley to KDM, October 13(?), 1923, MA.

7. Letter: Dr. Meyer to KDM, November 1923, MA.

8. Telegram: Stanley to KDM, January 10, 1924, MA.

9. Telegram: Stanley to Bentley, January 10, 1924, MA.

10. Letters between Katharine, Bentley, and Dr. Meyer between March 13 and April 23, 1924, MA.

11. Letter: Dr. Meyer to KDM, April 13, 1924, MA.

12. Letter: KDM to Dr. Timme, June 4, 1924, MA.

13. Examination of Mr. Stanley McCormick, at Riven Rock, Santa Barbara, CA, July 19 to 24, 1924, MA.

14. Letter: Dr. Meyer to Bentley, September 26, 1924, MA.

15. Letter: Dr. Brush to KDM, January 28, 1925, MA.

16. Letters: KDM to Dr. Meyer, January 28, 1925, and February 9, 1925, AMP.

17. Letter: Stanley to KDM, January 25, 1925, MA.

18. Letter: Dr. Meyer to Anita, April 24, 1925, MA.

19. Dr. Kraepelin's report on Stanley McCormick, April 28, 1925, AMP.

20. Letter: Dr. Meyer to KDM, June 25, 1925, AMP.

21. Clinical Opinion on Stanley McCormick by Dr. Charles H. Lawrence, June 29, 1925, AMP.

TWENTY-TWO

1. *Environmental Hazards and Community Response: The Santa Barbara Experience,* Public History Monograph no. 2, Public Historical Studies, University of Califor-

nia, Santa Barbara, 1979, provides a detailed description of the June 29, 1925, earthquake.

2. Letters: Bentley to Dr. Brush, February 21 and 22, 1926, and March 30, 1926, MA.

3. Young, pp. 91–95.

4. Young, p. 93.

5. Letter: Bentley to KDM, March 30, 1926, MA.

6. Letter: Sanger to KDM, July 31, 1926, MSP.

7. Notes of meetings between Anita and Dr. Meyer, July 9, 1926, MA.

8. Interview: Dr. Meyer and Bentley, July 14, 1926; letter: Bentley to Dr. Meyer, May 31, 1926; letter: Dr. Meyer to Bentley, June 4, 1926; letter: Dr. Meyer to Bentley, June 14, 1926; letter: KDM to Bentley, June 9, 1926, MA.

9. Study of Schizophrenia, Dr. Roy Hoskins proposal, no date, MA.

10. Letter: Dr. Meyer to Bentley, June 4, 1926, MA.

11. Letter: KDM to Dr. Meyer and Anita, November 10, 1926, MA.

TWENTY-THREE

1. Chesler, pp. 258–259; E. T. Douglas, *Pioneer of the Future: Margaret Sanger* (New York: Holt, Rinehart and Winston, 1970), pp. 196–197; catalog, World Population Conference, Geneva, Switzerland, August 31, September 1, 2, 3, 1927, Library of Congress.

2. Letter: Dr. A. A. Brill to KDM and Cyrus McCormick (copy for Dr. Meyer), July 13, 1926, MA.

3. A background on Dr. Edward Kempf can be found in *Who's Who, 1930*, p. 548.

4. Letter: KDM to Stanley, June 15, 1927, MA.

5. Dr. Meyer's report to Dr. Kempf, summarizing Stanley's medical history, May 1927. His introductory sentence began: "An unfortunate marital venture between a very intelligent and overconscientious, tense man and a strong-willed, self-confident, rather manipulative and unacceptable mate ended in the collapse of the husband." AMP

6. Excerpt from Dr. Kempf's testimony at the December 1929 trial, *McCormick v. McCormick*, MA.

7. Letter: KDM to Stanley, July 1, 1927, MA.

8. Medical Conference, KDM, Dr. Kempf, Dr. Hoskins, October 30, 1927, MA.

9. Telegram: KDM to Anita, November 11, 1927, telling her of the statement she sent to Dr. Kempf, MA.

10. Telegram: KDM to Anita and Harold McCormick, November 17, 1927, MA.

11. Telegram: KDM to Anita and Cyrus McCormick, December 30, 1927, MA.

12. Dr. Kempf's report to the Personal Care Board on Stanley McCormick's Illness and Treatment, from June 1927 to January 1, 1928, MA.

13. Letter: KDM to Personal Care Board, June 18, 1928, MA.

14. Ibid.

15. *New York Post*, May 26, 1929.

TWENTY-FOUR

1. *Santa Barbara Morning Press*, November 20, 1929.

2. *New York Times*, November 15, 1929.

3. All testimony comes from actual transcripts of the trial, Santa Barbara County Court House and daily articles in the *Santa Barbara Morning Press*.

4. A photograph of Katharine and Julia Roessing together appeared in the *Chicago Daily Times*, December 20, 1929, the caption under the picture stating: "Mrs. Katharine McCormick, wife of Stanley McCormick, America's wealthiest incompetent citizen, is shown with her best friend and constant companion, Mrs. J. B. Roessing."

5. The *New York Evening Graphic Magazine*, *Detroit Free Press*, *Los Angeles Times*, and *Chicago Daily Times* ran a series of Sunday features detailing the trial's events.

6. *Chicago Daily Times*, November 21, 1929.

7. *Los Angeles Times*, November 22, 1929.

8. *New York Graphic Magazine*, November 29, 1929.

9. *New York Times*, January 17, 1930.

TWENTY-FIVE

1. Letter: Dr. Brush to Dr. Meyer, March 15, 1930, AMP.

2. Letter: Sanger to KDM, July 2, 1930,

3. Report to the Chicago Probate Court, December 1932, MA.

4. The final decision by the probate court was made on April 1, 1933.

TWENTY-SIX

1. Chesler, pp. 346–348.

2. Chesler, pp. 373–374.

3. Telephone: KDM to Sanger, January 3, 1937.

4. Gertrude Calden was interviewed a number of times by the author. Her detailed recall of the years 1937 to 1947 at Riven Rock were extremely helpful in providing information and an understanding of Stanley and Katharine's situation during these years.

5. Letter: KDM to Sanger, April 27, 1937, MSP.

6. *Chicago Tribune*, November 19, 1937.

7. A detailed biography of Newton Baker was published in the *Cleveland Plain Dealer*, December 26, 1937. Baker's contributions to Cleveland are outlined in *The Encyclopaedia of Cleveland History* (Bloomington: Indiana University Press, 1947), pp. 66–68.

8. Letter: Sanger's secretary to KDM, January 18, 1938, MSP.

9. Letter: KDM to Sanger, August 15, 1938, MSP.

TWENTY-SEVEN

1. *The McCormick House: History of the Property*, Santa Barbara Museum of Art, no date.

2. Interview with Gertrude Calden, March 1, 1995.

3. *Noticias*, "Santa Barbara Art and Artists, 1940 to 1960," *Santa Barbara Historical Society*, Spring 1997, pp. 6–12.

4. Chesler, pp. 387–388.

5. Chesler, p. 391.

6. Chesler, pp. 392–393.

7. Chesler, p. 393.

8. Letter: KDM to Sanger, December 29, 1950, MSP.

9. Calden interview, February 8, 1995.

10. Letter: Anita to KDM, February 22, 1946, MA.

11. Stanley's death certificate, Santa Barbara County Court House.

12. *New York Times*, January 21, 1947.

13. Obituary written by Katharine for the *Santa Barbara News-Press*, January 20, 1947.

14. Last Will and Testament, Stanley McCormick, September 15, 1904.

TWENTY-EIGHT

1. Letter: KDM to Sanger, January 22, 1952, MSP.

2. Letter: KDM to Sanger, November 15, 1948, MSP.

3. Letter: KDM to Sanger, October 19, 1950, MSP.

4. Letter: Sanger to KDM, October 27, 1950, MSP.

5. Letter: KDM to Sanger, December 29, 1950, MSP.

6. Letter: KDM to Sanger, October 18, 1951, MSP.

7. Letter: Sanger to KDM, March 10, 1952, MSP.

8. Letter: KDM to Sanger, March 15, 1953, MSP.

9. L. McLaughlin, *The Pill, John Rock, and the Church* (Boston: Little, Brown, 1982), p. 92.

TWENTY-NINE

1. H. Hoagland, *Change, Chance, and Challenge* (Shrewsbury, MA: Worcester Foundation for Experimental Biology), chapter 5, no date.

2. McLaughlin, pp. 5–8, 16–23, 38–40, 153–173.

3. Letter: Pincus to Mrs. Peggy Blake, July 28, 1956, and August 2, 1956; Pincus to Mrs. Natalie Raymond, April 10, 1956, PP-LC.

4. Copies of monthly checks for $159.40 sent to Dr. Pincus by G. D. Searle. Pincus also owned 120 shares of Searle stock, which he signed over to his daughter, Elizabeth, PP-LC.

5. Copies of travel expenses, 1956–1960, PP-LC.

6. Letter: KDM to Sanger, September 28, 1953, MSP.

7. Letter: Sanger to KDM, October 5, 1953, MSP.

8. Letter: KDM to Sanger, November 13, 1953, MSP.

9. Letter: Sanger to KDM, February 13, 1954, MSP.

10. Letter: KDM to Sanger, February 17, 1954, MSP.

11. Letter: KDM to Pincus, March 31, 1954, PP-LC.

12. Letter: Sanger to KDM, March 26, 1954, MSP.

13. Letter: KDM to Pincus, March 31, 1954, PP-LC.

14. Letter: Pincus to KDM, April 3, 1954, PP-LC.

15. Letter: Sanger to KDM, April 1, 1954, MSP.

16. Letter: Dr. Stone to KDM, April 25(?), 1954, MSP.

17. Letter: KDM to Sanger, June 17, 1954, MSP.

18. Letter: Summary of meeting, June 22, 1954, Crawford (Worcester lab accountant) to KDM, PP-LC.

19. Telegram: KDM to Pincus, August 19, 1954, PP-LC.

20. Letter: KDM to Sanger, August 30, 1954, MSP.

THIRTY

1. Letter: KDM to Sanger, October 21, 1954, MSP.

2. Letter: KDM to Sanger, December 27, 1954, MSP.

3. Details of the Puerto Rico testing can be found in McLaughlin, pp. 128–133, 138–139.

4. Letter: Sanger to KDM, February 4, 1955, MSP.

5. Letter: KDM to Sanger, April 8, 1955, MSP.

6. K. Garber, "The Last Dexter," *Ann Arbor Observer,* June 1996, pp. 51–53.

7. Letter: KDM to Sanger, May 31, 1955, MSP.

8. Letter: KDM to Sanger, November 20, 1955, MSP.

9. Laughlin, pp. 128–130.

10. Pincus report to KDM, August 26, 1956, PP-LC.

11. Pincus and Rock report to KDM, October 10, 1956, PP-LC.

12. Letter: KDM to Sanger, November 20, 1956, MSP.

13. Letter: KDM to Sanger, January 3, 1957, MSP.

14. McLaughlin, p. 135.

15. Letter: KDM to Sanger, April 17, 1957, MSP.

16. Letter: KDM to Sanger, May 13, 1957, MSP.

17. Report: Dr. Rock to KDM, May 7, 1957, Dr. Rock's Papers, Countway Library, Boston.

18. Letter: KDM to Sanger, December 13, 1957, MSP.

19. Letter: KDM to Sanger, January 28, 1958, MSP.

20. Letter: KDM to Sanger, March 15, 1958, MSP.

21. Excerpts from Report of National Director, Planned Parenthood Federation of America at Board of Directors Meeting, April 9, 1958, Library of Congress.

22. Letter: KDM to Sanger, Pincus, and Rock, June 26, 1958, MSP.

23. McLaughlin, pp. 135–137.

24. Letter: KDM to Sanger, January 2, 1960, MSP.

THIRTY-ONE

1. Letter: KDM to Sanger, no date, MSP.

2. McLaughlin, p. 143.

3. McLaughlin, p. 142.

4. McLaughlin, p. 142.

5. McLaughlin, p. 145.

6. *New York Times,* May 12, 1960.

THIRTY-TWO

1. Letter: KDM to Sanger, June 15, 1960, MSP.

2. *Boston Globe,* April 12, 1960.

3. Speech by Katharine, October 7, 1963, at the dedication of Stanley McCormick Hall, MIT-A.

4. Letter: Pincus to KDM, December 6, 1960, PP-LC.

5. J. Rock, M.D., *The Time Has Come* (New York: A. A. Knopf, 1963).

6. Letter: Pincus to KDM, August 30, 1960, PP-LC.

7. Letter: Dr. Gamble to KDM, August 21, 1961, PP-LC.

8. Budget for Calendar Year 1965, Worcester Foundation for Experimental Biology, PP-LC.

9. For a complete history of Planned Parenthood of Santa Barbara, see M. J. Hungerford, *A Quiet Revolution* (Santa Barbara: Planned Parenthood of Santa Barbara, 1987).

10. Resolution given in honor of Katharine, Massachusetts Planned Parenthood, April 26, 1965.

11. Letter: KDM, a eulogy at Sanger's death, September 15, 1966, MSP.

THIRTY-THREE

1. *Chicago Tribune,* February 12, 1968.

2. Will of Katharine Dexter McCormick, MIT-A.

3. A Tribute to Katharine Dexter McCormick, 1875–1967, March 1, 1968, MIT-A.

4. C. Lane, "A Transforming Influence: Katharine Dexter McCormick," *MIT Spectrum,* 1975.

5. M. Resnick, "Katharine Dexter McCormick '04: Endowing Unpopular Causes with Credibility and Cash," *MIT Spectrum,* 1990.

Bibliography

BOOKS

Ad Hoc Advisory Committee. "FDA Report on Enovid." *Journal of the American Medical Association* 185 (1963).

Andersen, K. *After Suffrage*. Chicago: University of Chicago Press, 1996.

Asbell, B. *The Pill: A Biography of the Drug That Changed the World*. New York: Random House, 1995.

Banner, L. W. *Women in Modern America: A Brief History*. San Diego: Harcourt Brace Jovanovich, 1984.

Brady, K. *Ida Tarbell: Portrait of a Muckraker*. Pittsburgh: University of Pittsburgh Press, 1984.

Callahan, C. *Prairie Avenue Cookbook*. Carbondale: Southern Illinois University Press, 1993.

Chesler, E. *Woman of Valor: Margaret Sanger and the Birth Control Movement in America*. New York: Simon & Schuster, 1992.

Cott, N. F. *The Grounding of Modern Feminism*. New Haven, Conn.: Yale University Press, 1987.

Deacon, D. *Elsie Clews Parsons: Inventing Modern Life*. Chicago: University of Chicago Press, 1997.

Djerassi, C. *The Pill, Pygmy Chimps, and Degas' Horse*. New York: Basic Books, 1992.

Donnelly, M.C. *The American Victorian Woman*. Westford, Conn.: Greenwood Press, 1986.

Douglas, E. T. *Pioneer of the Future: Margaret Sanger*. New York: Holt, Rinehart and Winston, 1970.

Drury, J. "The Cyrus McCormick Mansion." In *Old Chicago Houses*. Chicago: University of Chicago Press, 1941, pp. 97–101.

Dubois, E. C. *Harriet Stanton Blatch and the Winning of Woman Suffrage*. New Haven, Yale University Press, 1997.

Flexner, E. *Century of Struggle: The Woman's Rights Movement in the United States.* Cambridge: Harvard University Press, 1982.

Fowler, R. B. *Carrie Catt, Feminist Politician.* Boston: Northeastern University Press, 1986.

Goldman, E. *Living My Life.* Salt Lake City: Peregrine-Smith, 1982.

Gordon, L. *Woman's Body, Woman's Right: A Social History of Birth Control in America.* New York: Penguin Books, 1990.

Grant, B. *Fight for a City: The Story of the Union League Club of Chicago.* Chicago, 1955.

Gray, M. *Margaret Sanger: A Biography of the Champion of Birth Control.* New York: Richard Marek Publishers, 1979.

Halberstam, D. *The Fifties.* New York: Fawcett Columbine, 1993.

Hale, N. G. Jr. *The Rise and Crisis of Psychoanalysis in the United States.* New York: Oxford University Press, 1995.

Horowitz, H. L. *The Power and Passion of M. Carey Thomas.* New York: A. A. Knopf, 1994.

Kerr, A. M. *Lucy Stone: Speaking Out for Equality.* New Brunswick, NJ: Rutgers University Press, 1992.

Lader, L. *A Private Matter: RU 486 and the Abortion Crisis.* Amherst, Mass.: Prometheus Books, 1995.

Lader, L. *The Margaret Sanger Story and the Fight For Birth Control.* New York: Doubleday & Co., 1955.

Lemons, J. S. *The Woman Citizen: Social Feminism in the 1920s.* Charlottesville: University Press of Virginia, 1973

Marks, L. V. *Sexual Chemistry: A History of the Contraceptive Pill.* New Haven, Conn.: Yale University Press, 2001.

Matthews, G. *The Rise of Public Woman.* New York: Oxford University Press, 1992.

McAllister, N. *Judge Samuel William Dexter.* Ann Arbor, Mich.: Thomson-Shore, 1989.

McLaren, A. *A History of Contraception: From Antiquity to the Present Day.* New York: Oxford University Press, 1994.

McLaughlin, L. *The Pill, John Rock, and the Catholic Church: The Biography of a Revolution.* Boston: Little Brown & Co., 1982.

Pincus, G. *The Control of Fertility.* New York: Academic Press, 1965.

Reed, J. *The Birth Control Movement and American Society: From Private Vice to Public Virtue.* Princeton, NJ: Princeton University Press, 1984.

Rock, J. *The Time Has Come.* New York: A. A. Knopf, 1963.

Romero, P. W. *E. Sylvia Pankhurst: Portrait of a Radical.* New Haven, Conn.: Yale University Press, 1987.

Rupp, L. J., and V. Taylor. *Survival in the Doldrums.* New York: Oxford University Press, 1987.

Schlereth, T. J. *Victorian America.* New York: Harper Perennial, 1991.

Schneider, D., and C. J. Schneider. *American Women in the Progressive Era, 1900–1920.* New York: Doubleday & Co., 1993.

Shaw, A. H. *The Story of a Pioneer.* New York: Harper & Brothers, 1915.

Simmerling, J., and W. Wolf. *Chicago Homes Facts and Fables.* New York: McGraw-Hill, 1995.

Stasz, C. *The Rockefeller Women.* New York: St. Martin's Press, 1995.

Tebbel, J. *An American Dynasty.* New York: Greenwood Press, 1968.

Tompkins, W. A. *Santa Barbara History Makers.* Santa Barbara: McNally & Loften, 1983.

Wheeler, M. S. (ed.). *One Woman, One Vote.* Troutdale, Ore.: Newsage Press, 1995.

Williams, D., and G. Williams. *Every Child a Wanted Child: Clarence James Gamble, M.D., and His Work in the Birth Control Movement.* Boston: Harvard University Press, 1978.

Young, L. M. *In the Public Interest: The League of Women Voters, 1920–1970.* Westport, Conn.: Greenwood Press, 1989.

ARTICLES

"A Breeze on Prairie Avenue." *Chicago Tribune,* November 1889.

"American Women: Mrs. Stanley McCormick." *Vogue,* May 1967, p. 184.

Bemis, W. H. "Remarks," program, Presentation of Stanley McCormick Hall, MIT, March 1, 1968.

Bogie, B. "How Coeducation Came About." *MIT Tech Review,* 1963.

Bushea, F. F. "Newton Baker Had Faith in Business Women." *Baltimore and Ohio Magazine,* May 1938.

Chiacos, E. "Women Donate to History." *Santa Barbara News-Press,* March 21, 1990.

"College Women's Dramatics." *College Women,* May 5, 1900.

"College Women's Suffrage League." *College Women,* November 24, 1900.

Davis, K. S. "The Story of the Pill." *American Heritage,* August/September 1978.

Doris, M. "Fertile Groundbreaking." *Worcester Phoenix,* March 3, 1995.

Excerpts from Minutes of the Massachusetts Woman Suffrage Association, March 2, 1900.

Garber, K. "The Last Dexter." *Ann Arbor Observer,* June 1996.

Garcia, C.-R., M.D., H. Rocamora, M.D., and G. Pincus, D.Sc., "Long-Term Effects of Oral Contraception," Proceedings of the Third and Fourth Annual Meetings of the American Association of Planned Parenthood Physicians, Chicago, May 1965.

"Garden Court Will Be Built at Art Institute." *Chicago Tribune,* January 9, 1959.

Halberstam, D. "Discovering Sex." *American Heritage,* May/June, 1993.

Hamilton, G. V. "A Study of Sexual Tendencies in Monkeys and Baboons." *Journal of Animal Behavior* 4, no. 5, September-October, 1914.

Head, F. "Wirt Dexter." *Chicago Historical Society Monthly Magazine,* April 1906.

Hoagland, H. "Birthplace of the Pill." *Worcester Sunday Telegram,* December 7, 1969.

Ireland, C. "McCormick Name Looms Large Here." *Santa Barbara News-Press,* May 13, 1984.

Irwin, S. "The Rustic Elegance of Stanley McCormick's Riven Rock." Montecito, no date.

"Katharine Dexter McCormick: Benefactress." Planned Parenthood Federation of America, no date.

"Keeping Up With the Neighbors on Millionaires Row." *Chicago Tribune,* June 14, 1987.

Lader, L. "Three Men Who Made a Revolution." *New York Times Magazine,* April 10, 1966.

Lane, Carla. "Katharine Dexter McCormick." *MIT Spectrum,* 1978.

Maisel, A. Q. "Where Do We Stand With the Birth Control Pill?" *Reader's Digest*, February 1961.

Marshall, L. H. "Early Studies of Primate Behavior in the U.S.A." American Psychological Association brochure, Los Angeles, August 26, 1981.

McMahon, M. "Ensconced In Mansion, McCormick Lived Life, Set History." *Santa Barbara News-Press*, October 4, 1994.

Meyer, P. "Mrs. Stanley McCormick of Santa Barbara (This Pill's For You)." *Independent*, May 4, 1969.

Miss Loring's School, Boarding and Day Pupils, brochure, September 26, 1889.

Monagle, K. "How We Got Here." *Ms.*, May-June 1995.

"Mrs. Stanley McCormick Gives Swiss Castle to U.S." *New York American*, October 3, 1962.

Murphy, L. R. "Stanley R. McCormick: The Youngest Reaper." *California Historical Society Quarterly* 48, no. 2, June 1969.

Noll, R., M.D. "Styles of Psychiatric Practice, 1906–1925: Clinical Evaluations of the Same Patient by James Jackson Putnam, Adolph Meyer, August Hoch, Emil Kraepelin and Smith Ely Jelliffe, Part I and II." Submitted for publication to *History of Psychiatry* (UK), December 30, 1995.

Park, M. W. Address to the Equal Suffrage League, February 8, 1906.

Park, M. W. "The Founding of the First College League." *Woman's Journal*, April 25, 1914.

"Prairie Avenue." *Chicago Tribune*, December 12, 1937.

"Prairie Avenue Finale." *Chicago Tribune*, June 22, 1949.

Reed, J. W. "The Birth Control Movement Before Roe vs. Wade." *Journal of Policy History* 7, no. 1, 1995.

Resnick, M. "Endowing Unpopular Causes With Credibility and Cash—Katharine Dexter McCormick '04," *MIT Spectrum*, Spring 1990.

Ridley, G. D. "Katharine Dexter McCormick." *Sojourner*, December 1, 1975.

Rouse, S. H. "Riven Rock—the Famed McCormick Estate." *Santa Barbara News-Press*, January 20, 1980.

Rouse, S. H. "When Stanley McCormick Lived Here." *Santa Barbara News-Press*, January 27, 1980.

Small, A. "Rush St. Retains Link to Past as Luster Fades." *Chicago Tribune*, January 17, 1954.

"Stanley McCormick—Class of 1895." Princeton University, Seeley G. Mudd Library.

Tilton, G. H. "A Visit to Riven Rock, Stanley McCormick's Wooded Estate." *Townsfolk*, April 1939.

"Wirt Dexter." Biography prepared by law colleagues in Chicago, 1890.

"Wirt Dexter Is Dead." *Chicago Tribune*, May 19, 1890.

Index

Abortion, 175, 284, 307
Adams, President John, 4
Addams, Jane, 15, 102, 118
American Birth Control Conference, 1921, 177
American Birth Control League (ABCL), 177, 180, 205, 235, 237, 241, 246
Anthony, Susan B., 11, 31, 76
Art Students' League, 42

Baker, Newton D., 129, 138–140, 142, 159, 171–172, 183–184, 189–190, 192, 197–198, 200–201, 206, 210–213, 216–218, 220–229, 231, 237, 239–240
Belmont, Alva, 116
Bemis, William, ix, 241, 244, 248, 250, 254, 265, 268, 271, 275, 280–281, 283, 286, 296, 303–306
Bentley, Cyrus, 70–75, 79, 81–82, 85, 95–98, 107, 131–134, 146–150, 165, 167–169, 184, 186, 188, 190, 192, 194, 197–198, 201, 206
Bernard, Col. Joseph H., 229–231, 237, 244
Beverly Farms, 33, 44, 47

Birth Control Federation of America, 246–247
Birth control movement, xi, 124–125, 176, 178–181, 185–186, 190, 198–199, 230, 235–236, 238–239, 243, 245–247, 254, 263, 265–266, 278, 281–282, 297, 299, 303, 307–308
Birth Control Review, 181
Blanch, Harriet Stanton, 100
Bly, Nelly, 32
Boardman, Dr. W. W., 228, 230
Bocker, Dr. Dorothy, 181
Boston Globe, x, 32, 163
Brandeis, Louis, 113
Brill, Dr. Abraham A., 152, 155–160, 163–165, 168–169, 178, 188, 206, 208
Brush, Dr. Nathanial, 133, 148–151, 165, 167–169, 171, 183–192, 195–198, 200–201, 205, 207, 209, 216, 220, 222, 224, 227–229
Burns, Lucy, 108

Calden, Gertrude, 237, 244, 248, 250
Catholic Church, 33, 91, 100, 179–180, 183–184, 235–237, 243, 246, 254, 264–265, 270, 277, 280, 284–285, 289–290, 299, 307

Catt, Carrie Chapman, xi, 76–77, 86,
    101, 103, 106, 111–112, 114, 116,
    118, 121–129, 137–139, 141–146,
    151, 159, 163, 165–166, 170–171,
    178, 185–186, 236
Cazenovia Seminary, New York, 6
Chang, Dr. Min-Chueh, 256, 261–264,
    267–268, 272–274, 277, 303
Château de Prangins, xi, 26–27, 52,
    56–57, 62, 106, 112, 160, 165, 182,
    190, 197, 205, 241, 255, 276, 280, 300
Chicago Art Institute, 303–304
Chicago fire, 7, 15, 38
Chicago Probate Court, 227, 230–231
Chicago Tribune, 6, 13, 16, 56, 58, 213,
    240, 303–304
Chopin, Kate, 32–33
Citizen's Committee for Planned
    Parenthood, 241, 243
Clews, Elsie, 21–23, 25–26
Clinical Research Bureau, 181, 186,
    190
College Equal Suffrage League
    (CESL), 32, 49, 52, 75, 101
Collyer, Reverend Robert, 16–17
Comstock Act, 124, 175–177
Comstock, Anthony, 175–176
Congressional Union, 114–116, 119,
    121
Contraception/contraceptive testing,
    xi, 175–177, 179–180, 182, 200, 236,
    239, 243, 245, 247–248, 253–256,
    261, 263–265, 267–268, 270–271,
    275, 277, 279, 282–283, 291, 297, 308
Council of Defense, 129

Deering Company, 42–43
de Excester, Richard, 3–4
DeFelice, Dr. Pasquale, 290–291
Dehy, Judge William, 215–218,
    220–221, 224–228
De Lancy, Sara, 301, 304
Democratic Party, 101, 122, 140, 144
Dennett, Mary Ware, 77, 91–93,
    101–102, 104, 110, 112, 124–125, 176
Dexter heritage, The, 10, 20, 26, 51,
    80, 157, 159, 184, 229, 240
Dexter, Josephine (Moore), 3, 6–11,

    13–17, 19–22, 25–27, 29, 34, 47–48,
    51–52, 56–57, 59–60, 63, 65, 69, 72,
    80, 86, 92, 100, 106, 112, 143, 151,
    157, 159, 165, 180, 183–184, 229,
    239–240, 300
Dexter, Michigan, 3, 5–6, 8, 15
Dexter, Millicent (Bond), 5–6, 8, 15,
    22, 276
Dexter, Samuel, 4
Dexter, Samuel, II, 4
Dexter, Samuel, III, 4
Dexter, Samuel (son of Wirt and
    Josephine), 6–16, 20–22, 86, 158, 240
Dexter, Samuel (son of Wirt and
    Kate), 6
Dexter, Samuel William, 3
Dexter, Samuel William, II, 4–5, 16
Dexter, Wirt, 3, 5–8, 10–17, 19, 22, 38,
    86, 158, 240, 303
Diaphragms, 181–182, 186, 189–190,
    197–198
Dusenberry, Kate Augusta, 6

Endocrine testing, 188–191, 194, 198,
    200–201, 207, 209–211, 217, 224
Enovid, 281, 283, 285–286, 289, 291,
    295, 298–299

Favill, Dr. Henry, 50–51, 73–75, 79–82,
    95–97, 107, 115, 131–133
Field, Marshall, 7–8, 14
Fitzgerald, Susan, 91–93, 102,
    109–110, 112, 118
Food and Drug Administration
    (FDA), 265, 279, 281, 286–287,
    289–291, 295
Freudian psychology, 155–156, 167,
    169, 217–218, 220–223, 226

Gamble, Dr. Clarence, 281, 299
Garcia, Dr. Celso-Ramon, 275, 283,
    303
Gardener, Helen, 113, 126
Garrett, John, 43
Goldman, Emma, 32, 176
Gordon Hall, 5–6, 8, 19, 276
Graceland cemetery, 16, 22, 240
Gray, Mrs. Katharine, 300–301

Hamilton, Dr. Gilbert Van Tassel,
    74–75, 79–84, 86–87, 95–96, 105,
    107, 115, 132–134, 148–149, 167, 224
Hand, Johnny and his orchestra, 14
Harper, Ida Husted, 100
Harriman, Averill, 243, 300
Harvard University, 4, 12, 15, 21, 27,
    261–262
Haven School for Boys, 8, 12
Hoagland, Dr. Hudson, 202, 255–257,
    261–263, 265, 267–268, 270–273,
    281, 283, 285, 291, 303
Hoch, Dr. August, 84–85, 133–134,
    146–149, 169, 224
Hoskins, Dr. Roy D., 200–201,
    209–210, 255, 262
Hotel Beau Rivage, 58, 112
Hughes, Charles Evans, 127
Humacao (Mexico), 281, 283–284, 286,
    298

Impressionist art, 60, 304
International Exposition, Paris, 43
International Harvester, 43, 64,
    252–253, 281
International Planned Parenthood
    Federation, 275, 283, 303
International Woman Suffrage
    Association (IWSA), 77, 101, 103,
    106, 112, 145, 165–167, 170,
    181–182, 185–186, 190

Jefferson, President Thomas, 4
Jelliffe, Dr. Smith Ely, 131–132, 169,
    224
Johnson, Cathrine, 10, 12
Johnson, Dr., 15, 16
Jung, Dr. Carl Gustave, 107, 156

Kempf, Dr. Edward, 206–212,
    216–220, 222–228, 250
Kennedy, Anne, 179, 181
Killian, James R., Jr., 302, 305
King, Henry, 6–7, 16
Kraepelin, Dr. Emil, 84–86, 133, 169,
    192–194, 198, 224

La Follette, Mrs. Robert, 102, 106
Laskar Award, 298–299
Lawler, Oscar, 216–225
League of Women Voters, xi, xii, 32,
    141, 143–146, 151, 159, 163–164,
    166, 170, 180, 185–186, 198–199, 297
League of Women Voters, 1921
    convention, 170
League of Women Voters, 1923
    convention, 185
League of Women Voters, 1925
    convention, 198
Lennon, Dr. Milton B., 228, 230
Leslie, Mrs. Frank, 125, 127
Lorch, Emil, 276
Los Angeles Times, 303, 306–307
Lowell, James Russell, 13

Malden, Massachusetts, 4
Margaret Sanger Research Bureau,
    268–269
Massachusetts Colony, 4
Massachusetts General Hospital, 299
Massachusetts Institute of Technology
    (MIT), ix, x, 28–33, 48–49, 52, 102,
    165, 224, 295–297, 302–305
Massachusetts State Insane Hospital,
    277–279
McCormick, Anita, 39–40, 49–50, 56,
    59, 63–64, 70–75, 79–82, 84, 87, 97,
    131, 133–134, 146–149, 165,
    167–170, 180, 183–184, 188, 192,
    194, 197–198, 200–201, 206–207,
    210–212, 216–217, 220, 222,
    225–228, 230, 238, 240, 248–249, 252
McCormick, Cyrus, x, 14–15, 34,
    37–38, 40, 47, 221, 303
McCormick, Cyrus, Jr., 40, 42–43,
    56–58, 63–64, 72–74, 184, 216, 248
McCormick, Edith (Rockefeller), 41,
    49–50, 62–63
McCormick, Harold, 40–41, 43, 49–51,
    56, 59, 62–64, 70–74, 82, 156, 169,
    184, 206–212, 216, 220, 222,
    225–228, 230–231, 238, 240, 248
McCormick, Harriet, 56–57, 167–169
McCormick, Mary Virginia, 40, 44, 50,
    70, 73, 82–83, 156, 207, 228, 248–249

McCormick, Nettie (Fowler), 15,
37–44, 49–53, 55–64, 70–74, 79–82,
84–85, 96, 106–107, 131–132,
156–158, 165, 167–170, 184,
186–188, 222, 248
McCormick, Ruth Hanna, 144
McCormick, Stanley Robert, x, 14,
33–34, 40–45, 47–53, 55–67, 69–75,
79–87, 92, 95, 97, 105–107, 111, 115,
117, 129, 132–134, 147–152,
156–159, 165–169, 171, 180,
183–184, 186–198, 200–201,
205–212, 216–226, 229–230,
237–240, 244, 248–252, 266, 297,
300, 303, 305–306
McKillop, Edward, 72–73, 79, 82–83,
86–87, 132–134, 147–149, 167–168,
186, 191, 195–197, 208, 216,
219–221, 228–229, 237
McLean Hospital, 66, 69–72, 74, 82
Meyer, Dr. Adolf, 73–75, 79–82, 84,
97–98, 115, 131, 133–134, 148–151,
165, 167–171, 183–194, 197–198,
200–202, 206–207, 216–217, 224,
228–229, 248–249
Miss Hershey's School for Girls, 20

National American Women's Suffrage
Association (NAWSA), 32, 75–77,
91–92, 99–103, 106–119, 121–130,
137–142, 144–146, 151, 166, 177, 180
National Birth Control League
(NBCL), 124–125
National Woman's Party (NWP),
126–128, 137–138, 140, 151
NAWSA Congressional Committee,
109–110, 114
NAWSA, 1909 convention, 31
NAWSA, 1910 convention, 100
NAWSA, 1911 convention, 102
NAWSA, 1912 convention, 107–109
NAWSA, 1913 convention, 113–114
NAWSA, 1914 convention, 117, 121
NAWSA, 1915 convention, 125
NAWSA, 1916 convention, 127
NAWSA, 1917 convention, 139
NAWSA, 1919 convention (Jubilee
Convention), 140, 143

NAWSA, 1920 convention (Victory
Convention), 146, 163–165
NAWSA-Massachusetts, 77, 91, 99,
101
New York Suffrage Party, 101,
124–125
New York Times, xi, 110–111, 215, 226,
250, 284, 291, 303, 307
New York World, 32
Nyons, France, 26, 56, 58–59, 106, 241,
255, 276

Ophuls, Dr. William, 228–231

Park, Maud Wood, 31–32, 75, 86, 118,
122–123, 125–126, 128, 163–164,
170, 185, 198
Paul, Alice, 108–111, 113–116, 118,
121–123, 126, 128, 138
Perkins, Secretary of Labor Frances,
235–236
Pill, The, 263, 265, 270, 272, 274,
277–287, 289–291, 295, 299, 301,
305–306
Pincus, Dr. Gregory, 255–257,
261–275, 277–286, 289, 291, 295,
298, 300, 303
Planned Parenthood Federation of
America (PPFA), xi, xii, 247,
254–256, 265–268, 281–284, 298,
302, 304
Planned Parenthood Federation of
Massachusetts, 301
Planned Parenthood Federation of
Santa Barbara, 300–301
Pollack, Dr. Lewis J., 231
Porter, Dr. Langley, 228–231
Prairie Avenue residence, 6–10, 12–14,
16, 19–20, 22, 27
Primate lab, 74, 80, 83, 96, 115, 133
Princeton University, 41–42, 113, 248
Progesterone, 263–264, 267–274, 279
Puerto Rico testing, 267–275, 277–286,
295, 298
Pullman, George, 7–8, 16
Putnam, Dr. James Johnson, 21–22,
66–67, 70, 106, 226

Radcliffe College, 28, 31–32
Rankin, Jeanette, 126, 128, 139
Relief and Aid Society, 7–8, 12, 15, 38
Republican Party, 101, 140, 144, 166
Rice-Wray, Dr. Edris, 278
Richards, Dr. Robert, 228–231, 237
Riven Rock, 82–87, 96–97, 105–107,
    115, 123, 130, 132–133, 146–151,
    158, 167–169, 171, 184, 186–189,
    192–198, 200, 206–207, 211,
    218–221, 223–224, 227–231,
    237–238, 244, 248–250, 253–254
Rock, Dr. John, 263–271, 273–275,
    277–287, 289–291, 295, 298, 303
Rockefeller, John D., 41, 43
Roessing, Mrs. Julia, 109, 123,
    126–127, 132, 140, 143, 146,
    151–152, 156, 159, 165, 181,
    209–211, 216, 224–226, 228
Roosevelt, Eleanor, xi, 235, 245
Rose, Dr. Kenneth, 246–247
Rublee, Juliet, 177, 181
Russell, Dr. Ernest, 237–238, 244, 248,
    250

Saginaw, Michigan, 5, 8
San Francisco Chronicle, 82
Sanger, Margaret, xi, 124–125,
    176–183, 186–187, 197–200, 205,
    229–230, 235–241, 245–247,
    253–257, 261, 265–272, 274–275,
    277–278, 280–284, 286, 289, 291,
    295, 299–300, 302
Santa Barbara earthquake, 194–197
Santa Barbara Museum of Art, 245,
    248, 303–304
Santa Barbara News Press, 215, 250,
    301, 303
Schizophrenia, 157, 201–202, 262
Science, 279–281
Searle, G. D., 264, 268, 281, 283–287,
    289–291, 298, 300–301
Searle pill (4642), 277–280, 283–284,
    286
Shaw, Reverend Anna Howard,
    76–77, 86, 101–102, 106–110, 113,
    116–118, 121–122, 125, 129, 159, 164
Stafford, O. A., 82

Stanley McCormick Hall, ix, 297–298,
    302, 304
Stanley McCormick Memorial
    Foundation for Neuro-Endocrine
    Research Corporation, 201–202,
    262
Stevenson, Adlai, 300
Stone, Dr. Abraham, 268–270, 274–277
Suffrage movement, The, 11, 32, 76,
    86, 91–93, 98–103, 107, 110, 112,
    115–116, 118, 121, 126–129, 137,
    139–141, 143–144, 151, 158–159,
    165, 176–177, 246, 297, 303
Suffragist, The, 111
Swing, Professor, 14, 16, 22
Syntex pill (759), 277–280

Terry, Ellen, 13
Thomas, M. Cary, 76
393 Commonwealth Avenue, 27, 32,
    52, 63, 65, 69, 101, 239, 243, 297,
    304
Time Has Come, The, 298
Tompkins, Martin, 72, 79, 82–83, 133,
    149, 196, 216, 228–229
Tyler, Dr. David, 270–271

University of Michigan, 6

Vogt, William, 266–268, 281–282, 284
Voting rights amendment, xi, 127,
    139–141, 144, 163, 166, 170, 243

War Services Department, 139,
    142–143
White, Dr. William A., 206–207,
    216–218
Williams, T. Talbot, 112–113
Wilson, President Woodrow, 109–110,
    113–114, 116, 121–122, 126–128,
    138–140, 164
"Winning Plan, The," 125, 127–128
Wirt, William, 5
Woman's Committee of the Council
    of Defense, 129
Woman's Journal, The, 106–107
Women's dormitories, 295–299, 303

Women's rights, 11, 31, 76–77, 102,
    108, 138, 152, 156, 166, 176, 178,
    180, 184, 245, 248, 303, 305–306, 308
Women's vote activities, 110, 115, 118,
    123–126, 138–140, 163, 166, 170, 243

Worcester Foundation for
    Experimental Biology, 256–257,
    262–263, 265, 271, 283–284, 295,
    298–300, 304
Worcester State Hospital, 262, 295

About the Author

ARMOND FIELDS is a social historian who is the author of eight biographies.